...dinavische Kritik
...anischer feministischer
...eologie

Critique scandinave de la théologie féministe anglo-américaine

Journal of the European Society of Women in Theological Research

Jahrbuch der Europäischen Gesellschaft für theologische Forschung von Frauen

Annuaire de l'Association Européenne des femmes pour la recherche théologique

Volume 15

**Bibliographical information and books for review
in the Journal should be sent to:**
Dr. Ursula Rapp, Kirchweg 12
A - 6800 Feldkirch, Austria

**Articles for consideration for the Journal
should be sent to:**
Prof. Dr. Sabine Bieberstein, St.-Getreu-Str. 17,
D - 96049 Bamberg, Germany

Scandinavian Critique of Anglo-American Feminist Theology

Skandinavische Kritik angloamerikanischer feministischer Theologie

Critique scandinave de la théologie féministe anglo-américaine

Editors:
Hanna Stenström, Elina Vuola, Sabine Bieberstein, Ursula Rapp

PEETERS - LEUVEN - DUDLEY, MA

A CIP record for this book is available from the Library of Congress.

Journal of the European Society of Women
in Theological Research, 15

© 2007, Peeters Publishers, Leuven / Belgium
ISBN 978-90-429-1974-7
ISSN 1783-2454
eISSN 1783-2446
D.2007/0602/116
Cover design by Margret Omlin-Küchler

CONTENTS – INHALT – TABLE DES MATIÈRES

Journal of the European Society of Women in Theological Research 15 (2007) 3-13.
doi: 10.2143/ESWTR.15.0.2022765

Elina Vuola and Hanna Stenström

Introduction

This ESWTR Journal will lead you into the world of feminist theology in Scandinavia, or, to use the terminology we ourselves use, the Nordic countries: Iceland, Norway, Denmark, Sweden and Finland. The Nordic countries have much of their history in common, a complicated history of both wars and unions. Although we can follow the history of all five countries back to the Middle Ages, three of them became independent only during the 20th century: Norway in 1905 (after being part of Denmark for centuries and in union with Sweden for about ninety years), Finland in 1917 (after being part of Sweden from the Middle Ages to 1809 and then part of Russia), while Iceland became an independent republic in 1944.[1] This reflects a history that is not just peaceful but also full of social, political and cultural tensions. However, in the past 50-60 years, the history of the Nordic countries has been a story of co-operation in all areas of society between five independent nations with distinct identities, a common history and many cultural affinities. There are examples of co-operation between organisations, institutions and individuals on all levels and in all fields of society. This ESWTR Journal is one example of Nordic co-operation, and it will hopefully do justice both to our similarities, and to our differences.

Although this is not the place for a complete description of the Nordic countries, something can still be said about the context in which this issue of the ESWTR Journal has been compiled.

During the second half of the 20th Century, all five Nordic states became welfare states, with similar, although certainly not identical, welfare models.[2] Three of them – Denmark, Sweden and Finland – now belong to the European Union. Four of the languages – Swedish, Norwegian, Danish and Icelandic –

---

[1] Iceland was part of Denmark until 1918, when it became an independent country in union with Denmark, i.e. Iceland and Denmark had the same king and a common foreign policy.

[2] For a brief but informative presentation of the social situation in Norway, Sweden and Finland see http://wrep.no-ip.info. See also Ninna Edgardh Beckman's article in this Journal.

are closely related, and speakers of the first three can communicate with one another using their native language, although not always without effort.

In all five countries, Lutheran national churches – in our languages called Folk Churches[3] – have historically dominated societal and religious life.[4] However, especially since the late 19th and early 20th century, other Christian churches and denominations than the Lutheran church have become part of the religious landscape. Various Christian revival movements have also found a place inside the Lutheran churches, Sweden being an exception, since there the majority of the revival movements left the Lutheran Church. In Sweden, there are therefore still a number of denominations of the Congregationalist, Baptist and Pentecostalist kind that are unique to that country. Since the late 19th and early 20th century, one can also find international churches (including the Roman Catholic Church) that are independent of the national churches in the Nordic countries.

Although about 80-90 % of the population still belong to the national churches, the Nordic countries are today regarded as more secularized than the USA and many other European countries. The Lutheran national churches are losing members. To take an example, the membership rate in Sweden is now (2005) 78.3% of the population. This is partly due to the immigration of people belonging to other churches or religions, but also to members leaving the Church. Today, all five countries are undergoing a process of change from more or less ethnically and culturally homogeneous societies to multicultural societies similar to the rest of Western Europe, with recognisable groups of immigrants representing a wide range of cultures, languages and religions. And, as in so many other Western European countries, many people find their spiritual nourishment in new religious movements of different kinds.

However, differences must not be disregarded. Cultural unity was not the whole story even 400 years ago. No history of Sweden, Finland or Norway is complete if the indigenous Sami people are not mentioned. The relation

---

[3]   In the following, we will use the term "national churches", not the Nordic terminology, since "Folk" (same as German *Volk*) may evoke other associations in some other European languages than in ordinary use in contemporary Nordic languages. To make a long and complex story short and simple, we can use "Folk" in names for a number of movements and social phenomena that are clearly part of our democratic societies, and it does not necessarily smack of a Nazi or communist use of Folk/*Volk*/People.

[4]   For a complete presentation of the Nordic national churches (although Iceland is almost absent) see Björn Ryman with Aila Lauha / Gunnar Heiene / Peter Lodberg, *Nordic Folk Churches: A Contemporary Church History* (Eerdmans: Grand Rapids 2005).

between the Sami and dominant society is a difficult and complicated history that includes Christian missionary work using force and violence. Other national and international minorities are also part of the history of the Nordic countries, although followers of non-Christian religions were only allowed to practice their religion gradually (the Jews, for example, were allowed to do so in the late 17th century in Denmark and the late 18th century in Sweden, but in both cases with restrictions). Culturally and linguistically, Finland is quite different from the other countries, Finnish not being an Indo-European language. During its history, Finland has belonged both to the west (Sweden) and to the east (Russia). This is still reflected in the fact that Finland has two national churches, the Lutheran (with the majority of the population as members) and the Russian Orthodox. Finland is also officially bilingual – Finnish and Swedish – although only 5.5% of the population has Swedish as their mother tongue. Politically, the Nordic countries include Greenland which is a dependency of Denmark.

In all the Nordic countries, women's social and political status is high. In the words of the Norwegian political scientist Helga Maria Hernes, one can even talk about "Scandinavian state feminism", i.e. the official response "from above" (from the state) to the demands "from below" (women's organisations).[5] This "state feminism" has had lasting effects on the development of the Nordic welfare societies: for example, gender equality in the job market and other areas of society is actively promoted both by legislation and social welfare systems.

Thus, all five countries are almost without exception among the first rankings in many statistics concerning the guarantee of women's human rights and women's full participation in societal life. To mention just a few examples, in 2005 the employment rates (i.e. the percentage of the working age population in employment) for women in Sweden and Denmark were the highest in the EU (71%) with the other Nordic countries not far behind and Iceland even somewhat higher. In 2005, 45.3% of the members of the Swedish parliament were women, which must place it at the top for female participation in European parliaments. The other Nordic countries are not far behind with between 30-42% in Finland (2007), which can be compared to Germany (31.8%), the Lower House of the Parliament in the Netherlands

---

[5] See Helga Maria Hernes, *Welfare State and Women Power: Essays in State Feminism* (Norwegian University Press: Oslo 1987), especially 10.11.15.

(36.7%), and the Lower House of the British Parliament (19.8%). The two Nordic countries that are republics, Iceland and Finland, have had two female presidents so far: Vigdis Finnbogadottir was elected President of Iceland in 1980 and was re-elected three times, in 1984, 1988 and 1992. She was the first woman in the world to be elected democratically as a president (Head of State). Tarja Halonen was elected president of Finland in 2000 and re-elected in 2006. The majority of the ministers in the current Finnish government are women (12 out of 20).

Although laws on abortion are liberal in all five countries and contraceptives are easily available (and their use actively promoted by society), the fertility rate is high in a European perspective. In Sweden, Denmark, Finland and Norway it has been 1.7–1.8 in recent years, while Iceland has the highest fertility rate in Europe (2.0). This can be compared with the average in the EU – 1.5 – and Greece and Spain, where it is about 1.3. One explanation is that the welfare policies guarantee paid *parental* leave (giving both parents the possibility of paid leave) without losing one's job and a well developed system of quality child care. Thanks to that, it is possible for women to combine work and children, and for parents to share the responsibility and the practical care for their children.

So, in the Nordic countries, the political support for gender equality seems to have succeeded in making Nordic women strong, independent, self-supporting, well represented in political assemblies, actively supported by the law in their aim to be equal to men – and at the same time, more often than not, they choose to be mothers. However, while there is much truth in this description, the reality is more complex. Although the employment rate for women is high, the labour market is still to a large extent divided along traditional gender lines. The "gender pay gap" is a reality in all the Nordic countries: in Sweden and Denmark it is 17% and in Finland 20% (2004), which is above the estimated average in the EU of 15%. In Sweden and Norway – in contrast to Finland and Iceland – about 40% of women in employment work part-time, which not only means lower incomes while working but also lower pensions when retiring. Although there are good numbers of women in the Parliaments, the number of female managers is low, especially in trade and industry. Generally – and this includes the universities – there is a good number of women at the bottom of all structures, but a stronger dominance of men the higher you come in the hierarchy. And, although a growing number of men exercise their right to parental leave, women still occupy the main part of it. Men participate in the household work to a higher degree than in the past, but in most cases women are primarily responsible for housekeeping.

Thus, there are still plenty of formal and informal mechanisms that maintain male dominance, including violence against women, both inside and outside the family, which has been made a public issue quite recently (often through feminist research and the work of the women's movement).

Finally, it may be mentioned that women can be ordained today in all the Nordic Lutheran national churches. Denmark was first, in 1948, while the first ordination of a woman in Finland took place as late as 1988, following a decision in 1987. Women are now a recognizable part of the clergy in all the Nordic countries. However, the responses to feminist theology in the churches vary. To give some examples, feminist theology has not made much impact on the life of the Lutheran Church in Finland, while the Lutheran national church in Iceland has a group called *Kvennakirkjan*, "The Women's Church", led by a pastor employed by the Church. In this group, women celebrate feminist services and participate in study groups about feminist theology as well as all kinds of issues relevant for women's lives. In the Church of Sweden, various groups and individuals have been working since the late 1970s in feminist theology, often by developing different kinds of feminist services. The work is actually often ecumenical. The issues of inclusive language are now on the official agenda when changes in rituals for worship, prayer books and lectionaries are discussed in the Lutheran national churches in Sweden[6], Norway and Iceland.

The immediate context of academic theology in the Nordic countries is quite different from that of many other, even other European, countries. In all the five countries, theological disciplines are primarily studied and researched only within secular state universities in which faculties of theology are usually the oldest ones. However, change is on its way. In Norway, Finland and Denmark there are privately funded conservative theological institutes, which were founded as a reaction to what was perceived as the secularization of the faculties of theology at state universities. Their present status varies. Unlike the ones in Finland and Denmark, the Norwegian *Menighetsfakultet* is today a recognized academic institution fully comparable to a university. In Sweden, due to changes in the system of higher education in the 1990s, some institutions (most of them seminaries for educating pastors in denominations other than the Church of Sweden) were developed into institutions for a basic theological education which is recognized by the state as equivalent to that given at state universities and open for students regardless of their confessional affiliations.

---

6 At least in Sweden these discussions are also on the agenda in some other Protestant churches.

Although some of these institutions are theologically conservative, this is certainly not true of all of them. Their aim is also to provide a possibility for students who want to be ordained to integrate theory and practice in a way that is not possible at secular universities.

Still, by and large, academic theology in the Nordic countries is non-confessional, in the sense that it is conducted in state universities which are by definition not affiliated to any church or denomination. Furthermore, today a growing number of scholars from "theological" disciplines – such as church history, biblical studies and ethics – work at departments for religious studies in faculties other than theology (e.g. education or the arts).

What this means for feminist theology is hard to assess in general terms, but one possible outcome is an understanding of feminist theology (and of theology in general) as primarily an academic enterprise. It is obvious that the relationship between academic theology and the churches (and other religious communities) in the Nordic countries is different from the relationship in church-related academic institutions, e.g., in the United States where many influential feminist theological works have been written. In the Scandinavian countries, the academic work of an individual theologian, feminist or not, does not necessarily have to reflect her or his religious convictions. This can be compared with the common presentation of feminist theologians in the United States where they are described in relation to their religious communities: they are either "reformists" or "post-Christian" or "rejectionists". By maintaining the Christian/post-Christian division, or by grouping themselves according to religious affiliations in general, feminist theologians themselves may in fact create an obstacle to the further development of non-confessional feminist research on religion as well as maintaining a rather unfruitful opposition. Thus, Scandinavian non-confessional theology may provide an interesting alternative in the international field of feminist theology.[7]

However, it must be admitted that a description of the Nordic theological faculties as "non-confessional" is not the whole truth. Although this is true formally – there are no Protestant or Catholic universities in our countries – the

---

[7] For the differences between Scandinavian and Anglo-American feminist theology, see also Jorunn Økland "Sex, gender and ancient Greek: a case-study in theoretical misfit", in: *Studia Theologica* 57 (2003), 124-142, here 124-130. Økland here also draws attention, as we do below, to the interest in feminist theory characteristic of much Scandinavian feminist theology, and to the differences between Scandinavian and Anglo-American feminist-theoretical discourse in general.

actual situations vary somewhat between our countries. For example, Norwegian Church law dictates that teachers in the faculty of theology at the University of Oslo (which is a state university) must be members of the Lutheran Church. The Faculty has as its task to educate pastors in the (Lutheran) Church of Norway. The ministry of culture and church affairs does, however, give dispensations from this rule. For a Swede, on the other hand, it seems almost absurd that the law could prescribe that the teachers at a state university should belong to a particular church.[8] Furthermore, there is of course, as always, in many places a tension between theory and practice, between explicit and implicit rules and truths. Since the theological faculties educate those who want to be ordained in the Lutheran churches, and since the majority of university teachers are Christians, there is in practice a Christian, often even a Lutheran, bias, which may be manifest (e.g. when a lot of resources are devoted to courses of particular relevance for would-be Lutheran pastors) or, even if not manifest, you can still feel it in the air. The degree and forms of Christian, or specifically Lutheran, bias vary not only between the Nordic countries, or between academic institutions in particular countries, but also between disciplines at a particular institution. During our work on this introduction, we realised that, even in our group, we had different opinions about how "non-confessional" our Nordic theological faculties actually are, depending on where we have worked, what comparison we made and on our personal convictions and perspectives.

The general theme we chose for this ESWTR journal, "Scandinavian critique of Anglo-American feminist theology", is related to all the issues mentioned above. Besides the non-confessional character of Scandinavian feminist theology, another related issue worthy of mention is the relationship between non-theological feminist theory and feminist theology. Several feminist theological dissertations in the five Nordic countries seem to be quite critical of some of the theoretical presuppositions and underpinnings of U.S. feminist theology, especially among the first generation of U.S. feminist theologians. While acknowledging the pioneering role of U.S. feminist theologians and often relying on their work, there seems to be an interest in epistemological issues that also easily leads to distancing oneself from the U.S. feminist theologies. How much this is a product of the academic and social setting described above is

---

[8]   It may be mentioned that a number of Catholic scholars work as teachers and researchers in various theological disciplines in Sweden.

hard to say. Especially in systematic theology, Scandinavians are strongly influenced by the tradition of analytical philosophy, which of course is not without problems for feminist theology. However, we are trained in a way that makes us pay attention to the use of conceptual categories, argumentation, and the bases for one's truth claims. This can be both a limitation and an enrichment for feminist theology.

But the situation of feminist theological research also differs between our countries. Generally speaking, one can say that the number of feminist theologians is growing, Sweden and Norway having the largest numbers of feminist theologians and the greatest diversity in terms of subjects studied. Two of the five Nordic countries have a permanent professor in feminist theology. One of them is located at the University of Oslo, Norway, where Kari Elisabeth Børresen was the first who has now been succeeded by Jone Salomonsen. The other is at the University of Reykjavik, Iceland, since Arnfriður Guðmundsdóttir has a permanent position as professor in systematic theology with an emphasis on feminist theology. In Sweden, there have been research positions for limited periods but no permanent professor.[9] And, as is shown elsewhere in this Journal, feminist theologians still have difficulties getting their work accepted in Finland. More examples could be added, but here it must suffice to say that the situation differs not only between the Nordic countries but also between different universities and university colleges within the countries and between academic disciplines. When feminist scholars are employed at the universities, it is mainly as doctoral students or for teaching, but not to do feminist research as post doctoral researchers or to create networks and other structures for promoting this kind of research. Finally, it should also be mentioned that, at least in Sweden, there are even a few men today who see themselves as doing feminist scholarship in various theological disciplines, and some men who work within gender studies but hesitate to call themselves feminists since they think that this designation should be reserved for women.

Finally, let us turn from the context of the Journal to the Journal itself.

This issue of the Journal has been co-edited by Hanna Stenström from Sweden and Elina Vuola from Finland.

Stenström received her doctorate in New Testament Exegesis from the University of Uppsala, where she is teaching, although she is now moving on to

---

[9] However, in some Swedish universities there are persons responsible for permanent gender seminars and for supporting gender studies in other ways as part of their work, but not full time.

a research position in the Church of Sweden. Elina Vuola has a doctorate in systematic theology from the University of Helsinki, and is a Research Fellow of the Academy of Finland working at the Institute of Development Studies at the same university. They have been supported by a reference group from the other Nordic countries:

- Arnfriður Guðmundsdóttir, who has a doctorate in systematic theology from the Lutheran School of Theology in Chicago and is now Associate Professor of systematic theology, with an emphasis on Feminist Theology, at the University of Reykjavik, Iceland
- Else Marie Wiberg Pedersen, who earned her doctorate in systematic theology at the University of Aarhus, Denmark, and is now Professor of Systematic Theology at the same university
- Lena Lybaek, who has a PhD in New Testament Exegesis from the University of Durham and is now working at the Department of Teacher Education at the University College of Buskerud in Hønefoss, Norway.

Although there is an overarching theme in the journal, there is also diversity, which makes this ESWTR Journal reflect some of the different contexts for theology in the Nordic countries today. The majority of the authors work at faculties of theology or religious studies. Some authors, however, are affiliated to other departments such as Gender Studies and Development Studies; some even work at Church based research institutions. Some of the authors have spent their academic life in their native country while others have worked in different countries and academic contexts. The authors represent different countries as well as different academic disciplines and also different academic contexts within their countries. Furthermore, there is also generational diversity in this Journal. The pioneer feminist theologian from Norway, Kari Elisabeth Børresen, represents the very first generation while some authors belong to the youngest generation – those who are still working on their doctoral dissertations. Some of the authors make their different confessional affiliations known – and they comprise both Catholics and Protestants, ordained and lay – while others do not. We included some articles that are not related to the theme in the "Forum" and "Women's traditions" sections in order to reflect more of the diversity of feminist theology in our countries. Since the field of feminist research – or, as some of us may say, gender studies – in theology is growing in the Nordic countries, it is more and more difficult to provide a general description. If asked, we could compile another issue of the Journal with a rather different content, covering other academic disciplines and introducing other topics tackled with other theoretical tools.

We also decided that this number would only cover theology, not comparative religion or research on women and religion in other fields, e.g. history or social anthropology. This was not an obvious choice, since the non-confessional character of our Nordic universities provides room for comparative religion (History of Religions) at faculties of theology, for researchers from non-theological disciplines (e.g. social anthropology) to work at faculties of theology[10] and for scholars from traditional theological disciplines to work in departments of religious studies outside the theological faculties. Important contributions to the study of gender and religion have also been made by scholars in disciplines such as folkloristics, history and anthropology. However, our decision to limit ourselves to the traditional theological disciplines was motivated by the fact that the majority of ESWTR members in the Nordic countries work in those disciplines, and that it is also in line with the situation in Europe in general.

There are different ways of finding contributors to a volume like this. One way gives the editors themselves a lot of power, choosing the theme and the contributors according to their own research interests and agendas. We, the editors and the reference group, wanted the Journal to be written by ESWTR members, and to make it possible for anyone of us to contribute. Therefore, we passed around a "call for articles" among the ESWTR members of our national sections. The Journal you are now reading is the response of members to this call.

In the Theme section, you will find an article reinterpreting understandings of Mary and motherhood (Cristina Grenholm, Sweden), an article on the Cross of Christ (Arnfriður Guðmundsdóttir, Iceland), critiques (marked by the contexts where they are formulated) of Elisabeth Schüssler Fiorenza (Anni Tsokkinen, Finland) and Daphne Hampson (Else Marie Wiberg Pedersen, Denmark), and an article on feminist sexual ethics (Sólveig Anna Bóasdóttir, Iceland). In all of these articles, the authors engage in critique of and dialogue with international feminist theology, especially from the Anglo-American world.

In the Forum section, the topics vary from the churches as agents of welfare in contemporary Europe (Ninna Edgardh Beckman, Sweden) to discussions of internationally well known and influential theologians in relation to Finnish contexts: Grace M. Jantzen (Annukka Kalske, Finland) and Ivone Gebara (Pauliina Kainulainen, Finland). Finally, you will find an article

---

[10] The actual organisation of the theological faculties, and of the relation between traditionally theological disciplines and general "religious studies", differs between our countries, but what is said above holds true on a very general level.

focusing on the problems of using birth giving as a metaphor in feminist contexts (Magdalena Raivio, Sweden). It may be mentioned that both Kainulainen's and Raivio's articles engage in discussion with ecofeminism. In "Women's traditions" you will encounter articles about two great Swedish[11] women from the past, Birgitta (Päivi Salmesvuori, Finland) and Queen Christina (Kari Elisabeth Børresen, Norway), as well as about the Catholic nuns in Norway during World War II (Else-Britt Nilsen, Norway). Finally, in "From the Countries", issues evoked by local contexts, but relevant for the international discussion, are brought to the fore by Elina Vuola (Finland) and Hanna Stenström (Sweden). We also decided to include a bibliography which, although selective, shows more of what is being and has been done, since a Journal can only cover a small part of all that is going on.

We wish to thank all those who contributed to this volume by translating articles into German and proofreading the English and French articles: Jenny Daggers (Liverpool, UK), Christiane Gäumann (Fribourg, Switzerland), Sylvie Gudin (Three Rivers, MI, USA), Isabelle Graesslé (Genève, Switzerland), Mary Phil Korsak (Linkebeek, Belgium), Charlotte Methuen (Oxford, UK and Hanau, Germany), Margaret Pater (Greifswald, Germany), Susan K. Roll (Ottawa, Canada) and Helga Voigt (Lüneburg, Germany), and last but not least Joachim Starkmann (Eichstätt, Germany) for his support in formatting the manuscripts.

So, finally, this is our Nordic contribution to the ongoing European discussion of feminist theology. We hope that it will promote further reflection and discussion.

Hanna Stenström – Elina Vuola
Uppsala and Helsinki in October 2006

In cooperation with Arnfriður Guðmundsdóttir, Reykjavik, Else Marie Wiberg Pedersen, Aarhus and Lena Lybaek, Hønefoss.

---

[11] Since Finland belonged to the Kingdom of Sweden at the time of Birgitta as well as that of Christina, these two women are also part of the history of Finland. In 1640, Queen Christina founded the Royal Academy of Turku, which was moved to Helsinki by the Russian rulers in 1828 and re-named the University of Helsinki in 1919 when Finland had gained its independence. The Christina Institute for Women's Studies at the University of Helsinki (founded in 1991) and its "Christina conferences", which are mentioned at some places in this Journal, are named after her, since she was not only the founder of the University of Helsinki but also a European intellectual woman, as is shown in Børresen's article.

Journal of the European Society of Women in Theological Research 15 (2007) 15-35.
doi: 10.2143/ESWTR.15.0.2022766

Cristina Grenholm

Mary Among Stereotypes and Dogmas
A Feminist Critique and Reinterpretation of the Patriarchal
Cornerstone of Motherhood

The purpose of this article is to analyze and reinterpret the conceptualization of motherhood in the perspective of a critical discussion of between contemporary Scandinavian and Anglo-American feminist theology in relation to Mary, the mother of Jesus, as an image of the mother. Mary strongly promotes both gender stereotypes and petrified Christian dogmas. My aim is not to save Mary or Christian faith. My concern is to add to the relatively sparse discussion on the conceptualization of motherhood, by asking: Can something be clarified about motherhood by approaching Mary and the story of the annunciation anew?

I give priority neither to experience nor to revelation. I understand revelation in a broad sense to include interpretations of biblical texts, tradition, and Christian teachings. For me, interpretation of experience and that of revelation are complex processes closely intertwined. Neither one can serve as the single point of departure. Rather, we must strive to clarify the processes of interpreting these two sources of faith. Our life-experience can be brought into dialogue with theological understandings of motherhood, or can be the basis for criticizing and even rejecting these understandings. Yet convictions based on life-experience about what characterizes motherhood can be corrected by an interpretation of the theological understanding of Mary's motherhood.

Motherhood as a challenge to gender studies
There is a tension between motherhood and other gender issues, which makes the topic both difficult and exciting. In contemporary Scandinavian and Anglo-American gender studies, body and sexuality are often the main focus; the theme of motherhood is almost absent.[1] Yet it can be found in the margins.

---

[1] It is significant that motherhood is not mentioned in Judith Butler, *Gender Trouble: Feminism and the Subversion of Identity* (Routledge: New York & London, 10th anniv. ed. 1999), James B.

With important exceptions, French feminism and ecofeminism stand outside the "mainstream"[2] of the Scandinavian and Anglo-American feminist debate.[3] The language barrier is a first explanation. Not many read French well enough to perform a qualified analysis of French feminism and to apply it in their own work. Another explanation is the accusation of gynocentrism, and sometimes also of essentialism, directed towards these movements. Although these accusations have often proved unjustified, they limited the entrance of these perspectives in the "mainstream" debate. Scholarly power plays that keep topics from the discussion are always intellectually unsatisfactory.

The tension between motherhood and Scandinavian and Anglo-American feminist studies is readily noticed by those who approach motherhood from a gender perspective. Swedish feminist philosopher Ulla Holm describes the field as mined, while also emphasizing the importance of clearing a path among explosive norms, values, emotions, reactions and reflections.[4] Grace Jantzen states that "…feminists have been anxious to resist romanticizing motherhood, either the labour of giving birth or the labour of bringing up children: still less is it a feminist view that womanhood should be equated with motherhood."[5]

Nelson / Sandra P. Longfellow (eds), *Sexuality and the Sacred: Sources for Theological Reflection* (Westminster / John Knox: Louisville 1992) and Ursula King / Tina Beattie (eds), *Religion, Gender and Diversity: Cross-Cultural Perspectives* (Continuum: London & New York 2004). Since 2000 there has not been a single article on this theme in *Journal of Feminist Studies in Theology*.

[2] I hesitate to use such an expression; I generally prefer to use descriptions less directly related to the scholarly power play.

[3] See Luce Irigaray, *Speculum of the Other Woman* (trans. Catherine Porter with Carolyn Burke; Cornell University Press: Ithaca, NY 1985 [1974]) especially the last section "Plato's Hystera". See also Julia Kristeva, "Stabat Mater", in: *Tales of Love* (trans. Leon S. Roudiez; Columbia University Press: New York 1987 [1983]), 234-263. Concerning ecofeminism see Carol P. Christ, *She Who Changes: Re-Imagining the Divine in the World* (Palgrave Macmillan: New York 2003) and Melissa Raphael, *Thealogy and Embodiment: The Post-Patriarchal Reconstruction of Female Sacrality* (Sheffield Academic Press: Sheffield 1996). Cf. Maria Jansdotter, *Ekofeminism i teologin: Genusuppfattning, natursyn och gudsuppfattning hos Anne Primavesi, Catherine Keller och Carol Christ* (Karlstad University Studies 2003:14; Karlstad University: Karlstad 2003) and David Kronlid, *Ecofeminism and Environmental Ethics: An Analysis of Ecofeminist Ethical Theory* (Acta Universitatis Upsaliensis: Uppsala Studies in Social Ethics 28; Elander Gotab: Stockholm 2003). Of course, there is also the feminist psychoanalysis with names like Nancy Chodorow, Jessica Benjamin and Dorothy Dinnerstein.

[4] Holm, Ulla M., *Modrande & praxis: En feministfilosofisk undersökning* (Daidalos: Göteborg 1993), 238.

[5] Grace M. Jantzen, *Becoming Divine: Towards a Feminist Philosophy of Religion* (Indiana University Press: Bloomington & Indianapolis 1999), 143f.

I believe it is possible to clear the path Holm refers to without falling prey to such romanticism.

The collective book, *Representations of Motherhood,* gives one explanation of why motherhood has received comparatively little attention from feminist scholarship. The editors claim that motherhood is over-determined on several levels: it is socially and culturally complex, while bringing difficulties and challenges at a personal level. According to them, motherhood raises too many questions at once.[6]

Before returning to these feminist reflections on motherhood, let me clarify the consequence of the tendency of gender studies to focus on the body and sexuality and to marginalize motherhood. What is so fascinating about motherhood, and yet often ignored, is that it is in fact located at the very intersection of the female body and its sexuality. Then, is motherhood a repressed phenomenon within gender studies?[7] Are there some reasons for not keeping it on the agenda? I can see three: a philosophical, a social, and a psychological reason. I also see reasons for changing this situation.

Philosophically, post-modern programmatic constructivism has made motherhood, with its obvious physical characteristics, difficult to approach. Almost everybody has been affected by the way this philosophical turn has challenged traditional – explicit or implicit, more or less – positivistic ways of thinking. Although most find it difficult to reduce reality to social constructions, one must account for the unclear border between "fact" and "conceptualization". In my opinion one should not reduce motherhood to biology. Neither should one confine reflection on pregnancy and delivery to the level of social or cultural constructions. Motherhood makes it necessary to reflect on the unstable borders between materiality, concepts, habits, political structures, etc.

Motherhood is clearly connected to the social patriarchal order and to women's lack of control. It runs the risk of being perpetually inscribed within the patriarchal circle. Therefore, it often seemed more productive for women's emancipation to focus on other spheres of life. Historically women's movements have sought to overcome the negative consequences of motherhood.[8]

---

6   Donna Bassin / Margret Honey / Meryle Mahrer Kaplan (eds), *Representations of Motherhood* (Yale University Press: New Haven 1994), 8f.
7   Irigaray claims it is. Grace Jantzen uses her philosophy of the repressed (m)other. Jantzen, *Becoming Divine*, 6-26, 128-155.
8   This is why radical feminism has favoured technological development in this area, as underscored in Shulamit Firestone, *The Dialectic of Sex: The Case for Feminist Revolution* (Morrow: New York 1970).

This includes issues of reproductive health, daycare systems, justice on the job market, marriage, and divorce legislation. Motherhood is an important part of the problem in the struggle for women's liberation. However, motherhood cannot be exclusively treated as a negative phenomenon. It also has positive values. Moreover, it is a common phenomenon. In Sweden, 85 percent of women over the age of forty have given birth.[9]

When considering the theme of motherhood, one immediately asks: who is to count as a mother? This is a sensitive psychological issue for many women. There is a close cultural connection between motherhood and womanhood. Yet we need not to accept this cultural view when approaching motherhood as a field for feminist inquiry. Rather, one of my aims is to confront such ideas. Of course, women can be mothers in different ways: adoptive mothers, foster mothers, extra mothers, stepmothers, surrogate mothers, etc. In each case somebody cares especially for a particular child. The fact that this article concerns motherhood that includes pregnancy and delivery does not imply that other kinds of motherhood are less valuable. However, I believe that the kind of motherhood I am analyzing should not be considered apart from the characteristic that distinguishes it from all other human relationships; namely, that one body has brought forth another. This makes biological motherhood unique, although not totally separated from other kinds of motherhood or human relationships. I do not make a distinction between real mothers and other mothers. We must consider differences in motherhood precisely as differences, which need not be evaluated, but which can be taken into account. Some seem to think that including pregnancy and delivery when reflecting on motherhood adds to the depreciation of women who do not give birth. I believe the opposite is true; such reflection offers a possibility to come to grips with the depreciation of other ways adults relate to children.

Motherhood in gender studies

That motherhood was neglected in feminist studies does not mean it was absent. Already Simone de Beauvoir highlighted the tension between motherhood and women's full participation and authorization in society at large.[10] During the 1960's and 70's others raised critical issues about motherhood.

---

[9] *På tal om kvinnor och män: Lathund om jämställdhet 2004* (Statistiska Centralbyrån: Stockholm 2004), 19, table over childlessness related to age.
[10] Simone de Beauvoir, *The Second Sex* (trans. & ed. H.M. Parshley; Vintage: London 1997 [orig. 1953]), 501-542.

Jessie Bernard is one of the pioneers, Adrienne Rich is another.[11] Still, as Bonnie Miller-McLemore pointed out, overall there was a tendency to focus on how women can have good life possibilities despite being mothers, rather than on how they can achieve this as mothers. Yet, note that this concerns motherhood in a patriarchal society. Feminists have not, as some of its critics claim, disregarded children. In fact, as Miller-McLemore also stresses, the women's movement has to a large extent focused on issues highly relevant for children, such as combating violence and sexism.[12] It also has made women aware of the injustices committed against them.[13]

Raising the issue of the link between injustice and motherhood is important. One must describe and critically assess the consequences of this link. But one must also evaluate motherhood positively for its contributions. Sara Ruddick has done pioneering and influential work on this. She describes the specific kind of thinking that mothers develop or should develop as "maternal thinking," characterized by the demands for preservation, growth, and social acceptability, which are met by preservative love, nurturance, and training.[14] The focus is ethical. Ruddick emphasizes that maternal thinking is not confined to the female gender.[15]

In Sweden Ulla Holm has taken up, criticized and developed Ruddick's work. Holm clarifies maternal ethics by relating it to Aristotelian thinking and describing maternal virtues in terms of the mean between vices.[16] After making a clear distinction between a) the biologically necessary, and thus gender specific, aspects of motherhood, and b) care for children, which is not gender specific, she focuses her analysis on the latter.

For me, in motherhood the distinction between biological necessities and what we make of them is not clear. It is also inappropriate to make it sharp, since that prevents us from raising important questions. While it is necessary to promote gender equality in parenting, one should not disregard that it is

[11] Jessie Bernard, *The Future of Motherhood* (The Dial Press: New York 1974); Adrienne Rich, *Of Woman Born: Motherhood as Experience and Institution* (W.W. Norton & Company: New York & London, 10th anniv. ed. 1986 [orig. 1976]).

[12] Bonnie J. Miller-McLemore, *Let the Children Come: Reimagining Childhood from a Christian Perspective* (Jossey-Bass: San Francisco 2003), 106-110.

[13] Cf. Sara Ruddick, *Maternal Thinking: Towards a Politics of Peace* (The Women's Press Limited: Aylesbury, Bucks, England, 2nd ed. 1990), 236-239.

[14] Ruddick, *Maternal Thinking*, 17.

[15] Ruddick, *Maternal Thinking*, 22.

[16] Holm, *Modrande & praxis*, 233-264.

women who get pregnant and give birth. Otherwise a realistic reflection on motherhood is impossible. Thus, my definition of motherhood seeks to take into account both its passive and its active aspects. The mother contains a process of creation and partakes in the creation of the human being that is her child.[17] And one should avoid identifying either pregnancy with the passive aspect of motherhood, or nurturing care for the child with the active. The pregnant woman cares for her future child and the child grows in and of itself when born.

Reflecting on the ethical aspects of motherhood is important, but not sufficient. We also have to ponder the concept of motherhood as part of the ongoing task of interpreting and understanding life. For this let us turn to biblical texts. I will retell the story of the annunciation in order to start the process of interpreting both experience and revelation.

The story of Mary encountering an angel

The story of the annunciation presents a specific problem for reflecting on motherhood, since it separates Mary's experience of discovering pregnancy from that of most women.[18] I will relate the image of Mary to a realistic understanding of motherhood, look for possibilities of identification with other mothers, and this without reducing mystery to either natural or supernatural "facts".

For this purpose, I read Luke 1:26-40, including the passage, which tells us that Mary after the visit of the angel went into the mountains to see Elizabeth.

> In the sixth month the angel Gabriel was sent by God to a town in Galilee called Nazareth, to a virgin engaged to a man whose name was Joseph, of the house of David. The virgin's name was Mary. And he came to her and said, "Greetings, favored one! The Lord is with you." But she was much perplexed by his words and pondered what sort of greeting this might be. The angel said to her, "Do not be afraid, Mary, for you have found favor with God. And now, you will conceive in

---

[17] Here it is enough to mention these two aspects of motherhood. However, note that I adopt a terminology of creation, and not of sin as many theologians do. Cf. Cristina Grenholm, *Moderskap och kärlek: Schabloner och tankeutrymme i feministteologisk livsåskådningsreflektion* (Nya Doxa: Nora 2005), 49f.

[18] For an overview of biblical, apocryphal and extra-canonical stories of annunciation see Antoinette Clark Wire, *Holy Lives, Holy Deaths: A Close Hearing of Early Jewish Storytellers* (Studies in Biblical Literature 1; Society for Biblical Literature: Atlanta 2001).

your womb and bear a son, and you will name him Jesus. He will be great, and will be called the Son of the Most High, and Lord God will give to him the throne of his ancestor David. He will reign over the house of Jacob forever, and of his kingdom there will be no end." Mary said to the angel, "How can this be, since I am a virgin?" The angel said to her, "The Holy Spirit will come upon you, and the power of the Most High will overshadow you; therefore the child to be born will be holy; he will be called Son of God. And now, your relative Elizabeth in her old age has also conceived a son; and this is the sixth month for her who was said to be barren. For nothing will be impossible with God." Then Mary said, "Here am I, the servant of the Lord; let it be with me according to your word." Then the angel departed from her. In those days Mary set out and went with haste to a Judean town in the hill country, where she entered the house of Zechariah and greeted Elizabeth. (Luke 1:26-40, NRSV)

The story can be retold as follows: Mary meets an angel. It is just the two of them in seclusion. Mary is frightened and perplexed, but she is told not to be scared. She receives a message that she will give birth; but instead of asking when, she asks how this will happen. This is remarkable. She is betrothed to Joseph, but does not understand the message as being about their future child. She says she has not been with a man, although she has her future planned with Joseph. The angel speaks of Holy Spirit and the power of the Most High. The angel does not mention Joseph, but points to Elizabeth. It is to her that Mary turns after the angel's visit.

The story is a vision, one of the biblical stories about people encountering angels, unlike common stories about other encounters. Such stories tell about a meeting point between heaven and earth, the transcendent and the immanent. We would not have been able to watch this encounter even if we had been there. The story is not historical in the ordinary sense of the word; it does not concern fact, but mystery. The parallel story of Zechariah and the angel is described as "a vision" (1:22).

The hidden mother
If motherhood is a repressed phenomenon in feminist studies, it is even more so in other fields, especially in theology. In one sense motherhood plays an important role in Christian theology, but at the same time the mother is constantly hidden behind the father. This is a basic presumption that has to be dealt with when approaching motherhood.

Sallie McFague has clearly described the role of the heavenly Father by classifying him as the dominating metaphor in Christianity.

It [God the Father as metaphor] suggests a comprehensive, ordering structure with impressive interpretive potential. As a rich model with many associated commonplaces as well as a host of supporting metaphors, an entire theology can be worked out from this model. Thus, if God is understood on the model of 'father', human beings are understood as 'children', sin is rebellion against the 'father', redemption is sacrifice by the 'older son' on behalf or the 'brothers and sisters' for the guilt against the 'father' and so on.[19]

Consequently, for McFague, the mother is made invisible and subordinate. Indeed, for many, the Father metaphor is foundational for Christianity, making masculinity the hidden norm of humanity.[20] Thus, we must keep in mind that motherhood is hidden, even as it is interwoven in the web of Christian thought. When we make it visible, something new happens. Motherhood simultaneously connects to tradition and changes it. Focusing on Mary as a pregnant woman in the story of the angelic encounter means that both the father and the son have to give way.

Beyond this, Swedish philosopher of religion, Kirsten Grönlien Zetterqvist, claims that Western philosophy, by insisting on the existence of the human subject and promoting autonomy, cannot do justice to the act of giving birth. It does not provide categories for describing it appropriately.[21] She shows that a woman cannot recognize her own experience of birthing. Grönlien Zetterqvist uses the image of having seen a new color. She says it is an open question how the mother wants to use this color in her image of life and emphasizes the difficulties she faces by claiming that "if I live in a culture that thinks red is unreal, spaced out, I may not use that color."[22] If that color is used in the interpretation of Mary and the angel, formerly hidden things can be seen.

Digging further into the implications of using the new color, Grönlien Zetterqvist holds that giving birth challenges the very distinction between body and mind.[23] She coins the concept of "body subject".[24] Sara Ruddick shares

---

[19] Sallie McFague, *Metaphorical Theology: Models of God in Religious Language* (Fortress Press: Philadelphia 2nd ed. 1984 [orig. 1982]) 23.

[20] McFague, *Metaphorical Theology*, 145f.

[21] Kirsten Grönlien Zetterqvist, *Att vara kroppssubjekt: Ett fenomenologiskt bidrag till feministisk teori och religionsfilosofi* (Uppsala universitet: Uppsala & Almqvist & Wiksell International: Stockholm 2002), 22-30.

[22] Grönlien Zetterqvist, *Att vara kroppssubjekt*, 113.

[23] Grönlien Zetterqvist, *Att vara kroppssubjekt*, 141.

[24] Grönlien Zetterqvist, *Att vara kroppssubjekt*, 75, 152.

much of the same view, stressing that giving birth above all challenges the traditional way of distinguishing between self and other.

Birth, more than any other experience except perhaps sexuality, undermines the individuation of bodies. The growing fetus, increasingly visible in the woman's swelling body, an infant emerging from the vagina, a suckling infant feeding off a breast, the mother feeding with and of her body express in dramatic form a fusion of self and other. Any man or woman might fear the obliteration of self that such an experience suggests.[25]

I think we have to move beyond Ruddick's presentation of this challenge in terms of a social relation. To gain a satisfactory view of motherhood we need an additional "color." Motherhood is not merely about a relationality that challenges the mother's autonomy; it is also about heteronomy.

Heteronomy as a characteristic of motherhood

Beyond relationality the challenge to autonomy points to its opposite, heteronomy. To be autonomous means to be independent and to make one's own decisions, to be in control of one's life. To depend on circumstances or other people in general, relationality, is not its opposite. Autonomy is always relative and limited; the individual is always in a web of relationality. The actual opposite of autonomy is the situation where one lacks control. "Auto" is Greek for self and "hetero" for other. Heteronomy means that somebody else is in control.[26]

Motherhood is not only characterized by the unclear border between mother and child, but also by the opposite of autonomy: heteronomy. The mother contains a process of creation she cannot control and the pregnancy results in a relationship she can neither leave, nor control. Motherhood is necessarily heteronomous. The mother can neither protect the child from all dangers, nor control its development. Heteronomy is also the basis for respect of the autonomy of the child. Eventually motherhood makes us face mortality; not just

---

[25] Ruddick, *Maternal Thinking*, 191.

[26] Daphne Hampson, "On Autonomy and Heteronomy", in: Daphne Hampson (ed.), *Swallowing a Fishbone? Feminist Theologians Debate Christianity* (SPCK: London 1996), 1-16. See also Cristina Grenholm, "Kvinnan och barnet: Självständighet – samhörighet – styrka", in: Sigurd Bergmann (ed.), *"Man får inte tvinga någon" : Autonomi och relationalitet i nordisk teologisk tolkning* (Nya Doxa: Nora 2001), 79-87.

that of the child, but also that of the mother, as Bonnie Miller-McLemore poignantly says.

> Letting go of children goes against the grain of human self-preservation precisely because to let go means to admit one's own finitude, limits, and fears.[27]

She adds a theological conclusion.

> For a religious person, perhaps the hardest spiritual lesson, or the most difficult virtue, to acquire through care of children is entrusting oneself and those most loved to God's care and protection.[28]

Heteronomy is frightening; it contains the possibility of extinction. Reflection on motherhood leads to the insight that we are not in control of life; neither our own, nor that of others. Heteronomy is also clearly related to female gender. According to the stereotype, femininity lacks control. Some would even argue women want it that way, a serious mistake in my view. Acknowledging the heteronomous character of motherhood simultaneously forces us to confront the patriarchal abuse of this phenomenon, as will become clear when I discuss the subtle distinction between vulnerability and exposure. Here I just want to highlight that, in the story of the angelic encounter, Mary is put in a situation characterized by heteronomy. It is a heteronomous situation that many women who are mothers can recognize in their own lives.

Although Ulla Holm (like Sara Ruddick) relates autonomy primarily to relationality, she conveys an awareness of the phenomenon of heteronomy. It may seem trivial, but she stresses that pregnancies originate beyond the control of parents.[29] Still, this is an important observation, since this is an often neglected point of connection between ordinary mothers and Mary.[30] Ulla Holm also refers to Agnes Heller's insistence that the ideal of the autonomous self is a dream and that heteronomy always has to be taken into account. For Holm feminists aiming for emancipation had a tendency to ignore this fact.[31] There

---

[27] Miller-McLemore, *Let the Children Come*, 157.
[28] Miller-McLemore, *Let the Children Come*, 157.
[29] Holm, *Modrande & praxis*, 140f.
[30] Cynthia L. Rigby, "Mary and the Artistry of God", in: Berverly Roberts Gaventa / Cynthia L. Rigby (eds), *Blessed One: Protestant Perspectives on Mary* (Westminster John Knox Press: Louisville / London: 2002), 145-158, here 155.
[31] Holm, *Modrande & praxis*, 202.

exist not only equal relationships, but also relationships that are necessarily asymmetrical.

> The children, the sick, the disabled and the old people will always exist among us. There are necessarily asymmetrical relationships between people, maybe not in the ideal world, but in this world in which we live. Where they prevail is the ideal of a free, autonomous "self" just a dream. The test for a relatively autonomous person is how she handles necessarily asymmetrical relations without either oppressing the weak or suppressing her own vital needs.[32]

Considering that the mother contains a process of creation and partakes in the creation of the human being who is her child, that she is hidden and simultaneously interwoven in theological thinking and, finally, that heteronomy characterizes the asymmetric relationship between mother and child, what can we learn from Mary?

Mother Mary, dogmatics and life

Mary is the Mother, not just in theology, but in broader circles. As Bonnie Miller-McLemore puts it, "…she gathers up all the free-floating desires that mothers evoke."[33] The tendency to neglect motherhood in feminist studies is also prevalent concerning Mary in feminist theology.[34] Still, there are exceptions. We can even perceive a growing interest in Mary in contemporary theology.

What is striking for me, a Scandinavian, is that discussions about Mary by theologians in the English-speaking world are much more guided by classic dogmatics than they are in my own setting. This cultural difference is especially apparent in the United States, where scholarly debates on Mary look like ecumenical discussions between churches. The tension between the Protestant critique of Marian devotion, and the Catholic and Orthodox veneration is constantly on the agenda. For instance, the Protestant editors of *Mary, Mother of God* point to their intention "to honor Mary in ways that are scripturally based, evangelically motivated, liturgically appropriate, and ecumenically sensitive".[35]

---

[32] Holm, *Modrande & praxis*, 202. When nothing else is stated, the translations from Swedish were made by me.

[33] Miller-McLemore, "Pondering All These Things", in: Gaventa / Rigby, *Blessed One*, 97-114, here 99.

[34] Miller-McLemore "Pondering All These Things", 102. See also Elisabeth Schüssler Fiorenza, *Jesus, Miriam's Child, Sophia's Prophet: Critical Issues in Feminist Christology* (SCM Press: London, 2nd ed. 1995).

[35] Carl E. Braaten / Robert W. Jenson (eds), *Mary, Mother of God* (William B. Eerdmans Publishing Company: Grand Rapids, Michigan / Cambridge U.K. 2004), viii.

Similarly, the editors of *Blessed One: Protestant Perspectives on Mary* announce that "[t]he time has come for Protestants to join in the blessing of Mary".[36] I use these books as examples for analysing interpretations of Mary in contemporary theology.

In these two volumes there is a clear tendency to make theological reflection self-referential within the theological system. For example, Robert Jenson states that rejecting that Mary is the Mother of God is simply heretical, since it was declared in the decrees of Chalcedon,[37] and thus concludes that for a Lutheran it is also acceptable to invoke the prayers of Mary.[38] Joel Green explicitly confronts the connection between Mary as blessed (Luke 11:27-28) and her motherhood. For him, Luke does not support the conventional view of women achieving their status as mothers; Mary testifies to God's initiative by embracing his word rather than meeting social expectations.[39] Mary is not so much a mother as a believer. In both cases Mary's motherhood returns to its hiding place, while conventional theological traditions of Marian devotion and Mary as the exemplary believer come to the fore.

For me, an important difference between the situation in Sweden and in the United States is related to the fact that there is a dominant folk church. As in Denmark, Finland, Iceland, and Norway, the Lutheran church has contributed considerably to the cultural and political coherence of Sweden. At the same time, affiliation, church buildings, and church ceremonies are not exclusively connected with institutional belief in God.[40] Consequently, one does not generally find a sharp distinction between a religious and a cultural sphere.[41] Indeed, for me this distinction is illusory. Thus, one is less concerned about

---

[36] Beverly Roberts Gaventa / Cynthia L. Rigby, "Introduction", in: Gaventa / Rigby, *Blessed One*, 1-6, here 1.

[37] Robert W. Jenson, "A Space for God", in: Braaten / Jenson, *Mary, Mother of God*, 49-57, here 50.

[38] Jenson, "A Space for God", 56.

[39] Joel B. Green, "Blessed Is She Who Believed: Mary, Curious Exemplar in Luke's Narrative", in: Gaventa / Rigby, *Blessed One*, 9-20.

[40] Björn Ryman with Aila Lauha / Gunnar Heiene / Peter Lodberg, *Nordic Folk Churches: A Contemporary Church History* (Eerdmans: Grand Rapids, 2005); Anders Bäckström / Ninna Edgardh Beckman / Per Pettersson, *Religious Change in Northern Europe: The Case of Sweden* (Verbum: Stockholm, 2004).

[41] For the opposite view cf. Nora O. Lozano-Díaz, "Ignored Virgin or Unaware Women: A Mexican-American Protestant Reflection on the Virgin of Guadalope", in: Gaventa / Rigby, *Blessed One*, 85-96.

proper Lutheran or Catholic views and more with the problem under discussion. One feels free to discuss alternatives, including when discussing Mary, unlike the discussion in the United States where there seem to be preset acceptable alternatives, such as those used by Jenson and Green. This freedom to consider alternative interpretations is, for me, a good thing for theological teaching and reflection. So that theology might ultimately serve as a reflection on life, dogmatics should be allowed to inform, but not to determine our span of thought.

Instead of letting dogmatics determine reflection, we should use experience as an equal partner. Instead of letting dogmatics choose the alternatives, we should also let other sources inform us. Theological reflection demands space for thought. Its primary aim is not to protect its own system, but to assist everybody in the task of interpreting ever changing life.

Here we find another important characteristic of Scandinavia when compared with many other parts of the world. Generally speaking, Scandinavian mothers have what many mothers lack. In Sweden the social security system provides good conditions for women's health and for combining motherhood and work. Mothers depend on the fathers of their children to a lesser degree than elsewhere in the world. As Hedvig Ekerwald has shown, this has been a rather fast development and today's mothers have possibilities that the generation before us could at best dream of.[42] This situation provides good soil for theological interpretations of motherhood that better correspond to the social reality of Scandinavian mothers.

Mary beyond the stereotype mother

Mary and her image strongly promote gender stereotypes and petrified Christian dogmas. In order to present a feminist critique and reinterpretation of this patriarchal cornerstone of motherhood we need to move beyond these gender stereotypes, as feminist studies always seek to do, but also beyond these petrified Christian dogmas. Why?

First, challenging Mary's stereotypical image of motherhood has to be done in relation to gender studies. While gender theory outside the field of theology has been eager to analyze gender stereotypes, it has been less interested in analyzing Christian beliefs. For example, Ulla Holm writes that Mary is a

---

[42] Hedvig Ekerwald, *Varje mor är en dotter: Om kvinnors ungdomstid på 1900-talet* (Symposion: Stockholm & Stehag 2002).

model for mothers in contemporary Sweden and describes her as "...she who gives up her own will and unconditionally obeys her almighty Lord, carries out his orders, adores and serves both him and the Son."[43] Since gender stereotypes and Christian fossilized dogmas are intertwined in this way, a task of primary importance is to confront both simultaneously from a feminist point of view. For this, one should not let conventional Christian terminology guide theological reflection.[44] Feminist theologians should critically examine and reinterpret the image of Mary's motherhood rather than make her attractive.

The second reason for confronting the petrified Christian dogmas of Mary's image has to do with the character of Christian teachings, as short, authorized formulations of the contents of Christian faith, such as "God is triune"; "Jesus is truly God and truly human"; "Mary is virgin and mother"; "human beings are justified sinners". Such formulations should be regarded as summaries of stories, reflections, and philosophical thinking.

Petrified dogmas and gender stereotypes alike unduly simplify what is complex. Summaries must not be identified with what is being summarized. Theological disputes tend to concentrate on the summaries rather than on the complex phenomena, in the same way that debates over gender and feminist studies tend to focus on stereotypes.

Summaries, taken in and of themselves, are deceptive. The same expression may not refer to the same thing to everybody. The titles of the books, *Blessed One* and *Mary, Mother of God*, testify to this. The dogmatic formulas, Blessed one and Mother of God, respectively, bring the contributors together, but do not make them agree on the meaning of these formulas.[45]

I am not arguing that creeds be changed or that certain topics be excluded from theological reflection. However, they should not always serve as our points of departure. This is why my retelling of Mary's encounter with the angel neither focuses on virginity, nor on incarnation. Rather, the pregnancy of a mother-to-be is highlighted.

---

[43] Holm, *Modrande & praxis*, 257.

[44] For an elaboration of my theological position in this respect in relation to Serene Jones, *Feminist Theory and Christian Theology: Cartographies of Grace* (Fortress Press: Minneapolis 2000) see Cristina Grenholm / Daniel Patte, "Introduction", in: Cristina Grenholm / Daniel Patte (eds), *Gender, Tradition and Romans: Shared Ground, Uncertain Borders* (Romans Through History and Cultures Series; T&T Clark International: New York / London 2005), 1-18, here 9-11.

[45] Cf. Grenholm, *Moderskap och kärlek*, 73-98.

Strategies for reinterpretation

Which strategies do feminist theologians use when approaching Mary as mother? Here are some examples.

First, as in feminist studies in general, motherhood is not focused. Theologians have a tendency to emphasize that Mary is "not only a mother" and then turn to something else. For example, Cheryl A. Kirk-Duggan holds that the Lukan stories of Mary and Elizabeth basically convey the message that "they were the right mothers for the right children at the right time."[46] Then leaving motherhood behind, Kirk-Duggan presents "Proud Mary" in a dialogue with a rock song, sang by Tina Turner. Mary is not only a mother, but also a powerful and brave person. The problem with this strategy is that, although it is helpful in other respects, it does not confront or critically discuss the stereotype of Mary's motherhood. However, this interpretation moves beyond traditional Christian teachings in seeking hermeneutical keys that do not originate in Christian tradition. Proud Mary is a praiseworthy invention.

A second strategy also moves beyond the motherhood of Mary, but remains within the formulations of Christian tradition. For example, Beverly Roberts Gaventa focuses on Mary as a model believer. She is then a mother in a more figurative sense as Mother of all believers.[47] Getting rid of Mary's stereotyped femininity and her concrete motherhood in order to describe her in less gendered terms often turns out to be just another way of putting her back into tradition, which in turn again promotes gendered stereotypes. This strategy lets Christian teachings determine interpretation, although with a feminist twist. I think it is helpful, but not sufficient.

A third strategy used by other scholars is to reinterpret Mary as mother in positive terms. For example, Bonnie Miller-McLemore sets out to relate Protestant attention to Scripture with contemporary experience of mothering in order to find inspiration and liberation.[48] Miller-McLemore underscores what Luke repeatedly says about Mary, namely that she ponders, as an expression of the practice of maternal thinking in Ruddick's sense.[49] This move takes her at least

---

[46] Cheryl A. Kirk-Duggan, "Proud Mary: Contextual Constructions of a Divine Diva", in: Gaventa / Rigby, *Blessed One*, 71-84, here 77.

[47] Beverly Roberts Gaventa, "'Nothing Will be Impossible with God': Mary as the Mother of Believers", in: Braaten / Jenson, *Mary, Mother of God*, 19-35. See also Beverly Roberts Gaventa, "'Standing Near the Cross': Mary and the Crucifixion of Jesus", in: Gaventa / Rigby, *Blessed One*, 47-56.

[48] Miller-McLemore, "Pondering All These Things", 99, 105.

[49] Miller-McLemore, "Pondering All These Things", 106.

one step away from pregnancy. Miller-McLemore's essay is not dogmatically determined, still she focuses on Mary as an ideal and limits herself to biblical terms and does not use other major analytical terms. The same strategy is adopted by Tina Beattie in a major Roman Catholic contribution to the debate, which explicitly confronts androcentrism by developing gynocentric narratives.[50] However, traditional symbols remain intact, although reinterpreted.[51] Biblical texts and traditional concepts from Christian teachings seem to be the goal, while other issues from experience such as maternal thinking, are at best an instrument. In my view this strategy is not satisfactory. Although it confronts the stereotype of motherhood, it does not challenge petrified dogmatics and thus becomes predetermined by it.

A fourth strategy is to bring forth the scandalous character of Mary's pregnancy, as Jane Schaberg did in her much discussed book, *The Illegitimacy of Jesus*.[52] She puts forth her argument in a delicate way, by describing it as a reading against the grain[53] and as the glass pieces in a kaleidoscope, which form a pattern, although it is fragile.[54] Mary can be seen as a single mother protected by God. Schaberg is aware of the danger in promoting the idea that God somehow uses sexual violation of a young girl for the higher purpose of human salvation.[55] However, there is another risk with her thought provoking interpretation. Is not the androcentric gaze still given priority? Does not the interpreter have to accept the prevalent view that mothers cannot guarantee the legitimacy of their children by themselves? Gender stereotypes prevail, while Christian teaching is indeed challenged.[56]

This last strategy is in my opinion the most promising, confronting both stereotypes of motherhood and fossilized Christian patterns of thought.

---

[50] Tina Beattie, *God's Mother, Eve's Advocate: A Gynocentric Refiguration of Marian Symbolism in Engagement with Luce Irigaray* (CCSRG Series 3; University of Bristol: Bristol 1999), 9. Another important contribution in this tradition is of course Elizabeth A. Johnson, *Truly Our Sister: A Theology of Mary in the Communion of Saints* (Continuum: New York 2003).

[51] "The maternal flesh, which, in a world of sin is associated with corruption and death, becomes a sign of purity and life in a world redeemed." Beattie, *God's Mother, Eve's Advocate*, 103.

[52] Jane Schaberg, *The Illegitimacy of Jesus: A Feminist Theological Interpretation of the Infancy Narratives* (Sheffield Academic Press: Sheffield 1995 [orig. 1990]). Cf. also Katharine Doob Sakenfeld, "Tamar, Rahab, Ruth and the Wife of Uriah: The Company Mary Keeps in Matthew's Gospel", in: Gaventa / Rigby, *Blessed One*, 21-31.

[53] Schaberg. *The Illegitimacy of Jesus*, 14f.

[54] Schaberg. *The Illegitimacy of Jesus*, 195.

[55] Schaberg. *The Illegitimacy of Jesus*, 90, 94f.

[56] For further discussion, see Grenholm, *Moderskap och kärlek*, 99-126.

However, Schaberg's privileging of the male gaze points to a problem, which her interpretation shares with several others. Feminist interpreters tend to choose between either a positive or a negative view of the motherhood of Mary. As I am aiming for a realistic understanding of motherhood, I want both aspects to be there. Viewing Mary either as the oppressed or as the strong woman becomes too one-sided and in that sense reductive. I believe that Schaberg is on to something important when she emphasizes the exposure of pregnant Mary. However, I do not want to equate Mary's situation with exposure or suppression. I believe the point of the story of Mary and the angel lies elsewhere and that it is vital to recover this point for understanding Mother Mary.

I want to argue that it is a story about vulnerability rather than exposure and a story of love rather than of oppression. Actually, the message is in the close relation between these two categories that we do not want to separate even though we should. The reader is left with an awareness of the ambiguity of vulnerability and exposure. She has a chance to reflect on her own responsibility in terms of a choice between love and oppression. In my view this interpretation offers new space for thought by avoiding the traps set by stereotypes of motherhood, by traditional dogmas, and also by gender stereotypes.

Which vulnerability?

The first reaction to the concept of vulnerability is often negative. It tells us that somebody is in need and we have to be careful. However, as soon as we start reflecting on it, we know that it also has powerful positive connotations.[57] To be able to show your vulnerability to somebody and be met with care is an experience of love. Still, we need to be cautious. A positive evaluation of vulnerability presupposes that there is a fair chance that it will not automatically be used against us. Although I see vulnerability as one of our life conditions, I am aware that human beings are always found in specific contexts and that should be taken into consideration. For example, Kirk-Duggan's proud Mary springs from a womanist perspective, where emphasizing the weaker sides of Mary would easily relapse back into reinforcing the virtue of self-sacrifice.[58]

---

[57] On the ambiguous character of the concept see Karen Lebacqz, "Appropriate Vulnerability", in: Nelson / Longfellow (eds), *Sexuality and the Sacred*, 256-261.

[58] Cf. the complex and much discussed idea of "marianismo", Elina Vuola, "Seriously Harmful for your Health? Feminism and Sexuality in Latin America", in: Marcella Althaus-Reid (ed.), *Liberation Theology and Sexuality* (Ashgate: Hampshire & Burlington 2006).

Vulnerability is not to be confused or identified with being exposed to subordination or oppression, although that is a permanent risk. We need to keep a clear distinction between exposure and vulnerability by looking closer to our modes of existence: autonomy, relationality and heteronomy.[59]

Autonomy and relationality do not need to be explained here. But heteronomy, as an ambiguous concept (and not merely as a negative concept), needs further clarification. Heteronomy is the mode of existence where we lack control. Indeed this is an occasion for exposure, opening the possibility of oppression, which always needs to be resisted. Feminist reflection has paid close attention to all forms of oppression – a legacy which is praiseworthy, to say the least. However, feminists also risk to miss the distinction between oppression and vulnerability. Vulnerability belongs to the heteronomous mode of existence and is characterized by a lack of control. What makes it different from exposure? According to the way it is received by the other. When heteronomy results in being exploited, then it is turned into exposure. If heteronomy is met with love and care, it is vulnerability and a source of empowerment.[60] This is what I learn from Mary's encounter with the angel.

Mary is a mother to be, struck by uncertainty regarding the presence of the father, as so many other women are. She is a woman who faces her irrevocable responsibility for an unknown growing life. To become a mother is to be connected to another person without being able to share that person's way through life. Indeed, Mary is unique, but not in every respect. She shares in heteronomy with all other mothers. People can easily use her heteronomy by elevating themselves and suppressing Mary, or by elevating Mary and suppressing themselves. But in this story heteronomy is primarily revealed, not exposed. The promise of the presence of the Holy Spirit implies that Mary's heteronomy is met with love. She is not an exposed mother, but a vulnerable mother.

When the story is interpreted neither in terms of the gendered stereotype of mothers, nor in terms of authorized Christian fossilized dogmas, it can reveal

---

[59] Cf. Cristina Grenholm / Daniel Patte, "Overture: Receptions, Critical Interpretations and Scriptural Criticism", in: Cristina Grenholm / Daniel Patte (eds), *Reading Israel in Romans* (Romans Through History and Cultures 1: Receptions and critical interpretations; Trinity Press International: Harrisburg 2000), 1-54, here 9-12.

[60] Cf. Sarah Coakley, "Kenosis and Subversion: On the Repression of 'Vulnerability' in Christian Feminist Writing", in: Daphne Hampson (ed.), *Swallowing a Fishbone? Feminist Theologians Debate Christianity* (London: SPCK 1996), 82-111.

other important things. Although heteronomy belongs to our modes of existence, it is unusually clear in the pregnancy of the mother. The common construction of motherhood as a primary locus of female weakness conceals the distinction between vulnerability and exposure. It also conceals that the effect of the heteronomy of motherhood is determined by the beholder. It is not feminine to lack control; but the gendered stereotype of mothers has led to the effect that mothers have been deprived of their need for love and care. Their heteronomy has been exposed and they have been oppressed sexually, in family life and on the job market. And the theology of Mary's motherhood has been part of that process. However, women's so called popular religiosity provides a source of experience, which fits better with this theological reinterpretation and could thus serve as a basis for further reflection.[61]

Our experience of and need for love

In this article I have related the image of Mary to a realistic understanding of motherhood by emphasizing its ambiguous relation to vulnerability and exposure. This makes possible Mary's identification with other mothers as well as their identification with her. But I have also claimed that this does not reduce Mary to just another mother. By pointing to her uncertainty regarding the presence of the father, I have not closed the door to the mystical dimension of the story. However, I believe that this mystery is less related to a fantastic explanation of the fatherhood of Jesus than to the fact that the story does not let us know more than Mary's heteronomous situation and the presence of God. Instead of continuing to ask for an explanation, we have to accept that the question remains unanswered.

This is in fact a recurrent theme in the Bible. Questions remain unanswered. There is a parallel scene with angels and women in Luke: the women at the empty tomb (Luke 24:1-12). They do not get to know how the tomb was emptied. They are perplexed. The answer of the angels adds to the puzzle. "Why do you look for the living among the dead?" The women find themselves in the open space created by the unanswered question of what has happened. This is what Elisabeth Schüssler Fiorenza calls "an ambiguous open space". Outside the open tomb is the space where visions of the unexpected possibilities of life can be formulated.[62] Maybe in the story of Mary and the angel the same

---

[61] See Vuola, "Seriously Harmful for your Health?".
[62] Schüssler Fiorenza, *Jesus, Miriam's Child, Sophia's Prophet*, 124f.

visions can be the effect of the insight that we do not get to know more than that Mary becomes the space for the creative process which forms the centre of Christian faith.

The *Wirkungsgeschichte* of the gendered stereotype of Mary understood in terms of the petrified dogmas of the Virgin Mother can illustrate how motherhood is located on the border between vulnerability and exposure. Mary should neither be reduced to the stereotype of the oppressed woman, nor to the ideal woman in weakness or strength, but should be interpreted in the direction of someone who shows us the close relation between oppression, love, exposure and vulnerability. There is no way to escape the flux of the changing life conditions of autonomy, relationality and heteronomy. Mothers, being socially exposed to their heteronomy, can also experience motherhood outside the constraints of patriarchy – as a reinterpretation of Mother Mary can clarify – and then experience this as the good heteronomy. Vulnerability has to be met with love. This is not just an ethical demand; it also is something which mothers experience and receive. This experience is not confined to motherhood, rather it is clarified by it. Still, it is important to acknowledge that motherhood is a rich source of experience when we need to distinguish between exposure and vulnerability, oppression and love.

Then, the point is not that Mary is an ideal mother, but that motherhood conveys the challenges of our life condition as heteronomous beings, ultimately lacking control. To me, this is also the starting point of Christian faith as belief in God as the one protecting human heteronomy with love, which in turn creates space for the development of autonomous persons in constructive and healing relationships.

Während Körper und Sexualität häufig im Zentrum von *Gender*-Studien stehen, ist dies im Blick auf Mutterschaft nicht der Fall. Das Ziel dieses Artikels ist es, Konzepte von Mutterschaft aus der Perspektive einer kritischen Diskussion zwischen skandinavischer und anglo-amerikanischer feministischer Theologie zu analysieren und neu zu interpretieren, und zwar in Bezug auf Maria, der Mutter Jesu, als eines Bildes *der* Mutter schlechthin. Maria bestärkt sowohl *Gender*-Stereotypen, als auch starre christliche Dogmen. Deshalb ist es unabdingbar, *Gender*-Stereotypen im Blick auf Mutterschaft und das Bild der jungfräulichen Mutter Maria gleichzeitig zu reflektieren. Die Strategien, die von zeitgenössischen feministischen Theologinnen angewendet werden, tendieren dahin, entweder *Gender*-Stereotypen oder die erstarrten religiösen Dogmen außer Acht zu lassen. Durch eine Neuinterpretation der Verkündigungserzählung wird eine Relektüre vorgestellt, die Maria weder in einer patriarchalen Sichtweise von Mutterschaft einsperrt, noch die Interpretation starren Dogmen unterordnet. Das Charakteristische von Mutterschaft: keine Kontrolle ausüben zu können (Fremdbestimmung), wird betont, doch gleichzeitig wird dem patriarchalen Missbrauch dieses Phänomens entgegengetreten. Maria sollte weder auf das Stereotyp der unterdrückten Frau noch auf das Ideal des verletzbaren Weiblichen reduziert werden, sondern sollte als eine vergegenwärtigt werden, die uns die enge Verbindung zwischen Ausgesetztsein, Unterdrückung, Verletzbarkeit und Liebe aufzeigt.

Alors que le corps et la sexualité constituent fréquemment l'objet principal des Etudes Genre, ce n'est pas le cas de la maternité. Le but de cet article est d'analyser et de réinterpréter la conceptualisation de la maternité dans la perspective d'une discussion critique entre théologies féministes scandinave et anglo-américaine, portant sur Marie, la mère de Jésus, en tant qu'image de *la* mère. Marie est tout autant à l'origine de stéréotypes de genre, que de dogmes chrétiens figés. C'est pourquoi il est important de mener une réflexion parallèle sur les stéréotypes de genre concernant la maternité et sur l'image de la mère vierge Marie. Les stratégies utilisées par les théologiennes féministes contemporaines tendent à laisser de côté, soient les stéréotypes de genre, soient les dogmes religieux figés. Une réinterprétation de l'histoire de l'annonciation permet de présenter une relecture qui n'enferme pas Marie dans une conception patriarcale de la maternité, ni ne laisse les dogmes figés déterminer l'interprétation. Le fait qu'une des caractéristiques de la maternité est de n'être pas maîtrisable (hétéronomie) est souligné, mais de même, l'abus patriarcal de ce phénomène est dénoncé. Marie ne devrait jamais être réduite au stéréotype de la femme opprimée ni à l'idéal de la femme vulnérable, mais devrait être considérée comme quelqu'un qui manifeste la proximité entre exposition, oppression, vulnérabilité et amour.

Cristina Grenholm (*1959) is professor of systematic theology at the University of Karlstad, Sweden. She is the director of The Center for Gender Research and serves presently as the dean of The Faculty of Arts and Education. Her research is characterized by the intersection of contemporary theology, feminist theology and biblical studies. Her most recent book was published in Swedish and concerns the themes of motherhood and love, *Moderskap och kärlek: Schabloner och tankeutrymme i feministteologisk livsåskådningsreflektion* [Motherhood and Love: Stereotypes and Space for Thought in Feminist Theological Reflection on Life] (Nya Doxa: Nora 2005). With Daniel Patte she is the co-editor of the Romans Through History and Cultures series and recently edited the volume *Gender, Tradition and Romans: Shared Ground, Uncertain Borders* (T&T Clark International: New York / London 2005).

Journal of the European Society of Women in Theological Research 15 (2007) 37-54.
doi: 10.2143/ESWTR.15.0.2022767

Arnfríður Guðmundsdóttir

Abusive or Abused?
Theology of the Cross from a Feminist Critical Perspective[1]

The growing awareness of the problem of violence against women has raised the call for action worldwide, including churches and other faith communities. As a follow-up to the Ecumenical Decade: Churches in Solidarity with Women 1988-1998, the World Council of Churches (WCC) confronted the challenge of violence directly by establishing a "Decade to Overcome Violence: Churches Seeking Reconciliation and Peace," (2001-2010).[2] While the WCC focuses on the manifold expressions of violence, violence perpetrated against women and children is among their target concerns.[3] Following on the heels of the WCC's call, the Lutheran World Federation (LWF), in its document *Churches say 'NO' to Violence against Women. Action Plan for the Churches* from 2002, called on its member churches to act on behalf of women victims of violence.[4] By offering this contribution to the WCC decade against violence, the LWF seeks to direct the focus of the international church community to the effect that violence is having on women in the home as well as in the church and in society at large. This document is significant for its attempt to consider violence against women as a theological problem instead of simply as a social one. As Ishmael Noko, the General Secretary of the Federation, writes in the Foreword to the document: "When those who are victimized suffer, so does God. Let us work together to overcome all forms of violence that are an offense against God and humanity."[5]

---

[1] I would like to extend my gratitude to Joy Ann McDougall, Elina Vuola and Hanna Stenström for their helpful editorial comments and critique.

[2] http://overcomingviolence.org

[3] Margot Kässmann, *Overcoming Violence. The Challenge to the Churches in All Places* (WCC Publication: Geneva 1998), 45-56.

[4] *Churches Say 'No' to Violence against Women. Action Plan for the Churches* (The Lutheran World Federation: Geneva 2002).

[5] *Churches Say 'No' to Violence against Women*, 5.

Pastoral care-givers and social workers, among others who work with women in abusive situations, claim that Christian theologies of the cross are one of the chief theological problems for such women. Theologies of the cross are frequently used to keep women in subjugated positions, by encouraging them to "be like Christ", i.e. by showing total obedience, submission and self-sacrificial behaviour towards their abusers.[6] Based on abused women's and their care-givers' testimony, feminist theologians have for over thirty years now scrutinized the Christian tradition's readings of the cross for their contribution to the problem. Here, Mary Daly's early criticism of the "scapegoat mentality" of Christianity pointed the way. Daly set the tone for the rejection of any positive interpretation of the suffering and death of Jesus. Following her lead, other feminist theologians have criticized the Christian tradition for providing a justification, or at least an excuse, for abusive or violent behaviour by means of a theology that glorifies suffering. While some feminist theologians have denounced Christianity on this basis as inherently *abusive*, others see the importance of a feminist critic of a theology of the cross that has often been *abused*, but still argue for the redemptive significance of the cross for women today.

This article highlights the key issues in this ongoing debate about the meaning of the cross of Jesus Christ within feminist theological literature in the United States. Feminist theologians in the United States have been pivotal to the international feminist debate about the cross and the possibility for a feminist retrieval of the cross as a hopeful symbol for women.[7] In what follows, I begin first by recalling briefly Mary Daly's pioneering work, *Beyond God the Father. Toward a Philosophy of Women's Liberation* (1973)[8] which more than

---

[6] See for example: Carol J. Adams / Marie M. Fortune (eds), *Violence against Women and Children. A Christian Theological Sourcebook* (Continuum: New York 1995); Carol J. Adams, *Woman-battering* (Fortress Press: Minneapolis, 1994); Susan Brooks Thistlethwaite, "Every Two Minutes: Battered Women and Feminist Interpretation", in: Judith Plaskow / Carol P. Christ (eds), *Weaving the Visions. New Patterns in Feminist Spirituality* (Harper: San Francisco, 1989), 302-313.

[7] The German theologian Elisabeth Moltmann-Wendel, asks in an article from the beginning of the nineties: "Will feminist theology become a theology without the cross?" In her article, Moltmann-Wendel expresses her concern about where the North American – European discussion on the cross is going. See: Elisabeth Moltmann-Wendel, "Is There a Feminist Theology of the Cross?" in: Yacob Tesfai (ed.), *The Scandal of a Crucified World. Perspectives on the Cross and Suffering* (Orbis Books: Maryknoll, New York 1994), 87-98, here 88.

[8] Mary Daly, *Beyond God the Father. Toward a Philosophy of Women's Liberation* (Beacon Press: Boston 1973).

any other sparked this critical discussion and also *Christianity, Patriarchy, and Abuse* (1989)[9], an essay collection, edited by Joanne Carlson Brown and Carole R. Bohn. Here, the main argument of one of the essays, "For God So Loved the World?" by Joanne Carlson Brown and Rebecca Parker, offers a classic example of a feminist theology "without the cross."[10] From here I turn to Rita Nakashima Brock and Rebecca Parker's much more recent book, *Proverbs of Ashes* (2001), which in many ways represents a logical outcome of the feminist critique of the theology of the cross over the past two decades. In their book, Brock and Parker ask pressing questions of Christian theologies of the cross, and provide powerful examples of women and children who have suffered from abusive representations of the cross.

In the second part of this article, I turn to the work of Wendy Farley and Elizabeth Johnson, as representatives of those feminists who critically retrieve the meaning of the cross as a source of hope, courage and strength for those who suffer – especially for women. By reinterpreting the power of God as *compassion*, Farley seeks to resolve the conflict between God's power and love. For Johnson, the symbol of a compassionate God then becomes a key to her understanding of a suffering God who expresses active solidarity with those who suffer. Third and finally, I will draw some conclusions from these divergent positions for the ongoing feminist discussion of the meaning of the cross in my context. While I consider the feminist critique of any abusive theology of the cross crucial, in my view the important distinction between an abuse and a constructive use of the cross has not always been given adequate attention in the feminist discussion. Here the danger is to lose sight of the cross as a symbol of a compassionate God, who shows solidarity in the midst suffering, gives reason to resist its passive acceptance, and offers ultimate hope.

I. The Cross of Christ: A Dangerous Message for Women

Mary Daly's radical criticism of Christianity and its abusive role in women's lives proved to be a landmark in the early development of the feminist critical

---

[9]   Joanne Carlson Brown / Carole R. Bohn (eds), *Christianity, Patriarchy, and Abuse. A Feminist Critique* (The Pilgrim Press: New York 1989), 1-30.

[10] Joanne Carlson Brown / Rebecca Parker, "For God So Loved the World?" in: Joanne Carlson Brown / Carole R. Bohn (eds), *Christianity, Patriarchy, and Abuse. A Feminist Critique* (The Pilgrim Press: New York 1989), 1-30.

approach to Christian theology. In her book, *Beyond God the Father*, Mary Daly accuses Christianity of advocating a "scapegoat mentality", by idealizing qualities such as sacrificial love and passive acceptance of suffering.[11] Because the Christian tradition has idealized these very same qualities in Jesus, Daly maintains that he is a dangerous model for women within a sexist society, who are in desperate need of a set of virtues to fight their victimized situation. Furthermore, Daly argues that since women have no chance to measure up to this ideal, and since they are unable to represent a male savior given their female sex, Jesus proves to be an impossible model for women. Moreover, since women are not able to follow the example of Jesus as a Victim, their victimization becomes even more oppressive. Thus, Daly concludes that, in order for women to break free from patriarchal oppression and to put an end to their victimization, they need to leave Christ and Christianity behind.[12]

While Mary Daly's writings have been instrumental for the critical discussion of the cross of Christ until today, the essay collection, *Christianity, Patriarchy, and Abuse. A Feminist Critique* (1989), represents a significant watershed offering a comprehensive critique of the abusive nature of a theology of the cross in Western Christianity. In their jointly authored article, "For God So Loved the World?", Joanne Carlson Brown and Rebecca Parker denounce any Christian theology that maintains that suffering is redemptive, including Jesus' suffering and death on the cross. Simply stated, they argue that not only does the image of the crucified Christ as the savior of the world give suffering a redemptive significance, but it also encourages self-sacrifice and total submission. Using the image of "divine child abuse", Brown and Parker compare the relationship between God the Father and the Son to the relationship between an abusive father and an abused child. Thus, Brown and Parker charge patriarchal Christianity with not only justifying but actually encouraging the abuse of women and children.[13]

In a co-authored, autobiographically-styled volume, *Proverbs of Ashes. Violence, Redemptive Suffering, and The Search for What Saves Us* (2001), the Protestant theologians Rita Nakashima Brock and Rebecca Ann Parker further develop the critical evaluation of the Christian tradition that they began in their respective articles in *Christianity, Patriarchy, and Abuse*. In a prelude to the

---

[11] Daly, *Beyond God the Father*, 77.
[12] Daly, *Beyond God the Father*, 77.
[13] Brown / Parker, "For God So Loved the World?", 2.

book, Rebecca Parker explains why the two of them chose this autobiographical style for their work:

> We were clear that the best way to show Christianity's complicity with violence would be to speak plainly. We needed to say how the theological sanctioning of violence has affected us and those we care about. Neither Jesus' death on the cross nor our own acts of self-sacrifice had saved us. But something had. We wanted to tell what we have tasted and seen ourselves of how life is saved.[14]

Brock and Parker's book is a collection of stories, their own together with those of people they have known, family and friends, and those that they have encountered in their work within the church and the academic world. By applying personal testimony to the correlation between violence and the Christian faith, Brock and Parker seek to provide firsthand evidence in support of their demand for a critical reevaluation of Christianity. More than any other theological theme, Brock and Parker point their finger at the cross-event as the source of the problem and the reason why they are searching for a "new theology", free of violence and abuse.[15]

Imitatio Christi
Rebecca Parker tells her own story of being sexually molested by a neighbor as a child, and her struggle to come to terms with the consequences of the abuse as an adult. A daughter of a pastor, Parker describes her parents as "good people", who by their examples taught their children the value of suffering silently, as well as the importance of being good and obedient and not disappointing those who loved them. For these reasons, Parker never told her parents about the abuse as a child. At the same time, she was obeying her abuser and keeping his crime a secret between the two of them.[16] In cases such as her own, Parker accuses the church of enforcing this silence by not addressing issues that are causing pain and suffering in people's lives. Based on her experience as a parish pastor, Parker claims that the church acknowledges illness and death as "acceptable troubles", which is not the case with pain caused by war-trauma, incest, homophobia, or domestic violence.[17]

---

[14] Rita Nakashima Brock and Rebecca Ann Parker, *Proverbs of Ashes. Violence, Redemptive Suffering, and The Search for What Saves Us* (Beacon Press: Boston 2001), 7.

[15] Brock and Parker, *Proverbs of Ashes*, 8.

[16] Brock and Parker, *Proverbs of Ashes*, 191.

[17] Brock and Parker, *Proverbs of Ashes*, 111.

Brock and Parker argue that the underlying reason for emphasizing silent suffering within the church is the example of Christ, who himself suffered silently and obeyed his father without resisting violence – even unto death. Here, too, Parker offers as evidence the testimony of a clergywoman who was abused by her father but kept silent about it, because she believed her father "would be crucified" if she told their secret:

> My friend's account of her childhood faith helped me see further the anguishing poverty of interpreting Jesus' death as a redemptive event. Elizabeth was a vulnerable child being violated by a parent. Her church taught her a good child honors her father as Jesus honored his when he consented to die at his father's request. At the same time it taught her to see herself as a sinner whose internal sense of resistance to abuse threatened the life of her father. By keeping silent she protected her father from "being crucified." Her silence "saved" him and trapped her in ongoing violation.[18]

Women in violent situations who believe they are to suffer "like Jesus" is a recurrent theme in Brock and Parker's book. They argue that the church expects women to be Christ-like, by which they mean that women are encouraged to remain passive and helpless in violent situations. Here again, Parker offers the testimony of another woman whose priest told her to tolerate her husband's violence because it made her Christ-like. This woman came to Parker because she hoped a woman priest would understand her problem and offer assistance:

> "I haven't talked to anyone about this for a while," she began, the smile fading, and sadness deepening in her eyes. "But I'm worried for my kids now. The problem is my husband. He beats me sometimes. Mostly he is a good man. But sometimes he becomes very angry and he hits me. He knocks me down. One time he broke my arm and I had to go to the hospital. But I didn't tell them how my arm got broken." I nodded. She took a deep breath and went on. "I went to my priest twenty years ago. I've been trying to follow his advice. The priest said I should rejoice in my sufferings because they bring me closer to Jesus. He said, 'Jesus suffered because he loved us.' He said, 'If you love Jesus, accept the beatings and bear them gladly, as Jesus bore the cross.' I've tried, but I'm not sure anymore. My husband is turning on the kids now. Tell me, is what the priest told me true?"[19]

Through encounters with women in violent situations, who had been told by the church to endure their sufferings, Brock and Parker became alarmed by

---

[18] Brock and Parker, *Proverbs of Ashes*, 28.
[19] Brock and Parker, *Proverbs of Ashes*, 20-21.

what they describe as a "spiritualizing of suffering" in Christianity. They point to how suffering is often given a spiritual significance as God's way to "edify or purify human beings."[20] This not only prevents people from resisting suffering, but renders them even more passive and acquiescent to it.[21]

Beyond this "spiritualizing of suffering," Christianity has (supposedly following Christ's example) promoted "self-sacrificial love" as the true and higher version of love, a love that focuses exclusively on the desire of the other (*agape*) instead of one's own (*eros*). Here, too, Brock and Parker claim a strong analogy between the abusive relationship of parent to child and the way Christian tradition has interpreted the cross-event. Brock explains:

> When the Christian tradition represents Jesus' death as foreordained by God, as necessary to the divine plan for salvation, and as obediently accepted by Jesus the Son out of love for God the Father, God is made into a child abuser or a bystander to violence against his own child. The seal of abuse is placed on their relationship when they are made into a unity of being. If the two are one, Jesus can be selfless, can give himself totally to God, a willing lamb to slaughter. I thought of this system as cosmic child abuse.[22]

Because Christians have not been willing to identify and protest against the violence that happened to Jesus, they have not been able to recognize and fight against the violence that is perpetrated against children in their midst.[23] Moreover, the authors insist that the image of God as a benevolent, almighty father, who does not spare his own son, has helped to explain away the violence exercised by earthly parents as a just expression of love.[24] Based on their experiences of working with abused youth, Brock and Parker argue that young people, who have put their trust in the benevolent protection of a powerful God, make the connection between their image of God and the abuse they have experienced, often at home, by interpreting "violence as divine intent, pain for their own good." They believe this impulse is supported by traditional theologies of the cross that, "uphold Jesus as a son who was willing to undergo

---

[20] Brock and Parker, *Proverbs of Ashes*, 44.
[21] Brock and Parker, *Proverbs of Ashes*, 157-8.
[22] Brock and Parker, *Proverbs of Ashes*, 157.
[23] Brock and Parker, *Proverbs of Ashes*, 199.
[24] Brock and Parker, *Proverbs of Ashes*, 30-31. Parker maintains that the relationship between the Father and the son which Jürgen Moltmann describes in his book, *The Crucified God*, is an abusive relationship (Brock and Parker, *Proverbs of Ashes*, 198).

horrible violence out of love for his father, in obedience to his father's will."[25] For this reason, they agree wholeheartedly with Daly about the dangerous example of Jesus Christ, who is interpreted as the obedient son who does not resist but silently accepts the will of his father.

Based on their own and others' experiences of violence and abuse, Brock and Parker demand a radical reinterpretation of the Christian message. In their view, what is needed is both a different understanding of the person and work of Jesus Christ, and a radical revision of the Christian image of God. Instead of a theology that spiritualizes suffering, supports victimization and helplessness regarding abuse, they call for a theology that empowers people "to affirm their own agency, to resist abuse, to take responsibility for ethical discernment, and to work for justice."[26] For Brock and Parker, this kind of theology is supported by a model of Jesus as "a prophet who confronted injustices and risked opposition"[27], whose death was "an unjust act of violence that needed resolution."[28] Such a theology does not have to cover up Jesus' death with a belief in resurrection, so as to avoid facing the horror and anguish of his death. Rather, it presents an image of God who "delights in revolutionary disobedience and spirited protest."[29] Parker wonders aloud what difference such an image of God might have made to the life of another woman whose husband abused and finally killed her. She writes:

> ... if Anola Reed had believed in a God who supported protest, might she have protested and resisted her husband's violence, rather than accepted and endured it? If her husband didn't regard God as the divine enforcer of obedience, would he have enforced obedience from his wife with violence. Would they have had more of a chance at life?[30]

A Crucified God: A Dangerously False Comfort?

For Brock and Parker, any attempt to redefine the meaning of the cross by mystifying violence offers a "dangerously false comfort" to suffering people.[31] In their view, the church, through its "spiritualization of suffering", suggests that all suffering comes from God who uses it "to edify or purify human

---

[25] Brock and Parker, *Proverbs of Ashes*, 148.
[26] Brock and Parker, *Proverbs of Ashes*, 156.
[27] Brock and Parker, *Proverbs of Ashes*, 31.
[28] Brock and Parker, *Proverbs of Ashes*, 60.
[29] Brock and Parker, *Proverbs of Ashes*, 31.
[30] Brock and Parker, *Proverbs of Ashes*, 31.
[31] Brock and Parker, *Proverbs of Ashes*, 48.

beings."[32] They use as their prime example the emphasis that liberal theology places on Christ as a model of self-sacrificial love (under the influence of Abelard's perfect moral example theory). Parker points out that such a christological ethos of self-sacrifice has been particularly damaging to women, who often suffer from a lack of a sense of self. This ethos makes it difficult for many women to offer love to others, while also claiming comfort, understanding, and the right to self-development for themselves. Parker detects a similarly dangerous ethos of self-sacrifice in contemporary liberation theology, which stresses opposition to oppressive and unjust systems often at the risk of one's personal safety:

> We are called to join Jesus in working to liberate people from all that diminishes life. We are asked to be courageous in this work. I agree with liberation theology's call to engagement. But I remain uncomfortable with its idealization of accepting violence and its glorification of the crucified people of God.[33]

Parker identifies the same problem in the theology of non-violence of Dr. Martin Luther King Jr., which, in her view, also borders on a glorification of suffering and sacrifice. Even if she agrees that non-violent resistance can be effective, she finds it dangerous to advocate acceptance of violence in order just to move perpetrators of violence to repentance. On the one hand, she questions the ability of all perpetrators to be touched by the suffering of the innocent; on the other, she refuses to prioritize the repentance of the perpetrator over the suffering of the victim. In short, Parker worries that such an ethos of self-sacrifice and non-violence will ultimately leave an abused child or a battered spouse defenceless. What is needed instead is a theology that takes seriously not only the healing of the world but also the victims of violence.

The Road to Recovery from Abuse
Preaching to her congregation during Lent, Parker warns her parishioners against escaping from the harsh reality of violence and evil by buying into a theology that transforms violence into divine providence:

> The mysticism of the cross teaches that violence is God's way of transforming people and communities into greater spiritual well-being. It clouds the realities of human violence in a haze of spiritual glory.

---

[32] Brock and Parker, *Proverbs of Ashes*, 44.
[33] Brock and Parker, *Proverbs of Ashes*, 39.

Instead of considering God as the source of suffering (and thereby being tempted to inflict pain on others or themselves), Parker encourages her parishioners not to look for such a spiritual escape from confronting harsh realities and grief, but rather to face such pain directly: "When grief and loss come to us, we cannot comfort ourselves by saying God is testing us or offering us a blessing that we don't yet understand. We have to face the pain without this divine sanction." Here, Parker worries that Christian spirituality's way of "covering over" suffering prevents people from grieving as they need to on their way to full recovery. Rather, victims of pain and violence (of whatever kind) have "to learn to grieve full out and face forward, without covering over the realities of human cruelty and violence." The road to recovery is always a passage through the "dark night of the soul."[34]

In the end, the authors of *Proverbs of Ashes* believe that hope can be found in the midst of suffering and pain. Given their pastoral experience of working through painful memories of violence and abuse, they believe truth-telling and rejection of self-sacrificial love is a critical first step. But they also insist theologically on rejecting any notion that God is the author of human violence or that God sanctions cruelty and torture in any form. Brock and Parker make it clear that violence destroys life and that recovery is sometimes beyond what is possible. Nevertheless, they are convinced that there is hope to be found for those who choose life, and that hope is to be found in "Presence", the presence of God and the presence of "steady witnesses" who "accompany the journey to healing."[35] It is "Presence" that makes it possible to face the harsh reality of violence and pain, and "Presence" makes it possible to tell the truth, both theologically as well as personally. In the end, survival for Brock and Parker is a matter of divine and human cooperation: "Presence burns fiercely, but Presence cannot override the decisions of perpetrators of violence. It is a human act to stay the hand of violence. Life is ours to choose."[36]

II. *Who* is God in the Midst of My Suffering and Pain?

The driving impulse behind *Proverbs of Ashes* is the profound experiences of suffering and violence perpetrated against women today. Such difficult experiences of harsh suffering often drive people to ask pressing questions about

---

[34] Brock and Parker, *Proverbs of Ashes*, 45.
[35] Brock and Parker, *Proverbs of Ashes*, 250.
[36] Brock and Parker, *Proverbs of Ashes*, 248.

God. Many ask: Where is God when I suffer? But no less pressing is the question: *Who* is God in the midst of my suffering and pain? Questions of God *vis à vis* the omnipresence of evil and suffering in the world have troubled believers within the Judeo-Christian tradition from early on. Even if Brock and Parker do not question the existence (or "Presence") of God in the midst of human suffering, they call for different understandings of *who* God is than the Christian tradition has provided thus far.

Criticism of unhelpful, even dangerous theories of God and redemption has been prevalent within feminist theological literature since the early seventies. Not all feminist theologians have been as pessimistic as Daly about Christianity's redeemability. Nonetheless, calls for a radical reinterpretation of basic categories of Christian discourse, especially the classical attributes of God and how they are reflected in the cross of Christ, have been widespread.

From early on, there has been a broad consensus within the Christian tradition about the all-powerfulness and all-goodness of God. Since the time of the Enlightenment, however, theologians have become increasingly open to rethinking these classical attributes in response to the *theodicy* question, that is, how it is possible to maintain God's omnipotence and perfect beneficence *vis à vis* the presence of evil and suffering amongst God's good creation. Many theologians of the twentieth century have made important attempts to write theology that takes the harsh realities of evil and suffering directly into account.[37]

A practical theodicy

In this wider discussion about God and human suffering, a Protestant theologian, Wendy Farley, has been one of the most influential feminist voices ever since the publication of her first book, *Tragic Vision and Divine Compassion. A Contemporary Theodicy* (1990).[38] Here, as elsewhere, Farley brings the relationship between theory and practice into sharp focus, by asking poignant questions about the meaning of the theoretical discussion of God's nature for those

---

[37] One example is Jürgen Moltmann's book on *The crucified God*, which in *Proverbs of Ashes* is dismissed as having neither liberating nor redeeming qualities. See Brock and Parker, *Proverbs of Ashes*, 47.

[38] Wendy Farley, *Tragic Vision and Divine Compassion. A Contemporary Theodicy* (Westminster/John Knox Press: Louisville, Kentucky 1990).

who are suffering.[39] Critical to Farley's "contemporary theodicy" is the category of *radical suffering*, which she defines as a suffering that "is destructive of the human spirit and that [it] cannot be understood as something deserved."[40] With her category of radical suffering, Farley rejects the necessary correlation between suffering and punishment suggested in the story of Adam and Eve in Eden. This does not mean that Farley thinks suffering can never be "good for people", in the sense that it can make them "stronger, more sensitive, more mature", which she admits it actually does at times. But this is exactly the basic difference, she contends, between suffering and *radical* suffering; the latter always "destroys its victims" instead of making them stronger.[41] Farley introduces the distinction between suffering and radical suffering in order to overcome the urge to find possible explanations or reasons for all suffering, which she rightly points out (like the author of Job) is in many cases simply not possible.

The concept of God's power is another important aspect of Farley's contemporary theodicy. Instead of interpreting the power of God as dominion or coercion, Farley suggests that we understand God's power as *compassion*. This is "a different *kind* of power,"[42] but still a real power, not simply a feeling or mood but "the kind of power that God exercises toward the world." Farley explains further:

> ... The power of compassion is the most real thing in the world, the signature of ultimate reality, and the name that truth bears in its active aspect. If we understand this – not in our heads but in our very bones – we will talk about God differently, interpret our scriptures differently, and relate to victims and perpetrators of violence differently. Compassion vitiates neat divisions between theory and practice, transforming theology into a practice of compassion even as it demands that all practice be rooted in the wisdom that discerns compassion as the signature of reality.[43]

---

[39] Wendy Farley, "The Practice of Theodicy", in: Margaret E. Mohrmann / Mark J. Hanson (eds), *Pain Seeking Understanding. Suffering, Medicine, and Faith* (The Pilgrim Press: Cleveland, Ohio 1999), 103-114, here 103. See also Wendy Farley, "Evil, Violence, and the Practice of Theodicy", in John S. McClure / Nancy J. Ramsay (eds), *Telling the Truth. Preaching about Sexual and Domestic Violence* (United Church Press: Cleveland, Ohio 1998), 11-20, here 11.

[40] Farley, *Tragic Vision and Divine Compassion*, 21.

[41] Farley, *Tragic Vision and Divine Compassion*, 22.

[42] Farley, *Tragic Vision and Divine Compassion*, 86.

[43] Farley, "Evil, Violence, and the Practice of Theodicy", 15.

By interpreting power as compassion (as a form of love), Farley resolves the conflict between God's power and love, that has often been the biggest issue within the theodicy question. In the midst of suffering, the presence of God as compassion makes the difference between the dehumanizing effects of radical suffering and restoring the broken human being to wholeness.

In her earlier writings, Farley appeals to her understanding of the cross of Christ without working out a full-fledged feminist theology of the cross.[44] For Farley, the cross of Christ is an example of radical evil, but it also represents "the incarnation of divine compassion in the midst of rupture."[45] Farley argues that the stories of Jesus' birth and crucifixion "tell us something deeply important about who God is and where God chooses to appear."

> ... It is in those places furthest from prosperity, fullness, beauty, honor, and power that Christians have had God revealed most distinctively to them. God, source of all reality, split the heavens to come to us in a cow shed so that God could be *with* us. And, as if the ridiculousness of being born in a manger weren't enough, God dies on a cross – as loathsome, humiliating, cruel, and helpless a death as imaginable – just in case we didn't get it... [46]

By presenting the cross as the locus where God's presence amongst those who suffer is revealed in a special way, Farley affirms the importance of the cross in revealing God's participation in the suffering of the world.

A Suffering God
Building explicitly on Farley's theology of divine compassion, the Roman Catholic theologian Elizabeth Johnson has made a further significant contribution to a feminist critical retrieval of a cross-centered theology. In her book *She Who Is. The Mystery of God in Feminist Theological Discourse* (1992), Johnson describes God's active solidarity with those who suffer as an expression of God's "compassion poured out."[47] Central to her understanding of a

---

[44] In her most recent work, Farley has developed further her position on Christ and the meaning of his suffering and death. See: Wendy Farley, *The Wounding and Healing of Desire. Weaving Heaven and Earth* (Westminster John Knox Press: Louisville, Kentucky 2005). Unfortunately, the constraints of this paper do not allow me to take up this work in detail.

[45] Farley, *Tragic Vision and Divine Compassion*, 132.

[46] Farley, "Evil, Violence, and the Practice of Theodicy", 15.

[47] Elizabeth A. Johnson, *She Who Is. The Mystery of God in Feminist Theological Discourse* (Crossroad: New York 1992), 246.

"suffering God" is her rejection of the classical idea of God's impassibility, which she thinks is both "morally intolerable"[48] and "not seriously imaginable."[49] At the same time Johnson warns against assuming that God suffers because God cannot do otherwise.[50] To affirm God's ability to suffer, has, on the contrary, to imply the notion that God, out of freedom of love, chooses to suffer with suffering people. Such a God is "the compassionate God", a God who helps by "awakening consolation, responsible human action, and hope against hope in the world marked by radical suffering and evil."[51]

Critical to Johnson's feminist interpretation of the cross of Christ (as well as her development of the symbol of a suffering God) is to renounce any view of redemption suggesting that God required Jesus' death as a payment for sin. For Johnson, such an idea is today "virtually inseparable from an underlying image of God as an angry, bloodthirsty, violent and sadistic father, reflecting the very worst kind of male behavior." On the contrary, Johnson insists that Jesus' death was an "act of violence", and a result of his message and behavior.[52] Instead of signifying a payment required for human sinfulness, Johnson describes the cross as a sign of God's identification with human beings in the midst of their suffering and pain. Borrowing a range of metaphors drawn from women's experience, she skillfully redresses the theology of the cross in feminist terms: The cross becomes a part of "the larger mystery of pain-to-life, of that struggle for the new creation evocative of the rhythm of pregnancy, delivery, and birth so familiar to women of all times."[53] Moreover, the belief in the risen Christ appears consequently as the expression of "the victory of love, both human and divine, that spins new life out of this disaster."[54] While the resurrection cannot be humanly imagined, Johnson argues that, in faith, it means that evil does not have the last word. In the resurrection, Sophia-God collects her child and prophet into new transformed life, a future for all God's creation. Here, Johnson encounters the feminist vision of wholeness, "of the

---

[48] Johnson, *She Who Is*, 249.
[49] Johnson, *She Who Is*, 253.
[50] Johnson, *She Who Is*, 253-254.
[51] Johnson, *She Who Is*, 269.
[52] Elizabeth A. Johnson, "Redeeming the Name of Christ", in: Catherine Mowry LaCugna (ed.), *Freeing Theology. The Essentials of Theology in Feminist Perspective* (Harper: San Francisco 1993), 115-137, here 124.
[53] Johnson, *She Who Is*, 159.
[54] Johnson, *Freeing Theology*, 124.

preservation of the bodily integrity of each, even the most violated, and the interconnectedness of the whole – at the very core of the Christian message."[55]

III. Abusive or Abused: Can the Cross of Christ Become a Source of Hope?

Let me conclude this brief survey of the North American debate by emphasizing three points that I view as critical with respect to a feminist critical retrieval of a theology of the cross today. First and most simply, there is indeed no consensus to be found within feminist theology about the role and meaning of a theology of the cross for women. While some feminists side with Daly's early assessment of the hopelessly oppressive character of Christianity, others insist upon the importance of Christ, without excluding his suffering and death, as a source of strength and courage to help women resist oppressive situations. In my view, it is critical that all these disparate voices be heard.[56] They need to be heard not least because they tell us important if uncomfortable truths about the praxis and preaching of the church. Feminist theologians like Rita Nakashima Brock and Rebecca Parker, who rely heavily on testimony to the abusive messages that are being preached and practiced by the church, are telling us something of great importance. They remind the church of its utmost responsibility in listening to and taking into theological account the experience of suffering people when it comes to theory-making concerning questions about God, the cross of Christ, and human suffering. This is particularly crucial since women's experiences of evil and suffering have been ignored, or even worse, silenced, in the theological tradition with devastating results.

A second conclusion I propose from the feminist discussion of the cross is the need for a fundamental distinction between a theology that is abusive in essence and a theology that is used for abusive purposes. In other words, I suggest that there is a basic difference between the use of a theology of the cross for abusive purposes, and the more radical claim that any theological

---

[55] Johnson, *Freeing Theology*, 125. On the cross as an important symbol of the *kenosis* of patriarchy, see Johnson, *She Who Is*, 160-1.

[56] For an interesting research on battered women's talk about their experience of God, see: Carol L. Winkelmann, *The Language of Battered Women. A rhetorical Analysis of Personal Theologies* (State University of New York Press: Albany 2004). On a feminist critical perspective on preaching about Christ, see: L. Susan Bond, *Trouble with Jesus. Women, Christology, and Preaching* (Chalice Press: St. Louis, Missouri 1999).

interpretation of the cross is guilty of justifying or even generating violent and abusive treatment of women and children. While the former is an example of an *abused* theology of the cross, the latter describes all theology of the cross as essentially *abusive*. For their part, Brock and Parker have given us critical insights into how a theology of the cross becomes abusive. A key to this abusive theology is the so-called *glorification of suffering*.

A clear sign of such glorification is what the authors call "a spiritualization of suffering", which not only prevents people from resisting the causes of their suffering, but, furthermore, renders them acquiescent to it. Here, suffering becomes a goal in itself, something to be sought out and endured because of its Christ-like character. Such a glorification of suffering must be stopped at all costs because of how harmful it can be. Here, the church must lead the way, speaking out against the danger of an abused theology, as for example in the WCC and the LWF's respective programs to combat violence and oppression. Such programs need to stress the importance of careful and judicious reading of biblical passages, such as the one where Christ encourages his disciples to "take up their cross" and follow him, so as to resist their cooptation for abusive purposes.[57]

Finally, an essential distinction needs to be made between an abusive and a constructive use of the cross. Only then can a theology of the cross be critically reclaimed for what it essentially is, namely, life-giving and hopeful.[58] Central to what I mean by a constructive use of the cross is to insist on the double edged character of the cross, namely, that it does not simply represent God's identification and solidarity with us in our suffering. There is also an *active* meaning to the cross as a symbol of empowerment and resistance to evil. For victims of violence to become empowered survivors, the importance of agency and resistance is critical. What one does with one's experience of suffering makes the difference between victim and survivor, between simply enduring suffering or transforming it into something else.[59] In order to experience something good coming out of what is intrinsically bad, a theology of

---

[57] Mt 16:24.

[58] On a feminist critical retrieval of a theology of the cross, see: Arnfríður Guðmundsdóttir, *Meeting God on the Cross. An Evaluation of Feminist Contributions to Christology in Light of a Theology of the Cross* (Diss, The Lutheran School of Theology at Chicago, 1995), 226-266.

[59] Marie M. Fortune, "The Transformation of Suffering: A Biblical and Theological Perspective", in: Adams / Fortune (eds), *Violence against Women and Children. A Christian Theological Sourcebook*, 85-91, here 90.

the cross brings in an *a posteriori perspective*. Only in light of the resurrection were the friends of Jesus able to see the cross as a symbol of life. What is bad is still bad, evil and suffering are still there. But because of who God is, and because God is with us in the midst of our suffering, we are able, *in retrospect*, to see God bringing life out of death, transforming evil into something good, making the victim into a survivor, which indeed is a powerful symbol of God's compassion poured out *pro nos*. Evil, indeed, does not have the last word.

Dieser Artikel setzt sich mit den Schlüsselthemen der laufenden Debatten über die Bedeutung des Kreuzes Jesu Christi innerhalb der nordamerikanischen feministisch-theologischen Literatur auseinander. Die Autorin ruft zunächst kurz Mary Dalys Pionierinnenarbeit *Beyond God the Father (1973; deutsch: Jenseits von Gottvater, Sohn & Co, 1980)*, an der sich die kritische Diskussion stärker als an allen anderen Untersuchungen entzündet hat, in Erinnerung, und sodann die Hauptthese des Essays "For God So Loved the World?" von Carlson Brown und Rebecca Parker, ein klassisches Beispiel einer feministischen Theologie "ohne Kreuz". Von hier aus wendet sich die Autorin dem Werk von Rita Nakashima Brock und Rebekka Parker, *Proverbs of Ashes* (2001) zu, das in vielerlei Hinsicht die logische Folge der feministischen Kritik an der Kreuzestheologie der letzten beiden Jahrzehnte darstellt. Im zweiten Teil des Artikels erörtert sie das Werk von Wendy Farley und Elizabeth Johnson als Repräsentantinnen derjenigen Feministinnen, die in einer kritischen Weise die Bedeutung des Kreuzes als einer Quelle von Hoffnung, Mut und Stärke für diejenigen, die leiden, wiedergewinnen wollen – speziell für Frauen. Drittens zieht sie schließlich einige Schlussfolgerungen aus diesen unterschiedlichen Positionen für die laufende feministische Diskussion über die Bedeutung des Kreuzes. Während die Autorin die feministische Kritik an jeglicher missbräuchlichen Kreuzestheologie für unabdingbar hält, wurde ihres Erachtens die zentrale Unterscheidung zwischen einem missbräuchlichen und einem konstruktiven Gebrauch des Kreuzes nicht immer in angemessener Weise beachtet. Hier besteht die Gefahr, eine Sicht auf das Kreuz als eines Symbols für den mitleidenden Gott zu verlieren, der/die sich inmitten des Leidens als solidarisch erweist, der/die zum Widerstand gegen das passive Ertragen des Leidens ermutigt, und der/die letztendliche Hoffnung schenkt.

Cet article aborde les questions fondamentales dans le débat en cours concernant la signification de la croix de Jésus-Christ dans la littérature féministe nord-américaine. L'auteure commence en rappelant brièvement le travail pionnier de Mary Daly: *Beyond God the Father* (1973), qui, plus que tout autre, est à l'origine de cette discussion critique. Elle discute ensuite la thèse principale de l'essai: "For God So Loved the World?" (« Car Dieu a tant aimé le monde ») de Joanne Carlson Brown et Rebecca Parker, thèse qui offre un exemple classique de théologie féministe «sans la croix». Ensuite, l'auteure se tourne vers le livre de Rita Nakashima Brock et Rebecca Parker, *Proverbs of Ashes* (2001), qui, de bien des façons, représente l'aboutissement logique de la critique féministe de la théologie de la croix de ces deux dernières décennies. Dans la deuxième partie de cet article, elle examine le travail de Wendy Farley et Elizabeth Johnson, en tant que représentantes de ces féministes qui se réapproprient la signification de la croix, en tant que source d'espérance, de courage et de force, pour ceux qui souffrent, et particulièrement les femmes. Enfin, elle tire des conclusions à partir de ces positions divergentes concernant la discussion féministe en cours sur la signification de la croix. Alors que l'auteure considère cruciale la critique féministe de toute théologie abusive de la croix, à ses yeux, la distinction primordiale entre une utilisation abusive et une utilisation constructive de la croix, n'a pas toujours reçu une attention suffisante dans la discussion théologique. Sur ce point, le danger est de perdre de vue la croix en tant que symbole d'un Dieu compatissant, qui manifeste sa solidarité au cœur de la souffrance, des raisons, qui donne des raisons pour résister à son acceptation passive, et nous procure l'ultime espérance.

Arnfríður Guðmundsdóttir (*1961) is an Associate Professor of Systematic Theology, with emphasis on feminist theology, at the Department of Theology, University of Iceland. She has a cand.theol. degree from the University of Iceland and was ordained within the Evangelical Lutheran Church of Iceland in 1987. She was a graduate student in theology at the University of Iowa, University of Chicago, and the Lutheran School of Theology at Chicago. She finished a Ph.D. degree from the Lutheran School of Theology in 1996. The title of her dissertation is: *Meeting God on the Cross. An Evaluation of Feminist Contributions to Christology in Light of a Theology of the Cross*.

Journal of the European Society of Women in Theological Research 15 (2007) 55-70.
doi: 10.2143/ESWTR.15.0.2022768

Anni Tsokkinen

BUT I wonder what SHE SAID
Some Contextual Remarks on Elisabeth Schüssler Fiorenza's Feminist Theology

Elisabeth Schüssler Fiorenza is probably the most widely read feminist theologian in Scandinavia. Her work has gained more scholarly attention here than the writings of other feminist theologians. Three aspects of Schüssler Fiorenza's thought have particularly interested Nordic researchers. Her feminist exegesis and biblical interpretation, the gender theoretical basis of her work, and her contribution to the liberation theological tradition have been critically analyzed.[1]

The reason why I decided to join the rank of Nordic Schüssler Fiorenza commentators grew out of my interest in liberation theology. After working as a pastor for about ten years in a Lutheran parish I was convinced that the central ideas of the liberation theological tradition should be taken seriously in our church. So I chose the "feminist liberation theology" of Schüssler Fiorenza as the object of my PhD study in the belief that it could offer me ideas and tools for formulating my own theological stance towards a church of which I had become quite critical. I could easily agree with Schüssler Fiorenza's criticism of a privatized and individualistic understanding of religion: The spiritual well-being of individuals should not be the primary concern of the Christian community in

---

[1] See especially Anne-Louise Eriksson, *The Meaning of Gender in Theology. Problems and Possibilities* (Acta Universitatis Upsaliensis. Uppsala Women's Studies A. Women in Religion 7; Almqvist och Wiksell International: Stockholm 1995), 87-106; ElinaVuola, *The Limits of Liberation. Praxis as Method in Latin American Liberation Theology and Feminist Theology* (Finnish Academy of Science and Letters: Helsinki 1997), 90-129; Hanna Stenström, *The Book of Revelation: A Vision of the Ultimate Liberation or the Ultimate Backlash? A study in 20th Century interpretations of Rev 14:1-5, with special emphasis on feminist exegesis* (Uppsala University: Uppsala 1999), 226-263.The working title of my forthcoming doctoral thesis (in Finnish) is *A Priviledged Gender? Elisabeth Schüssler Fiorenza on Women's Religious and Epistemological Authority*.

a world of devastating injustice and suffering. Nor should the church disregard the ethical and political dimensions of its preaching and dogma.[2]

Although my institutional position as a researcher has changed from systematic theology to women's studies, the basic motivation of my work has remained the same. I continue to wonder whether the work of Schüssler Fiorenza can offer me and other church members or theologically orientated persons in Finland guidelines for challenging the dominant voice of our Lutheran religion. My purpose in this article is to outline an answer to this question.

I begin with a preliminary remark. The contextuality of all theology is one of those often stated (and sometimes taken for granted) ideas that have become real during the years of my research. I have tried to understand what it means that all theology is situated, thought and written in a specific place and directed to a specific audience. The ground-breaking proposals of first-generation feminist theologians are no exceptions to this rule. Most of them can be equipped with a label: made in the USA. The contextual nature of feminist (and other) theologies does not, however, imply some kind of total regionality – to state what may be a self-evident fact. At the same time we should be aware of our inclination to see feminist theology done in North America as universal, or to put it another way, as goods on an international theology-market that can be exported and imported without difficulty. Little by little, I've had to give up my naive hope of finding in Schüssler Fiorenza's work a ready-to-use feminist theology for a Finnish audience. In what follows, I will discuss two concepts of Schüssler Fiorenza's theology – the *ekklesia* of women and gender – the analysis of which has opened my eyes to the difficulty of translating theological language from one context (language and culture) to another.

Struggling women of the ekklesia
Throughout her work Schüssler Fiorenza emphasizes the importance of emancipatory movements, especially the feminist movement, for offering a space for doing feminist theology. One of her central ideas is that feminist interpretation of the Christian faith and the Bible needs to position itself in a place which is the opposite of a patriarchal reality. Schüssler Fiorenza calls

---

[2] See, for example, Elisabeth Schüssler Fiorenza, *Jesus: Miriam's Child, Sophia's Prophet: Critical Issues in Feminist Christology* (Continuum: New York 1994), 7-9; Elisabeth Schüssler Fiorenza, *Bread Not Stone: The Challenge of Feminist Biblical Interpretation*, Tenth Anniversary Edition (Beacon Press: Boston 1995), 171.

this place *ekklesia of women*. When introducing this term in the 1980s, she also uses "women-church" as its equivalent. In her book *Bread Not Stone* (1984) she states that "the church of women is the gathering of all those women and men who...continue against all odds the struggle for liberation from patriarchal oppression in society and religion".[3] Thus, the *ekklesia of women* can be described as *a feminist movement* which does not exclude men.[4]

In her later works, Schüssler Fiorenza offers ever more detailed explanations of this key concept of her feminist theology. The meaning of the *ekklesia of women* also expands in a significant way. Using the dominant (feminist) terminology of the 1990s, Schüssler Fiorenza states that the *ekklesia of women* is to be regarded as a discursive counter-space to patriarchy. It is a "theoretical space from which to struggle" to change societal and religious institutions.[5] According to her, the meaning of the *ekklesia of women* thus comes close to what Chandra Talpade Mohanty has suggested with the notion of the "imagined community". In Schüssler Fiorenza's view, Mohanty's point is to argue that the basis of feminist struggles is not that all are of the same sex or race but that they share political views and goals of the same kind – that is, that they participate in the same "imagined community".[6]

Although Schüssler Fiorenza stresses the discursive nature of the *ekklesia* she does not want to detach this "imagined community" from concrete reality. She states that the *ekklesia of women* is "at once an historical and an imagined reality, already partially realized but still to be struggled for".[7] As "the congress of full decision-making citizens" the *ekklesia* "becomes embodied and realized again and again in debates and emancipatory struggles to change relations of domination, exploitation, and marginalization."[8] Thus, the being of the *ekklesia of women* can be depicted with a formula which has been used

---

3   Schüssler Fiorenza, *Bread Not Stone,* xiv.
4   Schüssler Fiorenza, *Bread Not Stone,* xiv-xv.
5   Elisabeth Schüssler Fiorenza, *But She Said: Feminist Practices of Biblical Interpretation* (Beacon Press: Boston 1992), 130.
6   Schüssler Fiorenza, *But She Said*, 130. See also Elisabeth Schüssler Fiorenza, *Wisdom Ways: Introducing Feminist Biblical Interpretation* (Orbis Books: New York 2001), 128.
7   Schüssler Fiorenza, *But She Said*, 130. See also Schüssler Fiorenza, *Jesus: Miriam's Child, Sophia's Prophet*, 28.
8   Elisabeth Schüssler Fiorenza, *Sharing Her Word: Feminist Biblical Interpretation in Context* (Beacon Press: Boston 1998), 112.

to describe the nature of the Kingdom of God (in the New Testament). According to Schüssler Fiorenza, the tension between "already" and "not yet" also characterizes the existence of the *ekklesia of women*.[9]

In her latest monograph, *Wisdom Ways* (2001), Schüssler Fiorenza clarifies her idea of the *ekklesia* as a concrete historical reality. She argues that various social movements in which women have struggled for their rights can be named "*ekklesia of wo/men*".[10] Her illustrative list of these movements includes for example "wo/men's struggle for the abolition of slavery, for religious freedom, for voting rights, against sexual violence, and against global capitalism".[11] Schüssler Fiorenza states that all these struggles and many more "provide the context of a critical feminist interpretation for liberation".[12]

From a Finnish perspective, *ekklesia of women* is a concept which clearly bears the marks of its birthplace. The whole idea of the *ekklesia* as "the decision-making assembly of full citizens" is, in my view, directed first and foremost at a Roman Catholic context and can surely be useful there: Thus critical edge of Schüssler Fiorenza's feminist theology is directed towards a patriarchal church which excludes women from religious and institutional authority, and the concept of the *ekklesia* crystallizes, accordingly, a vision of a community of equals. But I wonder if this basic concept of Schüssler Fiorenza's theology can hold its power elsewhere, for example, in churches and societies where the inequality between men and women is not as striking as in her own denomination.

Finland has often been called "the promised land of gender equality". In Europe, Finnish women were the first to gain the right to vote, in 1906. Moreover, gender equality has become a commonly shared goal in our society and it has been promoted by government efforts since the 1970s.[13] Feminism in Finland, as in other Nordic countries, has taken the form of the so called *state*

---

9 Schüssler Fiorenza, *But She Said*, 6.
10 Schüssler Fiorenza, *Wisdom Ways*, 81, 130. Her way of dividing the word "women" with the slash will be explicated later in this article.
11 Schüssler Fiorenza, *Wisdom Ways*, 80.
12 Schüssler Fiorenza, *Wisdom Ways*, 81.
13 My point is not, however, to argue that the ideal of gender equality has been achieved in Finland. I am more inclined to say that gender equality is in many respects an illusion. "For example, on the labour market and in the home relatively strong traditional gender patterns prevail, where women have the main responsibility for both unpaid and paid reproductive work", as Christina Bergvist notes in "The Nordic Countries – One Model or Several?" in: Christina Bergqvist *et al* (eds), *Equal Democracies? Gender and Politics in the Nordic Countries* (Scandinavian University Press: Oslo 1999), 5-13, here 6.

feminism which means that the state is seen as women's ally "having the potential to develop women-friendly features".[14] Women have worked for their goals mostly in and through political parties, and this is one of the reasons why the second wave ("new") feminist movement has been quite weak in Finland.[15] It is, therefore, no surprise that feminist activism has gained practically no footing in our main churches, the Lutheran and the Orthodox.

In the Lutheran church of Finland, the ordination of women – accepted in 1988 – cannot be described as an outcome of a *feminist* struggle. Women who were active in this long and exhausting debate have not wanted to name their case as a feminist one. In the political as well as the ecclesiastical sphere the overriding tendency has been to avoid controversies: most women have found it important to stress that they are not "feminists" fighting for their rights but doing their share for the common goal of advancing gender equality.

Schüssler Fiorenza's rhetoric of the *ekklesia* or the "struggling women" can therefore sound rather strange in our Finnish context. At the same time, it challenges us to think about one of the basic questions of feminist thought. How do we situate our feminist theologizing when the feminist (or some other social) movement is not the self-evident option? Of course I understand that seeing oneself as part of the worldwide feminist movement, or in Schüssler Fiorenza's words, the *ekklesia of women*, can be a strengthening experience or idea. But the question of positioning feminist theology looks quite different in those parts of the world where women cannot easily identify themselves as participants in a struggling feminist/emancipatory movement.

When describing the *ekklesia of women* as a theoretical space for feminist theology Schüssler Fiorenza seeks to distance herself from those ways of feminist thinking which she finds inadequate in their concept of gender theory. She targets her criticism especially against feminist theorists, such as Luce Irigaray and the other "French feminists", who, as she states, use "the feminist anthropological construct 'woman' or the 'feminine'" as the theoretical framework of their thought.[16] In order to assess the validity of this criticism, I will next

---

[14] Solveig Bergman, "Women in New Social Movements", in: Bergqvist *et al* (eds), *Equal Democracies*, 98-117, here 108.

[15] Bergman, "Women in New Social Movements", 105-106.

[16] Schüssler Fiorenza, *Jesus: Miriam's Child, Sophia's Prophet*, 28. See also Schüssler Fiorenza, *Discipleship of Equals: A Critical Feminist Ekklesia-logy of Liberation* (Crossroad: New York 1993), 340 where she writes: "The American reception of so-called French feminist theory and its concern with the feminine as methaphor and construct tends to reinscribe the cultural feminine...Thus the theory of the maternal-feminine sometimes comes dangerously close to

look at the way Schüssler Fiorenza herself deals with the question of gender in her work.[17]

Gender as an ideological and a sociopolitical structure

In her early writings of the 1970s and 80s, Schüssler Fiorenza makes only quite brief remarks about gender. She expresses her main point by claiming that the formulations of her critical feminist theology of liberation "are based on the radical assumption that gender is socially, politically, economically, and theologically constructed and that such a social construction serves to perpetuate the patriarchal exploitation and oppression of all women".[18] Also in her later works, Schüssler Fiorenza stresses the importance of seeing gender as socially constructed. Gender should be regarded as one of the relations of ruling which – together with race, class, ethnicity, and so on – constitute the pyramidal system of oppression. In Schüssler Fiorenza's view, we should not call this hierarchal structure "patriarchy" because this term is often used in a dualistic way to denote the domination of (all) women by (all) men. Instead of "patriarchy", Schüssler Fiorenza proposes her own term "kyriarchy" which refers to the rule of the lord (in Greek *kyrios*). Kyriarchy is thus to be understood as "a socio-political system of domination in which elite educated propertied men hold power over wo/men and other men".[19]

Schüssler Fiorenza's gender theoretical ideas are summed up in an encyclopaedia article on gender.[20] Her presentation is structured by a division according to which gender can be seen both as an ideological and a sociopolitical structure. When describing the operation of *gender as an ideology* she

---

reproducing in the language of deconstructivism the traditional cultural-religious ascriptions of femininity and motherhood – so familiar from papal pronouncements..."

[17] My aim here is not to present a detailed analysis of Schüssler Fiorenza's gender theorizing but rather give an overall picture of it. For example her ideas of *grammatical* gender are not dealt with in my article. This theme is discussed e.g. in Eriksson, *The Meaning of Gender in Theology*, 102-105.

[18] Schüssler Fiorenza, *Bread Not Stone*, 7.

[19] Schüssler Fiorenza, *Wisdom Ways*, 211. See also Schüssler Fiorenza, *But She Said*, 115. According to Schüssler Fiorenza, it is more accurate to speak of "kyriocentrism" instead of "androcentrism" and to understand it as "an intellectual framework and cultural ideology that legitimates and is legitimated by kyriarchal social structures and systems of domination". See Schüssler Fiorenza, *Jesus: Miriam's Child, Sophia's Prophet*, 14.

[20] Elisabeth Schüssler Fiorenza, "Gender", in: Robert Wuthnow (ed.), *The Encyclopedia of Politics and Religion* (Congressional Quarterly Books: Washington 1998), 290-294.

uses the "sex/gender system" as her main concept. She argues that the basic idea of the sex/gender system is that there exists two genders that are mutually exclusive or, at best, complementary: "one is either a woman or a man but not both".[21] Thus, according to Schüssler Fiorenza, "the cultural construct of male and female, masculine and feminine as both complementary and mutually exclusive categories constitutes the Western sex/gender system that correlates sex to cultural contents according to social hierarchies and values".[22]

Schüssler Fiorenza describes the sex/gender system as one of the most powerful ideologies in the West. In her view, the harmfulness of this "cultural symbolic structure of representation" lies in its way to reduce "the manifold differences between humans to a naturally given, metaphysically determined, or divinely ordained essential difference".[23] In other words, the sex/gender system presents the difference between men and women as the most basic difference of humanity, making it a "common sense" knowledge – either a natural or God-given fact.[24]

Alongside this ideological structure, Schüssler Fiorenza also describes gender as *a sociopolitical structure* or as a social institution. Drawing on the work of sociologist Judith Lorber she describes gender as a social status which is connected with generally accepted gender expectations. She also mentions the gendered division of labor and "gender scripts" prescribing behavior as ways to produce "gendered personalities" conforming to hegemonic gender roles. Schüssler Fiorenza thus states that "the inferior status of women is not achieved by force but in and through individual socialization".[25]

Schüssler Fiorenza's gender theorizing can, firstly, be characterized by the term "*social constructivist*". The main thrust of her arguments is to show that gender is not simply a natural-historical fact or a biological given but a socially constructed entity. Moreover, in her writings, descriptions of gender as an ideological structure prevail: Schüssler Fiorenza is primarily interested in the cultural (and at the same time, ideological) representations of gender. She writes far less about gender as a socio-political structure. Thirdly, what is generally

---

[21] Schüssler Fiorenza, "Gender", 290.
[22] Schüssler Fiorenza, "Gender", 291.
[23] Elisabeth Schüssler Fiorenza, *Rhetoric and Ethic: The Politics of Biblical Studies* (Fortress Press: Minneapolis 1999), 150.
[24] Schüssler Fiorenza, "Gender", 291.
[25] Schüssler Fiorenza, "Gender", 292-293. See also Elisabeth Schüssler Fiorenza, *Jesus and the Politics of Interpretation* (Continuum: New York 2001), 97.

typical of gender theories with a social constructivist emphasis also marks Schüssler Fiorenza's thinking: her interest seems to be directed almost exclusively to gender; and she says practically nothing about *sex* or the bodily realities of being a person, a woman or a man.

The inclusive term *wo/men*

Schüssler Fiorenza's gender theoretical ideas can be commented on more closely by looking at the way she uses the term "women". In her book *Jesus: Miriam's Child, Sophia's Prophet* she introduces a new way of spelling it, *wo/man*. Actually, Schüssler Fiorenza hardly ever uses this singular form but writes mostly about *wo/men* in plural. She also gives many reasons for her "unorthodox" usage of the term – as she herself calls it.[26]

First, Schüssler Fiorenza argues that her way of spelling *wo/men* seeks to indicate that "wo/men are not a unitary group and do not have a feminine nature and essence in common".[27] She sees the slash as her answer to those feminist critics who have rightly claimed that the term "women" has often referred to white women only. Thus, by adding the slash she wants to underscore the fact that wo/men are fragmented by structures such as race, class, and ethnicity. The slash is a sign and a reminder of those differences which divide individual wo/men.[28]

Secondly, Schüssler Fiorenza uses the term "wo/men" in an inclusive way, so that it also refers to marginalized men. Her way of writing it seeks to point out that those structures determining women's lives "also have an impact on men of subordinated races, classes, countries, and religions, albeit in a different way".[29] She continues: "Hence the spelling 'wo/men' seeks to communicate that whenever I speak of 'wo/men' I mean not only to include *all women* but also to speak of oppressed and marginalized men."[30] The expression "wo/men" should therefore be understood as a political category with no (gender) exclusions. As Schüssler Fiorenza states, the meaning of the term "wo/men" is often "people".[31]

Schüssler Fiorenza's third reason for splitting the word "wo/men" is to avoid expressions such as "women and minority men" or "women and other

---

[26] Schüssler Fiorenza, *Jesus: Miriam's Child, Sophia's Prophet,* 191.
[27] Schüssler Fiorenza, *Wisdom Ways,* 58.
[28] Schüssler Fiorenza, *Sharing Her Word,* 186. Schüssler Fiorenza does not explain what she means by differences within individual women.
[29] Schüssler Fiorenza, *Jesus: Miriam's Child, Sophia's Prophet,* 191.
[30] Ibid., 191. See also Schüssler Fiorenza, *Jesus and the Politics of Interpretation,* 57.
[31] Schüssler Fiorenza, *Rhetoric and Ethic,* ix.

oppressed groups". In her view, the idea of woman as the "other" is inscribed in these kind of phrases. They also present women as a unitary group which doesn't need to be described in more detail.[32]

Fourthly, Schüssler Fiorenza explains that the broken form of "wo/men" is intended to challenge androcentric language. The purpose is twofold: on the one hand, male readers are invited to think twice about whether or not they are included. In this way men have to engage in a similar thought process as that required of women in an androcentric language system in which the word "men" can refer to both men and women.[33] On the other hand, Schüssler Fiorenza sees the unconventional word "wo/men" as a means of changing language patterns. She argues that "wo/men as much as men are socialized into the mindsets and world-views of the dominant culture". Destabilizing customary expressions and finding new ones can thus be "a very important step toward the realization of a new consciousness".[34]

The divided term "wo/men" thus seems to crystallize some of the fundamental ideas of Schüssler Fiorenza's gender theorizing. I would argue that this inclusive word expresses clearly her point that the difference between men and women ought not to be seen as the most essential difference of humanity. That is, Schüssler Fiorenza argues that gender should not be prioritized in feminist analyses, but regarded only as one of the relations of ruling which intersect with race, class, and so on.[35]

I would further suggest that coining the inclusive term "wo/men" has been Schüssler Fiorenza's way of bringing together some central points of two traditions in their manifold expressions: feminist theory and liberation theology. Situating herself in the tradition of feminist theory, Schüssler Fiorenza directs her attention to the oppression and emancipation of *women*, but at the same time she wants to hold on to the idea expressed by, for example, Latin American liberation theologians that all theological reflection should begin with the experiences of oppressed *people*. Schüssler Fiorenza thus aims at constructing a "feminist theology of liberation" which does not exclude marginalized men.

---

[32] Schüssler Fiorenza, *Sharing Her Word*, 186.
[33] Schüssler Fiorenza, *Sharing Her Word*, 186.
[34] Schüssler Fiorenza, *Wisdom Ways*, 58.
[35] Schüssler Fiorenza wants to emphazise that she has taken into account the critique which Third World feminists have directed against the mainstream feminist theorizing of the West. See for example Schüssler Fiorenza, *But She Said*, 114-115; Schüssler Fiorenza *Wisdom Ways*, 117-118.

Against this background the introduction of the "wo/men" term can also be seen as a *practical* decision. Adding the slash relieves Schüssler Fiorenza of the necessity for speaking about "women and other non-persons" or "women and other marginalized people" as she had earlier done.[36]

Dividing the term "wo/men" can be characterized not only as a practical but also a *strategic* device. It is well in line with Schüssler Fiorenza's social constructivist gender theorizing which seems to be formed as a contrast to the understanding of gender as presented by the Vatican. Throughout her work she focuses her criticism on essentialist understandings of gender and argues that the difference between men and women should not be seen as naturally given or divinely ordained but socially and culturally constructed. She is also strongly opposed to the idea that women are "by their nature" – that is, because of their anatomical/biological sex – suited to some activities and roles in society – especially motherhood – and unsuited, for example, to be ordained to the Catholic priesthood. Thus, Schüssler Fiorenza's aim is to show that linking gender with anatomical facts (that is, conceiving gender as based on biology) is an untenable theoretical position.

Although I can, for the most part, understand the reasons why Schüssler Fiorenza has coined the word "wo/men", I also have reservations about the gender theoretical ideas implicit in it. In formulating my comments, I consider the question of the kind of gender theorizing which could meet the challenges posed by the (religious) situation in Finland.

Women without bodies and words of their own?

While Schüssler Fiorenza regards the slash as a sign of difference pointing to realities that separate women from each other, I see it also as expressing sameness between women and men. Again and again Schüssler Fiorenza's readers are reminded that the word "wo/men" refers both to women and marginalized men. [37] The difference between women and men thus seems to be given quite little weight in her writings.[38] Schüssler Fiorenza never actually considers the

---

[36] See, for example, Schüssler Fiorenza, *But She Said*, 4-5.

[37] See, for example, Schüssler Fiorenza, *Jesus and the Politics of Interpretation*, 4.

[38] I here come to a somewhat different conclusion than Anne-Louise Eriksson, who claims that Schüssler Fiorenza theorizes "women's experience as normative and epistemologically significant, thus underscoring difference between female and male gender..." Although Eriksson states that Schüssler Fiorenza defends the epistemologically priviledged standpoint of the *ekklesia of women* – the participants of which are both women *and* men – she still argues that Schüssler Fiorenza understands "*women's* experience" in a gynocentric way thereby construing

question of how men and women differ from each other. Nor is she interested in reflecting on the *reasons* for women's oppression, or asking why women – and not men – are subordinated worldwide and almost in every culture. When writing about the situation of women, Schüssler Fiorenza focuses on describing the structure of the system of domination which oppresses both women and men without elite status. The specific nature of women's subjection remains an undealt issue in her work.

What I find striking in Schüssler Fiorenza's gender theorizing is her silence on the bodily aspects or experiences of being a woman. In her writings women are depicted as social and political actors who can either conform to their oppressive situations or challenge them. Schüssler Fiorenza seems to write about women as if we (women) were almost bodiless beings characterized by our consciousness or rational, decision-making minds.[39] Her reluctance to pay attention to women's corporeality is understandable against her Roman Catholic background. In the anthropological teachings of the Vatican, long-lived Western ideas of women as "closer to nature" than men or "destined by their anatomy" are still very much alive. One way to resist this kind of thinking is to be silent about those experiences of women that can be linked to anatomy/biology, but I wonder if this solution can really do justice to women and the multiplicity of our lives and being. Surely a feminist theology which aims at having an effect on concrete, *real* women should take into consideration more aspects of women's lives than those proposed by Schüssler Fiorenza?[40]

---

gender as a separating category. However, I do agree with Eriksson that there is a tension between humanist (underlining the sameness of women and men) and gynocentric notions in Schüssler Fiorenza's writings. Unlike Eriksson, who has analyzed Schüssler Fiorenza's publications until 1993, I would nevertheless argue that the humanist emphasis is dominant in her writings since that time. See Eriksson, *The Meaning of Gender*, 4, 18, 95, 105.

[39] Notions of sex and gender articulated in the tradition of socialist-marxist feminism have been criticized especially by feminist theorists drawing on psychoanalytic theory. For example, Moira Gatens has argued that sex/gender theorizing which operates with the key concepts of "ideology", "consciousness", and "socialization" implies a "rationalist conception of the subject". This leads the promotion of feminist goals "as if women's *bodies* and the repression and control of women's bodies were not a crucial stake in these struggles". See Moira Gatens, "A Critique of the Sex/Gender Distinction", in: Senja Gunew (ed.), *A Reader in Feminist Knowledge* (Routledge: London and New York 1983), 139-157, here 154.

[40] In the women's studies' seminars where I have presented papers on Schüssler Fiorenza the theoretical and abstract nature of her work has been often commented on. I can not but agree with these observations. As one of the subtitles of *Wisdom Ways* shows, Schüssler Fiorenza

To contextualize my critique of Schüssler Fiorenza, I want to consider how a feminist theology which is silent about women's corporeality and questions of gender difference could be applied to a situation in Finland. As mentioned above, there have been female pastors in the Lutheran Church of Finland for almost twenty years. The days of rejoicing over the winning of the battle for the ordination of women therefore belong to the past. The wish to show that women can do the pastor's job as well as or even better than men was shared by many female pastors during their first working years. And the feedback from the vast majority of the church members has made it clear that women pastors have really earned their positions.

By and large, what characterized the struggle for the ordination of women has also marked the way in which female pastors understand their place and duty in the church. They have not wanted to make differences between men and women an issue. On the contrary, female pastors have emphasized that as ministers of the Word they share the same vision and vocation as men. Gender does not have any notable effect on the way the Christian message is proclaimed. Women pastors generally concur with the opinion that they usually do their work – for example in leading liturgy and officiating in church services – in a different manner than men. Among other things, women's courage and ability to show their feelings has been welcomed as a sign of a church which comes "closer to people" than ever before. Nevertheless, questioning the traditional and male-dominated ways of interpreting the Christian dogma has not been on the agenda of women pastors.

Some of the fundamental principles of so-called French feminism, which Schüssler Fiorenza strongly opposes, have helped me to consider the situation of Finnish female pastors from quite a different angle than that offered by her works. Grace Jantzen in particular has brought the insights of the French theorists of "sexual difference" into the feminist theological discussion.[41] In her

---

understands "women" primarily as a category of feminist analysis. Although she stresses the importance of taking "women's experiences" as the starting point of feminist theology she gives hardly any space for describing these experiences in her work. See Schüssler Fiorenza, *Wisdom Ways*, 107. In her study of 20th century interpretations of the Book of Revelation, Hanna Stenström has paid attention to the lack of concreteness in Schüssler Fiorenza's writings. In her opinion, it is quite surprising that as a feminist liberation theologian Schüssler Fiorenza does not refer to actual work with Revelation in concrete base groups or women groups. In this way, Schüssler Fiorenza's approach differs from methods commonly used by Latin American liberation theologians. See Stenström, *The Book of Revelation*, 246.

[41] As it is often noted, "French feminism" is a disputed term. It is commonly used to refer to "the big three" thinkers, Hélène Cixous, Julia Kristeva, and Luce Irigaray whose work has been

influential book *Becoming Divine* she has focused particularly on Luce Irigaray's understanding of women's subjectivity.[42] Taking a critical approach to the psychoanalytic theory of Jacques Lacan, Irigaray has searched for an answer to the problem of how women can become and live as subjects in a society in which not only language but also the rules and norms of social life – the broad conceptual patterns of civilization – are made by and for men. Using Lacan's terminology, Irigaray refers to this web or structure of interrelated signs, roles, and rituals as "the Symbolic Order". She sees the Judeo-Christian religion as being at the heart of the Western Symbolic Order (or Western Symbolism). A clear indication of this is, for example, the fact that the concept of God as Divine Father is still central to modern thinking, whether or not "his" existence is denied.[43] According to Irigaray, it is obvious that the religious symbolic order with its "male gods" has worked against women. For this reason it is time for women to create a new symbolic order of religion, and to start imagining God "according to our gender".[44]

On the basis of this very brief and somewhat superficial presentation of Irigaray's ideas I hope to take up some of the issues that following Grace Jantzen, I believe to be worth considering in the search for arguments to demonstrate

---

widely discussed by Anglo-American academics. Thus, "French feminism" does not demarcate an intellectual movement that travelled from France accross the Atlantic, but refers rather to "the way in which particular French writers were taken up, rather selectively, and used within Anglo-feminist circles". Because these writers cannot be said to be either "French" or "feminists" and since they see themselves as divergent thinkers it has been suggested that the term "French feminism" should be replaced by "the feminism of sexual difference". See "Introduction," in Morny Joy, Kathleen O'Grady and Judith L. Poxon (eds), *French Feminists on Religion. A Reader* (Routledge: London and New York 2002), 2-4.

[42] Grace M. Jantzen, *Becoming Divine: Towards a Feminist Philosophy of Religion* (Indiana University Press: Bloomington and Indianapolis 1999).

[43] Jantzen refers to Jacques Derrida's idea of the divine as the guarantor of meaning, noting that according to Derrida "it is the assumption of the divine presence (even when that presence is held to be absent, as in secularism) that ultimately grounds the system of signs". See Jantzen, *Becoming Divine*, 10.

[44] At the heart of Irigaray's thought is the idea that in order to achieve subjectivity, it is necessary for humans to have a horizon, an ideal of wholeness to which we can aspire. Drawing on Feuerbach, she argues that the symbolic order of religion, and especially the idea of God, has provided such a horizon. But the problem for women is that the God of the west "has been created out of man's gender". Thus, she states that "as long as woman lacks a divine made in her image she cannot establish her subjectivity or achieve a goal of her own". See Luce Irigaray, *Sexes and Genealogies*, trans. Gillian C. Gill (Columbia University Press: New York 1993), 62, 63. See also Jantzen, *Becoming Divine*, 12-15.

the necessity of feminist theology to a Finnish audience. Although I have some reservations about parts of the argument of Irigaray and Jantzen, I do believe that theorists of "sexual difference" have succeeded in spotlighting the male-dominance of our religious symbolic order which the commonly held view that Finns experience gender equality tends to hide.

To put it simply, it really seems not to be a matter of concern to women pastors that it is men who have constructed the symbolic order of our faith. In our Lutheran church, female pastors have continued to speak of "our Father in heaven". In women's language, God as Father is often depicted as more loving and close to people than in the language of men. But the basic idea of the heavenly hierarchy with the One God defined as masculine at the top has not really been questioned by women pastors. Expressed in a pointed way, women are speaking men's words, repeating faithfully what they have always said. Following Judith Butler, one can, of course, see the different tone in women's God-talk as a way of "repeat[ing] it differently". However, I would claim that more needs to be done than to polish the traditional language of the Divine. The question of gender difference needs to be thoroughly reflected on by women theologians. We should ask if we can truly consider ourselves equal with men when the core symbolic order of our religion in fact excludes us.[45]

On a continuum

After spending half a decade closely engaged with the works of Schüssler Fiorenza I cannot but subscribe to many of the issues which are often said to characterize feminist thinking and research. First, I have come to see not only that in order to understand somebody's ideas they have to be seen as *situated*, but that this is true also of the interpretations of such ideas. Second, in this article, I have evaluated two central concepts of Schüssler Fiorenza's thought from a perspective which can be described as *political*. Although as a researcher in women's studies my aim is to analyze her writings as objectively as possible, it is impossible for me to ignore the political dimension of my work.[46]

---

[45] Here my argument is similar to that of Hanna Stenström, who has considered Schüssler Fiorenza's minor interest in the symbolical dimensions of gender. One of the main points of Stenström's criticism of Schüssler Fiorenza's interpretation of Revelation is that the misogynist gender symbolism of the book is passed over too quickly. See Stenström, *The Book of Revelation*, 1999, 250, 252.

[46] My understanding of "objectivity" comes close to what Donna Haraway has suggested in her influential essay "Situated Knowledges: The Science Question in Feminism and the Priviledge of Partial Perspective," in: Donna Haraway *Simians, Cyborgs, and Women. The Reinvention of*

Inevitably, my interest is attracted to those aspects and ideas of Schüssler Fiorenza's thought which seem most problematic from my own context-dependent point of view.

In conclusion, I would suggest that the feminist liberation theology of Schüssler Fiorenza can be presented to the Finnish audience first and foremost as an example of those first generation feminist theologies done in North America which have been widely influential all over the world. Schüssler Fiorenza's work has led me and many others to the fascinating world of feminist theology and theory. Hearing her words has inspired me to listen to quite different feminist voices coming from this side of the Atlantic. Thanks to Schüssler Fiorenza and other North American feminist theologians, we have a head start when constructing our own feminist theologies here in Finland – theologies, which grow out of our own context.

Dieser Artikel diskutiert kontextbedingte Grenzen der feministischen Theologie Elisabeth Schüssler Fiorenzas. Zwei zentrale Konzepte ihres Werkes – die *Ekklesia* der Frauen und *Gender* – werden unter finnischer Perspektive betrachtet. Ziel ist es, herauszufinden, ob sie für eine feministische Theologie im sozialen und religiösen Kontext Finnlands von Bedeutung sind. Zunächst wird gezeigt, dass das Konzept der *Ekklesia* der Frauen, das feministische Theologie inmitten feministischer Kämpfe situiert, in einem Land, in dem man einen sukzessiven und (meist) konfliktfreien Fortschritt im Blick auf die Rechte von Frauen gewohnt ist, nicht ohne weiteres ein Echo findet. Zweitens wird Schüssler Fiorenzas *Gender*-Konzept als ungeeignet angesehen, um den Herausforderungen, die sich aus der religiösen Situation in Finnland ergeben, zu begegnen. Eine feministische Theologie, die sich über die Körperlichkeit von Frauen und über Fragen der Geschlechterdifferenz ausschweigt, bietet keine nützlichen Werkzeuge für eine feministische Kritik in einer lutherischen Kirche, in der die Gleichheit zwischen Männern und Frauen auf institutioneller Ebene das Problem der Männer-Dominiertheit unseres religiösen Symbolsystems zu verschleiern scheint.

Cet article discute des limitations contextuelles de la théologie féministe d'Elisabeth Schüssler Fiorenza. Deux concepts centraux dans son travail – L' *ekklesia* des femmes et le genre – sont étudiés à partir d'une perspective finlandaise. L'objectif est de découvrir si ces concepts peuvent être utilisés pour créer une théologie féministe significative dans le contexte social et religieux de la Finlande. D'abord, nous

---

Nature (Routledge: New York 1991), 183-201, here 190: "Feminist objectivity is about limited location and situated knowledge, not about transcendence and splitting of subject and object."

affirmons que le concept de l'*ekklesia* des femmes qui situe la théologie féministe au cœur des luttes féministes ne trouve pas facilement d'écho dans un pays habitué à ce que les droits des femmes progressent de façon graduelle et (presque) sans conflits. Ensuite, le concept de genre d'Elisabeth Schüssler Fiorenza ne paraît pas approprié pour faire face aux défis posés par la situation religieuse en Finlande. Une théologie féministe muette sur les questions de la corporéité des femmes et de la différence de genre, n'apporte pas d'instruments utilisables par la critique féministe dans une Église luthérienne où l'égalité entre hommes et femmes au niveau institutionnel semble occulter le problème de la domination masculine de notre symbolique religieuse.

Anni Tsokkinen (*1962) is an ordained minister in the Evangelical Lutheran Church of Finland. She is currently working as a lecturer in systematic theology at Diaconia University of Applied Sciences. She is also revising her doctoral dissertation in Women's Studies at the University of Helsinki. Her latest publication in English is "Elisabeth Schüssler Fiorenza on the Authority of the Bible", in: Charlotte Methuen *et al* (eds): *Holy Texts: Authority and Language* (Yearbook of the ESWTR 12; Peeters: Leuven 2004), 133-142.

Journal of the European Society of Women in Theological Research 15 (2007) 71-87.
doi: 10.2143/ESWTR.15.0.2022769

Else Marie Wiberg Pedersen

God as a Something: Daphne Hampson's Post-Christian Religion

This article is about Daphne Hampson's Post-Christian religion as she has formulated it between 1990 and 2001. I will consider her critique of Christian theology and her own theological deliberations in her major publications within this
time span, a task that has not been done before. What is of particular interest is
to observe how Hampson, who claims never to have been a Christian feminist,
confronts, not conservative male theology, but diverse forms of Christian feminism in her search for a religion in which gender is of no significance. Notwith-
standing, Hampson is a feminist and as such delivers both sharp observations
and fine critiques of patriarchal systems. But she is no longer a Christian, and
this has made her pose daring questions to feminist Christian theology, which
I see as both necessary and welcome. Hampson daringly and seriously questions
whether Christian feminists' Christology is really Christian and not something
else instead. This question could be posed to a range of Christologies through
the history of Christianity, and by her way of criticising Christian feminist theologians Hampson seems to end up in asserting a rather conservative understanding of Christian theology, which one might expect her to contest. The
question I will address is, if Hampson by way of her picture of Christian theology, which very much looks like a conservative theism, and by way of her
picture of feminism, which is presented as a particular ethos, contrary to her
vision of an egalitarian theology in fact fixates the ugly broad ditch between past
and present, and between not only women and men but also between women.

A Woman with a Quest
From her often autobiographical publications one gets an idea of both the theologian Daphne Hampson and the person behind the theologian:[1] a person

---

[1] In general, all Daphne Hampson's publications contain a certain amount of self-biographical
   material and personal notes. A more condensed version can be found in her article "Exodus or

with a quest, first to become ordained to priesthood, then to make feminist values the matrix of human behaviour. With a Free Church background she had been visiting the Quakers, and while remaining a member of the Presbyterian Church of England, she was drawn to Anglicanism though sceptical of the Anglican Church's opposition to ordain women. The wish to be ordained has been the incentive of Hampson's life, and the fact that the Anglican Church was against women's ordination had been the fuel of her profession as a theologian. Thus she founded the Group for the Ministry of Women in that church and wrote the theological statement arguing in favour of the ordination of women to the priesthood that was circulated to all members of the General Synod of the Church of England before the vote on women's ordination in 1978. However, having lost the yearlong fight, she decided that the resistance to women's ordination among traditionalist Christians reflected not only their limited understanding of the gospel but the very limits of Christianity *per se*. Without recognizing that an increasing number of Christian churches were ordaining women to the priesthood[2], she finally decided to follow Mary Daly's Post-Christian stance and exodus from the church, which she had almost witnessed some twenty years earlier at Harvard in 1971. What made her a Post-Christian was the fact that after twenty years of struggle she still could not be ordained in the Anglican Church.[3] Her vision was to establish an egalitarian theology where women could be autonomous. And suddenly, Hampson after her Post-Christian

---

Not?", in: Angela Berlis et al. (eds), *Women Churches. Networking and Reflection in the European Context* (Yearbook of the European Society of Women in Theological Research 3; Kok Pharos: Kampen / Grünewald: Mainz 1995), 73-83.

[2] The Evangelical-Lutheran Church in Denmark ordained women from 1948, the Church of Sweden voted for 1958 and ordained the first women in 1960, followed by a steadily increasing number of Lutheran churches during the 1960'es and 1970'es, long before Hampson deemed Christianity as a whole limited. The Anglican Church in Great Britain voted for in 1992. Admittedly, there is still an unpleasant resistance against ordination of women to be found even within some of the Lutheran churches (the Roman Catholic Church and the Orthodox churches go without mentioning). Patriarchal structures persisted in these churches as also a group of persistently conservative pastors, but it is worth stressing that the resistance and the patriarchal structures decrease rapidly the very moment women pastors are a fact. See Else Marie Wiberg Pedersen (ed.), *Se min kjole. De første kvindelige præsters historie* (Samleren: Copenhagen 1998).

[3] See Hampson, "Exodus or Not?", 73. Note that this biographical article was based on a talk given in 1994 at the University of Groningen to mark the twentieth anniversary of Mary Daly *Beyond God the Father: toward a philosophy of Women's liberation* (Beacon: Boston 1973).

conversion turned rather ambivalent, if not even opposed, to women's ordination.

Hampson's Post-Christian Theology

In both her Post-Christian manifestos *Theology and Feminism*[4] and *After Christianity*[5], Hampson criticises Christian theology generally and Christian feminist theology specifically. Here she renders Christianity not only truly conservative, a past history about a particular man of the past, but also to be only true if it is a conservation of a particular interpretation of the Chalcedonian theology, which made it impossible for it to accept and ordain women. Hampson interprets Christian doctrine as if it were a fixed and firm teaching since the fifth century. Furthermore, though allowing various male theologians such as Thomas Aquinas, Luther, Schleiermacher, Barth and even Bultmann and Tillich to take Christian doctrine out of the freezer and cook it, she does not allow female theologians to do the same. In Hampson's estimation, there is but one way of understanding the "unique revelation in Jesus as the Christ", and if one does not correspond with that one understanding, one cannot be a Christian with one's integrity intact:

> It is inevitable then that I should exit from the church and from Christianity. Why? Because nothing else is intellectually honest or morally possible. If one wishes to be a religious person, not least – as I do – one must have a certain integrity. I do not admire women who try to twist Christianity to mean anything that they would have it be. Christianity must mean something. What Christians have always stood for in human history is the claim that there was a unique revelation in Jesus as the Christ.[6]

Hampson's aim is to move "away from a myth which is held to be objective and true and which, in turn governs us", and so to move away from "a transcendent God 'above' the world, by which all else is to be measured" and also to be more loose about dogmatic beliefs.[7]

As a theologian and theist she stayed in the academy to teach theology despite her animosity toward Christian dogmatics. She defends this "internal

---

4 Daphne Hampson, *Theology and Feminism* (Blackwell Publishers: Oxford 1990).
5 Daphne Hampson, *After Christianity* (SCM: London 1996).
6 Hampson, "Exodus or Not?", 76.
7 I here refer to Hampson, *After Christianity*, 292, but these statements are recurrent also elsewhere in her publications.

exodus" strongly in cultural terms, in that she perceives of herself as part of the Western tradition, however only the great Christian fathers "without whom she cannot think", as she puts it. Thus:

> I teach Schleiermacher by choice because here was a man, whom I can admire, who commenced from human awareness of God, of which I also wish to speak. In that he went on to conceptualise this awareness in Christian form, Schleiermacher took a path that I cannot follow. But his work is a starting point. I do not teach women from the past (there were no great women theologians), though I do incidentally teach the thought of some present day feminist theorists.[8]

Hampson's choice to stay within the field of theology has to do with her wish to drop a "rather big bomb" to shake and change theology by way of her "new ethic, new way of conceiving of the self, a new vision". The bomb must be dropped precisely in theology because it is "that discipline within which people have always expressed their highest aspirations" – and which therefore "must not be left to the men".[9] I think she does right in not leaving theology to men. But how does she explain the apparent incoherence between a mainly male theology's "high aspirations" and her view of male theologians' hegemonic bad ethics (patriarchal) on the one hand and her view of female and feminist theologians who thinks differently on the other hand? Despite her call to women to give one another space, a close reading of her statements reveals instead that Hampson only has space for those who "pursue [her] thoughts with [her], and with whom [she] can inter-change ideas", for – as she bluntly announces – "I learn more from women in feminist theory than from people of a different outlook within theology".[10]

Feminism as the death-knell of Christianity

Since women are the pivotal point of Hampson's Post-Christian project and her view of feminism shapes her understanding of Christianity,[11] it is important to see what her feminism is about and how it reflects on women and men.

---

8   Hampson, "Exodus or Not?", 81.
9   Hampson, "Exodus or Not?", 82-83.
10 Hampson, "Exodus or Not?", 81-82. Hampson was at the time working on supplying her much criticised definitions of feminism and Christianity launched in Hampson *Theology and Feminism*. In this book she mainly referred to such theorists as Gilligan and Chodorow. In Hampson *After Christianity* she tried to meet some of the criticism by adding French feminist theory such as Luce Irigaray and Julia Kristeva.
11 Hampson, *Theology and Feminism*, 4; Hampson, *After Christianity*, 84: "My thesis is that feminists (for all their differences) have a radically different understanding of the self-in-relation

Hampson discerns between female, feminine and feminist. "Female" she employs in contrast with male for the biological difference between men and women, whereas "feminine" to her has solely negative connotations in that the meaning of this term is a cultural construct reflecting men's sexist suppositions about women. "Feminist", a term she decidedly uses not in a descriptive but a prescriptive way, then by contrast designates "a certain set of views ... about equality of the sexes and the need for example for non-hierarchical relationships".[12] In other words, to Hampson feminism is a moral principle (as categorical as Kant's imperative), a way we all should behave since there must be a complementarity between the sexes, as she formulates it.

Having presented feminism as an ethical formula, Hampson in *Theology and Feminism* immediately enmeshes her understanding of feminism with her understanding of Christianity in a circular move. Therefore she goes on to state that Christianity can also be employed as pure moral teaching, in which case, however, it is no longer Christianity but sheer humanism. Exactly for this reason, so Hampson argues, feminism will be "the death-knell of Christianity as a viable religious option."[13] In this feminist ethics, the question of the theodicy is not: if God is so good why is there evil? – But: "why if God be good, has any harm come to women?" Hence, theodicy is reduced to a matter of gender, as is theology as such:

> There is then a theological question posed for one who takes the feminist agenda seriously and believes in human equality, as to how this revelation can be a revelation of God. The question then as to whether feminism and Christianity are compatible is that of whether the equality of women is compatible with a religion which has come from a past patriarchal age.[14]

Feminism means a shift of paradigm in relation to the Enlightenment which, in its part, already meant a discontinuity of the Christian story, and feminism will inevitably make Christianity, a mere myth, "seem not only untrue but immoral". Thus, in Hampson's view, feminism will totally reverse the Enlightenment's paradigm of Christianity as the absolutely true and moral and reveal

---

from that which has been built into Western theology. It is from this perspective of this different understanding that feminists critique the theology that we have known."

[12] Hampson, *Theology and Feminism*, x.
[13] Hampson, *Theology and Feminism*, 1.
[14] Hampson, *Theology and Feminism*, 11.

it as absolutely untrue and immoral. But is it possible to hold such an absolute claim in this day and time of immense fluidity and flexibility?

In Hampson's circular argument, equality of women immediately collapses with her talk of an egalitarian God, rapidly eclipsing the talk of human equality. Likewise, in her endeavours to define an egalitarian God, she deconstructs first a conservative Christology, then various Christian feminist Christologies, all in her view making the past normative; before she eventually establishes her own religious position where the present is normative. For Hampson, neither liberal Christians nor Christian feminists represent true Christianity, since the former (coined the "Kairos approach") is ethically incoherent, whitewashing the hierarchical and unjust past of Christianity, and the latter (coined the "golden thread approach") has an "ethical *a priori* position" to which it adjusts Christianity. Hampson holds two theses:

1. Christianity and feminism are incompatible. Feminism proclaims equality between men and women, whilst Christianity proclaims inequality, hierarchy and sexism. Feminism, the crown of the Enlightenment project, promotes a discontinuity with the irrational past, whereas Christianity promotes continuity between past and present though at the same time standing in discontinuity to our post-Enlightenment rational knowledge.
2. Religion and feminism are compatible. God is something which is always available, not someone bound to any particular history or person. God is something just and egalitarian which cannot be found in either Christ or the Trinity.

How much feminism and Christianity are enmeshed can be seen also in the chapter on "Feminist Anthropology", where anthropology is immediately translated into "theological anthropology".[15] Hampson poses the question whether women have another kind of anthropology, and must admit that there are limitations. But though not fully developed, she argues, feminist theology can at least point to something new in terms of politics and ethics. It is of particular importance that feminism constitutes a shift in the perception of the self and of the relationship between oneself and others in the ordering of the world. According to Hampson, women in their way of conceiving of reality focus on the sphere of praxis.

Hampson received much criticism of *Theology and Feminism* from particularly liberal theologians. Men and women alike found her definitions rather

---

[15] Hampson, *Theology and Feminism*, chapter 4, 116-147, here especially p. 116.

superficial and inconsistent, both of feminism and of its coherent deconstruction of not least feminist theologians who seriously try to break the male monopoly on the Christian tradition from within.[16] What was contested was not the criticism of patriarchy or feminism's impact on Western culture. Hampson's critique of patriarchy and feminism can hardly be discerned from that of Christian feminist theology:

> By Christian feminist theology I mean a reflection on God and all things in the light of God that stands consciously in the company of all the world's women, explicitly prizing their genuine humanity while uncovering and criticizing its persistent violation in sexism, itself an omnipresent paradigm of unjust relationships. In terms of Christian doctrine, this perspective claims the fullness of the religious heritage for women precisely as human, in their own right and independent from personal identification with men.[17]

The main criticism had to do with the fact that she from her own construction takes an essentialist stance from which she attacks other feminist theologians (men and women) with a constructivist approach to Christian theology, whether in biblical studies, church history or systematic theology. In addition, she never delivers a substantial study either of the bible, church history or dogmatics, as there is no discussion of hermeneutics. Being so fundamentally essentialist and prescriptive from her own imposed standards, she makes the scientific fallacy of deducing an "is" from an "ought" in her feminist anthropology, whereas she in her estimation of Christian theology makes the peculiar deduction from an alleged male ontology to an "ought not". It is problematic that her argumentation contains so many contradictions: theology is a human construct, still this does not go for Christianity, and definitely not for Hampson's constructed God who is as "God has always been"; and the "internal exodus" that she defends on her own part she attacks Christian feminists for making.

Hampson does not allow for anyone, whether male or a female, to take a feminist critique seriously and yet being Christian. She ignores that neither the Christian tradition nor feminism is one but many, and have been so each of them from their very inception. Instead of making the diversity of the two,

---

[16] One of the most important contributions was Rosemary Radford Ruether, "Is Feminism the End of Christianity? A Critique of Daphne Hampson's *Theology and Feminism*", in: *Scottish Journal of Theology* 43 (1990).

[17] Elizabeth A. Johnson, *She who is: The Mystery of God in Feminist Theological Discourse* (Crossroad: New York 1994), 8.

both the feminist movement and the Christian tradition, a resource to avoid a simplistic either/or thinking and the "flamboyance of a dramatic and decisive choice, as it were, between two opposed singular entities,"[18] Hampson discards diversity. She rejects revisionist feminist theologians such as Ruether, McFague, Trible, and Fiorenza, and in effect supports the conservative critique of these theologians. Concurrently, conservative theologians on their side favour Hampson for her uncompromising understanding of Christian theology, not least due to her critique of feminist Christian models. So for example Carl Braaten, a conservative Lutheran who a few years ago converted to Catholicism, in protest of the alleged relativism of today's Lutheran theology, has employed Hampson in this fashion: "No one who reads her book will find it easy to scoff at her thesis, as disconcerting as it may seem to those whose project is to reform the Christian faith on a feminist model."[19] Hampson thus theologically supports the Christian radical orthodoxy to which she is ideologically opposed.

In *After Christianity*, Hampson tries to meet the criticisms but fails, her main argument recurrently being that: "I am constantly misunderstood". Thus the most significant change is a terminology shift from feminist "anthropology" to feminist "ethics" only. But still she speaks in an essentialist way, though rather insubstantially, of feminism:

> My thesis is that feminists (for all their differences) have a radically different understanding of the self-in-relation from that which has been built into Western theology. It is from this perspective of this different understanding that feminists critique the theology that we have known.[20]

---

[18] Paul R. Sponheim, "On Being and Becoming before God: A Response to Daphne Hampson", in: *Word & World* XV (1995), 332-341, here 332. Apart from Hampson *Theology and Feminism,* Sponheim is also responding to Hampson "Luther on the Self: A Feminist Critique", in: *Word & World* VIII (1988), 334-342.

[19] Carl Braaten, review of Hampson *Theology and Feminism*, in: *Dialog* 31 (1992), quoted in Sponheim, "On Being and Becoming", 333. Hampson has never responded to Sponheim's critique on this point (see note 18), as far as I know, though he invites to a further conversation. Instead we see her confirming his criticism as she in a later book, Daphne Hampson, *Christian Contradictions: The Structures of Lutheran and Catholic Thought* (Cambridge University Press: Cambridge UK 2001), lists Braaten along with other conservative theologians in her acknowledgement, whereas she never mentions Sponheim whose references to Luther texts nonetheless seems to have inspired her.

[20] Hampson, *After Christianity*, 84.

Hampson admits there are differences amongst women and feminists, but she does not want to enter into dialogue with those of a different opinion. Instead, she contends that women, in spite of such differences, have a common understanding of self, a feminist ontology, profoundly different from that of Western theology, also ontologically conceived. She finds these commonalities through a scanty feminist reading of art, psychoanalysis and political science that all come together in a feminist discourse which has given us a new perspective from which to analyse the past.

> …when humanity comes to an ethical divide of the magnitude represented by feminism, anything which does not conform to our new ethical awareness needs to be cast aside. It will be judged and found wanting. Ethics and religion correlate closely, so that it must be impossible in the long run to hold to a religious position which embodies paradigms that we cannot consider ethical. For God is supposed to be good, and religion to speak to our highest aspirations.[21]

It would be interesting to see Hampson enter into a serious dialogue with those who firmly point to feminist theology as a contextual enterprise where no commonalities between women, not even within one "continent", can be found. How would she answer for example Nami Kim, who engages in a theology of what I would call "shared diversity" in a rapidly changing global context, and who with Kwok Pui-Lan warns against "indiscriminate appropriation and mindless borrowing" from other religious traditions, here specifically "Asian" (another colonial generalisation) traditions?[22]

Another important question is, what Hampson's "self-in-relation" feminism actually entails? This she expounds by way of the term "autonomy", for the use of which she also finds herself constantly misunderstood. Unlike the fathers of Enlightenment, she explains, she uses it in the sense of "inter-dependent

---

[21] Hampson, *After Christianity*, 88. Hampson's notion of the divergences of feminist theories is here reduced to a matter of a cleavage between the "French" and the "Anglo-Saxon", see p. 105. See also Margaret D. Kamitsuka, "Reading the Raced and Sexed Body in *The Color Purple*: Repatterning White Feminist and Womanist Theological Hermeneutics", in: *Journal of Feminist Studies in Religion* 19 (2003), 45-46.

[22] Nami Kim, "My/Our Comfort *Not* at the Expense of 'Somebody Else's': Toward a Critical Global Feminist Theology", in: *Journal of Feminist Studies in Religion* 21 (2005), 75-94, (see her note 69). There are several other warnings against a colonization of feminist theology, but Kim's suggestion of "shared diversity" seems to me one of the most promising in inviting to a dialogue.

autonomy", advocating as she and other feminists are for a self centred in relation.[23]

> Women who have come under the sway of feminist ideas will be unwilling to bow to heteronomous relationships, demanding a rightly defined autonomy ... The self which feminists are advocating is neither on the one hand enclosed within itself, nor on the other hand does it sacrifice self in the service of others. It does not know isolated pride, but equally wishes to avoid self-deprecation.[24]

But how inter-dependent is it, if Hampson really denounces the service of others as mere sacrifice and not as relational? Nevertheless, she maintains that women traditionally have acted in a self-relational way in decidedly equal and non-hierarchical relationships among themselves, which men will immediately disrupt when present, as competitive as men and male relationships always are.[25] Her romantic view of women may coincide with the bourgeois ideal of "woman" of the nineteenth century, but does it hold in today's reality in a rapidly changing global context? Is it not so that when it comes to competition (in work or research) or power and organization of power, women and men very often act very similarly? At any rate, I do not believe that a Margaret Thatcher was more compromising or more relational than a Tony Blair.

In *After Christianity*, Hampson rejects the criticisms of her views as misunderstandings, and instead she absolutizes her arguments,[26] formulating a theology exclusive of those women who broke men's monopoly on interpreting scripture and doctrine, and who in their own right interpret and employ the Christian message. In Hampson's view, these women are automatically made subordinate to continue serving their female virtues of motherhood, which also goes for those (Protestant) women, whom she seemingly self-contradictory contends, have joined the boys' club by being ordained.[27] Her ethics claims to

---

[23] Hampson, *After Christianity*, 104 and 106.

[24] Hampson, *After Christianity*, 115.

[25] Hampson, *After Christianity*, 112 -115.

[26] This was a move, which Sponheim foresaw in Sponheim "On Being and Becoming", 341.

[27] Hampson, *After Christianity*, 204. Hampson places this argument in a broader renunciation of Protestant theology which is peculiar in the light of her later positive attitude to Lutheran theology in Hampson *Christian Contradictions*, and particularly peculiar is this renunciation of women's ordination in the light of her attitude to ordination both in her earlier struggle and in the same work where she about 100 pages earlier has raised the question if not "transgressive practices (possibly even – within the realm of the church – ordaining women) themselves [can]

be universal (to women), yet non-inclusive. This paradox is based on an alleged universalism of women's experiences of consensus, opposed to an alleged universalism of men's non-experiences of consensus: "men simply have not had the experience ... of consensus decision-making within the context of a large group or a work situation".[28] By such contentions, Hampson presents a social reality so relentlessly and deliberately gendered that her actual ethical *a priori* position, her critique of Christian feminists, in effect is a double standard.[29] For while Christian theology is rejected as idolatrous because it allegedly conforms to the male psyche only (projecting solely men's hopes and fears) and therefore is immoral and untrue, a theology that reflects women's experience (or psyche?) is uplifted to being the only ethical and true.[30]

It is a good question how true Hampson's empiricist ethics is, and not least how ethical her essentialist standards are. As to the recurrent critique of her essentialism, her reply rather than solve the problem makes it more serious: "That depends how one defines 'essentialism', doesn't it?"[31] For how does one deal with a relativistic essentialism that even divides humanity into two incompatible "species" characterized by two incompatible ethics according to somebody's own standards. Hampson does not acknowledge the problem, however that her perspective is a construction in which people are trapped no matter what they say or do:

> ...the problem is that, with the best will in the world men can only begin from the constructed position that Hampson *needs* to deconstruct if her hope is ever to be fulfilled. She needs men to be men in the first place if they are to have any hope of understanding her position.[32]

I would like Hampson to explicate how essentialism can be relativistic, and the possibility of holding universals of empiricism in our time. Also, I would like

---

bring about a theological and indeed also a social shift" (Hampson, *After Christianity*, 105). I wonder.

[28] Hampson, *After Christianity*, 114-117. Hampson is here in line with the observation of first and foremost Judith Butler.

[29] See further Angela West, "Justification by Gender – Daphne Hampson's *After Christianity*", in: *Scottish Journal of Theology* 15 (1998), 99-115, here 101.

[30] Hampson, *After Christianity*, 119 and 84-118. See also Hampson, *Theology and Feminism*, 116-145.

[31] Hampson, *After Christianity*, xxi.

[32] David Jasper, "Book review of *After Christianity* 2. ed.", in: *Literature and Theology* 17 (2003), 474-477, here 475.

Hampson to deliver a thorough explication of women's common experience (deemed by most contemporary feminist theologians as a colonial white claim) and how this can form an ethical and true theology.

A Post-Christian God

Most parts of Hampson's Post-Christian books are dedicated to deliberations on Christian theology's immoral and untrue God: whereas women have monolithically been depicted as Virgin Mary and bride of the Christ in a subordinate relation to God the Father, God has always and univocally been understood as Lord, King, Judge or Father, the patriarch of patriarchs, on top of a human hierarchy. Hampson knows but does not waste much space on such trifles as Christianity's different strings from its very inception, revealed in scripture's collection of very diverse rendition of Jesus as the Christ, and in the creeds' compromises of very diverse understandings of Christology. Hampson knows that neither scripture nor the creeds underline the maleness of Christ, but rather the humanity and love of Christ. Hampson knows that Christian theology does not claim to be an enclosed doctrine but "a living community in history, which does not just have a past, but a present and a future", and which in the particular language of every time and place continually reads, interprets and re-evaluates itself from within the community.[33] Hampson knows that in this tradition there have always been strands focusing on, not the man Jesus as male, but the man Jesus as a human being. Hampson knows that it is only certain very conservative strands that reduce God's incarnation in the man Jesus to mean that God is male and male divine, and then use this distortion to exclude women from ministry. Nevertheless, she decides to give in and let the conservative party win the struggle for the true Christian God, eventually renouncing this God.

Considering her renunciation of the Christian God, which she reduces to be the male God of conservative theologians, what kind of God does Hampson believe in? Before attempting to answer that, Hampson, in continuation of Daly's critique in the 1970's, states that feminists must not be content with simply renaming God, which will be but a conceptualization of a God that is still a product of patriarchy. In order to reconstruct the notion of God compatible with feminism, the notion of God must be reshaped:

---

[33] Ruether, "Is Feminism the End of Christianity", 396.

The task of feminists working in theology is (as I conceive it) to formulate a conceptualization of God which is true both to what we may in the late twentieth century think the world to be, and moreover to the norms and values which feminists hold. I am not, then, saying that God is a human projection. I believe the word God to refer, and that moreover some theologies may better fit what we may believe to be the case than others. What seemed credible in one age no longer seems credible today. Furthermore it is not the case that ethically there is nothing to choose between different conceptualizations of God. Feminists claim that their way of conceiving reality, their way of understanding the self in relation to others, is ethically superior to the oppositional stance of male thought and behaviour. They may then well also believe that a conceptualization of God which embodies such an ethic and is commensurate with such a sense of relationality will both reflect and also tend to legitimate a social order which they would promote.[34]

Interestingly enough, Hampson here allows for the relativity that she refuses to allow for Christianity, simply due to her understanding of revelation. But Hampson's God in order to be the universal God – the God for all people at all times, which Christianity also claims – cannot be related to a particular revelation in a particular man.

Whereas Hampson's "after-Christianity" concept of the Christian God is fixed (and as immutable as the God concept of Aristotle), her concept of the Post-Christian God is rather blurred: "God is something which is always available, however much people in some ages, or some people in each age, may appear to be more aware of God".[35] It is unclear whether she in some way intends to promote Daly's concept of God as "it", in a retelling of Alice Walker's Shug in *The Color Purple*. To denounce God as a "someone" seems problematic, given her need for a God of prayer. As Kamitsuka has pointed out, it is a misunderstanding of Walker and African American theology to translate this "it" into an impersonal God, when it is rather an accentuation of a personal God's relation to the forsaken.[36] It is difficult to see what Hampson intends, and suddenly she shifts to talking about God as a word that "refers", even as a "thou" in prayer:

---

[34] Hampson, *Theology and Feminism*, 150.

[35] Hampson, *Theology and Feminism*, 8.

[36] See Kamitsuka, "Reading the Raced and Sexed Body in *The Color Purple*", 53-56, where she treats of Hampson's use of Alice Walker's *The Color Purple* in *Theology and Feminism*. Kamitsuka denounces Hampson's interpretation as an example of "how white feminist theology can impose a universalizing, color-blind grid on Walker's text", missing the "African American

I am very clear then that for me the word 'God' refers. It is not simply a construct in language; however profoundly our conceptualization of God be shaped by the linguistic and cultural tradition to which we belong. Nor is using religious language for me simply a way of naming the world, a way of affirming (for example) that there is an underlying goodness. (Though such a faith may indeed be prerequisite to construing the world religiously.) To affirm that the word 'God' refers is however not necessarily to believe that the word refers to a kind of entity, one which could be distinguished from all else that is. It has always been recognized in theology that there is a necessary problem in naming God – and mystics have deliberately chosen negative language, saying what God is not, rather that falsely confine our sense of God through inadequate vocabulary. The word God names what one concludes must be the case, the other level of reality which one believes to exist. If it were not that prayer is effective, I cannot see what grounds there could be for using the word God.[37]

The blurred concept of God is not less blurred when Hampson concludes by scoffing at modern theology for being profoundly secular, whilst her own 'God' is a "dimension of all that is", particularly as her own self in the daring words of Catherine of Siena: "My real me is God."[38] But it seems Hampson still does not even know if she will continue using the word 'God' for what she intends, whatever that is.[39] Is it something like pantheism? Or what is the something for which Hampson is searching?

Post-Christian Contradictions

When going through Hampson's publications, it is obvious that no Christian theology is able to pass the Hampson test, either because it reflects the strangely fossilised and monolithic entity which she conceives to be true Christianity or because it reflects that living, heterogenic complex of traditions and interpretations which Christianity has truly always been but which according to her is not Christianity. This is clearly demonstrated in the book which followed her post-Christian manifestos, namely her *Christian Contradictions* (2001). Here she confronts Catholicism with Lutheranism freezing them as two different, and in her rendition extremely undifferentiated, paradigms

---

Christian subtext" of Shug's song, which is not a distancing from God the Father, but a seeing God as mother to the motherless and father to the fatherless.

[37] Hampson, *Theology and Feminism*, 169-170.
[38] Hampson, *Theology and Feminism*, 169-171; Hampson *After Christianity*, 251-252.
[39] Hampson, *After Christianity*, 253.

(Catholicism being linear, Protestantism dialectic), and which she deems as incompatible as Christianity and feminism. For "choosing a particular structure one is also committed to a whole outlook".[40] In consequence, she dismisses any kind of ecumenical Christian theology just as she dismisses any kind of feminist Christian theology.

The contradiction looming large in her book, though, is that the dedicated Post-Christian Hampson engages in discussing mainline Christian theology with the purpose of making Lutheranism understandable to Catholics. But Hampson claims a connection between this book and her previous post-Christian publications:

> It was in part in wrestling with the issues which I discuss in this book that I moved outside and beyond Christianity. (It was simply too difficult to explain to readers of the feminist work that there was no way in which, within Christianity, I could see the self both as grounded in God and as able to inter-relate with God.) The questions which I discuss in this book were at one time of acute personal moment for me. But it is not that I have resolved them. Rather have I moved to a position where they have become inapplicable, in that I have come to think of 'God' in very different terms.[41]

The issues in question are those central to the Reformation of 16th Century Western Christianity, the Lutheran doctrine "justification by faith alone" and the coherent Lutheran principle *simul justus et peccator*, and it is Hampson's thesis that these have often been (purposefully) misunderstood by Catholic theologians, including the most liberal and ecumenical of them.

Unlike in *After Christianity*, Hampson is here outspokenly sympathetic to Lutheranism, as she here demonstrates a less monolithic understanding of Western theology, by thus depicting two different paradigms of Christian theology. But although I as a Lutheran find her sympathetic reading of Lutheran confession intriguing, I find it problematic that most of the central publications used by her are from before 1970, quite a number of them from between 1940-65 and some more recent publications are actually just new editions of older books[42] – whilst she constantly and blatantly asks why Catholics do not read

---

[40] Hampson, *Christian Contradictions*, 285.
[41] Hampson, *Christian Contradictions*, 7.
[42] The only exceptions from this are the publications relating to the Catholic-Lutheran dialogue on justification, from about 1970-1995/99, and the research done by the Finnish Luther scholarship from the late 1980'es and on.

Lutheran or Luther's own texts before they judge it. What Hampson understands as true Lutheranism and true Catholicism are again frozen definitions, not allowing for change and ongoing deliberations. Her paradigm shift stands and falls with a static understanding of theology, which especially for Lutheranism, if it should maintain its Protestant principle *ecclesia reformata semper reformanda*, is highly problematic. Both the employment of old literature and conservative interpretations of theology confirms the impression of Hampson as in fact a very conservative theologian.

Conclusion

It is hard to disagree with Hampson that the feminist movement has provided Western culture with a new and enriching perspective, and that societies within Western culture at large have gained from bringing in this perspective as well as from recognizing women as an immense resource on par with men. Hampson's feminism is more than understandable, and her daring questions to feminist Christian theology both necessary and welcome. What is less understandable is her essentialism, which seems so idiosyncratic, and which she seems to impose on the world at large as an "ethical *a priory* position". Since Hampson is looking for a gender free theology, why does she in her theological deliberations primarily confront Christian feminists' endeavours for the same, whilst consulting conservative theologians, identifying conservative theology with orthodox doctrine *per se* as *the* truth? It would be interesting to see something more essential of her theology.

Dieser Beitrag überprüft die theologischen Überlegungen Daphne Hampsons, angefangen von ihrem post-christlichen Manifest *Theology and Feminism* (1990), bis hin zu ihrem "innerchristlichen" Buch *Christian Contradictions* (2001). Es wird gezeigt, wie Hampson in ihrem Bemühen, eine neue egalitäre Theologie zu entwerfen, sich, anstatt konservative männliche christliche Theologen zu entlarven, gegen feministische ChristInnen wendet und ihre Theologie als falsch verurteilt. Nach ihrer post-christlichen Wende betrachtet Hampson Christentum und Feminismus als unvereinbar. Die Autorin verficht die Ansicht, dass Hampson, indem sie als Essentialistin KonstruktivistInnen entgegentritt, durch ihre Argumentationsweise tatsächlich einen konservativen Theismus verstärkt, von dem man ansonsten erwarten würde, dass sie ihn ablehnt – während sie gleichzeitig die Unterschiedlichkeit christlicher Theologie vollständig ignoriert. Sucht man nach Hampsons eigener positiv formulierter Theologie, ist es schwierig, ein klares Bild zu gewinnen, kommt sie doch nicht über eine verschwommene Skizzierung Gottes als ein "etwas, das sich bezieht", hinaus.

Cette contribution se veut une étude critique des réflexions théologiques de Daphne Hampson, de son manifeste post-chrétien *Theology and Feminism* (1990) à son livre «d'un christianisme intériorisé» *Christian Contradictions* (2001). Elle démontre comment Daphne Hampson, qui entreprend d'établir une nouvelle théologie égalitaire plutôt que de se confronter aux théologiens chrétiens conservateurs, s'oppose aux chrétiennes féministes et réfute leur christologie, la considérant fausse. Après son virage post-chrétien, Daphne Hampson considère que le christianisme et le féminisme sont incompatibles. L'auteure affirme que Daphne Hampson, une essentialiste confrontant des constructivistes, propose une argumentation qui, de fait, confirme une thèse théiste et conservatrice – ce que l'on s'attendrait par ailleurs à ce qu'elle conteste – tout en ignorant complètement la diversité de la théologie chrétienne. Il est difficile de se faire une idée claire de la théologie de Daphne Hampson telle qu'elle la formule, car elle ne mentionne Dieu que de façon assez floue, ne dépassant pas le référant.

Else Marie Wiberg Pedersen (*1956) is Professor of Systematic Theology at the Faculty of Theology at the University of Aarhus, Denmark. She earned her doctoral degree at the University of Aarhus for a thesis on Beatrice of Nazareth and her vernacular theology. She has been engaged in ecumenical work, and from 1997-2001 she was part of international core group of the LWF/DTS project on ecclesiology. Her areas of research include women's issues, Mariology and ecumenism. Her publications include: *Om nåden og den fri vilje* (Anis, 2006), *Cracks in the Wall* (Peter Lang, 2005), and *For All People. Global Theologies in Contexts* (Eerdmans, 2002). She is Chair of the Aarhus University's Equal Opportunities Committee since 2002 and was Vice President of the ESWTR 2001-2003.

Journal of the European Society of Women in Theological Research 15 (2007) 89-102.
doi: 10.2143/ESWTR.15.0.2022770

Sólveig Anna Bóasdóttir

Pleasure and Health
Feminist Theological Discourse on Sexuality, Religion and Ethics[1]

For at least twenty years, Western feminist theologians working in the field of sexual ethics have been wrestling with questions about human sexuality.[2] Critical of oppressive, androcentric perspectives in Christian sexual ethics, feminist scholars have argued for a comprehensive revision of Christian thought in sexuality issues. In 1994, Christian ethicist James B. Nelson and his colleague Sandra P. Longfellow observed in their book, *Sexuality and the Sacred: Sources for Theological Reflection*, that a new theological understanding of sexuality had emerged. This understanding, they argued, was "largely spurred by feminist theologians and by gay and lesbian theologians."[3]

Recognized as the pioneer of Christian feminist liberation ethics, Beverly W. Harrison was one of the first scholars to criticize traditional Christian sexual ethics for being oppressive for women, denying them the moral right to control their own bodies.[4] This is especially evident in terms of marriage,

---

[1] I want to stress that I am aware of some major differences regarding issues of sexuality and religion between the North American context wherefrom my main sources come and the Scandinavian context in which I stand. In this article, however, I am not focusing on the differences but rather on the similarities, arguing that feminist theologians in a Christian-Western context have an important contribution to make to global ethics and global health. Feminist theologians in the field of sexual ethics, whether their context is Scandinavian or something else, share a global moral vision of all women's rights to well-being and health and mutuality in sexual pleasure.

[2] My use of the the word *Western* in this article most often refers to feminist theological work within the Judeo-Christian context. The fact that most of this work derives from US feminist theologians does not necessarily reflect their normative status, but rather indicates that over the last twenty-five years North American feminist theologians have laid a foundation in the field of sexual ethics which cannot be ignored.

[3] James B. Nelson / Sandra P. Longfellow (eds), *Sexuality and the Sacred. Sources for Theological Reflection* (Westminster/John Knox Press: Louisville 1994), xv.

[4] Beverly W. Harrison, *Our Right to Choose: Toward a New Ethic of Abortion* (Beacon Press: Boston 1983).

sexuality and reproduction. Harrison finds the drive for rethinking human sexuality, as well as resources for change, mainly in discourses of social justice movements, which affirm the goodness of sexuality, respecting women's "bodyself" and "bodyright".[5] Harrison maintains that feminist ethicists should turn to critical theory in their analyses of women's subordination. In its critical approach to what is called "social reality", critical theory is concerned with knowing this social reality from the perspective of the oppressed. In order to change the conditions of oppressed women, Harrison argues, one must know their social and material realities. Knowledge on these issues, however, requires interpretation.[6]

The theoretical impact of Harrison's work is strong in recent contributions to feminist theological sexual ethics.[7] She offers an inductive theoretical approach which does not abandon the notion of women as a universally identifiable and frequently oppressed group. Such a feminist theoretical model, to be sure, does not doubt whether such a category as the *subject* exists.[8] On the contrary, it stresses that without a unified category of "woman" there can be no political possibility of the ending of women's oppression. Women exist, as do women's experiences of oppression.

---

[5] I build this claim on my knowledge of Harrison's writings in theological sexual ethics over twenty-five years.

[6] Carol Robb (ed.), *Making the Connections: Essays in Feminist Social Ethics* (Harper & Row: San Francisco 1985)

[7] See e.g. Christine Gudorf, *Body, Sex and Pleasure: Reconstructing Christian Sexual Ethics* (The Pilgrim Press: Cleveland 1994); Marie F. Fortune, *Love Does No Harm: Sexual Ethics for the Rest of Us* (Continuum: New York 1995); Marvin M. Ellison, *Erotic Justice: A Liberating Ethic of Sexuality* (Westminster/John Knox Press: Louisville 1996); Sólveig Anna Bóasdóttir, *Violence, Power, and Justice: A Feminist Contribution to Christian Sexual Ethics* (Acta Universitatis Upsaliensis. Uppsala Studies in Social Ethics 20; Uppsala University: Uppsala 1998).

[8] Here I am referring to the feminist theoretical debates of the late 1980s and the 1990s concerning postmodernism, deconstruction, identity and difference. See e.g. Luce Irigaray, *Ethique de la Différence Sexuelle* (Editions de Minuit: Paris 1984); Judith Butler, *Subjects of Desire: Hegelian Reflections in Twentieth-Century France* (Columbia University Press: New York 1987); Rebecca S. Chopp, "Feminism's Theological Pragmatics: A Social Naturalism of Women's Experience", in: *The Journal of Religion* 67, 239-256; Sharon Welch, "Sporting Power", in: C.W Maggie Kim / Susan M. St.Ville / Susan M. Simonaitis (eds), *Transfigurations: Theology and The French Feminists* (Fortress Press: Minneapolis: 1993); Mary McClintock Fulkerson, *Changing the Subject. Women's Discourses and Feminist Theology* (Fortress Press: Minneapolis 1994); Susan J. Hekman, *Moral voices, Moral selves: Carol Gilligan and Feminist Moral Theory* (The Pennsylvania State University Press: Pennsylvania 1995).

Harrison's theoretical legacy then, which, in my view, is apparent in recent feminist theologians' sexual ethics, implies at least two things: one on a theoretical level, another on a practical level. Firstly, global ethical systems and universals, applied to sexual ethics, can exist. This point does not mean that feminist ethicists have to give up their powerful critique of particularistic ethical theories masquerading as ethical universalism. On the contrary, while doing so, they can continue to support a genuine, rather than a false, universalism in ethics, which includes everyone, both women and men, in moral and social life.[9] Secondly, feminist politics is possible and it is imperative to develop it.[10] This means that concrete legal and political solutions concerning women's oppressive conditions can and ought to be fought for. One powerful instrument to use is the notion of universal human rights. Many feminist scholars use human rights approaches to address oppressive features of institutions and traditions within which women's agency may be limited.[11] The conceptual framework of human rights, I am convinced, can and should be developed more by feminist theologians working in the field of sexual ethics. This, I would argue, includes us feminist theologians in a Scandinavian context. As an Icelandic feminist, working in the field of theological sexual ethics, I want to emphasize the global thinking in Western feminist theological ethics that stresses that major structural injustices tend to override local boundaries. A feminist goal has always been to advance the well-being of women across diverse cultures and traditions. Awareness of local and contextual experiences and knowledges does not necessarily mean that one should turn away from global thinking.

In this article I focus on some crucial issues in recent analyses of sexuality, religion and ethics put forward in the field of Western feminist theological sexual ethics. However, much will be left out in the interest of space. In the first section, I discuss the recurrent feminist view that sexuality is socially and

---

[9] A good example can be found in feminist bioethics, see e.g. Rosemarie Tong / Anne Donchin / Susan Dodds (eds), *Linking Visions: Feminist Bioethics, Human Rights, and the Developing World* (Rowman & Littlefield: Oxford 2004).

[10] Over more than ten years feminist scholars and activists have been extending the human rights discourse. Especially important in this regard are the two conferences: the United Nations Conference on Human Rights, held in Vienna in 1993, and the Fourth World Women's Conference in Beijing in 1995. At these conferences, feminists urged that human rights must be reconceptualized in crucial ways if they were to address the multiple and serious ways in which the rights of women were violated because they are women.

[11] The work of feminist ethicist Susan Moller Okin, *Is Multiculturalism Bad For Women* (Princeton University Press: Princeton 1999), is particulalry important in this area.

culturally constructed. Then, I illustrate how feminist theologians in the field of sexual ethics have been working to reconstruct the concepts of justice, sexual pleasure and well-being, challenging the patriarchal legacy of Western Christian culture. Finally, I consider grounds for the inclusion of a human rights framework within feminist theological sexual ethics, reflecting on how feminist theologians can strengthen their work towards global social change.

Sexuality as socially constructed

At the center of feminist theory lie two understandings: that Western culture is patriarchal, and that it is a culture that eroticizes gender inequality.[12] Patriarchal ideology and patriarchal culture, many feminist theologians argue, contribute towards socializing men to implement power over others. Women, under the same cultural circumstances, are socialized to accept dependency, emotionality and weakness.[13] Crucial to all feminist struggles is the countering of the idea of biological determinism, which claims that sexuality is a natural, biological and psychological phenomenon, different for women and men. Thus, contemporary feminist theological sexual ethicists fully agree that sexual experiences must be understood as social constructions, meaning that one should make a distinction between a) sexuality as activity, and b) sexuality as a set of attitudes and beliefs. It is the latter point which needs critical scrutiny and that is what feminists have done.

Some have pointed out that sexuality is constructed as exclusively heterosexual, automatically precluding gay and lesbian sexuality, viewing "heterosexism" as a reasoned system of prejudice as well as a pattern which pervades most dimensions of Western cultural life.[14] Others focus on the constructed

---

[12] Beverly Harrison observed in 1985 "the tragedy of our so-called sexual morality is that mutual respect and erotisicm are utterly separated in the lives of most people", see Robb (ed.), *Making the Connections*, 148.

[13] See e.g. Karin Lebacqz, "Love Your Enemy: Sex, Power, and Christian Ethics", in: Lois K. Daly (ed.) *Feminist Theological Ethics. A Reader* (Westminster John Knox Press: Louisville 1994), 246-247.

[14] For this critique, see e.g. Patricia B. Jung / Ralph F. Smith, *Heterosexism: An Ethical Challenge* (State University of New York Press: New York 1993); Robert E. Goss, "Gay Erotic Spirituality and the Recovery of Sexual Pleasure", in: Marvin M. Ellison / Sylvia Thorson-Smith (eds), *Body and Soul. Rethinking Sexuality as Justice-Love* (The Pilgrim Press: Cleveland 2003), 201-217.

sexist difference in power between men and women by virtue of gender.[15] Graze M. Jantzen complements these views with her conviction that sexuality is not only heterosexist and sexist in its usual constructions, but is even racist. Through colonialism and missionary activity, Jantzen argues, Christian European ideals of good sex have historically been imposed on colonized countries for them to internalize.[16]

Justice-focussed sexual ethics

In broad terms, a recurring theme in the discourse of Western feminist theologians is that of *justice*. The ethicist Christine Gudorf claims that traditional Christian sexual ethics fails to mirror God's reign of justice and love which Jesus proclaimed.[17] Marvin Ellison puts forward a justice-centered liberating theological sexual ethics.[18] These two strains, the critique and reconstruction, are imperative in all theological feminist ethics.

Let us begin with the critique.

This focuses, first, on the devaluation of sex in the Christian tradition. The negative focus on sexuality in Christianity, as well as the low status of sexual pleasure in the Christian tradition, is seen as highly problematic.[19] Platonism, one dominant force in the development of Christendom, was distrustful of the body in general and of sex in particular. This view was readily adopted as the writings of all the major fathers in the early Church reveal.[20]

---

[15] See e.g. James B. Nelson, *Embodiment. An Approach to Sexuality and the Christian Theology* (Augsburg Publishing House: Minneapolis 1978); Karin Lebacqz, "Love Your Enemy"; Gudorf, *Body, Sex, and Pleasure*.

[16] Graze M. Jantzen, "Good Sex: Beyond Private Pleasure", in: Patricia B. Jung / Mary E. Hunt / R. Balakrishnan (eds), *Good Sex: Feminist Perspectives from the World's Religions* (Ruthgers University Press: London 2001).

[17] Gudorf, *Body, Sex, and Pleasure*, 2.

[18] Here I mention Marvin M. Ellison, *Erotic Justice*, as well as Marvin M. Ellison, *Same-Sex Marriage? A Christian Ethical Analysis* (The Pilgrim Press: Cleveland 2004)

[19] Theologian James B. Nelson was an early critic of the Christian sexual tradition. In several books, a recurring theme is that the Jewish and Christian traditions have contributed to sexual alienation and sexual distortions instead of offering nurture to sexual wholeness and sexual healing. Nelson diagnosed seven sinful problems regarding sexuality in both Judaism and Christianity: spiritualistic dualism, sexist or patriarchal dualism, heterosexism, self-rejection, legalistic sexual ethics, sexless spirituality and privatized sexuality. See e.g. James B. Nelson, *Body Theology* (Westminster/John Knox Press: Louisville 1992).

[20] See Grace M. Jantzen, *Power, Gender, and Christian Mysticism* (Cambridge University Press: Cambridge, 1995), chapter 2.

Of all the Church fathers, however, the most influential was St. Augustine, who made close connections between sin and sex.[21] Christine Gudorf argues that he regarded sexual pleasure as dangerous because he considered it irresistible. Seen as irresistible, sexual pleasure in St. Augustine's view is a powerful and unmanageable passion, resulting in the loss of rational control. Overpowering sexual passion leads to carelessness and neglect of moral duties toward our neighbors. Sexual passion, in Augustine's view, makes a person focus on his or her own individual satisfaction, and therefore tempts them to be selfish.[22] The low value given to sexual pleasure, Gudorf argues, can also be attributed to Thomas Aquinas, who stressed that sexual pleasure is something we have in common with animals.[23] According to Aquinas, sexuality is part of human lower nature, not the higher rational nature that links us to God. In Aquinas' view, sexual pleasure, as such, is not morally wrong, but in order to be justified, it must be oriented to a more human end. That end was procreation.[24] Feminist theologians claim that the close connection between sexuality and procreation are due to male experience; because orgasm is nearly equivalent with ejaculation for men, the exclusive purpose of sex was constructed as procreation.[25] Against this view, Brazilian theologian Wanda Deifelt maintains that this sexual construction is at the expense of the health and even survival of women and their children.[26]

A second element to be critically highlighted is the neglect of women's well-being in Christian sexual ethics.[27] One reason for this inadequacy, many feminists argue, is that men, rather than women, have shaped the theological discourse in sexual ethics, and that they have failed to take into consideration the

---

[21] Augustine, *The City of God*, Ch. 14, in: *The Fathers of the Church*, vol. 14, trans. G. Walsh and G. Monohan (Father of the Church, Innc.: New York, 1952); Augustine, "On Marriage and Concupiscence", in: Philip Schaff (ed.), *The Nicene and Post-Nicene Fathers* I:17 (Wm. B. Eerdmans: Grand Rapids, MI 1971).

[22] Gudorf, *Body, Sex, and Pleasure*, 82-83.

[23] Thomas Aquinas, *Summa Theologiae* 1:82:1,1 (McGraw-Hill: New York, 1964).

[24] Gudorf, *Body, Sex and Pleasure*, 82-83.

[25] Patrica B. Jung, "Sanctifying Women's Pleasure", in: Jung / Hunt / Balakrishnan, *Good Sex*, 77-95, here 91.

[26] Wanda Deifelt, "Beyond Compulsory Motherhood", in: Jung / Hunt / Balakrishnan, *Good Sex*, 96-112, here 108.

[27] See e.g. James Nelson, *Embodiment: An Approach to Sexuality and Christian Theology* (Augsburg Press: Minneapolis 1978); James Nelson, *Between Two Gardens: Reflections on Sexuality and Religious Experience* (Pilgrim Press: New York 1984); Robb (ed.), *Making the Connections*; Carter Heyward, *Touching Our Strength. The Erotic as Power and the Love of God*

different experiences of women. The sexual well-being of women during intimate sexual activities was never considered from a Christian standpoint, Patricia B. Jung argues, "so foreign was it to the experience of most men."[28] Karen Lebacqz argues that conventional androcentric perspectives in Christian sexual ethics do not recognize the links between violence and sexuality in the experiences of women.[29] To be able to do that, one has both to view sexuality as ideologically and culturally shaped, and to account for women's experiences. To stress the ideological/cultural dimension means, as we have seen above, to approach sexuality from a social constructionist point of view. Not doing this is inadequate in normative sexual ethics, Lebacqz concludes. According to her, men's dominance is eroticized in Western culture. As a result, sexuality and violence are linked in the experiences of women. Ignoring this social reality and urging women to seek intimacy in an arena which is unsafe for them, fraught with sexual violence and power struggle, is ethically questionable.[30] Essentially, then, the challenge for feminist theological sexual ethics has been to deconstruct the androcentric foundations of Christian moral traditions that underlie the harmful construction of women's sexuality.

Let us now turn to the next step in feminist theological sexual ethics, to develop and reconstruct a Christian teaching on sexuality.

Sexual pleasure as a source of power for women

The focus on sexual pleasure in feminist theological work is considered by many to be a healthy approach to justice work in a wider sense. Audre Lorde, in her study *Sister Outsider*, writes about the Erotic as a source of power and life-force. This power has, however, been distorted by a racist, patriarchal and anti-erotic culture. For women, Lorde writes, "this has meant a suppression of the erotic as a considered source of power and information within our lives."[31] To fight oppression, powerlessness and suffering, Lorde maintains that women must accept their most profoundly creative source of power.[32]

(Harper Publishers: San Francisco 1989); Gudorf, *Body, Sex, and Pleasure*; Ellison, *Erotic Justice*.

[28] Jung, "Sanctifying Women's Pleasure", 91.
[29] Karen Lebacqz, "Love Your Enemy", 244.
[30] Karen Lebacqz, "Love Your Enemy", 246.
[31] Audre Lorde, "Uses of the Erotic: The Erotic as Power", in: Nelson / Longfellow (eds), *Sexuality and the Sacred*, 75.
[32] Lorde, "Uses of the Erotic", 78-79.

In a related vein, Harrison and Heyward acknowledge sexual pleasure as fundamentally life-enhancing at an individual level.[33] Their project, however, is different from Lorde's: they offer a critical analysis in the role of Christianity in developing and sustaining structures of alienation, such as heterosexism, sexism, racism and class exploitation, which have led to the confusion of sex and dominance, pain and pleasure. Harrison and Heyward are deeply troubled by the Christian dualistic anthropology which associates the female – and thus females – with flesh, darkness and evil. According to them, anti-woman and anti-body dualisms laid the groundwork for the Christian romanticization of suffering, and even contributed to the sex-phobic and sex-preoccupied focus of the Christian sexual ethic.[34] The core of Harrison's and Heyward's transforming project is to stress the significance of the idea of sexual mutuality rather than the idea and image of domination. Our whole culture, they claim, must struggle for the eroticization of mutuality.[35]

Mutuality in sexual pleasure

Combining the views of Lorde, Harrison and Heyward, Christine Gudorf goes on to argue that Christian sexual ethic should encourage sexual pleasure in its social as well as its individual functions. Sexual pleasure, she remarks, is good because it feels good. So understood, it is a premoral good.[36] However, pleasure as such is not a sufficient condition for moral goodness. To qualify for that end, it must be mutual. This is what Christian sexual ethics must make normative: mutuality in sexual pleasure.

Any failure to include one's partner in sexual pleasure is, first, a violation of the Christian imperative to love one's neighbor, and second, a rejection of the social function of sex which is dependent upon the mutuality of pleasure.[37]

---

[33] Beverly W. Harrison / Carter Heyward, "Pain and Pleasure: Avoiding the Confusions of Christian Tradition in Feminist Theory", in: Nelson / Longfellow (eds), *Sexuality and the Sacred*, 130-137.

[34] Harrison / Heyward, "Pain and Pleasure", 134-135.

[35] Harrison / Heyward, "Pain and Pleasure", 133.

[36] A premoral good means that something is good before we morally evaluate its role in any particular situation. An example of premoral goodness is when the author of Genesis pronounces the creation good.

[37] Gudorf, *Body, Sex, and Pleasure*, 139.

However, what does mutual sexual pleasure really imply? First, it is clear that mutual sexual pleasure implies mutual consent to sex. That can, of course, be seen as an extremely radical moral criterion, given existing sexual practice both in Western society and elsewhere. Mutual consent to sex is, however, a much less radical criterion than mutuality in sexual pleasure. To explain the difference, Gudorf takes some examples where sex has been formally consented to but, because of power differences, does not aim at mutual pleasure. Her examples include sex with children, with prostitutes or between superiors and subordinates in the work-place [one might add – between therapists or doctors or priests and their clients / patients / parishioners]. Her point is that, especially if repeated, such sexual activity is unhealthy, being destructive to both relationships and self-esteem.[38]

Gudorf goes on to explore how restrictive her two ethical criteria might be: 1) that sexual activity should be pleasurable, and 2) that both those involved should experience pleasure. She concludes that these criteria would indeed be transformative of the sexual landscape in current Western societies as well as other cultures.[39] First, all sexual violence, such as rape, sexual abuse and sexual coercion and harassment, violates these criteria. Second, they would preclude cultural practices like genital mutilation, which has as a purpose the removal of pleasure from sex for women through surgery, as well as criticize cultures – including Western culture – which seek to achieve the same result through socialization.

Thus, her criteria would require a major resocialization of both men and women with regard to their roles in sexual activity.[40] Third, if both women and men are to take responsibility for achieving mutual pleasure in their sexual activity, society must support this through sexual education, addressing among other things old and new fears, such as fear of pregnancy, AIDS and other sexually transmitted diseases. Other important themes in sex education would be, for instance, domestic violence, rape, child sexual abuse, sexual harassment and homophobia.[41] The essence in Gudorf's message regarding her two ethical criteria can be summarized thus: "if sex is to be as fully pleasurable as possible, both individual behavior and social policy must change in many ways."[42]

---

[38] Gudorf, *Body, Sex, and Pleasure*, 141-142.
[39] Gudorf, *Body, Sex, and Pleasure*, 143-154.
[40] Gudorf stresses that this point applies both to heterosexual and homosexual relationships.
[41] Here I would add to her examples patriarchal marriages.
[42] Gudorf, *Body, Sex, and Pleasure*, 155.

Recognition of "bodyright" – a precondition for full personhood and moral agency in humans

Spiritualistic dualism, or mind/body dualism, sees life composed of two antagonistic elements: spirit, which is good and eternal, and flesh or matter, which is temporal, corruptible and corrupting.[43] The heritage of this pervasive dualism in the Christian West, Christine Gudorf argues, is the failure to recognize bodyright.[44] In her view, the absence of bodyright in Western culture is directly attributable to patriarchy. But what is bodyright? The answer Gudorf gives is that it is a moral right that humans have to control their own bodies. The incapability to implement that control seriously hinders a person's ability to become responsible a moral agent.[45]

According to Gudorf, bodyright is the most foundational human right of all. Evidence of pervasive sexual violence against women and children, drawn from all over the world, shows that this is one of the most violated human rights. Global research reveals that sexual violence has appalling effects on the victims:

> Sexual violence transforms the victim's relationship to others, world, self, and often God, but that the principal injury is to victim's self-concept. The victim feels stripped of self-esteem, dignity, strength, the love and respect of others, that ability to trust others, the ability to feel secure, and even the ability to trust herself and her own judgment.[46]

The struggle to move Western Christian culture toward more complete respect for bodyright is both a feminist and a theological claim. Gudorf does not stand alone among feminist theologians when she claims that theology must purge the Christian tradition of unhealthy images of God as dominion and as autonomous power over other.[47] The link between theology and the moral claim of bodyright show her alternative vision of God as the loving parent

---

[43] Nelson, *Body Theology*, 3.

[44] Gudorf, *Body, Sex, and Pleasure*, 162.

[45] Gudorf, *Body, Sex, and Pleasure*, 161.

[46] Gudorf, *Body, Sex, and Pleasure*, 190.

[47] Suffice it to mention but a few examples of feminist theology in which feminists explore this theme: Mary Daly, *Beyond God the Father. Toward a Philosophy of Women's Liberation* (Beacon Press: Boston 1974); Sallie McFague, *Models of God. Theology for Ecological, Nuclear Age* (SCM: London 1987); Rosemary Radford Ruether, *Gaia & God. An Ecofeminist Theology of Earth Healing* (Harper: San Francisco 1992).

who created our bodyselves and calls all persons into full adulthood as co-creators of the universe. Gudorf's moral vision is that all sexual relationships, including marriage, would change if bodyright were respected. This would happen if all sexual unions would be based in mutuality. A clear feminist vision is, however, that the recognition of bodyright would rule out traditional hierarchical sex roles as well as all domestic violence. The greatest challenge, however, of respecting bodyright would occur in child-rearing practices. A radical shift from the present focus on achieving socially desirable behavior in one's children, to successfully transferring power and responsibility to one's children, would take place.

> These are not minor changes in our religious tradition or our secular culture. Purging the image of God will be a long, gradual affair of sifting through scripture and the theological tradition piece by piece and self-consciously rejecting divine images of domination for use in prayer, song, or liturgy, while making a point at all levels of Christian education to indicate the inadequacies of divine images of domination, and how they entered the tradition without serious critique because they were tide to prevailing social structures and institutions.[48]

To summarize, within theological feminist sexual ethics, mutuality in sexual pleasure is understood to be a liberating process which involves challenging inequality in love and in sexual activity. Feminist theologians have paid a great deal of attention to this issue because they understand Christian repression of sexual pleasure, its pervasive fear of sex and of strong passion to have led to a violent and unhealthy culture which is especially dangerous to women, but problematic also for men and for sexual minorities, i.e. gays/lesbians and bisexual people. Feminists working in the field of theological sexual ethics seek to confront this in their writings. Their aim is to try to move unhealthy cultures throughout the world towards more respect for women and their human rights.

Sexual health and well-being

In their diverse approaches to theological sexual ethics, feminist theologians usually share three ambitions: 1) to evaluate and critique actions, practices, systems, structures and ideologies that perpetuate women's subordination; 2) to develop morally acceptable ways to resist the dissimilar causes of women's subordination; and 3) to visualize morally feasible alternatives to the sexist,

---

[48] Gudorf, *Body, Sex, and Pleasure*, 201.

heterosexist and racist culture that many of us identify within Western Christian civilization.[49] We have seen examples of all three purposes above.

I wish to argue that feminist theologians working in the field of sexual ethics have an important contribution to make to global feminist ethics and even to the fields of international human rights laws and development theory. Here I am thinking especially of the moral principles of human well-being and mutuality in sexual pleasure, fundamental in feminist theological discourse on sexual ethics. These offer potential resources as well as correctives for social change. In this respect, feminist theologians *have already* made a valuable contribution to the improvement of human sexual health and well-being across the globe, as can be discerned in a recent document, *Promotion of Sexual Health* (2001), published jointly by the *Pan American Health Organization* (PAHO), the *World Health Organization* (WHO) and the *World Association for Sexual Health* (WAS), which focuses on a number of recommendations for action.[50] Under the headline *Rationale*, some of the most important developments concerning sexual health in the past twenty-five years are considered.[51]

Three out of eight areas in this development are recognized by the document as directly linked to feminist scholarly thinking and feminist activist work. These areas include feminist contributions on 1) the social construction of gender and human sexuality,[52] 2) sexual violence[53] and 3) women's human rights and sexual rights.[54] All three areas mentioned in the document represent important areas of commitment in the feminist theological struggle to enhance

---

[49] Alison Jaggar, "Feminist Ethics", in: Lawrence Becker with Charlotte Becker (eds), *Encyclopedia of Ethics* (Garland: New York 1992), 364-367.

[50] http://www2.hu-berlin.de/sexology/GESUND/ARCHIV/PSH.HTM

[51] The World Health Organization started its work on human sexuality in 1974, which was also a period in which feminism gained in significance and influence.

[52] "Formation of a solid body of knowledge originated in the writings and views of feminist scholars. This knowledge indicated that societies are articulated and regulated by a complex and pervasive set of rules and assumptions that permeate every aspect of the society and the very construction of knowledge. The gender perspective has shown that any consideration of human sexuality cannot be completed if it ignores the cultural concepts of "masculinity" and "femininity" (http://www2.hu-berlin.de/sexology/GESUND/ARCHIV/PSH.HTM)

[53] "Recognition of violence, including sexual violence, especially against women, children and sexual minorities, as a serious public health issue" (http://www2.hu-berlin.de/sexology/GESUND/ARCHIV/PSH.HTM)

[54] "Recognition of sexual rights as human rights. Sexual rights have been explicitly recognized and stated by groups such as the International Planned Parenthood Federation and by the World Association for Sexology. However, sexual rights have often only been recognized in their

women's health and well-being across cultural and national boundaries, as will be clear from the discussion above. The commonalities which are seen in both feminist theological sexual ethics and the field of sexology and sexual health, include the rights-based moral framework which in both fields is intended to develop conditions which are able to shape human health and well-being across the globe. Another similarity is the understanding of the concept of health, namely in terms of well-being: a healthy human sexuality is seen as essential to the totality of both personal and corporal well-being. The theologians I have examined in this article all stress this view. Awareness of this fact, which may also be called the product of cross-fertilization between the fields of sexology, sexual health and feminist theology, should be theoretically stimulating for all fields.

Conclusion

Feminist thinking in the field of theological sexual ethics puts forward visions of wholeness, health and healing in their understanding of human sexuality, visions that describe sexual health and well-being both at individual and societal level. The development within feminist theological sexual ethics has paralleled the development of social justice movements, especially the women's movement. The point of departure in both feminist studies and feminist activism is that the personal is political. It therefore is essential that personal experiences of sexual violence and alienation be linked to public and social institutions and norms.

At the outset of this article, I pointed out that recent feminist approaches apply human rights perspectives to address oppressive features of institutions and traditions within which women's agency may be limited, and noted that I believe that feminist theologians working in the field of sexual ethics have contributed to this development in a fruitful way. Indeed, feminist theological ethics can be said to have already laid the groundwork for this. In its global concern about the health and well-being of all in this world, in its conceptual moral framework which understands human rights as flowing from human material embodiment and social relations, feminist theological sexual ethics

---

reproductive dimension as in the 1994 Interanational Conference on Population and Development (ICPD) in Cairo, as well as the Fourth World Conference on Women (Beijing, 1995). A more comprehensive stance needs to be taken to achieve full recognition of sexual rights." http://www2.hu-berlin.de/sexology/GESUND/ARCHIV/PSH.HTM

have begun explicitly to incorporate human rights perspectives, thereby supporting the global human rights movement. The main reason for doing this is moral: in this way feminists, working in the field of theological sexual ethics, forcefully struggle to enhance women's health and well-being in the world.

Dans cet article, l'auteure affirme que les théologiennes féministes occidentales travaillant dans le domaine de l'éthique sexuelle ont apporté une contribution importante à l'éthique féministe globale, ainsi que dans le domaine des droits humains internationaux et de la théorie du développement. Cette contribution se réfère aux principes moraux de la santé et du bien-être des humains et à la réciprocité dans le plaisir sexuel, principes fondamentaux dans le discours théologique féministe de ces vingt dernières années. L'auteure affirme que ces principes moraux peuvent (et devraient) être appliqués dans un contexte global, exhortant les théologiennes féministes travaillant dans le domaine de l'éthique sexuelle, à faire le lien entre les cadres conceptuels de l'éthique sexuelle féministe et ceux des droits humains.

In diesem Artikel unterstreicht die Autorin den wesentlichen Beitrag, den westliche feministische Theologinnen, die auf dem Gebiet der Sexualethik forschen, sowohl zur weltweiten feministischen Ethik, als auch zur internationalen Menschenrechts-Gesetzgebung und Entwicklungstheorie geleistet haben. Dieser Beitrag ist in den moralischen Prinzipien menschlicher Gesundheit und Wohlergehens sowie in der Gegenseitigkeit sexueller Lust zu finden, was in feministisch-theologischen Diskursen seit zwanzig Jahren grundlegend ist. Diese moralischen Prinzipien können und sollen gemäß der Autorin in einem weltweiten Kontext angewendet werden, um feministische Theologinnen aus dem Gebiet der Sexualethik dazu zu bringen, Verbindungen zwischen den konzeptionellen Rahmen feministischer Sexualethik einerseits und Menschenrechten andererseits zu ziehen.

Sólveig Anna Bóasdóttir (*1958), studied theological ethics in Uppsala, Sweden, and was awarded her doctoral degree by Uppsala University in 1998. She was a lecturer in ethics at the Faculty of Theology, Uppsala University, 1998-2001. Since 2001 Sólveig Anna Bóasdóttir works as a researcher in feminist sexual ethics at Reykjavik Academy and as a teacher in theological ethics at Iceland's University, Reykjavik, Iceland. She has published *Violence, Power, and Justice. A Feminist Contribution to Christian Sexual Ethics* (Acta Universitatis Upsaliensis. Uppsala Studies in Social Ethics 20: Uppsala 1998). She currently works on a project on feminist sexual ethics.

Journal of the European Society of Women in Theological Research 15 (2007) 103-118.
doi: 10.2143/ESWTR.15.0.2022771

Ninna Edgardh Beckman

Die Rolle der Kirchen in der Wohlfahrtsarbeit – eine Genderperspektive

Der Rahmen

In den späten Fernsehnachrichten sehe ich eine alte Frau, die weint. Sie beugt sich über ein Fotoalbum und zeigt auf ein Foto ihres Mannes. Mit einer vor Alter zitternden Stimme, doch in festem Ton und voll Autorität sagt sie: „Ich habe diesen Mann fast fünfzig Jahre lang geliebt, und ich liebe ihn immer noch. Doch ich möchte nicht, dass er nach Hause kommt!"

Langsam folgt die Kamera der Frau Ida, fest auf ihren Gehwagen gestützt, aus dem Wohnzimmer in die Küche. Im Laufe der Geschichte erfährt man, dass ihr Mann nach einem Schlaganfall schwer behindert ist. Er ist bettlägerig und kann nicht einmal selbst essen oder ins Bad gehen. Er ist immer noch im Krankenhaus, doch die medizinische Behandlung ist abgeschlossen, und das Krankenhaus möchte ihn so schnell wie möglich loswerden. Was der schwer behinderte alte Mann jetzt braucht, ist gute Pflege, rund um die Uhr, Tag und Nacht.

Idas Fall ist ein Beispiel für die Auswirkungen der Kürzungen, die in den 1990er Jahren in Schweden bei der Pflege alter Menschen vorgenommen wurden. Aufgrund der finanziellen Einschränkungen sind Bemühungen unternommen worden, um die Kosten von der medizinischen Pflege im Krankenhaus auf die Heimpflege zu verlagern, für die die kommunalen Behörden zu sorgen haben. Für die kommunalen Behörden fiel das zusammen mit der schnell ansteigenden Zahl von über Achtzigjährigen. Angesichts dieser doppelten Belastung mussten die Behörden den bedürftigsten Menschen den Vorrang geben, so dass die übrigen Alten auf häusliche Pflege angewiesen blieben, die vornehmlich von Frauen wie Ida geleistet wird. Man geht davon aus, dass ihr Mann zu Hause gepflegt wird, mit der Hilfe – so hofft man – von Hauspflegepersonal. Das macht Ida verzweifelt. Sie ist 87 Jahre alt und schafft es kaum, für sich selbst zu sorgen. Sie ist nicht fit genug, um rund um die Uhr die Pflegerin ihres Mannes zu sein.

Der Reporter redet ihr zu und sagt, dass die Sozialdienste mehrmals am Tag kommen und helfen werden. Doch Ida schüttelt einfach den Kopf und weint still vor sich hin. Sie kann voraussehen, was passieren wird: die Frustration, wenn ihr Mann etwas schnell braucht und es noch Stunden dauern wird, bis das Pflegepersonal für einen kurzen Besuch vorbei kommen wird; wie erschöpft sie sein wird, wie gedemütigt, wenn sie nicht in der Lage ist, ihm zu helfen. Ida lebt in einem Wohlfahrtsstaat, den man oft zu den besten in der Welt gezählt hat im Blick auf die Sorge für Gruppen wie Frauen, alte und kranke Menschen – und sie ist verzweifelt.

Wohlfahrtsarbeit in Europa

Die Geschichte von Ida ist an den schwedischen Kontext gebunden, wo hohe Erwartungen an den öffentlichen Sektor gestellt werden hinsichtlich der Sorge für die Bedürfnisse der Bürgerinnen und Bürger. Die Geschichten aus anderen Ländern über die finanziellen Einschränkungen, denen das Sozial- und Gesundheitssystem ausgesetzt ist, werden anders aussehen. Die Besonderheiten der jeweiligen Probleme hängen vom Typ des Wohlfahrtssystems, der finanziellen Situation des Landes usw. ab; doch die Schwierigkeiten, ein Grundmaß an sozialer Sicherung für alle Bürger aufrecht zu erhalten, sind in allen Ländern ähnlich.[1]

Das ist der Hintergrund für das Forschungsprojekt *Wohlfahrt und Religion in einer Europäischen Perspektive* (*Welfare and Religion in a European Perspective* – WREP) mit Schwerpunkt auf der Rolle der historischen christlichen Mehrheitskirchen in der Sozialfürsorge.[2] Das Projekt stellt die Frage, wie die

---

[1] Einen Überblick bietet u. a. Gøsta Esping-Andersen, *Why We Need a New Welfare State* (Oxford University Press: Oxford 2001). Die Begriffe „Wohlfahrtsstaat" und „Wohlfahrt" haben im deutschen Kontext einen anderen Klang als im britischen oder im skandinavischen Raum. Aus historischen Gründen wird der Begriff Wohlfahrtsstaat sowohl in der politikwissenschaftlichen wie auch in der öffentlichen Diskussion mit einem umfassenden sozialen System verbunden, in dem ein (über)mächtiger Staat die soziale Versorgung dominiert und damit die Freiheit der nichtstaatlichen Wohlfahrtsorganisationen und Anbieter sowie der Bürgerinnen und Bürger einschränkt. Der Wohlfahrtsstaat wird vom positiv besetzten Sozialstaat unterschieden, vgl. z.B. Jens Alber / Martin Schöllkopf, „Sozialstaat / Wohlfahrtsstaat", in: Dieter Nohlen (Hg.), *Wörterbuch Staat und Politik* (Bundeszentrale für Politische Bildung: Bonn 1998), 705–714. Der Begriff „Wohlfahrt" ist zwar im Deutschen gebräuchlich, zum Beispiel für die freie „Wohlfahrtspflege" oder die „Wohlfahrtsverbände". Er ist aber nicht so verbreitet und eindeutig positiv besetzt wie in Nordeuropa oder Großbritannien. Für die Übersetzung des englischen Wortes „welfare" wurden daher – je nach Zusammenhang – unterschiedliche Begriffe (wie Wohlfahrtsarbeit, Sozialfürsorge oder soziale Sicherung) gewählt.

[2] *Välfärd och religion i europeiskt perspektiv. Projektbeskrivning / Welfare and Religion in a European Perspective. Project description* (Diakonivetenskapliga institutets skriftserie 4: Diakonivetenskapliga institutet, Uppsala 2003). Ich verwende im Folgenden den Begriff „Mehrheitskirchen", obwohl ich weiß, dass er die bikonfessionelle Situation in Deutschland mit den

Mehrheitskirchen in Europa auf die laufenden Veränderungen reagieren. In welchem Maße üben sie die Funktion von Anbietern von Wohlfahrtsdiensten aus? Wie wirken sie als öffentliche Meinungsbildner? Tragen sie zu einem Geist der Solidarität und der Zugehörigkeit zur Gesellschaft bei, und wenn ja, wie geschieht das?

Die Arbeitsweise ist vergleichend und bezieht acht Länder ein: Schweden, Finnland, Norwegen, England, Deutschland, Frankreich, Italien und Griechenland. Die Länder umfassen Mehrheitskirchen römisch-katholischer, orthodoxer und verschiedener protestantischer Traditionen, einschließlich der lutherischen Kirchen Nordeuropas und der anglikanischen Kirche in England. Christliche Minderheiten und nicht-christliche Traditionen sind nicht berücksichtigt.

Das Material ist zusammengetragen aus Fallstudien in mittelgroßen Städten in den einzelnen Ländern. Die Daten enthalten umfangreiche Beschreibungen der aktuellen Rolle, die die Kirchen auf lokaler Ebene spielen. Die Methoden sind vornehmlich qualitativ und beziehen Dokumente und Interviews mit ein. Die endgültigen Ergebnisse des Projektes werden im Laufe des Jahres 2007 in zwei zusammenhängenden Bänden von *Ashgate Publishing* veröffentlicht. Mir geht es in diesem Artikel um einige einleitende Überlegungen zur Beziehung zwischen Theologie und Gender in der Wohlfahrtsarbeit der Kirchen.

Dabei gehen meine Überlegungen grundlegend in folgende Richtung:

Das Angebot von Sozialdiensten in Europa ist ein Bereich, in dem die Genderperspektive in hohem Grade relevant ist, weil getrennte Rollen für Frauen und Männer vorausgesetzt werden, wobei die Frauen im Wesentlichen die Dienstleisterinnen sind. Dieses Modell der Rollenverteilung verliert jedoch in ganz Europa an Bedeutung, was auf eine Reihe von Veränderungen in der Lebensgestaltung, vor allem der Frauen, zurückzuführen ist. Das geht Hand in Hand mit einem zunehmenden Bedarf und führt zu einem „Pflegedefizit".

Die europäischen Mehrheitskirchen sind wichtige potentielle Ressourcen im Blick auf dieses Defizit. Das soziale Wirken der Kirchen hat eine solide theologische Grundlage, doch es ist offensichtlich auch eng mit Traditionen im

---

beiden Volkskirchen und ihren regional sehr unterschiedlichen Mehrheitsverhältnissen nicht zutreffend beschreibt. Wir haben innerhalb des Projekts dennoch an diesem Begriff festgehalten, weil er sich für alle anderen Fallstudien als sinnvoll und hilfreich erwies.

Blick auf Familie und Rollenbilder für Mann und Frau verbunden. Das bedeutet, dass die potentiellen Rollen der Kirchen in ihrem Engagement im sozialen Bereich ambivalent sind angesichts der europäischen Bestrebungen nach einer zunehmenden Gleichstellung von Frau und Mann.

Wohlfahrtsarbeit und Gender

Die Bereitstellung von sozialen Diensten scheint in allen europäischen Ländern in hohem Grade geschlechtsbezogen zu sein. Seit Anfang der 1990er Jahre ist viel über diese Beziehungen geschrieben worden.[3] Diese Literatur weist auf die Tatsache hin, dass sich die Organisation der Pflege- und Erziehungsarbeit sowie der Sozialen Arbeit in Europa nach dem Zweiten Weltkrieg auf einen Familien-bezogenen Geschlechtervertrag stützte, wobei von einem männlichen Ernährer und einer weiblichen Fürsorgerin ausgegangen wurde. Einige Länder wie die nordischen sind im Laufe der Zeit einen weiten Weg gegangen, bis dahin, dass sie Frauen in den Arbeitsmarkt einbezogen haben, zumindest in Teilzeit und in bestimmten Arbeitsbereichen. Doch immer noch wird der Hauptanteil der Sozialen Arbeit und der Pflege- und Erziehungsarbeit – sei es nun in der Familie, im ehrenamtlichen Bereich oder in bezahlten Tätigkeiten – von Frauen geleistet.[4]

„Mit dem Körper einer Frau geboren zu sein, bedeutet, eine potentielle Fürsorgerin zu sein", so fasst Renita Sörensdotter die Situation in einer kürzlich erschienenen Anthologie über Pflegearbeit in Schweden zusammen, die aufzeigt, wie Frausein und Pflege traditionell durch soziale und kulturelle Prozesse miteinander verknüpft worden sind.[5]

Zum normativen Bild der Weiblichkeit gehört es, fürsorglich, sensibel und einfühlsam zu sein, symbolisch dargestellt in der Madonna mit ihrem Kind. Viele der Fähigkeiten, die mit Pflege und Fürsorge in Verbindung gebracht werden, werden auch mit dem Frausein in Verbindung gebracht. Fürsorge scheint mit dem Weiblichen gleichgesetzt zu werden und sich als ein natürliches weibliches Merkmal eingebürgert zu haben.

---

[3] Einen guten Überblick bietet Mary Daly, *The Gender Division of Welfare. The impact of the British and the German Welfare State* (Cambridge University Press: Cambridge 2000), 19-44.

[4] Mary Daly / Katherine Rake, *Gender and the Welfare State. Care, Work and Welfare in Europe and the USA* (Polity Press: Cambridge, UK 2003), 48-69.

[5] Renita Sörensdotter / Inga Michaeli (Hg.), *Att vara i omsorgens mitt* (Gidlund: Hedemora 2004), 50.

Ein Pflegedefizit

Untersuchungen über die Veränderungen der Wohlfahrtssysteme stellen heute ein allgemein verbreitetes „Pflegedefizit" in den europäischen Gesellschaften fest, und zwar als Folge einer Reihe von Herausforderungen, denen die Organisation des Sozial- und Gesundheitswesens gegenüber steht.[6] Mit den Worten von Mary Daly und Katherine Rake, die die Frage von Wohlfahrt und Gender untersucht haben, kann die Situation so zusammengefasst werden: „Der Bedarf an Pflege nimmt in dem gleichen Maße zu, in dem das Angebot privater Pflege in der Familie abnimmt".[7]

Die Krise in der pflegerischen Versorgung im Kontext der Familie hat verschiedene Wurzeln. Die Familienbande sind allgemein in der Auflösung begriffen. Paare leben zusammen, ohne verheiratet zu sein. Eltern ohne Kinder und alleinstehende Erwachsene sind allgemein verbreitete Haushaltsformen, wohingegen es seltener vorkommt, dass die Generationen zusammenleben. Ehescheidungen nehmen zu; und es ist nicht selbstverständlich, dass die Familie die ganze Zeit zusammen lebt angesichts der Tatsache, dass der Arbeitsmarkt von den Arbeitnehmern in zunehmendem Maße Mobilität verlangt.

Die Frauen passen sich zunehmend dem Lebensmuster der männlichen Arbeitnehmer an und verdienen ihr eigenes Geld. Das ist auch die Situation, die sich die Menschen wünschen. Nach einer Statistik der OECD würden sogar noch mehr Menschen das Modell des männlichen Ernährers aufgeben, wenn die Umstände es ihnen erlaubten.[8]

Viele der oben erwähnten Veränderungen haben zweifellos positive Auswirkungen, nicht zuletzt für Frauen, die eine neue Freiheit als Individuen erfahren. Was weniger erkannt wird, ist die Tatsache, dass die Veränderungen eine neue Ordnung des ganzen Pflegebereichs erfordern. Wie die schwedische Wirtschaftswissenschaftlerin Agneta Stark gezeigt hat, erkennen die europäischen Politiker das nur widerstrebend an.[9] Dieses Widerstreben hat damit zu tun, dass der Geschlechtervertrag, wonach die Frauen die Verantwortung für die Pflege der Mitglieder des Haushaltes und die Betreuung der Kinder haben,

---

6   Thomas P. Boje / Arnalug Leira, „Introduction", in: Thomas P. Boje / Arnalug Leira (Hg.), *Gender, Welfare State and the Market. Towards a New Division of Labour* (Routledge: Florence, KY USA 2000), 1-19.

7   Daly / Rake, *Gender and the Welfare State*, 168.

8   Daly / Rake, *Gender and the Welfare State*, 169f.

9   Agneta Stark / Åsa Regnér, *In Whose Hands. Work, Gender, Aging and Care in Three EU-countries* (Tema Genus; Linköpings Universitet: Linköping 2002).

kein förmlicher, rechtlicher Vertrag ist, der als Ergebnis von politischen Entscheidungen geschlossen worden ist, sondern ein informeller Vertrag, der sich auf die oben erwähnten Vorstellungen von der Fürsorge als einem natürlichen Wesenszug der Frau stützt. Statt die Defizite bei den Finanzmitteln für die Pflege als ein gemeinsames politisches Problem zu betrachten, besteht die Tendenz, dies als ein Problem der Frauen und der Gruppen zu betrachten, die der Pflege bedürfen.

Eine individuelle Lösung für den Mangel an Ressourcen für Pflege und Kinderbetreuung besteht bei jungen Leuten häufig darin, das Kinderkriegen hinauszuschieben oder sich zu entscheiden, keine Kinder zu bekommen. Die Frauen in Europa bringen sehr viel weniger Kinder zur Welt als frühere Generationen, und die Mütter sind älter, wenn sie ihr erstes Kind bekommen. Zusammen mit der höheren durchschnittlichen Lebenserwartung führt das zu einer Überalterung der Bevölkerung. Eine schwindende Zahl von Erwerbstätigen muss eine zunehmende Anzahl von Älteren unterhalten. So wächst der Bedarf an Pflege, statt dass er verringert wird.

Eine andere Lösung, die überall in Europa, vor allem aber in den südeuropäischen Ländern immer üblicher wird, ist die, eine Immigrantin einzustellen, um die Lücke im Haushalt zu schließen.[10] Der geschlechtsbezogene Charakter der Pflege erhält damit eine ethnische Komponente, und die Last des Pflegedefizits wird von uns auf „die anderen" verschoben, das heißt auf das Land, aus dem die Immigrantin kommt.

Die politische Lösung der nordischen Länder bestand lange Zeit darin, die Pflege öffentlich zu organisieren, wobei sie zwar immer noch vornehmlich von Frauen geleistet wird, nun aber als bezahlte Arbeit. Diese Lösung gerät jedoch immer häufiger in Konflikt mit der angespannten Finanzlage und dem Druck zur Kostensenkung. So sind in den letzten Jahren Anstrengungen unternommen worden, die Verantwortung an die Familie zurückzugeben, und dort vor allem an Frauen, wie im Fall von Ida in meiner einleitenden Geschichte.[11]

Welche Lösung man auch immer anstreben mag, der Mangel an Ressourcen im Bereich der Pflege wird von vielen Frauen als eine unvermeidliche

---

[10] Barbara Ehrenreich / Arlie Hochschild, *Global Woman. Nannies, Maids and Sex Workers in the New Economy* (Metropolitan Books: New York / Granta Books: London 2003).

[11] Marta Szebehely, „Care as employment and welfare provision – child care and elder care in Sweden at the dawn of the 21st century", in: Hanne Marlene Dahl / Tine Rask Eriksen (Hg.), *Dilemmas of Care in the Nordic Welfare State* (Ashgate: Aldershot 2005).

Last an Schuld erfahren. Das radikalste Beispiel einer solchen Schuldzuweisung, das mir je begegnet ist, kam kürzlich in einer britischen Debatte zur Sprache, die durch einen Artikel von Alison Wolf, Professorin für Management im öffentlichen Sektor am King's College in London, ausgelöst wurde. In der Titelgeschichte von *Prospect Magazine* im April 2006 behauptete sie, dass wir uns heute „dem Ende des weiblichen Altruismus" gegenübersehen und damit die Familien und der ehrenamtliche Tätigkeitsbereich ihrer Hauptquelle beraubt werden. Das ist zurückzuführen auf „den Bruch in der menschlichen Geschichte", der durch die Öffnung aller Sektoren des Arbeitsmarktes für Frauen entstanden ist. Während – nach Alison Wolf – die ehrenamtliche Arbeit der Frauen im Sozial- und Pflegebereich von idealistischer, unbefangener religiöser Sprache und religiösen Werten durchtränkt war, findet das weibliche Ideal unserer Zeit Ausdruck in dem ikonenhaften Bild der Werbung, das dich dazu auffordert, in die eigene Schönheit zu investieren, „weil du es wert bist".[12]

Alison Wolf gelang es offensichtlich, an einen wunden Punkt in der britischen Gesellschaft zu rühren. Ihr Artikel fand Echo in den Tageszeitungen. Die *Times* veröffentlichte ihre Geschichte unter der Überschrift „Das egoistische Geschlecht?" Der Artikel wurde durch ein ganzseitiges Foto einer älteren Frau illustriert, die mutmaßlich nicht bereit war, ihre natürliche Fähigkeit zur Fürsorge einzubringen, da sie alleine da stand.[13]

Wie ich zu zeigen versucht habe, gehen die meisten Lösungen, die vorgeschlagen werden, um das „Pflegedefizit" zu beheben, noch immer von der Vorstellung aus, dass es die Frauen sind, die die Hauptlast der Pflege tragen. Der renommierte Forscher in Sachen Wohlfahrtsstaat, Gøsta Esping-Andersen, vertritt jedoch in einem vor wenigen Jahren erschienenen Buch die Auffassung, dass für die europäischen Wohlfahrtsstaaten der einzige Weg nach vorn in einer Veränderung der Lebensgestaltung bei den Männern besteht, vergleichbar der, die bei den Frauen schon stattgefunden hat.[14] So wie Frauen in den letzten Jahrzehnten neben den Männern zu Ernährerinnen geworden sind, so müssen die Männer neben den Frauen zu Fürsorgern werden, wenn das Wohl der gegenwärtigen Generation und der zukünftigen Generationen gesichert werden soll.

---

[12] Alison Wolf, „Working Girls", in: *Prospect Magazine* 121, April 2006.
[13] Michelle Henery, „The Selfish Sex"?, in: Times 2, 29. März 2006.
[14] Gøsta Esping-Andersen, „A New Gender Contract", in: Esping-Andersen u.a., *Why We Need a New Welfare State*, 68-95, hier 70.

Kirchen als Ressourcen im Sozialsystem

Welche Rolle spielt nun die Religion bei den derzeitigen Veränderungen und Herausforderungen? Das ist ein Fragenkomplex, der bisher noch kaum berührt worden ist, weder in der Literatur über die sozialen Sicherungssysteme noch in den feministischen Veröffentlichungen, die die Relevanz der Genderperspektive in die Diskussion einbringen.

Der Hauptanspruch unseres Projektes ist es darum, die Religion als einen höchst relevanten Faktor in die Diskussion einzubeziehen. Ein Grund dafür hängt mit der historischen Rolle zusammen, die die Kirchen in der europäischen Kultur gespielt haben. Es ist unmöglich, die Geschichte irgendeines Aspekts der Wohlfahrt darzustellen – sei es im Bereich der Medizin, der Armenhilfe oder der Erziehung in Europa – ohne die Geschichte der christlichen Kirchen zu berücksichtigen. Durch ihre Lehre und ihre Praxis haben sie alle auf verschiedene Weise zu einer bestimmten Wertebasis beigetragen, die quer durch die verschiedenen Typen von Wohlfahrtssystemen zu bestehen scheint, und sind zu der Erkenntnis gekommen, dass es eine gewisse Solidarität *geben müsste*, das heißt, dass wir nicht nur auf unsere eigenen Bedürfnisse, sondern auch auf die unserer Nächsten blicken sollten.

Der zweite Grund dafür, die Religion in die Diskussion über die Wohlfahrt mit einzubeziehen, ist die historische Rolle, die die verschiedenen kirchlichen Traditionen bei der Entwicklung der verschiedenen Typen von Wohlfahrtssystemen gespielt haben, die heute in Europa vorherrschend sind. Die Wohlfahrtssysteme in den nordischen Ländern haben sich in Verbindung mit den lutherischen Volkskirchen entwickelt, die sich theologisch die „Zwei-Reiche-Lehre" zueigen gemacht haben, die dem Staat und der Kirche in der Gesellschaft strikt getrennte Rollen zuweist, wobei der Staat für die weltliche Ordnung und die Kirche für die Verkündigung des Evangeliums verantwortlich ist.

Die Wohlfahrtssysteme von Mittel- und Südeuropa hingegen sind vornehmlich durch die römisch-katholische Kirche und ihre Soziallehre beeinflusst worden.[15] Vor allem das Subsidiaritätsprinzip, nach dem Hilfe möglichst nah an der hilfsbedürftigen Person geleistet werden sollte, das heißt zumeist in der Familie, ist bis heute ein Eckpfeiler dieser Art von Wohlfahrtssystem.[16]

---

[15] Gøsta Esping-Andersen, *The Three Worlds of Welfare Capitalism* (Polity Press: Cambridge 1990), 61.

[16] An dieser Stelle kann ich nicht ausführlicher auf das Subsidiaritätsprinzip und seine umfassende sozialpolitische und theologische Wirkungsgeschichte eingehen, die in Deutschland beispielsweise zum bedingten Vorrang der freien Wohlfahrtspflege führte, der jahrzehntelang die

Zu den anderen Varianten von Wohlfahrtssystemen gehören der liberale Typ, der in unserem Projekt durch England mit seiner anglikanischen Tradition vertreten ist, und der südliche Typ in Griechenland, der von der griechischen Orthodoxie beherrscht wird. Wenn sie sich in ihrer Art auch sowohl vom protestantischen Norden als auch von den katholischen zentral- und südeuropäischen Ländern unterscheiden, so haben diese beiden kirchlichen Traditionen doch Einfluss auf die Entwicklung der entsprechenden Wohlfahrtssysteme gehabt.

Einige Einzelheiten dieser historischen Entwicklung sind im Hintergrundmaterial dokumentiert, das für das Projekt „Welfare and Religion in a European Perspective" zusammengestellt worden ist.[17] Unsere Hauptaufgabe war es jedoch, Daten zusammenzutragen über die Rolle, die die Kirchen heute spielen.[18] Unser Dokument über die Fallstudien bezeugt eine erstaunlich aktive Rolle der Mehrheitskirchen in allen acht Ländern, wenn auch die Rolle je nach dem Typ des Wohlfahrtssystems unterschiedlich ausgeübt wird.[19]

In den nordischen Ländern wird die Rolle der Kirchen als Ergänzung und oft in enger Zusammenarbeit mit den öffentlichen Wohlfahrtseinrichtungen gestaltet. Es könnte z.b. durchaus sein, dass die Lösung der Probleme, die Ida in meiner einleitenden Fallgeschichte erfahren hat, von der Ortsgemeinde durch ihren ehrenamtlichen Besuchsdienst angeboten wird. Vielleicht können sie die

---

Arbeitsteilung im sozialen Bereich bestimmte. Einen Einblick in die Diskussion gibt zum Beispiel: Sylvia Ettwig, *Subsidiarität und Demokratisierung der Europäischen Union. Die Verbände der freien Wohlfahrtspflege als sozialpolitische Akteure vor den Herausforderungen einer europäischen Sozialpolitik* (Deutscher Verein für Öffentliche und Private Fürsorge: Frankfurt am Main 2000).

[17] Die Hintergrundberichte sind als Arbeitspapier 1 des WREP-Projekts veröffentlicht. Das Arbeitspapier ist erhältlich unter dvi@svenskakyrkan.se: Ninna Edgardh Beckman (Hg.), *Welfare, Church and Gender in Eight European Countries. Working Paper 1 from the project Welfare and Religion in a European Perspective* (Diakonivetenskapliga institutets skriftserie 9; DVI: Uppsala 2004).

[18] Wenn wir uns hier auf Kirchen beziehen, schließt dies auch die kirchlichen Wohlfahrtsorganisationen wie Diakonie oder Caritas mit ein, die in einigen der untersuchten Länder eine wichtige Rolle spielen und die Mehrzahl der sozialen Dienste mit kirchlichem Profil anbieten. Dies gilt z.B. (wenn auch in unterschiedlicher Weise) für Italien und Deutschland.

[19] Die Ergebnisse der Fallstudien sind als Arbeitspapier 2 und 3 des WREP-Projekts veröffentlicht und unter dvi@svenskakyrkan.se verfügbar: Anne Yeung / Ninna Edgardh Beckman / Per Pettersson (Hg.), *Churches in Europe as Agents of Welfare – Sweden, Norway and Finland* (Diakonivetenskapliga institutes skriftserie 11; DVI: Uppsala 2006) und *Churches in Europe as Agents of Welfare – England, Germany, France, Italy and Greece* (Diakonivetenskapliga institutes skriftserie 12; DVI: Uppsla 2006).

Unterstützung leisten, die Ida braucht, um die Situation zu bewältigen, die durch die Lücken im schwedischen Wohlfahrtsnetz entstanden sind. Niemand unter den Befragten der schwedischen Studie möchte, dass die Kirche die Rolle des öffentlichen Sektors übernimmt. Es wird jedoch ausdrücklich von der Kirche erwartet, dass sie diejenigen schützt, die als schwache Gruppen in der Gesellschaft betrachtet werden, und zwar sowohl im Blick auf tatsächliche Hilfeleistungen als auch auf das Eintreten für diese Gruppen in der öffentlichen Diskussion.

Ganz anders ist die Situation für die Frauen, die im Rahmen einer Kirche in Thiva in Griechenland eine Suppenküche aufgemacht haben, um Arme zu unterstützen. Aus soziologischer Sicht ist jedoch klar, dass sie ein wichtiges soziales Engagement der Kirche darstellen angesichts der enormen Lücken, die die rudimentären sozialen Dienste der griechischen Behörden aufweisen.

Sowohl in Deutschland als auch in Italien spielen die freien kirchlichen Wohlfahrtseinrichtungen eine entscheidende Rolle, während in Frankreich mit seiner strikten Trennung von religiösem und säkularem Bereich die Rolle der Kirche sehr viel subtiler ist und weitgehend durch kirchliche Vereine ausgeübt wird.

Die europäischen Wohlfahrtssysteme sind das Ergebnis unterschiedlicher Mischungen, in denen Akteure wie der Staat, der Markt, Non-Profit-Organisationen und Familien zusammenwirken. Unsere Fallstudien bieten reichhaltige Beispiele dafür, dass die Stimmen und die Dienste der Kirchen immer noch in jeder Mischform von Wohlfahrtspflege gefragt sind. In den meisten Fällen scheint der Bedarf nach kirchlichen Beiträgen in dem Maße zuzunehmen, wie der Druck auf die verschiedenen Akteure im sozialen Bereich wächst.

Die ambivalente Stellung der Kirchen

Vor dem oben aufgezeigten Hintergrund sieht es so aus, als hätten die Mehrheitskirchen Europas wichtige Beiträge zu leisten in einer Situation, in der die Mittel für Pflege, Betreuung und soziale Arbeit geringer werden, während der Bedarf steigt. Wenn man die Unterschiede zwischen den Kirchen in Betracht zieht, ist es unmöglich zu verallgemeinern, doch es scheint immerhin einige gemeinsame Merkmale zu geben.

Erstens: Die Kirchen haben eine Theologie, die für Werte wie Solidarität und Fürsorge eintritt, die in dem immer härter werdenden Klima im Europa des 21. Jahrhunderts bedroht sind. Hilfe für die Armen und Kranken hat eine feste theologische Grundlage sowohl in der Bibel als auch in der kirchlichen Tradition. Von dieser Basis her haben die Kirchen ein Potential, um als kulturelle Gegenkräfte zu wirken und ihre prophetische Stimme zu erheben. Was die

Kirchen daraus machen, kommt darauf an; doch die Basis dafür ist jedenfalls gegeben.

Zweitens: Die Kirchen haben eine flächendeckende Struktur zu ihrer Verfügung, die einsatzbereit ist für Dienste an denen, die von anderen Leistungen ausgeschlossen sind. Die finanzielle Lage der Kirchen ist unterschiedlich, doch im Vergleich zu anderen Organisationen scheint dieses Merkmal ihnen gemeinsam zu sein.

Drittens: Keine andere Organisation kann mit den Kirchen konkurrieren, was die Unterstützung durch die Bevölkerung betrifft. Die Mitgliederzahlen bei den von der Studie erfassten Mehrheitskirchen variieren von etwa 50% der Bevölkerung in England bis hin zu 95% in Griechenland; doch selbst 50% sind immer noch die Hälfte der Bevölkerung.[20]

Viertens: Die an die Kirchen gestellten Erwartungen im Blick auf ihr soziales Handeln zugunsten der schwachen Gruppen sind in den europäischen Bevölkerungen im Allgemeinen hoch. Wir haben nicht aus jedem Land die Zahlen zur Verfügung; doch unsere Projekt-Mitarbeiterin in Deutschland berichtet, dass die Wohlfahrtsaktivitäten und die diakonische Arbeit als relevante Gründe dafür gelten, in der Kirche zu bleiben, und dies auch bei Menschen, die ansonsten nicht religiös aktiv sind.[21] Untersuchungen in den nordischen Ländern zeigen, dass 90% der erwachsenen Bevölkerung es für wichtig erachten, dass „die Kirche Finanzmittel investiert, um den Alten und Kranken zu helfen".[22]

Es gibt also starke Argumente dafür, dass die Mehrheitskirchen in Europa eine aktivere Rolle in der Wohlfahrtsarbeit spielen. Es gibt viele Gründe für die Kirchen in einem zunehmend säkularen Europa, dem Ersuchen nach einem vermehrten sozialen Engagement nachzukommen. Abgesehen von den theologischen Gründen könnte ein solches Engagement ihre Unterstützung durch die Bevölkerung fördern, die in unterschiedlichem Maße durch die anhaltenden Prozesse der Säkularisierung bedroht ist.

Wenn man in Betracht zieht, was oben über die enge Beziehung zwischen den laufenden Veränderungen im Blick auf geschlechtsbezogene Rollenbilder

---

[20] Auch hier unterscheidet sich die bikonfessionelle Situation in Deutschland von den anderen Ländern. Wenn man die Zahlen der beiden Volkskirchen zusammenzählt, kommt man auch in Deutschland auf 60-70 % Unterstützung.

[21] Annette Leis-Peters, „Protestant Agents of Welfare in Germany – The Case of Reutlingen", in: Yeung / Edgardh Beckman / Petterson (Hg.), *Churches in Europe as Agents of Welfare – England, Germany, France, Italy and Greece*, 56-122.

[22] Anders Bäckström / Ninna Edgardh Beckman / Per Pettersson, *Religious Change in Northern Europe. The Case of Sweden* (Verbum: Stockholm 2004), 98.

und Familie und die Krise des Wohlfahrtsstaates gesagt worden ist, mögen einige Warnungen angebracht sein. Es scheint allgemein notwendig zu sein, dass die Kirchen unterscheiden zwischen den Traditionen sozialen Engagements, die Ausdruck ihrer theologischen Identität sind, und dem Ballast traditioneller Werte im Blick auf Gender und Familie, der eng mit diesen Traditionen zusammenhängt.

Um noch einmal zu Alison Wolfs Artikel zurückzukehren: Sie stellt interessante Überlegungen dazu an, wie stark die Religion in den letzten Jahrhunderten in der ehrenamtlichen Fürsorgetätigkeit der Frauen verankert war. „Im 19. und frühen 20. Jahrhundert ist eine Fülle von Wohltätigkeitsvereinen mit religiösem Hintergrund entstanden, von denen viele die Frauen im Blick hatten und fast alle sich stark auf das weibliche Ehrenamt stützten", schreibt Alison Wolf.[23] Ihre Schlussfolgerung ist, dass die Zeit für dieses Engagement vorüber ist und es keine Rückkehr dahin gibt. Wenn man die Daten aus unseren Fallstudien analysiert, ist es jedoch fraglich, ob das Ethos, auf das Alison Wolf sich bezieht, sich wirklich so verschlechtert hat, wie sie befürchtet. Im Gegenteil, ihre Beschreibung der „Fülle von Wohltätigkeitsvereinen" mit religiösem Hintergrund scheint eine ganz gute Zusammenfassung des Spektrums von sozialen Aktivitäten zu sein, die in den Berichten des WREP-Projekts über die Fallstudien dokumentiert sind, und die sich stark auf ehrenamtlich tätige Frauen stützen.

In einer Hinsicht ist das natürlich positiv und eine wirkliche Hilfsquelle für die Kirchen und die Gesellschaft. In einer anderen Hinsicht jedoch macht das Angewiesensein auf weibliche ehrenamtliche und niedrig bezahlte Dienste die Kirchen abhängig von Gender- und Familienmodellen, die die Gesellschaft im Großen und Ganzen zunehmend hinter sich lässt. Die Mehrheit der von uns Befragten aus verschiedenen Ländern scheint es für normal zu halten, dass die Frauen in den Kirchen eine fürsorgende Rolle übernehmen, die sich von der der Männer unterscheidet. Männer können auch helfen, doch auf andere Weise als Frauen oder – wie eine Befragte aus Griechenland es formuliert:

„Stellen Sie sich einen Mann vor, der sich anschickt, eine ältere Frau zu waschen. Das wird nicht vorkommen. Doch es ist natürlicher für ihn, zu kommen, um im Garten zu arbeiten oder Backgammon mit den Alten zu spielen. Auch das ist *diakonia*".[24]

---

[23] Wolf, „Working Girls".

[24] Effie Fokas, „The Greek Orthodox Church as an Agent of Welfare – the Case of Thiva and Livadeia", in: Yeung / Edgardh Beckman / Pettersson (Hg.), *Churches in Europe as Agents of Welfare – England, Germany, France, Italy and Greece*, 249.

Selbst wenn nicht alle dem zustimmen würden, dass Backgammonspielen natürlicher ist für Männer als Schmutz zu beseitigen, so herrscht doch in unserem ganzen Material die Meinung vor, dass die Geschlechter sich ergänzen.[25]

Solche Auffassungen werden durch theologische Argumente legitimiert, denen zufolge die Berufung von Mann und Frau sich radikal unterscheiden. Die römisch-katholische Kirche ist in dieser Sache am deutlichsten, erklärt sie doch offiziell, dass Frauen und Männer unterschiedliche Gott-gegebene Rollen haben.[26] Standpunkte wie diese nehmen in den Medien einen breiten Raum ein und tragen zu dem Eindruck bei, dass die Kirchen in Fragen von Geschlecht und Familie weit hinter der übrigen Gesellschaft herhinken.

Das mag nicht in jeder Hinsicht zutreffen. Die eigentliche Spaltung in diesen Fragen geht mitten durch die Kirchen hindurch und verläuft weniger zwischen Kirche und Gesellschaft. Die römisch-katholische Kirche nimmt hier insofern eine Sonderstellung ein, als sie eine Hierarchie hat, die die offizielle Lehre für die weltweite Kirche festlegt. Doch die Gläubigen dieser Kirche sind nicht einer Meinung in Sachen Familie und Gender; und die umstrittenen Fragen – von Empfängnisverhütungsmitteln bis hin zu gleichgeschlechtlichen Beziehungen – verursachen interne Konflikte in den meisten Kirchen.

Da die Gleichstellung der Geschlechter heute ein Wert ist, der in ganz Europa anerkannt wird – wie viel auch noch zu tun bleibt, bis er in der Praxis voll und ganz verwirklicht ist –, werden die Standpunkte der Kirchen in Sachen Gender und Familie sich vermutlich auf ihre Glaubwürdigkeit als soziale Kraft auswirken. Hier geht es um interne Probleme wie die Frage, wer die Sozialarbeit der Kirchen leistet und unter welchen Bedingungen und wer versorgt wird und wie. Auch externe Probleme sind im Spiel wie die Frage, welche Position man in Sachen Gender und Familie beziehen soll. Das gilt sowohl für einzelne Kirchenvertreter auf lokaler Ebene wie auch für Stellungnahmen auf offiziellerer Ebene. Die Position der Kirchen in allen diesen Fragen und auf allen Ebenen wird sich auf die Rolle auswirken, die sie in der Gesellschaft im Blick auf die Gender spielen.

Eine schwedische Diskussion mag veranschaulichen, was für Machtfragen hier im Spiel sind. Es sind zunehmend Befürchtungen geäußert worden, dass

---

[25] Beispiele finden sich in den oben erwähnten Berichten über die Fallstudien des WREP-Projekts.

[26] Glaubenskongregation, *Schreiben an die Bischöfe der katholischen Kirche „Über die Zusammenarbeit von Mann und Frau in der Kirche und in der Welt"*, 31. Juli 2004.

gemeinnützige Organisationen, unter ihnen auch die Kirche, in einer Situation knapper Finanzen Gefahr laufen, „städgummor" in der Gesellschaft zu werden. Der Ausdruck ist eine leicht herabsetzende Bezeichnung für Putzfrauen und legt verschiedene Bedeutungen nahe im Blick auf das Geschlecht ebenso wie die soziale Schicht und die ethnische Zugehörigkeit. Eine „städgumma" ist eine Person, die ohne viel Einfluss auf die Arbeitsbedingungen oder den Inhalt ihrer Arbeit, einen Job leistet, den andere verachten.

Wenn die Kirche zu einer „städgumma" in der Gesellschaft wird, wird „sie" wohl geschätzt werden, wenn auch nur als eine untergeordnete Größe. Sie wird diese Rolle wahrscheinlich nur einnehmen können, indem sie selbst echte Menschen in untergeordneten Stellungen einstellt und benutzt und diese dafür nach Geschlecht, sozialer Schicht und ethnischer Zugehörigkeit auswählt. Es könnte eine positive Alternative für die Kirche geben, nämlich die Rolle einer „Putzfrau" als Ausdruck eines wirklichen Interesses für das Wohl der Menschen zu übernehmen. Eine solche Rolle könnte Ausdruck einer konter-kulturellen Neubewertung der Fürsorge für andere sein, dem Dienst Jesu entsprechend, der seine Jünger ermutigte, seinem Beispiel zu folgen und Diener der anderen zu sein.

Damit eine solche konter-kulturelle, auf dem Evangelium basierende Rolle verwirklicht werden kann, müsste die „Putzrolle" jedoch mit einer prophetischeren Rolle verbunden sein, die bewusst negativen Verbindungen zwischen Fürsorge, weiblichem Geschlecht, fremder ethnischer Zughörigkeit und niedriger sozialer Schicht entgegenwirkt. In einer spät-modernen Gesellschaft ist es keine haltbare Strategie für die Kirchen, die Gläubigen dazu zu ermutigen, den Machthabern der Welt zu dienen und sich ihnen zu unterwerfen. Die fürsorgende Rolle muss mit einer kritischen und prophetischen Rolle verbunden sein, insbesondere im Blick auf die Verflechtung von Gender, Klasse und ethnischer Zugehörigkeit und die Bedrohung der menschlichen Würde, die damit verbunden ist.

Die Machtfragen, um die es geht, wenn die Kirchen sich am Sozialsystem beteiligen, kann an dem deutschen Fall im WREP-Projekt verdeutlicht werden. Der Bericht über die Fallstudie zeigt, wie die kirchlichen Wohlfahrtsorganisationen, die vom Staat damit betraut sind, eine Reihe von Sozialdiensten zu übernehmen, zunehmend gezwungen sind, mit privaten Unternehmen um die billigsten Dienste zu konkurrieren, und wie sie ständig der Gefahr ausgesetzt sind, Kompromisse zu schließen im Blick auf die Qualität und die ethischen Werte, die sie verteidigen möchten. Der deutsche Fall weist auf die Notwendigkeit für die Kirchen und kirchlichen Wohlfahrtsorganisationen hin, ihre

Unabhängigkeit gegenüber den Behörden und anderen Dienstleistern zu bewahren.[27] Die Rolle des Dienens muss freiwillig sein und auf theologischen Argumenten basieren; das gilt sowohl für die Menschen, die die Dienste leisten, als auch für die Kirchen als Organisationen.

Die europäischen Mehrheitskirchen haben die Möglichkeit, Männern und Frauen eine Plattform zu bieten, um füreinander zu sorgen und ihre Stimmen für soziale Veränderungen zu erheben. In dem Maße, in dem dies geschieht, können die Kirchen eine prophetische Mission erfüllen, die tief im Evangelium verwurzelt *und* dringend notwendig ist in einem säkularen postindustriellen Europa. Es besteht jedoch die Gefahr, dass die Kirchen es vorziehen, passiv auf jedes Ersuchen von außen zu reagieren und sich dabei darauf zu verlassen, dass die Frauen ihre ehrenamtliche Tätigkeit in der traditionellen Weise fortführen, ohne Rücksicht auf die laufenden Veränderungen im Blick auf die Genderrollen und die Familienstrukturen. In dem Maße, in dem die Kirchen sich für diesen Weg entscheiden, werden ihre Beiträge aller Wahrscheinlichkeit nach nur von vorübergehender Wirkung sein und eher als ein Ausdruck von Unterlegenheit als von prophetischer Kraft wahrgenommen werden.

Übersetzung aus dem Englischen: Helga Voigt

Due to a number of reasons European welfare states today face a common crisis in the provision of care for the young, the sick and the elderly. The Research Project "Welfare and Religion in a European Perspective" documents how several big church traditions in Europe react to this situation on the local level. The social activity of the churches is closely related to their basic theological self-understanding, but it is also highly influenced by attitudes related to gender and family. The author argues that the ambiguous position of the churches in these issues risk to threaten the credibility of the churches as agents of welfare, not least from a gender perspective.

Pour un certain nombre de raisons, les États européens ayant un système de sécurité sociale sont confrontés à une crise commune en ce qui concerne les jeunes, les malades et les personnes âgées. Le Projet de Recherche «Sécurité sociale et Religion dans une Perspective Européenne» apporte des informations sur la façon dont plusieurs grandes traditions ecclésiales d'Europe font face à cette situation à un niveau local. L'action sociale des Eglises est fondée sur leurs conceptions théologiques particulières, mais elle est aussi fortement influencée par les comportements envers le genre et la famille. L'auteure affirme que la position ambiguë des Églises sur ces questions risque de mettre en danger la crédibilité de leur engagement social.

---

[27] Annette Leis-Peters, „Protestant Agents of Welfare in Germany – the Case of Reutlingen".

Ninna Edgardh Beckman (*1955), Dr. theol. der Universität Uppsala, Schweden. Sie ist spezialisiert auf dem Gebiet von Gender und Religion und schrieb ihre Dissertation 2001 über Feminismus und liturgische Erneuerung. Sie arbeitet zur Zeit an verschiedenen internationalen Projekten mit, die sich mit religiösen und sozialen Veränderungen unter besonderer Berücksichtigung der Fragen von Wohlfahrt, Minderheiten und Gender befassen. Es liegen zahlreiche Veröffentlichungen von ihr auf Schwedisch und Englisch vor. Zu den jüngsten Publikationen auf Englisch gehören die Mitautorinschaft an dem Band *Religious Change in Northern Europe. The Case of Sweden* (2005) sowie die Herausgabe von drei Bänden von Arbeitspapieren des Projekts *Welfare and Religion in a European Perspective*.

Journal of the European Society of Women in Theological Research 15 (2007) 119-129.
doi: 10.2143/ESWTR.15.0.2022772

Annukka Kalske

BECOMING … SANCTIFIED
A Finnish Perspective on Grace Mary Jantzen's Approach to Protestantism

> The Post-Enlightenment western cultural symbolic … especially as that has been informed by Protestantism, places enormous emphasis on truth … in the sense of true beliefs … Indeed in much of Protestantism it is precisely whether one has true beliefs or not that is decisive for salvation, where salvation is understood ultimately in terms of life after death … The correlation between the emphasis on truth claims and the investment in a symbolic of mortality and other-worldliness could hardly be clearer.[1]

> Protestant Christendom in particular has chosen to fasten on the idiom of salvation rather than that of flourishing … that choice both reflects and reinforces the necrophilic imaginary and its obsession with dominance, mastery and escape.[2]

Philosopher Grace M. Jantzen's critique of philosophy of religion and the Protestant tradition is severe. Jantzen argues that philosophy of religion has been perverted into a one-sided affair. Rationality has become a disembodied virtue, which lacks dependence on anything remotely tied to physical facts of life. Jantzen links this tendency to necrophobia: a fear of the material, fear of the maternal and eventually fear of limits. She attributes the philosopher's phobic tendency to a conception of humanity, which Jantzen sees portrayed as a negative state in the Protestant tradition. In her view, emphasis on salvation in religious doctrines leads to a passive human condition, from which one needs salvation from the outside. Jantzen suggests a philosophy of flourishing as a remedy to the philosophy of religion.

In this article I take a closer look at Jantzen's concepts of necrophobia and flourishing and compare notes with Lutheran theology to see whether her

---

[1] Grace M. Jantzen, *Becoming divine: Towards a feminist philosophy of religion* (Manchester Studies in Religion, Culture and Gender; Manchester University Press: Manchester 1998), 21.

[2] Jantzen, *Becoming divine*, 157.

premises are to be taken at face value. My test case is the Finnish Lutheran context, from which some of Jantzen's comments seem unfair (at best).

I intend to operate on a similar general theological and philosophical level to that on which Jantzen's criticism of Protestant culture is proposed. Therefore I draw my examples from the latest Lutheran theology,[3] without going systematically through the theological practices or all the doctrinal interpretations of different church sects in Finland[4]. This method coincides well with the atmosphere of Jantzen's *Becoming Divine*[5].

Limit and Beginning – Necrophilia and Natality as key concepts in Philosophy of Religion

Jantzen points out that Western culture[6] seems to be both fascinated by and fearful of death. One of the basic tenets in its masculine ethos has been the inability to bear limits. Thus, the tradition of looking into other worlds has

---

[3] I resort mainly to an innovative interpretation of Luther's theology by contemporary Finnish theologians. Therefore many of my sources are in Finnish, but similar handling of the topics can be found in English and German translations for the interested reader. A good collection of critical articles is published in Carl E. Braaten / Robert W. Jenson (eds), *Union with Christ: The New Finnish Interpretation of Luther* (William B. Eerdmans Publishing Company: Cambridge 1998).

[4] Finnish religious culture, although mostly Lutheran in denomination and closely associated with Finnish culture (and the Finnish state for that matter), is peculiarly divided into at least five strong revivalist movements. All of these movements have stayed within the Evangelic-Lutheran Church of Finland, but have their own interpretations of the Bible and theological practices. This has lead to a relatively wide variety of pragmatic interpretations of the Lutheran doctrines and therefore rather than talking generally of a Finnish Lutheran culture as a whole, one needs to specify the geographical and theological context of the interpretations. Thus I shall resist the temptation of giving culturally specific pragmatic examples of any given abstraction in this article, because although they might be of use, they are always very contextual and can accurately be related to only a specific case.

[5] Jantzen's vast critique of the western culture and philosophy of religion is impossible to sketch out in the limited space of this article. To get the whole picture I urge the reader to familiarize oneself with Jantzen's persuasive argumentation in full.

[6] With the "western culture" she refers to European and Anglo-American [Protestant] culture. Her outlook on philosophy of religion is decidedly Anglo-Protestant and alien at times to the readers from Nordic or Eastern European cultures. It has been noted that her writing echoes curiously catholic tones and the philosophers she refers to as a cure of this culture are for the most part from [unrecognised] Jewish cultural backgrounds. Cf. Tina Beattie, "Redeeming Mary: The potential of Marian symbolism for feminist philosophy of religion", in: Pamela Sue Anderson / Beverly Clack (eds), *Feminist Philosophy of Religion: Critical Readings* (Routledge: London 2004), 107-122.

been an attempt to escape the limits of our finite being. This attempt has then produced a necrophilic (-phobic) symbolic, which aims to enable eternal existence via eliminating any otherness as threat and imposing hierarchies attempting to ensure the untouchable nature of the ones on top of it. The irony is of course that in posing a seemingly stable, controlled environment in Western culture, the means of that position have been destructive practices of mastery.

The attempt to escape limits has not only practical consequences in this world, but also in the concept of God.

> The traditional concept of God is directly connected to the assumption that only the infinite could be divine. From this follows the necessity of monotheism (since it would be impossible for more than one being to be infinite), of omnipotence (infinity of power), eternity (infinity in relation to time and space), omniscience (infinity of knowledge), omnipresence (infinity in relation to space) and of course incorporeality (since bodies are by definition finite in at least some of the above respects.[7]

An image of God who is so much unlike anything we can ever be as living people, has consequences in our not accepting ourselves and in our aiming at other worlds instead of this one. Jantzen argues that Western philosophy has promoted thought processes along the line of necrophobia (and with the intense preoccupation with death, necrophilia). She finds in Feuerbach's writings an explicit desire to avoid death at all costs and thus to aim towards immortality through invention of a God who guarantees life after death, which also involves control over things reminiscent of mortality, namely women, earth or bodiliness.[8]

Jantzen also suggests that the preoccupation with deathly images is directly linked with gender in philosophy and theology. In Plato's worldview the soul is captured in the body's prison, from which death sets the soul free. Bodily involvement is seen as a weakness, above which one must rise. In women's case this does not seem to be an option. In Augustine's theology, mortality and embodiment is directly linked with sinfulness, and although later thinkers such as Thomas Aquinas struggle to combine this with the idea of resurrection, the idea that arises is none the less an idea of a resurrected spiritual body. Current philosophers of religion such as Swinburne have introduced an idea of a new

---

[7] Jantzen, *Becoming Divine,* 128-130, 155.
[8] Jantzen, *Becoming Divine,* 135.

body (or no body) in life after death. The immanent body, born out of a woman and imperfect, must be left behind once progressing to God's realm.[9]

Jantzen points out that it is hardly in the feminist agenda to deny human mortality or the importance of religious and philosophical reflections of it. What she is opposed to is the position death has taken in Western thinking. "It is in relation to death – one might say as an answer to death – that the western symbolic takes shape, especially in its religious dimensions."[10] Jantzen argues that this cultural symbolic should be transformed to enable human flourishing rather than anticipation of death or life after it. Instead Jantzen suggests an analysis of Western culture, through which natality[11] can be seen as the unrecognized other of mortality, and birth as the unacknowledged foundation under the symbolic of death.[12]

From a philosophical perspective a shift from an illusionary view from nowhere and insistence on mortality to embodied knowledge and a preoccupation with natality is massive. Jantzen points out that in the case of salvation, there is a huge difference between a philosopher who is concerned with salvation of the soul after death (thus being preoccupied with theorizing the terms of salvation in the afterlife) and a philosopher who is concerned with salvation of the embodied subject (thus being preoccupied with diminishing suffering of people in real life).[13]

Together alone – Salvation at the heart of Protestant Theology

There has been significantly more emphasis on the theological concept of salvation than there has been on the concept of flourishing. Jantzen points out, that both concepts have their roots in the biblical literature. There is undeniably more emphasis on salvation than on flourishing in the scriptures, but, as Jantzen points out, disregarding the one totally in favor of the

---

[9] Jantzen, *Becoming Divine,* 132-140.

[10] Jantzen, *Becoming Divine,*132.

[11] Jantzen relies in her account of natality on Hannah Arendt's works, where natality as a concept does not only imply infancy, but rather our physical origin and a birth into a web of life. Although we arrive into this world as strangers, we are welcomed into the community of surrounding people. Thus instead of Arendt's teacher's Heidegger's views on human existence as Being-unto-Death and having been thrown into the world, Arendt herself underlines the natality and a person's relations to the surrounding community and the world.

[12] Jantzen, *Becoming Divine,* 141.

[13] Jantzen, *Becoming Divine,* 148.

other is an active choice in the course of tradition. What, then is the difference between these metaphors? Jantzen underlines the etymological roots of both terms, where to flourish implies positive thriving or blossoming and salvation denotes rescue from something negative. Salvation implies strong dependence on something, which makes the rescuing possible, whereas flourishing implies a more independent act of dynamic well being and self-fulfillment.[14]

Salvation and flourishing are but metaphors describing a relationship between God and humans. What Jantzen notes, however, is that salvation as a term is so heavily invested in the tradition of especially Protestant theology, that the meaning of the term is more dogmatic than metaphorical. Thus, it is important to think: What does this investment in salvation mean to the practice of philosophy of religion and theology?

First of all, thinking in terms of salvation, the human condition appears a negative one, from which one must be delivered. God can be pictured as an external savior, whose incarnation, the heroic Jesus-figure, sweeps in and saves the world from everlasting separation of God through sin. In terms of flourishing, the picture would seem quite different. Jantzen underlines that flourishing as a term carries with it the potential for full humanity: it is possible for humans to develop and thrive, drawing from inner sources in addition to the web of life surrounding an individual. A God in this picture would be thought of in terms of a well-spring rather than an external supernatural force. Should "flourishing" be a key concept in this sort of new theology, then the problematic act of atonement could be cast aside. The life of Jesus could be seen rather as an example of incarnation, a living proof of what life can be lived to the fullest in justice of God; what it is to become divine.[15]

Jantzen argues that the preoccupation with salvation as a central doctrine in Christianity has resulted, in Protestantism, to a road of individualization and privatization of religion alongside with preoccupation with the life after death. As salvation is by definition individual, it is not a central point of interest what happens to the community around us.

> (...) [S]alvation is individual. A particular individual can be saved, singled out for rescue, though all others around her perish. The combined influence of Luther and

---

[14] Jantzen, *Becoming Divine,* 156-160.
[15] Jantzen, *Becoming Divine,* 161-162.

Calvin on Protestant theology has made an individualized aspect of salvation central to much subsequent theological thought (…) Bunyan's Pilgrim's Progress is (…) one of many spiritual autobiographies (…) in which the grace of God was observed at work in the inner self, the soul standing naked and alone before God, rescued by divine grace from eternal catastrophe, deserting wife and family and fleeing all companionship to undertake a spiritual journey to the celestial city. The links between individualism, patriarchy, and an imaginary of death could hardly be clearer.[16]

Jantzen quite happily pulls together Luther, Calvin and Bunyan as examples of the emphasis on individuality in models of salvation. She totally ignores the not so fine lines between these theologians' views on salvation (Luther's emphasis being on God's grace and forgiveness and on the role of the community of believers; Calvin being preoccupied with predestination and Bunyan expressing his views from an Anabaptist background, emphasizing the importance of the choosing of faith for salvation in the afterlife). In doing this, Jantzen opens herself to justified criticism of her reference to Protestantism and its implications.

According to contemporary Lutheran scholars, Protestant tradition can be seen as a phenomenon, which carries Lutheran and Reformed Churches' traditions in it along with bits and pieces of modern German philosophy. This modern Protestantism lacks accurate boundaries and precise, defining doctrines, and has in many ways been sidetracked from the original goals and findings of the Reformation period.[17]

The general ethos of modern Protestantism hints at a view of humanity where one is thoroughly changed after receiving faith. The former humanity is left behind and the new woman of faith is thus something totally different than before, leaning towards transcendence and in many ways being quite beyond the human condition from this point. This conception does imply a negative view of humanity, as being a state from which one needs to be recovered into something wholly "Other". This view implies that human potential is something one needs to abandon after receiving faith, that human environment and community is something one no longer needs after the change and

---

[16] Jantzen, *Becoming Divine,* 164.

[17] Antti Raunio, "Onko olemassa luterilaista spiritualiteettia?" in: Olli-Pekka Vainio (ed.), *Johdatus luterilaisen spiritualiteetin teologiaan* (Theologica Systemica, Kirjapaja: Helsinki 2003) 11-38, here 18-19.

that immanence is something that will be left behind as one enters phase two in one's lifespan.

Such a picture is conventionally painted by Protestant churches, due to the understanding that the human condition and its potential are tainted by the perversion of sin and thus need to be disregarded on the whole. A spiritual subject must constantly pay attention to a tendency to hubris; as one thinks one is on the right path, one is once again misled by one's illusions of grandeur. God cannot be reached by a human being. A path of divinisation (like one of the Eastern Orthodox Church) is thus a sin in this Protestant view.[18]

This also leads to another problematic view. Where one's conscience is constantly on the alert and it is stressed that one needs to be aware of the sinful nature of the human condition in order to hear the freeing Gospel and feel redemption, there is a constant negative self-image at play. The negativity of this view of humanity has given rise to conceptions of God such as those of Nietsche and Freud. God in these views is quite rightly a judgemental psychological projection, which one needs to be freed from in order to become healthy again.[19]

To love and be loved – The individual process of sanctification in a community

This one sidedness of modern Protestantism is due to an emphasis on justification of the sinner and what happens after that in the righteous person. Protestant theology has thus leaned towards the end rather than the beginning of human life. In this theological emphasis the theme of creation has been forgotten. Instead of interpreting the act of justification as setting things right again, reinstating the gifts and capacity of humans on the right track, justification has become a borderline between the old and the new state of humanity, between which there is not any continuity.[20] This interpretation of the

---

[18] Raunio, "Onko olemassa luterilaista spiritualiteettia?" 18-19.

[19] Raunio, "Onko olemassa luterilaista spiritualiteettia?" 16-18.

[20] Raunio, "Onko olemassa luterilaista spiritualiteettia?" 14-19. Tuomo Mannermaa, "Kristuksen kuvan kaltaisuuteen muuttuminen", in: Pekka Kärkkäinen (ed.), *Johdatus Lutherin teologiaan* (Theologica systematica, Kirjapaja: Helsinki 2001), 320-332. The Melanchtonian translation underlines Christ's action in this justification, where human being is the object of the [mental] act. One is sanctified/reformed after justification. Luther's view was, that whilst one was being in the centre of the justification process, the act itself is really happening to and in a righteous person whilst God is actually in the act itself and in the righteous person as well. The former view, which separates the act of justification and sanctification/participation in God to separate affairs, became the mainstream of Lutheran interpretations *Die Bekenntnisschriften der*

human condition is not a necessity according to Lutheran doctrine, but is rather a historical interpretive current, which has become mainstream, but which need not remain so in the future. Lutheran spirituality can be seen first and foremost as the receiving of God's gift. This gift of grace is something that cannot be obtained by any human action. However, this does not necessarily imply total passivity by a woman's part. The Holy Spirit, which both is God and the gift, revives one, cherishes one and guides one to recognise and receive God's work in the world. This all enables human beings to be active subjects in faith.[21]

Jantzen blames preoccupation with salvation for being depoliticized and introverted. A philosophy of religion built around the idea of flourishing could never be that. The traditional philosophy of religion has emphasized salvation and with it a view of humanity, where the sinful disposition of an individual is negative to start with. If that disposition is to be in any way improved, one needs to be rescued from the very essence of humanity itself.

In regard to flourishing, humanity is natality, connected to the surrounding ecosystem and people in it, with a very positive potential for a full existence in flourishing. Thus Jantzen underlines that a philosophy of religion which takes flourishing seriously would not be based on dichotomies such as soul over body but would be holistic, even in its spiritual nature. Jantzen concludes that a transformed philosophy of religion would involve itself with pressing issues in this life as well.

---

evangelisch-lutherischen Kirche IV [CA IV], (Vandenhoeck & Ruprecht: Göttingen 1967), 159-169. This leads to an implication of separatedness, a view of justification where human being is solely a passive object of God's work. Luther's teaching underlines the equal giving of forgiveness in "favor" and presence in "donum Dei". Participation in God after justification is a constant transition phase from sin to grace. This transition phase also means transition towards becoming like the image of Christ. This does not imply becoming a fuller self or living a life of individual divinisation but living a life that is the life of Christ in a Christian. Martin Luther, *Doctor Martin Luthers Werke. Kritische Gesamtausgabe. Briefwechsel, Weimar 1883-* [WA] 2, 414, 12-15, WA 2 33-415, 6, WA 2, 548, 26-29. This in turn implies passivity, estrangement in terms of one's own, old self; the aspirations and achievements one has had. In this also lies the real difference between Jantzen's view of the process of becoming divine and the Lutheran view of the process of sanctification. In Jantzen's writing it seems, that one is to fulfil a promise of subjectivity one has within, actualising potentiality for one's own sake. In Luther's writing this same potentiality is originally set and eventually actualised by and for God. The divinity in Jantzen's writing appears as a vehicle for personal growth. The divinity in Lutheran doctrine is the eventual goal of any growth in the world.

21 Raunio, "Onko olemassa luterilaista spiritualiteettia?" 21-23.

Since flourishing involves the physical and communal realities of a person's life, as already discussed, a philosophy of flourishing could not content itself with looking piously to an afterlife where present injustices will be abolished, while doing nothing in the struggle for their abolition her and now. For this reason a social and cultural order reflecting a symbolic of flourishing would not be able to avoid confrontation with issues of domination, whether in terms of poverty, class, race, sex, or any other form of injustice; since these are things which prevent people and communities from flourishing. A philosophy of religion which took the model of flourishing seriously would necessarily be political philosophy which confronted social and economic issues not as marginal philosophical interests but as central to philosophical thought.[22]

Jantzen argues that the culture of necrophobia/-philia is destructive and must be left behind in favor of a symbolic of flourishing. Philosophy of religion must focus on natality instead of mortality. This shift would require a change in the way humanity is viewed. In theological thought this would mean reviewing the concept of salvation.

Jantzen's criticism of Protestantism may be justified in some contexts. Had she familiarized herself with Lutheran theology, though, she might have found something of the emphasis on love and communal acts of God that she was looking for in her own philosophy. The human condition can be seen in Lutheran theology as both good and evil, as in terms of being created by God one is good but in terms of being sinful and selfish one is also evil. The division can also be made between the old and the new self, where the old self is referred to as the flesh and the new self as the spirit. This division implies first and foremost thought and action, which is pervasive to the whole human being, both the body and the mind. Self-centred egoism is of flesh, whereas considerate and altruist action is of spirit.[23] With faith, it is possible for a woman to act in the world in loving relation to fellow human beings, trying to place herself into another's position and to see, which action would be mutually beneficial. Spiritual life is not only of a private contemplation, but is communal. According to Lutheran theology, the love of God is received, demonstrated and shared in a caring and supporting community.[24] It is hard to picture a fuller picture of human flourishing.

---

[22] Jantzen, *Becoming Divine,* 164-170.
[23] Raunio, "Onko olemassa luterilaista spiritualiteettia?" 24.
[24] Raunio, "Onko olemassa luterilaista spiritualiteettia?" 25-36.

After the gift of faith, the religious person is on the way to sanctification. In Lutheran theology this sanctification is linked to the act of justification, but not interpreted as something that turns a person to a wholly other at once. The process of sanctification is such that the acts of a spiritual self become more and acts of the flesh less in the process of time. The righteous person becomes more of the self God created her to be. This happens in an active relation to the community of faith as well, the emphasis being in receiving the gift of God through sermon and material sacraments.[25] This is the part that seems to be lacking from Jantzen's view of the process of becoming divine. One is thus left to wonder, whether the becoming divine she refers to, is in fact a more individual process, than the [Lutheran] process of sanctification could ever be.

Grace M. Jantzen kritisiert eine Religionsphilosophie, die es Menschen nicht ermöglicht, göttlich zu werden. Nach Jantzen ist dies die Folge einer Kultur, die nicht in der Lage ist, Grenzen zu ertragen, und die deshalb von der Sterblichkeit als der letzten Grenze des menschlichen Lebens in Bann gehalten wird. Die kulturelle Anziehungskraft des Todes oder Nekrophilie/-phobie, wie Jantzen es nennt, hat ihre Wurzeln in philosophischen und theologischen Traditionen. Besonders ProtestantInnen betonten die Erlösung und das Leben nach dem Tod auf Kosten einer ethischen Konzentration auf das Leben hier und jetzt. Nach Jantzen ist die Kultur der Nekrophilie/-phobie destruktiv und muss zugunsten einer Symbolik des Blühens und Gedeihens (*flourishing*) aufgegeben werden. Religionsphilosophie muss Gebürtigkeit und nicht Sterblichkeit ins Zentrum stellen und die Art und Weise, in der menschliches Leben betrachtet wird, verändern. Für das theologische Denken würde das bedeuten, das Konzept von Erlösung neu zu durchdenken. Dieser Artikel untersucht aus einer lutherischen Perspektive Jantzens Argumentation und besonders ihre Perspektive auf Protestantismus und Rettung. Die Autorin hält gegen Jantzen fest, dass lutherische Theologie durchaus in der Lage ist, menschliches Blühen und Gedeihen (*flourishing*) zu ermöglichen.

Grace M. Jantzen critique la philosophie de la religion ne permettant pas d'accéder à l'état divin. Grace M. Jantzen affirme que c'est la conséquence d'une culture incapable de supporter des limites et donc fascinée par la mortalité, la mort étant l'ultime limite de la vie humaine. La séduction culturelle de la mort, ou

---

[25] Juntunen, "Jumalan olemus ja työ spiritualiteetin näkökulmasta", in: Olli-Pekka Vainio (ed.), *Johdatus luterilaisen spiritualiteetin teologiaan* (Theologica Systemica, Kirjapaja: Helsinki 2003), 39-58, here 56-58. Vainio, "Luterilaisen spiritualiteetin ongelmakohtia", in: Olli-Pekka Vainio (ed.), *Johdatus luterilaisen spiritualiteetin teologiaan* (Theologica Systemica, Kirjapaja: Helsinki 2003), 59-84, here 77-78.

nécrophilie/-phobie, ainsi que Grace M. Jantzen la nomme, a ses origines dans les traditions philosophiques et religieuses. Les protestants, en particulier, ont mis l'accent sur le salut et la vie après la mort, au détriment d'une éthique portant sur la vie humaine ici et maintenant. Grace M. Jantzen affirme que la culture de la nécrophobie/-philie est destructrice et doit être abandonnée en faveur d'une symbolique de l'épanouissement. La philosophie de la religion devait mettre l'accent sur la natalité plutôt que sur la mortalité, et faire évoluer le concept d'humanité. Dans la pensée théologique, cela signifierait revoir le concept du salut. Cet article étudie l'argumentation de Grace M. Jantzen à partir d'une perspective luthérienne et, en particulier, sa conception du protestantisme et du salut. Kalske maintient, à l'inverse de Jantzen, que la théologie luthérienne est capable de favoriser l'épanouissement des êtres humains.

Annukka Kalske (*1975) majored in Systematic Theology from the University of Helsinki in 2001. She is currently working on her PhD under the working title "Feminist Epistemology in Philosophy of Religion". She has published an article about the general outlines of feminist epistemology in Philosophy of Religion in *Teologinen Aikakausikirja* 1/2006 and is about to publish another about feminist symbolic in *Uskonnollinen Kommunikaatio Toimintana* (ed. Arto Kuorikoski), forthcoming in fall 2007.

Journal of the European Society of Women in Theological Research 15 (2007) 131-139.
doi: 10.2143/ESWTR.15.0.2022773

Pauliina Kainulainen

Wisdom Theology and Finnish Nature Spirituality Reflections on Ivone Gebara's Ecofeminism

Introduction

What kind of Christian theology could be designated as *ecologically sensitive* and capable of meeting today's ecological challenges in a meaningful way? Personally, I perceive as the most promising direction the attempts to revive the old understanding of theology as Wisdom (Lat. *Sapientia*). A renewal in our ways of conceiving the function of theological reflection could result in an original contribution to the larger ecological debate. This does not imply a rejection of more analytical and strictly academic forms of theology. On the contrary, wisdom theology is in constant need of interacting with other forms of theological pursuit.

In addition, I argue that an ecologically relevant theology cannot overlook the impact that feminist consciousness has brought to the global theological discussion. My point of view in this article is strongly influenced by several insights from ecofeminist theology, especially by the thinking of the Brazilian ecofeminist philosopher and theologian Ivone Gebara.[1] Gebara writes from "the margin" as well as I do – I live and work in Eastern Finland. I am also going to reflect on some features of the Finnish way of life that still carry life-enhancing elements. I do this in order to find beginnings of paths that could lead to concretisation of an ecologically sensitive way of life.

Theology matters. Age-old philosophical and theological patterns influence the way modern women and men form their attitudes and subsequent actions towards the earth. Ivone Gebara holds the conviction that a significant change in attitudes and actions requires a change at the metaphysical level of concepts of reality and knowing. A turn to a more holistic way of understanding

---

[1] I did my theological dissertation on Ivone Gebara's thinking at the University of Joensuu in 2005: *Maan viisaus. Ivone Gebaran ekofeministinen käsitys tietämisestä ja teologiasta [The Wisdom of the Earth. Ivone Gebara's Ecofeminist Concept of Knowing and Theology]*.

the world could have tremendous ethical consequences. Theology is needed in this project, and, according to Gebara, theology is required in its mystical form, updated to meet today's challenges. I agree with her and add that especially a holistic wisdom theology – a twenty-first century form of ethical mysticism – can provide us with symbols powerful enough to make a difference, to restore to post-Enlightenment Western world the dimensions of meaning, emotion, the poetic and the intuitive that have been neglected for centuries.[2]

Loss of Meanings

For many Finns, the forest has deep spiritual value. The forest is experienced as a place of healing and consolation, possibly also of prayer. People often claim that they experience the sacred in the forest. The forest contains meanings.

In my childhood I used to walk along a beautiful path through a forest to a lakeshore, often with my father whom I assisted in net fishing. Beside the path there were special places where rare flowers and mushrooms used to grow. One day the forest was cut down and the path with all these meanings disappeared. I shed tears.

This loss of meanings may serve as a metaphor for the loss of meanings that many people experience in their lives in this fragmented culture of ours in the Western world. This is an issue of concepts of reality. The dominant way to understand the world in the West since the seventeenth century is mechanistic. It brings along a concept of knowing that aims at growing specialization. Our knowing becomes fragmented and communication between different areas of knowing becomes more difficult.

The loss of meanings and the nature of knowing are important themes for Ivone Gebara.[3] Gebara strives for a post-patriarchal theology based on a holistic concept of reality. According to her, this kind of thinking is best suited to bringing back meanings and thus helping people to recover a more respectful

---

[2] I have encountered the idea that we need powerful enough symbols in the texts of the eco-theologian Larry Rasmussen. See especially Larry Rasmussen, *Earth Community, Earth Ethics* (Orbis Books: Maryknoll NY 1996).

[3] Ivone Gebara was born in 1944 in São Paulo, Brazil. She became a Catholic nun in the order of Sisters of Our Lady. She holds a doctorate in philosophy in the Catholic University of Sao Paulo and a doctorate in theology in Louvain. Gebara lives in Camaragibe, near Recife. She works outside ecclesial or academic institutions, mainly with women's groups in Brazil and abroad.

attitude towards the earth. Gebara is working for the flourishing of the earth and of humans in all their diversity:

> Each new generation must rediscover, through mutual aid and surely also by learning from its past, new forms of shared living that will permit, to the greatest possible extent, the flourishing of the life of all beings and the development of each individual. This presents to us the challenge of thinking through an ethic with new foundations ...[4]

This quest for new foundations takes us to the level of the basic structures of our thinking, that is, to the metaphysical level of concepts of reality and knowing. An epistemological turn towards more holistic views will also have a profound effect on how the function of theology is understood.

An Alternative Way: Organic Thinking

Many people are interested in the possibility of reviving the old organic concept of reality. Its root metaphor is an organism, a living body. The world is construed of mutual relations and all parts are essentially interdependent. The reality is understood in holistic terms which means that the totality is more than the sum of the parts. The organic model has sometimes been used to maintain hierarchical power structures if the individual has been forced to submission for the benefit of the whole community. But today's ecofeminists, like Ivone Gebara, insist that an updated version of the organic thinking must respect diversity.[5]

The concept of knowing linked with organic thinking can be described as integrating. Ivone Gebara has devoted much energy to create a vision of knowing that can bring together important dimensions of reality and help to tackle the complex global problems of our time. Gebara, who lives in Northeast Brazil in a relatively poor urban setting, combines ecological awareness with a feminist view and with a perspective of poverty. In addition, Gebara wants to emphasize the aspect of spirituality. According to her understanding, an ecologically and socially relevant contemporary theology must return to value the

---

[4]   Ivone Gebara, *Longing for Running Water. Ecofeminism and Liberation* (Fortress Press: Minneapolis 1999), 98.

[5]   See also Carolyn Merchant's analysis of the influential concepts of reality in the West: Carolyn Merchant, *The Death of Nature. Women, Ecology, and the Scientific Revolution* (Harper & Row: San Fransisco 1980). Gebara's ecofeminist thinking is best expressed in her *Longing for Running Water*.

mystical current of theology that has been long suppressed in the West. Mystical knowing appreciates experience, emotion and bodiliness as sources of knowing. Knowing is connected with loving, often with erotic passion. All senses have epistemological significance. Surely also the mystical current of Christian theology has been deeply affected by dualistic and sometimes exceedingly ascetic practices, but nevertheless it offers important perspectives to the discussion of the function of theology that is relevant now.

We can also call the mystical current of Christian theology "wisdom theology". A distinction between the sapiental and sciential functions of theology was made already by Augustine, but his thinking evolved in a platonistic frame which impeded him from appreciating the many holistic possibilities of mysticism. Lately, Robert Schreiter has constructed a model of the forms of theological expression. I raise two of them in the discussion here: theology as wisdom (*sapientia*) and theology as sure knowledge (*scientia*).[6]

Sapiental theology shows a strong interest in integrating all parts of the cosmos into a single, meaningful whole. It aims at spiritual growth and uses metaphors such as *path* or *way*. Sapiental theology also prefers poetic language that is seen as capable of respecting the divine mystery. In contrast, theology as sure knowledge is interested in forming definitions and constructing systems to explain the world. Sciential theology has flourished in Western theology since the Middle Ages and this orientation has led to more and more refined methods and clearly defined subdisciplines.

Return of the Sacred

Human greed needs something to restrain it and symbols that are powerful enough to shatter the existing models of thinking. One symbolically far-reaching change would be the return to concepts of the charm and sacrality of nature. This turn would not be such a major shift for Christian theology as it would be for the modern Western project of continued progress and growth. In Christian sapiental theology the sacramental tradition and the panentheistic concept of God have always maintained alive the sense of the sacred connected to the concrete materiality and the earth. Together with the whole wisdom tradition these emphases have been undervalued in the West but today they must be brought centre-stage. The Eastern Church has preserved a more holistic understanding of the cosmos.

---

6   Robert Schreiter, *Constructing Local Theologies* (Orbis Books: Maryknoll NY 1985).

In my Eastern Finnish context it is natural and inspiring to seek relevant theological paths together with Orthodox colleagues.[7] But also some sources in my own Lutheran tradition contain a potential for a more ecologically sensitive theology. In the core of Martin Luther's theology is a panentheistic concept of the presence of God/Christ in every minute detail of the creation.[8] Luther's thinking has been rather thoroughly studied in Finland, but so far no Finnish theologian has recognized the contribution of his theology to the ecological debate.

If the symbolism of the sacrality of the earth is revived it can bring practical consequences in the ways human beings understand their relationship with the earth. To the notion of holiness are associated ideas of respect and inviolability, as well as awe and wonder. Gebara adds to this vision of reality the theme of beauty that has been important to earlier mystics as well. She writes of death as the return to the Sacred Body of the earth:

> We will welcome the transformation of our individual bodies into the mystery of our Sacred Body. And we will do this precisely because life rushed into this universe and became vibrantly mortal. Similarly, the love of this instant must be intense, respect for all things is a duty, the struggle for justice is a light for us all, and happiness is possible and is the right of all things. There is a beauty in this indissoluble unity and the intercommunion that invites us to develop life options that refuse to put off justice and tenderness until tomorrow, or happiness until some imagined eternity.[9]

There are two significant aspects in this passage. First, Gebara wants to remind us of the interdependence of spirituality and ethics. In her thinking, a feeling of communion with the earth causes people to refrain from manipulating the secrets of the earth and from destroying it.[10] Her thinking resembles that of Dorothee Sölle, who sees that the sense of unity, of kinship with all living, can at its best lead to concrete political action for example in resistance groups.[11]

---

[7] The University of Joensuu has a theological faculty since 2002. The faculty is unique in the world because it consists of two units, one for Orthodox theology and one for Western theology.

[8] See for example Rasmussen, *Earth Community, Earth Ethics*.

[9] Gebara, *Longing for Running Water*, 57.

[10] See also Gebara, *Longing for Running Water*, 157.

[11] See Dorothee Sölle, *The Silent Cry. Mysticism and Resistance* (Fortress Press: Minneapolis 2001), 110-111.

Secondly, the above text from Gebara about death shows that this kind of holistic, panentheistic theology is sometimes uneasily located inside the borders of the Christian tradition. There is evidently no need for strict borders and clear definitions in sapiental theology which strives for the respect of the freedom of the divine mystery to express itself in new and surprising ways. But continuity has value, too, if one's goal is to renew the tradition and not to detach oneself from it. After all, Christianity is the largest religion in the world – its turn to a more holistic and subsequently a more ecologically sensitive thinking would make a difference. Gebara is inclined to stress the immanence far more than the transcendence, in her concept of death as well as in her interpretation of Jesus, for example. A balanced panentheism needs both poles, a transcendence included in the immanence.

One promising vision that Gebara, among others, has developed is a new interest in Trinitarian theology. For Gebara, the Trinity means basically the unity in the diversity of the cosmos. One can argue that the whole emphasis in her thinking as well as more broadly in today's theological discussion on spirituality is an attempt to restore the dimension of the Holy Spirit to serious theological consideration. Ecotheology by and large has paid a lot of attention to the themes of creation and Creator (though this is not actually the case with Gebara). Ecologically sensitive theology seems to be able to restore to Western theology a more balanced, non-hierarchical approach to the Trinitarian mystery. Of course, this line of theology needs to be much further elaborated.

Nevertheless, a vigorous new approach to the Trinity may prove to be a source of that kind of powerful imagery that is needed in Christian theology. This kind of theology hopefully can genuinely appreciate the earth-bound wisdom of many cultures, like those of the world's indigenous peoples. The stress on creation and on spirit opens up possibilities for dialogue where finally, after centuries of blind triumphalism, also Christians can find a spirit of humility and learning.

Finally, using all these ecofeminist epistemological and theological insights as a background, I turn to view my own Finnish culture. I am going to reflect briefly and tentatively, on whether my culture contains some sapiental elements that could be brought into dialogue with Christian tradition. Unfortunately, as in so many corners of the world, Christianity invaded Finland predominantly in an arrogant manner, despising the existing traditions that included in several ways respect for nature. We cannot alter the course of history, but we can strive now, in the twenty-first century, to relinquish some heavy burdens of history and think anew. What kind of Christianity could be born of the intimate interconnection between Christian wisdom theology and the still vibrant tradition of Finnish nature spirituality?

Finnish Forest Mysticism?

With Finnish nature spirituality I refer among other things to the respect for trees, the respect for silence and the meaning of the sauna as a holy place in my culture.

Traditionally, Finns have respected and worshipped trees. There were several trees that were considered sacred, the most important of them was the rowan. The red berries of the rowan had also a connection with the menstrual cycles and fertility of women. When Christianity arrived, some trees were seen as good and some as bad trees, mostly following their "usefulness" to humans. Consequently, for example pine and spruce were good while some others were called "the devil's trees". The general attitude of Christian missionaries and priests was that the worshipping of trees was anti-Christian superstition that had to be – literally – uprooted. The church was efficient in destroying ancient places of worship and cutting down holy trees. There existed some resistance but with time this meant the loss of the sense of the sacredness of trees and with them of all nature.[12]

It is striking that the biblical symbol of the *Tree of Life* has not hindered this development. Nevertheless, some elements in Finnish Christian spirituality survived that carry on the tradition of reverence and communion with the earth. The Orthodox tradition is more deeply imbued with the sense of union but also the Lutheran tradition has traits of it, for example in its hymns that adore the beauty of the creation. Lutheran church architecture has also used a lot of wood and wooden art. Lately, many new chapels (for example in tourist centers in Lapland) make the most of the surrounding landscape: usually behind the altar are big windows that let the landscape become a vital part of the sacred space.

Outside the Christian tradition, old Finnish religious beliefs like the deep respect for trees are raising more and more interest. I think that it would be beneficial to these different religious traditions to seek dialogue and common ground for ethical action. Dialogue with the traditional Finnish nature spirituality can also open eyes for the existent but long neglected nature-oriented elements at the core of the Christian tradition.

---

[12] An artistic guide to the meaning of the trees to Finns in past and present is Ritva Kovalainen / Sanni Seppo, *Tree People* (Kustannus Pohjoinen: Oulu 2006). This book contains photos, historical texts and collected experiences that contemporary Finns have told.

Another important feature in the Finnish everyday life is respect for silence. It is part of the Finnish conversation culture which people from different cultural backgrounds sometimes experience as an awkward lack of social skills. But many Finns also actively search for possibilities to retreat to silent places, preferably near lakes and forests. Every summer weekend there is a huge traffic to summer cottages, an escape from cities. Many men find ways of meditation at silent fishing trips during light summer nights, women often prefer picking forest berries or they participate in organized retreats of silence.

The third element important in everyday Finnish nature spirituality is our sauna culture. It is also linked with the respect of silence; cellular phones and every kind of noise are a sacrilege in the sauna. Traditionally saunas are located on the watershore. The sauna has been a cosmic meeting place of the elements: earth, water, air and fire. It has been and is a place of renewal or rebirth, with the oldest form of sauna, the smoke sauna, especially being often experienced as a dark womb.

The sauna is a holy place. It used to be a place of giving birth and of washing the dead. The Finnish word *löyly* that means the hot vapour from the sauna stones is of the same root as the word for *soul* in our language. Even today Finns experience bathing in the sauna as a possibility to holistic purification and relaxation. The sauna is a place where hierarchies lose their meaning. The sauna culture with its natural attitude to nakedness also encourages a positive relationship with one's body.

These three features are a living reality to a great amount of Finns. It is time to highlight their neglected epistemological and theological importance: there is already a lot to build on in our way to an ecologically sensitive thinking and action. This kind of nature spirituality is able to heal some of the wounds that the religious battle and later Enlightenment have inflicted. The time is ripe to make peace between ancient traditions and Christianity and seek a form of Christian faith that respects people's earthbound wisdom. Maybe that future form could be called *Finnish forest mysticism*?

For me personally my physical context is of crucial importance. I have chosen to live in a rural setting in Eastern Finland, in a landscape of forests and lakes that is my "soul landscape" since my childhood. I feel privileged to live in a place where there is abundantly silence and a possibility to live in intimate touch with the different seasons. It is a way of meditation for me just to see the beauty of the lake. Another form of meditation is a trip to pick forest berries. I feel interconnected with the animals of the forest (bears, wolves etc). I also feel enriched by the closeness of many ancient holy places of the Finns and the living presence of the Orthodox tradition. In addition to my Lutheran background, I wish to draw from all these sources in my theologising. Finally, I suggest as a central symbol powerful enough to bring change the phrase *the earth is sacred*. It needs explanation in order not to become confused with pantheism. It is panentheism, which can prove to be a truly significant emphasis of ecologically sensitive theology. It is on a continuum with the thinking of many earlier Christian mystics. The idea of sacredness brings along restrictions to the human greed and arrogance vis à vis the rest of nature. It is connected to the idea of living better with less things, that is, to the old ideal of simple lifestyle in Christian wisdom theology. There are pitfalls in this imagery but that should not prevent us from seeing the urgent need to reconsider our understanding of the contribution of Christian theology to ecological change.

La théologienne brésilienne écoféministe, Ivone Gebara, base sa réflexion sur un concept holistique de la réalité et un concept intégrant de la connaissance. Elle élabore une théologie post-patriarcale pouvant conduire à recouvrer un comportement respectueux envers la terre. Les idées développées dans cet article incitent à réfléchir à quelques caractéristiques de la spiritualité finlandaise de la nature toujours existantes actuellement: le respect pour les arbres et le silence, et la signification du sauna en tant que lieu sacré.

Die brasilianische ökofeministische Theologin Ivone Gebara stützt sich in ihrem Denken auf ein ganzheitliches Konzept von Wirklichkeit und ein integrierendes Konzept von Wissen. Sie bemüht sich um eine postpatriarchale Theologie, die Menschen dazu befähigen kann, wieder zu einer respektvollen Haltung gegenüber der Erde zu finden. In diesem Artikel geben ihre Ideen Anstoß, über einige noch existente Besonderheiten Finnischer Natur-Spiritualität nachzudenken: den Respekt vor den Bäumen und der Stille und die Bedeutung der Sauna als eines Heiligen Ortes.

Pauliina Kainulainen (*1968), Doctor of Theology, pastor. Studied theology first at the University of Helsinki, focusing on Latin American liberation theology, especially its spirituality and feminist hermeneutics. She earned her doctorate in theology at the University of Joensuu in 2005 with a dissertation on Ivone Gebara's ecofeminism. She works as a Lutheran Pastor in Joensuu, Finland.

Journal of the European Society of Women in Theological Research 15 (2007) 141-152.
doi: 10.2143/ESWTR.15.0.2022774

Magdalena Raivio

Transforming Reality or Reinforcing Stereotypes?
On the Use of Birth-Giving as Metaphor in a Spiritual Ecofeminist Context

Introduction

In this article, I interpret *God giving birth* (1968), the most well known painting by the late artist and spiritual ecofeminist Monica Sjöö (1938-2005), in which she depicts a woman giving birth, presenting it as gynocentric metaphor of creation.[1] By interpreting this painting, I wish to rise and discuss some of the questions of relevance when using "birth-giving" as metaphor in a spiritual ecofeminist context.[2] I argue that even though there are a number of gender related problems in such a project, there are other possibilities. Especially if it is defined as part of the project of resacralization of the natural world and of "the female", as understood by Melissa Raphael, and if it is framed by the post-modern project of contesting normative universal worldviews.[3] Even

---

[1] Monica Sjöö was born in Sweden but lived and worked in Great Britain most of her life. Sjöö has been discussed as a feminist artist in a number of articles, mainly focusing on the painting *God Giving birth*. See e.g. Amy Mullin, "Pregnant Bodies, Pregnant Minds", in: *Feminist Theory* 3, no. 1 (2002), 27-44.

[2] "Spiritual ecofeminism" here mainly refers to ecofeminism within the field of Post-Christian religious feminism or goddess spirituality/thealogy. In Raphael's writings however, the words *spiritual feminism* are used. By speaking of "spiritual ecofeminism" I stress the common trait of a religious and feminist worldview *and* the ecological awareness that is always present in these authors' writings. Raphael discusses Monica Sjöö's written work in Melissa Raphael, *Introducing Thealogy: Discourse on the Goddess, Introductions in Feminist Theology* (The Pilgrim Press: Cleveland, Ohio, 2000) and in Melissa Raphael, *Thealogy and Embodiment: The Post-Patriarchal Reconstruction of Female Sacrality* (Sheffield Academic Press: Sheffield 1996).

[3] "The female" is understood by Melissa Raphael as women's own self-definition of what is to be considered as female. "Femininity" is then the patriarchal view of women and of woman, cf. Raphael, *Thealogy and Embodiment*, 71. She makes a critical feminist analysis of the concepts sacred and profane as used by Mircea Eliade and Rudolph Otto, and argues that it is

141

though representations of birth-giving can be understood as a symbol of motherhood and at worst risk reinforcing the patriarchal stereotyped ideal of femaleness, I show that there are other possible interpretations when birth-giving is used as metaphor. What are the gender related problems of using birth-giving as a metaphor? Why and how are feminists in spite of these problems striving to transform the meaning of "the female" and of birth? What does resacralization mean? And, finally, how may birth be interpreted when it is depicted in such a painting as *God Giving Birth*, thanks to a certain model of critical interpretation of visual images and the spiritual ecofeminist understanding and usage of the concept of "resacralization"?

The feminist dilemma of using birth as metaphor
Within feminist theory there has been a great deal of criticism and controversy concerning essentialist, romanticizing and universal spiritual feminist starting points.[4] Spiritual ecofeminism is seen by some as not at all feminist, but rather "feminine" in its (supposed) usage and its valorisation of traditional stereotyped views of women, men, femininity and masculinity.[5] However, Raphael argues that the "essentialism" within spiritual ecofeminism is not simplistically essentialist, but that spiritual ecofeminists derive meanings from female biological processes assuming that female being does not have one fixed essence but is as she puts it: "suggestive and open to a number of biophilic ways of being".[6] Instead of discussing essentialism, I will focus on: a) Romanticizing birth-giving and certain aspects of being a woman, thereby ignoring the actual risks of giving birth or reinforcing traditional gender stereotypes. b) Overestimating the possibility of universalizing female experience, when using birth-giving as an epistemological ground for knowledge, but also acting ethnocentric and generalizing through ignorance of the differences among women and their different situations.

I will start with the risk of romanticizing and making one aspect of womanhood superior to another, making becoming or being a mother the

---

possible to redefine the meaning of the sacred and the profane considering the present situation, cf. Raphael, *Thealogy and Embodiment*, 31-50.
4   See e.g. Rachel Alsop / Anette Fitzimons / Kathleen Lennon (eds), *Theorizing Gender* (Polity Press: Cambridge 2002).
5   See e.g. Victoria Davion, "Is Ecofeminism Feminist?" in: Karen Warren (ed.), *Ecological Feminism* (Routledge: London and New York, 1994), 8-28.
6   Raphael, *Thealogy and Embodiment*, 69.

"hegemonic femininity". There are obvious problems in the glorification *and* demonization of motherhood and of woman that exist side by side within the patriarchy of western culture.[7] In the images of motherhood given by the media for example, a young woman finds very few and often stereotype role models for how to manage life as a mother in all its complexity. If the focus on birth as a metaphor is too one-sided and idealized it would probably also be found non-relevant and even offending to those who for different reasons do not give birth to any children. Idealizing interpretations of birth as a metaphor is also problematic considering all the women that are forced to give birth to more children than their bodies or situations can endure: dying while giving birth or watching their unborn or newly born dying.

The dangers and the sometimes lethal consequences of birth-giving mentioned above are, according to Raphael, also dealt with by spiritual ecofeminists, and giving birth is thus understood as both a physically challenging and sacred experience.[8] In many spiritual ecofeminists' understanding of "the female", motherhood is included in a trinity model of the virgin, the mother and the crone or witch, and thus it is not seen as *the main* aspect of womanhood. When they include aspects and behaviour that are traditionally connected to men and masculinity in their understanding of "the female", the traditional female gender stereotype is also contested. Raphael claims, that the spiritual ecofeminists' usage of birth as metaphor is totally unsentimental and far from romanticizing, since they base it on an acknowledgment of both the life bringing and destructive aspects and powers of birth and motherhood.[9]

---

[7] This is discussed in e.g. Grace M. Jantzen, *Becoming Divine: Towards a Feminist Philosophy of Religion* (Manchester Studies in Religion, Culture and Gender; Manchester University Press: Manchester 1998), 143-145, and Cristina Grenholm, *Moderskap och kärlek: Schabloner och tankeutrymme i feministteologisk livsåskådningsreflektion* (Bokförlaget Nya Doxa: Nora 2005), 45-62.

[8] The key to understand this thinking lies, I think, in the spiritual ecofeminist redefining of both "the sacred" and of God (as the Goddess), contesting the view of life and death as the opposites in a dichotomy. I will come back to this. In Raphael *Thealogy and Embodiment*, 267-268. Raphael discusses spiritual ecofeminist use of birth as metaphor.

[9] See e.g. Barbara Mor / Monica Sjöö, *The Great Cosmic Mother: Rediscovering the Religion of the Earth* (Harper & Row: San Francisco 1987; reprint, 1991), xviii-xxi; Monica Sjöö, *The Norse Goddess* (Dor Darma Press: Penzance 2000), 4. These are also seen as the three ages of women: the young growing women, the adult fertile and creative woman and the old wise woman according to Raphael, *Thealogy and Embodiment*, 56-57.

I move on to the problem of using gynocentric experiences as epistemologically relevant for claiming universal knowledge. As a gender theoretical dilemma this has been discussed mainly when it comes to whether it is epistemologically relevant to regard "women's experiences" as different from "men's experiences" or not, and when discussing the tendency to regard particular women's experiences as "every woman's experiences" in a generalizing way in gender theory or epistemology.[10] However, Raphael shows that spiritual ecofeminism consists of a multitude of understandings – each person generally using her own experiences and interpretations of life to understand her self, and assuming femaleness as a political and spiritual identity for strategic reasons.[11]

Resacralizing "the female" and reconstructing the understandings of birth
As mentioned, feminists as well as spiritual ecofeminists use the image of God as a woman to contest the patriarchal image of a male God and also to deconstruct the dichotomy constructed in the history of ideas between the transcendent creator and the created world. Spiritual ecofeminists want to contest the Christian view of creation by articulating a view of creation as ongoing co-creativity, where creator and creation are not separated, but instead seen as related as in a pantheistic or pan-en-theistic worldview.[12] According to Raphael, the spiritual ecofeminist view of the Goddess as both immanent and transcendent and "the embodied immanence of the Goddess in women or 'female' modes of being makes all biophilic creativity cosmogonic to some degree".[13] One argument – in spite of its shortcomings – for using the gynocentric image of God is that the male image has to be complemented by female ones.[14] Raphael refers to Starhawk's pragmatic view that the image of the Goddess inspires women to see themselves as divine, their bodies as sacred, and the changing phases of life and all the aspects of being woman as holy.[15]

---

[10] This is indeed a problem since a great deal of spiritual ecofeminism has been written by white, middle class, heterosexual, western women. See Alsop / Fitzimons / Lennon (eds), *Theorizing Gender*, and Gayle Letherby, *Feminist Research in Theory and Practice, Feminist Controversies* (Open Univ. Press: Buckingham 2003).

[11] Raphael, *Introducing Thealogy*, 164.

[12] See also e.g. Raphael, *Introducing Theology*, and Carol P. Christ, *She Who Changes: Re-Imagining the Divine in the World* (Palgrave, Macmillian: New York 2003).

[13] Raphael, *Thealogy and Embodiment*, 265.

[14] Sallie McFague, *Models of God: Theology for an Ecological Nuclear Age* (Fortress Press: Philadelphia, reprint, 1997), 97.

[15] Raphael, *Thealogy and Embodiment,* 56.

According to Raphael, resacralization is to be understood in a post-modern context as the effort to socially and spiritually re-empower women by regaining the ontological vision of nature and women and "the female" as sacred.[16] The sacredness that in some cultures and times has been understood as connected to women and women's lives was – according to the mainstream spiritual ecofeminist view of history – devalued, hidden and destroyed by patriarchy.[17] The patriarchal "profanizing" of the female and of women, their bodies and their creative powers, is one of the main answers to why the resacralization of birth is central within the spiritual ecofeminist movement.

Feminists have different strategies for reconstructing the idea of birth. Grace M. Jantzen chooses to focus on the fact that everyone has *been born*, and she writes of *natality* (a concept from Hannah Arendt), in her philosophy of flourishing, and does not focus on the female experience of giving birth.[18] There are, according to Swedish feminist theologian Cristina Grenholm, several other feminist philosophers besides Jantzen who choose to disconnect the philosophy of birth from the philosophy of motherhood, to avoid making it only a "women-preferably mothers-philosophy".[19] Grenholm herself argues that the inclusion of birth is central to a realistic and non-reductive image in theological and philosophical reflections of motherhood.[20] Swedish philosopher of religion Kirsten Grönlien Zetterqvist regards the philosophical split between motherhood and birth as part of the patriarchal dichotomising of body and mind.[21] She shows (as do Jantzen and American art scholar Amy Mullin), how philosophically the split was made between actual birth-giving and the idea of birth. Grönlien Zetterqvist uses Plato's "cave metaphor" as an example of how the metaphor of birth has been used within the androcentric western philosophical heritage. In the split between actual birth-giving and the *idea* of birth

---

[16] Raphael, *Thealogy and Embodiment*, 63.

[17] Raphael, *Thealogy and Embodiment*, 61-63. I am well aware of the criticism of the theories of matriarchal pre-history. See e.g. the discussion in some of the articles in *Feminist Theology* 13, no. 2 (2005). Here I just want to describe the spiritual ecofeminist view.

[18] Jantzen, *Becoming Divine*.

[19] Grenholm refers e.g. to Ulla Holm and Sara Ruddick and their ethics of mothering, cf. Grenholm, *Moderskap och kärlek*, 50-51.

[20] Grenholm, *Moderskap och kärlek*, 51.

[21] Kirsten Grönlien Zetterqvist, *Att vara kroppssubjekt: Ett fenomenologiskt bidrag till feministisk teori och religionsfilosofi* (Studia Philosophiae Religionis 23; Uppsala universitet: Uppsala & Almqvist & Wiksell International: Stockholm 2002).

(birth as metaphor), the body was separated from the spirit, the mother from the virgin. Following the value hierarchy in Plato's dualistic theory of principles, there was also a depreciation of the mother / cave wall / actual birth and an overestimation of the virgin / the mirror / birth as metaphor.[22]

Mullin points to how philosophers such as Plato and Nietzsche and many (male) artists throughout history have used metaphors drawn from experiences of pregnancy and child birth to express intellectual or artistic creativity. Philosophical and artistic creativity (the "birth" of an idea or a piece of art) was then presented as an original and spiritual pregnancy, and a radical distinction was made between this and the woman's bodily pregnancy and birth-giving, the latter being seen as insignificant and to be valued only through its outcome.[23] Jantzen supplements this analysis by recognising that the male appropriation of birth has (historically) been linked to men becoming divine.[24] She illustrates how Christian male appropriations of birth, are to be found in the New Testament, where, as Jantzen puts it: "it is only by this rebirth, which redoes or undoes the maternal birth, that it is possible to be a 'child of God', to become divine".[25]

God giving birth – a spiritual ecofeminist act of resacralization

Like most of Sjöö's paintings, *God giving birth* is in oil on masonite. God is depicted as a powerful naked birth-giving woman of indeterminate race, half black and half white, looking the observer straight in the eye.

When interpreting Sjöö's painting I am not interested in looking for *the* meaning of birth-giving in it. I use Gilligan Rose's model for critical interpretation of visual images, in which the meanings are created in the relation between the visual image and its spectators, although there are actually three sites where meanings of an image are made: The site of production, the site of the image itself, and the site where it is seen by various audiences.[26] Rose's approach, in part influenced by the theory of semiotics, gives me the (responsible) choice of what to focus on when looking at and "reading" the painting, even though the painting in itself, through its composition and content, also

---

22 Grönlien Zetterqvist, *Att vara kroppssubjekt*, 29.
23 Mullin, "Pregnant Bodies, Pregnant Minds", 28-30.
24 Jantzen, *Becoming Divine*, 141.
25 Jantzen, *Becoming Divine*, 143.
26 Gilligan Rose, *Visual Methodologies: An Introduction to the Interpretation of Visual Materials* (Sage Publications Incorporated: London 2001), 15-17.30.

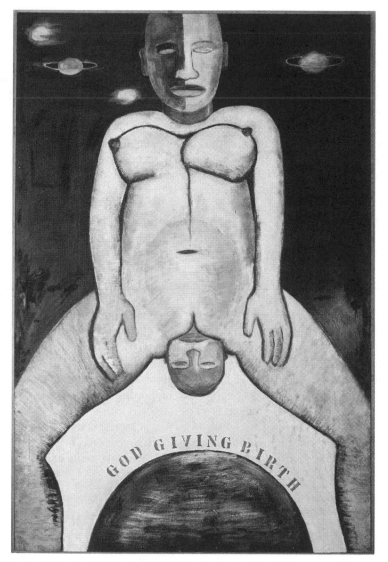

(Monica Sjöö, God Giving Birth, 1968, oil on masonite, 185 × 125 cm, Museum
Anna Nordlander, Skellefteå, Sweden)

suggests to me what should be of a central interest in the meaning made of it.[27] Rose gives three criteria for such an approach: To take the image seriously, to think about the social conditions and effects of visual objects and to consider our own way of looking at images.

In *God Giving birth* the representation of the body of a woman giving birth is central, as is the text written below the woman, telling the spectator this is to be understood as God giving birth. This makes the image powerful in the sense that forces me *not only* to see what I see, but also to intellectually reconsider my visual impression, and thus to consider if this could actually be an image of God, and if birth could be seen as metaphor of the moment of creation. The image without the text *God Giving Birth* would have made it easier for me as a spectator to simply consider this as the representation of a naked woman giving birth. Instead the focus is, as I see it, therefore not on motherhood or on the baby being born, but rather on the relation between how to understand the process of giving birth and the process of creation.[28]

Art critic Amy Mullin writes of *God Giving Birth* that it views women as both spiritually and physically creative and thus can be said to "present, represent and explore pregnant bodies in ways that contest both the dichotomy between bodily and spiritual pregnancy and the priority given to the latter".[29] However, she also criticises the fact that the body of the woman depicted does not show enough evidence of the experience of radical physical and psychological changes Mullin finds significance for women involved in pregnancy. And the fact that the woman depicted is God makes it difficult to imagine her being transformed or challenged by the event in the way mortal women often are. She also criticises Sjöö's painting for supporting the valorisation of pregnancy solely for its end-product.[30].

I still think *God giving birth* can be seen as a representation of the experience of the powers set in motion when the birth process has begun, especially when the site of production and the site of the painting being exhibited to its

---

[27] For a more exhaustive presentation of semiotics see Mieke Bal, *Double Exposures: The Subject of Cultural Analysis* (Routledge: New York, London 1996).

[28] Elizabeth E. Green has discussed the issue of how birth as metaphor for creation is to be understood theologically and in relation to the question of God's transcendence or immanence. "The Transmutation of Theology: Ecofeminist Alchemy and the Christian Tradition", in: Elizabeth Green / Mary Grey (eds), *Ecofeminism and Theology* (Yearbook of the European Society of Women in Theological Research 2/1994; PUBLISHER: CITY YEAR, 48-57).

[29] Mullin, "Pregnant Bodies, Pregnant Minds", 30.

[30] Mullin, "Pregnant Bodies, Pregnant Minds", 34.

audience are taken in account. The criticism that the pregnant woman depicted as God, is non-changing and opposed to human experience, does not take into account those views of the Goddess that are common in spiritual ecofeminism: the goddess understood as immanent, feeling with and caring for created beings, and as ever changing.[31] Sjöö's view of the Goddess and of the nature of creation is expressed both in her art and in her writings.[32] When it comes to the use of female bodies as metaphor, Sjöö's view might well fit into Raphael's description: In spiritual ecofeminism

(a) woman's body can mark the passage of the sacred through the world in the numinosity of her experience of its continuous change: conception, birth (not only of babies), ageing or decay, rotting and rebirth into non-human life forms.[33]

"The Great Mother" or "Mother Earth" are the images of God used in most of Sjöö's writings, and thus probably the main metaphors of her choice, even though her work includes many other images. Even though the gynocentric image of God is used throughout her work, the image of the Mother is also as in most other spiritual ecofeminism accompanied by those of the virgin and the crone or hag. Birth-giving is indeed one of Sjöö's more frequently used metaphors for creation, but as in other spiritual ecofeminism there are also others such as "dance", "alchemy", "crafting" or "change".[34]

Furthermore, some social conditions are to be recognised as sites of meaning when interpreting a painting. I will here focus on the context of the production of *God giving birth*, and the social or political and personal impact of the existence of the painting. The painting is explicitly inspired by the artist's experience and conceptualisation of what she experienced in body and mind while giving birth. In several of her texts, Sjöö refers to this occasion, and the transforming physical and spiritual experience she had while giving birth at

---

[31] Christ, *She Who Changes*; Raphael, *Introducing Thealogy*, 52-74; Raphael, *Thealogy and Embodiment*.

[32] There are several more motifs on the theme of birth-giving within Sjöö's art, e.g. *Birth and struggle for Liberation* from 1969 (not included in the online exhibition) where the motif is more related to the everyday life and struggle of women, and *Universal creation/Sheela Na Gig*, oil on hardboard 1978, and *Sun Goddess at Stonehenge*, mixed media 1992 where the theme of birth/creation is explicit.

[33] Raphael, *Thealogy and Embodiment*, 41.

[34] Mor and Sjöö, *The Great Cosmic Mother*, 46-65; Raphael, *Thealogy and Embodiment*, 262-297.

home to her second son.[35] On the website where the painting is exhibited she writes:

> For the first time I experienced the enormous power of my woman's body, both painful and cosmic and I "saw" in my mind's eye great luminous masses of blackness and masses of radiant light coming and going. The Goddess of the universe in her pure energy body. This birth changed my life and set me questioning the patriarchal culture we live in and its religions that deny the life-creating powers of the mothers and the Great Mother.[36]

Seeing Sjöö's painting as a phenomenological and existentialist representation of experience along with the aspects of the image itself and the intertextual aspects mentioned above, suggests that the motif of the painting can be understood to contest the idea of birth-giving solely as a profane "material matter": birth is also a sacred act.

Finally, there is the social and political context surrounding the exhibitions of the painting: When Sjöö first showed *God Giving Birth* at the Arts Council sponsored arts festival in St. Ives in 1970, when she later showed it in London at the Swiss Cottage Library, and in 1973, when Sjöö cooperated in a collective women's art show called "5 Women Artists – images and Womanpower", she was attacked and threatened by angry Christian men who were provoked by the painting. At some point she nearly ended up in court for charges of obscenity and blasphemy.[37] I think this proves it a powerful painting, as it actually engaged a whole group of men in trying to prevent its being shown. However, it is not only provocative, it is also empowering, as an event in 1993 makes clear. Sjöö and *Ama Mawu*, a Bristol women's spirituality and politics group, then carried a poster of the painting *God Giving Birth* into Bristol cathedral during the Sunday mass. This was a demonstration meant to tell the priest that he and the church were being blasphemous towards the Mother Goddess.[38] This event, plus the interpretation of the painting, clearly makes it a political force

---

[35] E.g. in Monica Sjöö, *Return of the Dark/Light Mother or New Age Armageddon: Towards a Feminist Vision of the Future*, 2 ed. (Plain View Press: Austin 1999), xix.

[36] Sjöö, *Through Space and Time the Ancient Sisterhoods Spoke to Me*. See the text underneath the painting of *God Giving Birth*.

[37] Monica Sjöö, *Kvinnligt konstnärligt skapande är mänskligt skapande: Några kommentarer till Monica Von Stedingk, "Kvinnokonstmuseum som idé"* (Skellefteå: Museum Anna Nordlander 2003), 12.

[38] Sjöö, *Through Space and Time the Ancient Sisterhoods Spoke to Me*.

for social change empowering not only the artist herself but also a whole group of women protesting against the patriarchal tyranny they felt women had experienced, in this case in the Christian church. Raphael defines the demonstration as an example of spiritual ecofeminist "resacralization of place".[39]

Birth as a transforming metaphor

It is time to sum up this article. Mullin finds Sjöö's work challenging, as it rejects the tendency to view the physical and the spiritual as distinct. It is also challenging as the artist's exploration of bodily pregnancy through artworks, since artworks are treated by both Nietzsche and Plato as the products of (male) "spiritual pregnancy" and the artist is in this case a woman. However, Mullin thinks that the painting is stuck with the thought that pregnancy is valued mainly for its outcome, failing to place value on the birth-giving process as such. She also thinks that this painting fails to stress the significance of change in birth-giving. In opposition to Mullin I suggest that the experience and expression of change or process may well be found to be central in an interpretation of the painting *God giving birth* when based on the model for critical interpretation of visual images I have used.

The painting may also, through a semiotic reading and when seen as an act of spiritual ecofeminist resacralization, be regarded as both personally and politically challenging and powerful. Including the painting in the post-modern spiritual ecofeminist project of the resacralization of the natural world and of the female, the matter of creation, the body of the birth-giving woman and the process of birth-giving are affirmed as sacral. This does not, as shown, automatically lead to a glorification of motherhood or the romanticizing of women's experiences of birth-giving. Nor is it to be understood as universal. To destabilize the western androcentric gender marked dichotomising of body and spirit, and the devaluation of physical birth as philosophically less relevant than spiritual or creative birth, I interpret birth-giving as depicted in *God giving birth* as a metaphor for a socially transforming physical and sacred process or change. I see the painting as both challenging and transforming, able to provoke its viewer to consider women's practice of birth-giving as sacred, but also to make the viewer ponder whether birth-giving may be a possible metaphor for a creating and created, sometimes dangerous, but always changing, sacred reality.

---

[39] Raphael, *Thealogy and Embodiment*, 230-33.

Dieser Artikel interpretiert das Gemälde *God Giving Birth* von Monica Sjöö, das eine gebärende Frau darstellt, und stellt dies als eine gynozentrische Metapher für Schöpfung vor. Einige der Fragen, wie Gebären in spirituellen ökofeministischen Rekonstruktionen als Metapher verwendet wird, werden ausgeleuchtet und diskutiert. Raivio argumentiert, dass es – trotz einiger *Gender*-spezifischer Probleme bei einem solchen Unterfangen – auch Möglichkeiten gibt, die dargestellte Geburt als eine sozial transformierende Metapher innerhalb des spirituellen ökofeministischen Projekts der Resakralisierung der natürlichen Welt und "des Weiblichen" zu interpretieren, wie es von Melissa Raphael beschrieben wird. Dieses spirituelle ökofeministische Projekt muss im Horizont des postmodernen Projekts verstanden werden, das normative universale Weltsichten ablehnt.

Cet article donne une interprétation du tableau *God Giving Birth* de Monica Sjöö. Il s'agit d'une femme accouchant présentée comme une métaphore gynocentrique de la création. Certaines des questions concernant l'utilisation de la métaphore de l'accouchement dans les reconstructions spirituelles éco-féministes sont mises en lumière et discutées. Magdalena Raivio affirme que, bien qu'une telle entreprise présente des problèmes liés au genre, elle offre aussi la possibilité d'interpréter l'accouchement représenté dans le tableau comme une métaphore de transformation sociale dans le cadre spirituel éco-féministe de la re-sacralisation du monde naturel et du « féminin » selon Melissa Raphael. Cette entreprise éco-féministe doit être située dans le cadre de la perspective post-moderne qui conteste l'existence de visions universelles normatives.

Magdalena Raivio (*1972) finished her MA in Religious studies (Faiths- and Ideologies with a special focus on Feminist theology and Gender studies) in 2004. She is now working on a PhD thesis at the Department of Religious studies and the Centre for Gender Studies at Karlstad University in Sweden. The overall topic of the thesis is "spiritual ecofeminist and sustainable development". Magdalena Raivio also teaches "faiths and ideologies" and gender studies at the Faculty of Arts and Education at Karlstad University.

God Giving Birth is reproduced by courtesy of Museum Anna Nordlander, Skellefteå, Sweden.

Journal of the European Society of Women in Theological Research 15 (2007) 153-162.
doi: 10.2143/ESWTR.15.0.2022775

Päivi Salmesvuori

Establishing the Authority
Birgitta of Sweden and Her Calling Vision

In the high Middle Ages, female saints used to be noble virgins. Thus, as a wife and a mother of eight children the noble Swedish lady Birgitta (1303–1373) was an untypical candidate for sanctity. However, she was canonized in 1391 only 18 years after her death and became a role model for many late medieval mothers and widows. Already during her lifetime she was regarded as a holy woman, as a "living saint", i.e. a person who was seen as saintly while she or he was alive. The medievalist Aviad Kleinberg has given an apt definition for living saints:

> The living saint could be given no formal (papal or other) recognition, for one could never be certain about his or her future activities. The saintly status of a living person was never established once and for all; the tacit 'pact' between saint and community had to be constantly renegotiated.[1]

Thus, a living saint needed an audience for whom she performed signs of her sanctity.[2] One could not become a living saint in an isolated place, in solitude. The saint needed followers, devotees, supporters, who determined whether he or she was a saintly person. The interaction between the saintly person and her audience created a living saint. It is this interplay between Birgitta and her audience that interests me and especially what kind of elements of power it involves.

---

[1] Aviad Kleinberg, *Prophets in their Own Country: Living Saints and the Making of Sainthood in the Later Middle Ages* (University of Chicago Press: Chicago & London 1992), 6.

[2] Kleinberg, *Prophets in their Own Country*, 6. Besides Kleinberg, a good introduction to the concept of the living saint is Gabriella Zarri, "Living Saints: A Typology of Female Sanctity in the Early Sixteenth Century", in: Daniel Bornstein / Robert Rusconi (eds), *Women and Religion in Medieval and Renaissance Italy*. Translated by Bargery J. Schneider (University of Chicago Press: Chicago & London 1996), 219–303.

Women's traditions in Europe
Frauentraditionen in Europa
Traditions des femmes en Europe

There are naturally several systems of power active in the life of a saintly person, affecting the person directly or indirectly and vice versa. I am especially interested in Birgitta's ability to use and have power in different contexts. Along with the concept of power, *authority* is another key issue in my study. One who has power, usually also has authority. That living saints had authority, meant that people listened to them. Their speech and other utterances were found significant.

During the Middle Ages, institutional power and authority were exclusively in the hands of churchmen and secular male leaders. However, I argue that Birgitta used a different kind of power than men. This becomes evident in the ways she influenced secular and clerical authorities. Birgitta's authority was principally based on her mysticism and on her ascetic way of life and on a vivid collaboration with important people. In this article, I concentrate especially on how Birgitta established authority and her status as a living saint in Sweden.

The Death of Ulf Gudmarsson and the Calling Vision

In Birgitta-scholarship, the death of Birgitta's husband, Ulf Gudmarsson, has often been seen as the birth of the visionary Birgitta. To take an example, Bridget Morris claims that Ulf's death came as "... a release from earthly pressures and pleasures ..."[3] I completely agree that Ulf's death seemed to be a relief to Birgitta. However, she did not leave "the earthly pressures" – on the contrary, her activities, for example among the politicians, were only about to begin. She was now free to follow her hagiographic role models and ready to create a model of her own. She had struggled to live a virtuous life as a married woman. She was now ready for the transformation from wife to bride.

The so-called calling vision only a few days after Ulf's death has been interpreted as a decisive turning point in Birgitta's life. It has been maintained that it was only after she became a widow that she started to have heavenly revelations, and that earlier she had had only few such experiences. However, Birgitta had already been having revelatory experiences a few years before her husband died and she was already gaining some kind of fame as a living saint in her surroundings. The time of the calling vision is nevertheless important since it represented a crucial change in Birgitta's social status.

---

[3] Bridget Morris, *St. Birgitta of Sweden* (Boydell Press: Rochester, NY 1999), 62.

There are two versions of the calling vision in the Birgittine corpus. The longer one is in the *Life of Birgitta*, the *Vita*[4], and the shorter one is the *Extravagantes* 47.[5]

In the *Ex.* 47 it is told that few days after her husband's death Birgitta was worrying about her changed status. Suddenly, the inflaming spirit of God had surrounded her. She was rapt in spirit and saw a bright light and heard a voice saying to her: "I am your God, who wants to speak with you." According to the revelation, Birgitta was terrified because she feared the "illusion of the enemy". Then she heard the voice speaking comfortingly:

> Do not be afraid. For I am the creator of all and am not a deceiver. You should know that I do not speak to you for your sake alone, but for the sake of the salvation of all Christians. Therefore, hear what I say. For you shall be my bride and channel and you shall hear and see spiritual things and heavenly secrets, and my Spirit shall remain with you until your death. Therefore, believe firmly that I am he who was born from the pure virgin, who suffered and died for the salvation of all souls, who rose from the dead and ascended into heaven, and who now with my spirit speaks with you.[6]

This moment implied Birgitta's transformation from wife to bride and channel. Through her, Jesus wanted to declare spiritual things and heavenly secrets.

The longer version in the *process vita* underlined how terrified Birgitta was to have such a revelation and that she feared it was "an illusion". The longer calling vision seems to be also more formal than the shorter one:

> After some days, when the bride of Christ was worried about the change in her status and its bearing on her service of God, and while she was praying about this in her chapel, then she was caught up in spirit; and while she was in ecstasy, she saw a bright cloud; and from the cloud, she heard a voice saying to her: 'Woman, hear

---

4 For the Latin life of Birgitta see: Isak Collijn (ed.), *Acta et processus canonizacionis Beate Birgitte* (Samlingar utgivna av Svenska fornskriftsällskapet. Serie 2, Latinska skrifter 1; Uppsala 1924–1931) [*Acta*], 73–101. This is also called the *process vita*. It is translated into English by A. Kezel in Marguerite Tjader Harris (ed.), *Birgitta of Sweden. Life and Selected Revelations* (The Classics of Western Spirituality; Paulist Press: New York 1990), 69–98.

5 Lennart Hollman (ed.), Birgitta of Sweden, *Revelaciones Extravagantes* (Samlingar utgivna av Svenska fornskriftsällskapet, Ser. 2, Latinska Skrifter 5; Almqvist & Wiksell: Uppsala 1956) [*Ex*].

6 *Ex.* 47. Translated by Claire Sahlin in: *Birgitta of Sweden and the Voice of Prophecy* (Studies in medieval mysticism 3; Boydell: Woodbridge 2001), 45.

Women's traditions in Europe
Frauentraditionen in Europa
Traditions des femmes en Europe

me.' And thoroughly terrified, fearing that it was an illusion, she fled to her chamber; and at once she confessed and then received the Body of Christ. When at last, after several days, she was at prayer in the same chapel, again that bright cloud appeared to her; and from the cloud, she heard again a voice uttering words like those before, fearing that the voice was an illusion. Finally, after several days, when she was praying again in the same place, she was indeed caught up in spirit and saw the bright cloud, and, in it, the likeness of a human being, who said this: 'Woman, hear me; I am your God, who wish to speak with you.' Terrified, therefore, and thinking it was an illusion, she heard again: 'Fear not', he said; 'for I am the Creator of all, and not a deceiver. For I do not speak to you for your sake alone, but for the sake of the salvation of others. Hear the things that I speak; and go to Master Matthias, your confessor, who has experience in discerning the two types of spirit. Say to him on my behalf what I now say to you: you shall be my bride and my channel, and you shall hear and see spiritual things, and my Spirit shall remain with you even to your death.'[7]

When compared with the shorter version, it is evident that the longer version puts weight on Birgitta's fear of deception, which she calls "an illusion". The call was repeated three times before Birgitta was confident that it was her Lord who was speaking. The main reason for that was that the voice said it was not speaking for the sake of Birgitta in the first place but for the sake of the salvation of others. Birgit Klockars has pointed out that the longer calling vision is very similar to the calling visions of the biblical prophets Isaiah, Jeremiah, Ezekiel and Daniel.[8]

In both versions, Birgitta is called to be the bride and channel. The purpose of her calling is to bring salvation to as many as possible. The main differences between these two calling visions are that in the longer one the call is repeated three times and at the end there is the exhortation to reveal the visions to Master Matthias. His task was to check the authenticity of the revelations.

I think that the first calling experience – which I believe Birgitta *did* have soon after Ulf's death – did not contain Master Matthias at all.[9] He was first needed after some revelations were written down. The longer version seems

---

[7] *Acta*, 80–81. Tjader Harris (ed.), *Birgitta of Sweden*, 78.

[8] Is 6, Jer 1, Ez 1–2, Dan 10:9. Birgit Klockars, *Birgitta och böckerna: en undersökning av den Heliga Birgittas källor* (Kungl. Vitterhets-, historie- och antikvitetsakademiens handlingar, Historiska serien 11; Almqvist & Wiksell: Stockholm 1966), 63.

[9] Sahlin implies this also by calling the *Ex. 47* the original prophetic call. Sahlin, *Birgitta of Sweden and the Voice of Prophecy*, 45. Morris takes up only the longer version. Morris, *St. Birgitta of Sweden*, 64.

to have been reworked to convince especially the readers of the *Canonization Acts* of Birgitta's prophetic role. For that reason it is built up like the callings of prophets in the Hebrew Bible.[10]

I suppose that the simple and short version in the *Ex.* 47 is the primary calling vision. The following revelation in the *Extravagantes* also supports this idea. In the *Extravagantes* it is said that after the calling vision Birgitta had another vision about having her revelations written down in Latin.

Sub-prior Peter's Authorization

In *Ex.* 48 Birgitta is exhorted to tell Sub-prior Peter of Alvastra Cistercian monastery to listen to her words and write them down in Latin. Birgitta often visited the monastery and knew Peter well. Christ spoke in the revelation and told that he sent his words through this woman out of his love and promised Peter that he would have an eternal treasure for every single word. The *Ex.* 48 is a compilation of Peter's narration and Birgitta's words. I think it reflects Peter's impression about Birgitta's calling vision and the events immediately after it.

In *Ex. 48* Prior Peter told that Birgitta had gone to him immediately after she had heard Christ's words and asked him to do as told. Peter had hesitated. The same evening he had stood in the church of the Alvastra monastery and had decided not to help Birgitta with the writing, for two reasons: First, he felt unworthy of that task and, second, he was afraid that the revelations were the work of the devil. Straight away, after making up his mind, he had felt as if something had hit him. He fell down and lay on the floor as though paralysed. The other monks found him lying there and carried him to his cell. He lay in his bed, and was still not able to move, but his mind was clear. He started to think that perhaps the reason for his illness was the refusal to assist Lady Birgitta. He prayed God to help him, saying if it were His will he would take on the writing job. Right away after this prayer he became well and hurried to Birgitta.

---

[10] Because of its elegant style, Sara Ekwall suspected that it was Birgitta's Spanish confessor Alphonse of Jaen who had modified the process *vita*'s longer version. According to her the Swedish confessors could not have written such passages because of their modesty. Ekwall, *Vår äldsta Birgittavita,* 47. I find this a peculiar claim, because the style is not especially elegant in the C15 and on the other hand Master Peter's style in *Sermo Angelicus* or Prior Peter's bold testimonies in the *Acta et processus canonizazionis* prove their apt ability to compose Latin texts.

Women's traditions in Europe
Frauentraditionen in Europa
Traditions des femmes en Europe

Birgitta interpreted the cause of Peter's illness to be his rejection to write. Christ had told Birgitta that it was he who had hit and also cured him. In the end of his account, Peter told that he had started immediately to write and translate the revelations given to Birgitta.[11] The last sentence gives the impression that there was a bunch of revelations ready in Swedish, which Peter started to translate into Latin.

The story is interesting because it reveals that Sub-prior Peter, who supposedly knew Birgitta well, was not immediately convinced about her authority as a visionary. He had reason to hesitate since, as Rosalynn Voaden has stated, the fortune of the spiritual director depended on the success of the visionary; Peter's career was at stake.[12] Naturally the story has hagiographic flavor, but if it is put together with the shorter calling vision they build a very plausible chain of events. According to them Birgitta had had visionary experiences, which she had written down in Swedish. After Ulf's death, she had experienced the special call to make the revelations known.

She had started the writing in the vernacular, as was customary among visionary women in the fourteenth century.[13] Naturally, it would not have made any sense to write in Latin for Swedish recipients of the revelations. Nevertheless, after having revelations for some time – it is difficult to estimate for how long – Birgitta seems to have felt that the revelations should be written in Latin. There are two main reasons for that. First, she had messages for foreign people, therefore writing in Swedish would not have been sensible, and second, she felt that her revelations should be examined by the leading theologians of her time. In that case the more official language Latin would be a good choice. It would also bring more authority to the revelations. She needed a capable person for the translation, the best possible choice being a theologian who mastered both the church doctrines and the Latin language. Birgitta found Sub-prior Peter the most suitable man.

Birgitta's case differs from many known relationships between visionary women and their confessors. The confessors usually told the visionary women

---

[11] *Ex.* 48.

[12] Rosalynn Voaden, *God's Words, Women's Voices. The Discernment of Spirits in the Writing of Late-Medieval Women Visionaries* (York Medieval Press: York 1999), 60.

[13] Bernard McGinn, *The Presence of God: A History of Western Christian Mysticism, Vol 3: The Flowering of Mysticism* (Crossroad: New York 1998), 20–24; Barbara Newman, *God and Goddesses: Vision, Poetry, and Belief in the Middle Ages* (Middle Ages Series; University of Pennsylvania Press: Philadelphia 2002), 296–298.

to write their visions or religious experiences down in order to be able to decide whether they stemmed from God or not.[14] But Birgitta acted on her own initiative – although commissioned through a divine revelation – and arranged for her revelations to be both translated and presented to the clergy. She acted from a very practical point of view; she needed help with Latin and the publishing of her revelations. But in the eyes of the church leaders this looked also as if Birgitta submitted herself to clerical control. This was important because: "... doctrinal affirmation of redemptive equivalence forced the church to tolerate female mystics and prophets, on the condition that they submitted to clerical control of their activities and writings."[15] Thus, the definition of prophecy worked for women in given frames, offering them a channel to act publicly. Nevertheless, Birgitta probably valued the doctrinal checking of her revelations, since she did not have the same kind of formal education as her confessors.

The Meaning of the Calling Vision

Why was the calling vision needed? One reason is given in the calling vision itself: Birgitta was worried about her changed status as a widow; the new mission was given to her in the calling vision. The good side in becoming a widow was that with regard to heavenly matters her status rose from thirty-fold to sixty-fold fruit. Hundredfold fruit was reserved to virgins. Nina Sjöberg has noted that Birgitta must have been well aware of this hierarchical grading but, surprisingly, does not use it explicitly herself. This might be due to her efforts to raise the status of wives and widows compared to the highly esteemed status of a virgin.[16]

Still, as a woman and a layperson, Birgitta did not have any authority in the matters of religion. The only chance for her was to get the authority directly from God. As mentioned above, Birgitta's calling resembles the calling of the Hebrew prophets. The biblical pattern of calling visions was familiar to her.[17]

---

[14] Catherine M. Mooney (ed.), *Gendered Voices. Medieval Saints and Their Interpreters* (University of Pennsylvania Press: Philadelphia 1999).

[15] Kari Elisabeth Børresen, "Birgittas teologi: eksemplarisk intesjon, uanvendelig innhold", in: Tore Nyberg (ed.), *Birgitta, hendes værk og hendes klostre i Norden* (Odense University Studies in History and Social Sciences vol. 150; Odense Universitets förlag: Odense 1991), 21–72, here 21.

[16] Nina Sjöberg, *Hustru och man i Birgittas uppenbarelser* (Acta universitatis Upsaliensis: Studia historico-ecclesiastica Upsaliensia, 41; Uppsala universitet, Uppsala 2003), 76.

[17] For example 1 Sam, Is 6, Jer 1, Ezek 1–2, and Dan 10:9. Klockars, *Birgitta och böckerna*, 63; Sahlin, *Birgitta of Sweden and the Voice of Prophecy*, 76.

Women's traditions in Europe
Frauentraditionen in Europa
Traditions des femmes en Europe

The explicit calling visions in the Hebrew Bible as well as of many medieval mystics, such as Hildegard of Bingen, marked a notable change in the person's social status. For example, Hildegard felt that she was called to fulfill a new assignment. Very similarly to Birgitta, Hildegard called herself "a vessel", through which God could pronounce truths. The writer of her *Life*, Theoderic, compared her especially to prophet Deborah.[18] Perhaps most importantly, the status of the prophet meant for women stepping from the private to the public sphere.

Concerning Sub-prior Peter his recognition of Birgitta's authority was fundamental for the whole enterprise to succeed. This was also a risk for Peter; his reputation was at stake if Birgitta were found by others to be a false prophet. But after his own experiences he was convinced and ready to take the chance. I assume that the monks from Alvastra supported him, because had they been against Peter's collaboration with Birgitta, it would not have been possible for those two to work with Birgitta's revelations. Sub-prior Peter was thus Birgitta's first assistant who translated the revelations into Latin. He is also called in the sources Birgitta's confessor. This was important, because it should guarantee the orthodoxy of the revelations.

Sub-prior Peter was at last convinced because of his own experience. I find this paradoxical, when compared to how women's experiences were commonly interpreted. Peter interpreted his box on the ear to stem from God and nobody questioned his interpretation. Instead, women's religious experiences were, as Grace Jantzen noted, continually subject to social control. If a woman mystic claimed to have direct access to the divine truths, in a patriarchal society this had to be tested.[19] This had to do with the concept of knowledge. As Ronald Surtz puts it in his study on Mother Juana de la Cruz (1481–1534): There are two types of knowledge: "that acquired through formal studies by the lettered that is to say, by males, and the infused science closely associated with women."[20] Sub-prior Peter had the theological schooling; he was seen as being able to interpret his own experience. According to the sources, this is exactly

---

[18] Monica Klaes (ed.), *Vita Sanctae Hildegardis* (Corpus Christianorum, Continuatio Medievalis 126; Turnholti: Brepols 1993), 24.

[19] Grace Jantzen, *Power, Gender and Christian Mysticim* (Cambridge University Press: Cambridge 1995), XII.

[20] Roland Surtz, *The Guitar of God: Gender, Power, and Authority in the Visionary World of Mother Juana de la Cruz (1481–1534)* (University of Pennsylvania Press: Philadelphia 1990), 2.

what happened. But the divine experiences of women visionaries' had to be carefully tested. Birgitta passed the test in her immediate entourage but not without struggle.

I find it fruitful to compare the situation in Sweden with that in fifteenth century Castile, where there seemed to be a very positive attitude towards visionary people. According to Surtz, they corresponded to the needs of those who were not satisfied with traditional access to the divine through ecclesiastical hierarchy. Visionaries provided "a more direct way of contacting the supernatural. The visionary functioned as a locus of spiritual power, a channel of grace, a direct pipeline to the eternal."[21] In the sources of fourteenth century Sweden it is hard to find similar common enthusiasm for visionaries. Revelations and visions were not totally unknown in Sweden though, there are some descriptions even in the sources about Birgitta. What I think is extraordinary is that apart from Birgitta, all the other Swedish visionaries were men, either monks or lay brothers who lived in a monastery.[22] Thus, the circumstances in Sweden were quite different from those in Spain and other European countries in which female visionaries were a familiar sight. Perhaps this was due to the shorter history of Christianity in Scandinavia.

Very often the change in the status of a visionary is described as a struggle; the chosen person herself did not dare to follow the call but was forced to do so by God. This is what is said to have happened in, for example, Hildegard of Bingen's case. But in the case of Birgitta, there seems to have been a clear and simple calling experience, about which Birgitta told her confessor. It appears as if she had been prepared for this task during the years in marriage when her will to live a more pious life grew. The calling grew in her gradually. Thus, perhaps it could be said that the purpose of the calling vision was especially to effect transformation from a wife and widow to a bride publicly known and confirmed. As a channel of Christ she should have authority, which in practice meant that she should be listened to.

The calling vision and Sub-prior Peter's box on the ears were performances which convinced the people near Birgitta about her divine call and made her new status known. It is not possible to know what really happened, but since the sources are written with the aim of proving Birgitta's saintliness and while many who had personally known Birgitta were still alive, I assume that the

---

[21] Surtz, *The Guitar of God*, 2–3.
[22] *Ex.* 55 tells about the lay brother Gerekinus.

Women's traditions in Europe
Frauentraditionen in Europa
Traditions des femmes en Europe

description of the events is quite accurate, after wiping some of the hagiographical cream away. Assuring Sub-prior Peter and having him as a translator of the revelations was decisive for Birgitta's career. With his help Birgitta could gain credibility for her revelations and even move to the international arena.

In diesem Artikel wird Aviad Kleinbergs Konzept "Lebende/r Heilige/r" (*living saint*) als Verständnisrahmen für Birgitta von Schweden (1303-1373) verwendet. Als eine "lebende Heilige" wurde Birgitta schon zu Lebzeiten als heilig anerkannt, wenngleich dieser Heiligenstatus nicht fest etabliert war, sondern immer wieder neu erlangt werden musste. Ihr frommes Leben und Offenbarungen, die als himmlisch angesehen wurden, überzeugten viele Menschen. Deshalb untersucht der Beitrag das Wechselspiel zwischen Birgitta und den Menschen ihrer Umgebung, besonders Subprior Peter, der ihre Offenbarungen als erster ins Lateinische übersetzte. Ein Schwerpunkt liegt auf Birgittas Berufungsvision; denn die Untersuchung der Ereignisse, die ihrer so genannten Berufungsvision folgen, zeigen viel über die sozialen Dynamiken um sie herum. Als eine "lebende Heilige", die Offenbarungen von Gott empfangen hatte, übte Birgitta theologische Autorität aus, obwohl sie eine Frau und Laiin war.

Dans cet article, le concept de « saint vivant » présenté par Aviad Kleinberg, est utilisé pour comprendre Brigitte de Suède (1303-1373). La sainteté de Brigitte était déjà reconnue de son vivant; cependant ce statut n'était pas fermement établi et devait être sans cesse reconfirmé. Sa vie pieuse, et les révélations qui lui ont été faites, étaient considérées comme divines, et donc convaincantes. Cet article traite donc des rapports entre Brigitte et son entourage, particulièrement le prieur Pierre, qui, le premier, traduisit ses révélations en latin. L'article met l'accent sur la vision qu'a eue Brigitte quand elle a reçu son appel car l'étude des événements entourant cet « appel » est très révélateur des dynamiques sociales de son temps. Sainte de son vivant et recevant des visions de Dieu, Brigitte exerça une autorité théologique, en dépit du fait qu'elle était une femme et une laïque.

Päivi Salmesvuori (*1963) is researcher and teacher in the Department of Church History, University of Helsinki. She is currently finishing her dissertation *Revelation as Female Power: Birgitta of Sweden 1303–1373*. Her subjects of research are sexuality and the position of women in the history of Christianity, especially the medieval period. She is co-editor and co-writer of a collection of articles: *Taivaallista seksiä. Kristinusko ja seksuaalisuus* [Heavenly Sex. Christianity and sexuality], and has published "The Church and Society. How Religion affects Images of Women and Humanity", in: Anna Moring (ed.), *Politics of Gender. A Century of Women's Suffrage in Finland* (Nytkis, Otava: Helsinki 2006).

Journal of the European Society of Women in Theological Research 15 (2007) 163-176.
doi: 10.2143/ESWTR.15.0.2022776

Kari Elisabeth Børresen

CHRISTINE, REINE de SUEDE: Autonomie et foi rationelle

Brigitte et Christine

Après la prophétesse médiévale Brigitte de Vadstena, morte à Rome en 1373, canonisée en 1391 par Boniface IX pour être invoquée contre son rival à Avignon (cf. le grand schisme 1378-1419) et proclamée sainte co-patronne de l'Europe en 1999, Christine (1626-1689) est la femme scandinave la plus importante dans l'histoire occidentale des idées. Abdiquant son trône en 1654 pour quitter aussitôt la Suède, officiellement convertie au catholicisme en 1655, cette fille unique du grand chef protestant de la guerre de Trente Ans, le roi Gustave II Adolphe, a été longtemps considérée en Suède comme trahissant à la fois sa patrie et sa foi luthérienne. Cette attitude négative, d'inspiration à la fois nationaliste et confessionaliste, pourrait expliquer que ses écrits soient restés si longtemps sans édition critique.[1] En contraste, les *Reuelaciones* de l'héroïne nationale, *sancta Birgitta*, sont impeccablement publiées.[2] Christine a laissé plus de 1600 Maximes, *Les Sentiments Héroïques et L'Ouvrage de Loisir,* des essais historiques, son autobiographie inachevée et une grande correspondance de genre philosophique et théologique.

Etat des recherches

L'activité de la reine en tant que protectrice des arts ainsi que sa vaste collection de manuscrits et de livres sont très bien étudiées, tandis que ses propres écrits sont restés dans l'ombre. Par conséquent, la reine Christine a souffert

---

[1] Edition en préparation, financée par L'Academie Royale des Lettres, Histoire et Antiquités: Eva Haettner Aurelius / Marie-Louise Rodén (éds.), *The Literary Works of Queen Christina of Sweden (1626-1689),* (Stockholm 2008). A présent, Christine est citée selon la transcription en français moderne par Jean François de Raymond, *Christine Reine de Suède: Apologies* (Editions du Cerf: Paris 1994).

[2] *Reuelaciones Sanctae Birgittae,* Libri I-VII, SSFS. Ser. 2, VII, 1-7 (Uppsala 1967-2001); *Reuelaciones extrauagantes,* SSFS. Ser. 2, V (Uppsala 1956); *Opera Minora Sanctae Birgittae,* SSFS. Ser. 2, VIII, 1-2, (Uppsala 1972, 1975).

Women's traditions in Europe
Frauentraditionen in Europa
Traditions des femmes en Europe

d'un jugement fort ambivalent et demeure défigurée par une anti-hagiographie diffamatoire, tandis que Brigitte reste encombrée de stéréotypes hagiographiques. Déjà au XVIIIe siecle, le finlandais Johann Arckenholtz, bibliothécaire à Kassel, a voulu défendre la reine contre les falsifications diffamatoires, surtout d'origine française. Repérant les sources concernant Christine dans les archives européennes, ce vaste dossier fut publié entre 1750 et 1760.[3] Il est regrettable que les transcriptions faites par Arckenholtz sont souvent embellies ou même eronnées. Entre 1837 et 1842, l'historien allemand Wilhelm Heinrich Grauert a présenté une analyse très sobre de la documentation relative à Christine, tant vérifiable que fabriquée.[4] En 1887, l'historien suédois Martin Weibull a bien démasqué la propagande française lancée contre Christine.[5] Son fils, l'historien Curt Weibull, a poursuivi cette réhabilitation de la reine par des études également solides. Il a d'ailleurs montré que l'exécution de Monaldeschi pour haute trahison à Fontainebleau en 1657 fut conforme à la juridiction royale sur sa cour, que Christine exerçait après l'abdication.[6] Malheureusement, cette érudition publiée en langue vernaculaire reste inaccessible à la recherche internationale. Ainsi, un historien français de littérature, René Pintard, a repris l'interprétation de Christine comme adhérente au "libertinage érudit", en attribuant aux pamphlets diffamatoires du XVIIe siecle une valeur historique qu'ils n'ont pas.[7]

Heureusement, des études impeccablement documentées sont maintenant accessibles en langue anglaise. L'historien norvégien Oskar Garstein a écrit une oeuvre magistrale sur la contre-Réforme en Scandinavie.[8] Son compte-rendu

---

[3]   Johann Arckenholtz (éd.), *Mémoires concernant Christine, Reine de Suède* I-IV (Amsterdam, Leipzig 1750-1760).

[4]   Wilhelm Heinrich Grauert, *Christina, Königin von Schweden und ihr Hof* I-II (E. Weber: Bonn 1837; 1842).

[5]   Martin Weibull, "Om 'Memoires de Chanut'", in: *Historisk Tidskrift* 7 (1887), 49-80, 151-192; *Historisk Tidskrift* 8 (1888), 1-28, 131-166.

[6]   Curt Weibull, *Drottning Christina: Studier och forskningar* (Natur och Kultur: Stockholm 1931); Curt Weibull, *Drottning Christina och Mondalesco* (Natur och Kultur: Stockholm 1936); Curt Weibull, *Christina of Sweden* (Natur och Kultur: Stockholm 1966).

[7]   Rene Pintard, *Le libertinage érudit dans la première moitié du XVIIe siecle* I-II (Paris 1943). Cf. la mystification de la reine libertine, reprise même par des auteurs suédois: Sven Stolpe, *Från Stoicism till Mystik: Studier i drottning Kristinas Maximer* (Bonniers: Stockholm 1959); Susanna Åkerman, *Queen Christina of Sweden and her Circle: The Transformation of a Seventeenth-Century Philosophical Libertine* (Brill: Leiden 1991).

[8]   Oskar Garstein, *Rome and the Counter-Reformation in Scandinavia* I-IV, (Brill: Leiden 1963-1992), spécialement IV: *The Age of Gustavus Adolphus and Queen Christina of Sweden 1622-1656.*

des textes relatifs à la conversion de Christine, laissés par ses interlocuteurs jésuites et ses biographes contemporains, est désormais indispensable pour comprendre l'abdication survenue en 1654. La carrière romaine de Christine et la collaboration avec son ami intime et fidèle, le cardinal Decio Azzolino, sont soigneusement etudiées par l'historienne suédoise Marie-Louise Rodén.[9] Il faut aussi signaler un étude approfondie sur l'éducation de Christine et une biographie précise de la reine, publiées récemment en suédois.[10]

Analyse du genre

Comme je l'ai fait pour Brigitte[11], il est important de considerer l'oeuvre de Christine dans une perspective de *Gender Studies*, où le caractère sexué de tout être humain, à la fois biologiquement programmé et culturellement déployé, sert de catégorie analytique principale.[12] En interprétant le discours de Christine sur Dieu et l'humanité comme structuré par son expérience humaine de femme, cette méthodologie pourrait clarifier son destin apparemment ambigu.[13] Pourquoi Christine a-t-elle renoncé solennellement au trône

---

[9] Marie-Louise Rodén, *Church Politics in Seventeenth-Century Rome: Cardinal Decio Azzolino, Queen Christina of Sweden and the Squadrone Volante* (Almqvist & Wicksell: Stockholm 2000).

[10] Leif Åslund, *Att fostra en kung: Om drottning Kristinas utbildning* (Atlantis: Stockholm 2005); Peter Englund, *Silvermasken: En kort biografi över drottning Kristina* (Bonniers: Stockholm 2006).

[11] "Birgitta of Sweden: a Model of Theological Inculturation", in: Kari Elisabeth Børresen / Kari Vogt, *Women's Studies of the Christian and Islamic Traditions: Ancient, Medieval and Renaissance Foremothers* (Kluwer Academic Publishers: Dordrecht 1993), 277-294; "Birgitta's Godlanguage: Exemplary Intention, Inapplicable Content", in: Øyvind Norderval / Katrine Lund Ore (éds.), *From Patristics to Matristics: Selected Articles on Christian Gender Models by Kari Elisabeth Børresen* (Herder Editrice: Roma 2002), 171-230; "Religious Feminism in the Middle Ages", in: Louise D'Arcens/Juanita Feros Ruys (éds.), *Maistresse of My Wit: Medieval Women, Modern Scholars* (Making the Middle Ages 7; Brepols: Turnhout 2004), 295-312.

[12] Ursula King, "Introduction: Gender and the Study of Religion", in: Ursula King (éd.), *Religion and Gender* (Blackwells: Oxford, 1995), 1-38.

[13] Kari Elisabeth Børresen, "Concordia Discors. La pensée de Christine de Suède sur Dieu et l'humanité. Esquisse préliminaire", in: *Augustinianum* 36 (1996), 237-254; "Christina's Discourse on God and Humanity", in: Marie-Louise Rodén (éd.), *Politics and Culture in the Age of Christina* (Suecoromana IV; Stockholm 1997), 43-53; "La religion de Christine de Suède", in: Börje Magnusson (éd.), *Cristina di Svezia e Roma* (Suecoromana V; Stockholm 1999), 9-20, "Le portrait de Christine du Suède selon ses écrits", in: Olivier Bonfait / Brigitte Marin (éds.), *Les portraits du pouvoir* (Académie de France: Rome 2003), 67-75, 104-105.

Women's traditions in Europe
Frauentraditionen in Europa
Traditions des femmes en Europe

de Suède, tout en désirant le récupérer après la mort du roi successeur en 1660? Déjà en 1656, elle avait cherché l'appui du cardinal Mazarin pour devenir reine de Naples. En 1668, elle voulait être élue reine de Pologne. Pourquoi Christine s'est-elle convertie à l'Eglise combattue par son père et territorialement amputée par la paix de Westphalie en 1648, résultant de sa propre habileté politique? Je propose de considérer l'abdication et la conversion de Christine comme également motivées par son désir fondamental d'autonomie. Comme femme intelligente, la reine refusait et de se soumettre au mariage et d'accepter une foi sans raison.

Devenir mâle

Née en 1626, Christine hérita du royaume après la mort de son père à la bataille de Lützen en 1632. Elle fut élevée comme un prince, installée comme reine régnante "contra naturam per legem" en 1644 et couronnée comme roi en 1650. Les écrits de Christine démontrent qu'elle a entièrement intériorisé le caractère viril de royauté sacré. En effet, cette formation anormale l'a fait régresser à l'androcentrisme foncier du christianisme primitif, où Adam en tant que prototype du genre humain imite le pouvoir royal de Dieu (Gen 1,26-27a; 2,7). Ce privilège de l'*imago Dei* est ensuite hérité par les fils d'Adam, tandis qu'Eve et ses filles ne sont théomorphes parce qu'elles sont créées en état de subordination (Gen 2,18-21; I Cor 11,7). D'autre part, dans l'ordre du salut, les femmes sont promues à l'image divine en devenant mâles par incorporation baptismale au Christ ressuscité (Gal 3,28; Col 3,10-11; Eph 4,13, EvThom 114). Il faut noter que dans l'Eglise ancienne, cette transformation en fils de Dieu et frères du Christ est ardemment poursuivie par les femmes elles-mêmes, et le thème de vertu virile est repris par les éloges patristiques des saintes martyres, vierges et veuves.[14]

C'est dans ce contexte de devenir mâle, c'est-à-dire pleinement humaine, que Christine se valorise par une déféminisation vertueuse, rendant grâce à Dieu d'être promue à la royauté virile:

> Il faut ici Seigneur, que je vous fasse un remerciement contraire à celui de ce grand homme, qui jadis vous remercia de l'avoir fait naître homme, et non pas femme. Car moi Seigneur, je vous rend grâce de m'avoir fait naître fille, d'autant plus que

---

[14] Le développment doctrinal est analysé dans Kari Elisabeth Børresen (éd.), *The Image of God: Gender Models in Judaeo-Christian Tradition* (Fortress Press: Minneapolis MN 1995). Cf. Kari Vogt, "'Becoming Male': a Gnostic, Early Christian and Islamic Metaphor", in: Børresen / Vogt, *Women's Studies of the Christian and Islamic Traditions*, 217-242.

vous m'avez fait la grâce de n'avoir fait passer aucune faiblesse de mon sexe jusque dans mon âme, que vous avez rendue par votre grâce toute virile, aussi bien que le reste de mon corps. Vous vous êtes servi de mon sexe pour me préserver des vices et des débauches du pays où je suis née; et après m'avoir condamnée au sexe plus faible, vous avez voulu m'exempter de toutes ses faiblesses ordinaires. Vous avez voulu m'emanciper aussi de toutes ses dépendences, en me faisant naître sur un trône où je devais commander seule. (Vie de Christine 4, 93).

Il faut noter que Christine fait ici allusion à l'action de grâces attribuée à Platon, d'être né Grec et non pas Barbare, homme et non pas femme. Cette combinaison ethno-androcentrique se trouve également dans la prière du Juif mâle, remerciant Dieu d'être créé Juif et non pas Gentil, homme et non pas femme. Choisie par Dieu pour excercer une autonomie de Roi, Christine est de ce fait devenue mâle, en transcendant son sexe subordonné. Curieusement, ce texte a été mal compris par quelques chercheurs ignorants de théologie historique, au point même de postuler une masculinisation physique de la reine!

Les deux corps de la reine

Pour Christine il en résulte une scission entre "the queen's two bodies", c'est-à-dire son corps politique andromorphe et son corps naturel féminin.[15] Ce conflit existentiel s'accentue par le devoir d'enfanter un héritier à son royaume. En effet, le mariage chrétien est de structure foncièrement hiérarchique, symbolisant l'union entre le Christ comme nouvel Adam théomorphe et l'Eglise comme nouvelle Eve non théomorphe (Eph 5,32). Tout en supprimant le mariage sacramentel comme symbole de l'union indissoluble du Christ avec l'Eglise, la doctrine luthérienne valorisait le *pater familias* comme représentant de la *patria potestas* du Dieu Père. Christine refuse donc de soumettre son corps naturel à un mari, trouvant insupportable de sacrifier ainsi son autonomie personnelle. Le mari proposé était le duc Charles Gustave de Pfalz, un

---

15 Pour le caractère théomorphe du roi, voir Ernst H. Kantorowicz, *The King's Two Bodies: Studies in Medieval Theology* (Princeton University Press: Princeton NJ 1957). Elizabeth I, sans accent sur "sex/gender", est étudiée par Marie Axton, *The Queen's Two Bodies: Drama and the Elizabethian Succession* (Studies in History; Royal Historical Society: London 1977). Carole Levin souligne que "Mary and Elizabeth were legally kings, that is males, for the purpose of ruling", *The Heart and Stomach of a King: Elizabeth I and the Politics of Sex and Power*, 110 (University of Pennsylvania Press: Philadelphia PA 1982). Cf. l'étude solide en suédois, Karin Tegenborg Falkdalen, *Kungen är en kvinna: Retorik och praktik kring kvinnliga monarker under tidigmodern tid* (Umeå University Press: Umeå 2003), summary 207-211: "The King is a Woman".

Women's traditions in Europe
Frauentraditionen in Europa
Traditions des femmes en Europe

cousin né en Suède. L'électeur Frédéric Guillaume de Brandenbourg, candidat humainement plus adéquat et qui restait son ami, était inéligible car calviniste.

En 1647 le Conseil Royal déclara que Christine garderait son autonomie de reine régnante après son mariage. Néanmoins, en 1649 Christine affirma devant ce Conseil son choix definitif du célibat. Afin de sauvegarder la monarchie héréditaire, Christine réussit à imposer Charles Gustave comme prince héritier du royaume avec droit de succession pour sa descendance mâle. Approuvée par le *Riksdag* (Parlement) le 7 octobre 1650, cette émancipation de Christine de son devoir procréatif fut suivie par sa coronation solennelle le 20 octobre, selon le cérémonial du sacre des rois suédois.

Il est significatif que dans l'autobiographie, Christine manifeste une nette ambivalence envers son rôle de reine autonome, qu'elle a d'ailleurs très efficacement rempli:

> Mon sentiment est que les femmes ne devraient jamais régner; et j'en suis si persuadée, que j'aurais ôté sans doute tout le droit de succession à mes filles, si je me fusse mariée. Car j'aurais sans doute plus aimé mon royaume que mes enfants, et c'est les trahir que de permettre que la succession tombe aux filles. Je dois être crue d'autant plus que je parle contre mon propre intérêt. Mais je fais profession de dire la vérité à mes dépens. Il est presqu'impossible qu'une femme se puisse acquitter dignement des devoirs du trône, soit qu'elle gouverne pour elle-même, ou pour son pupille. L'ignorance des femmes, la faiblesse de leur âme, de leur corps et de leur esprit, les rendent incapables de régner (Vie de Christine 9, 135).

En effet, ce texte illustre la situation existentiellement anormale de Christine, qui par son éducation mâle a intériorisé l'androcentrisme classique sans être dressée à la subordination féminine. Il en résulte une misogynie sociobiologique, comme elle l'exprime sans ambages:

> Le sexe féminin est d'un grand embarras, et d'un grand obstacle à la vertu et au mérite. Ce défaut de la nature est le plus grand qu'on saurait avoir; il est presque incorrigible et peu de personnes se sont tirées avec honneur de cet embarras. (Les Sentiments Héroïques 340, 357).

Foi et raison

A partir de 1646, Christine apprécia le catholicisme éclairé d'Hector-Pierre Chanut, un diplomate érudit qui représentait la France à Stockholm jusqu'en 1651. Dans une lettre au Secrétaire d'Etat (datée du 1er février 1648), Chanut souligne que Christine fut plus intéressée par la relation entre foi chrétienne et raison philosophique, que par les controverses des variations protestantes.[16] Aussitôt, Chanut établit le contact entre son ami René Descartes et la reine, d'abord en lui communiquant leur propre correspondance philosophique.[17] Dans une lettre adressée directement à Christine (datée du 20 novembre 1647), Descartes lui présente un traité sur Dieu comme le Souverain Bien.[18] Le philosophe se montre ici foncièrement catholique, en présupposant une affinité commensurable entre Dieu et l'être humain créé à l'image divine. Descartes se rattache donc à la notion patristique de *theosis*, dans le sens que Dieu s'est fait homme afin que l'humanité soit divinisée. En accentuant que "le libre arbitre est de soi la chose la plus noble que puisse être en nous", ce volontarisme rationnnel est entièrement incompatible avec l'anthropologie protestante, tant calviniste que luthérienne, qui élimine toute coopération humaine en faveur de la souveraineté totale de Dieu. Invité à Stockholm en 1649 et contraint de se présenter devant la reine à cinq heures du matin pour des séances surtout consacrées à la mathématique, Descartes mourut le 11 février 1650 d'une grippe virulente. Il faut noter un certain désillusionement réciproque des deux personnages. Avant de rencontrer la reine (lettre à Chanut, datée du 26 février 1649), Descartes exprime son admiration pour la capacité intellectuelle de Christine:

> Il me semble que cette Princesse est bien plus créée à l'image de Dieu que le reste des hommes, d'autant plus qu'elle peut étendre ses soins au plus grand nombre de diverses occupations en même temps.[19]

Plus tard, écrivant à sa femme savante préférée, la princesse palatine Elisabeth (lettre datée du 9 octobre 1649), Descartes critique l'intérêt exagéré de Christine pour les textes anciens: "Elle est extrêmement portée à l'étudies des lettres; mais, pour ce que je ne sache point qu'elle ait encore rien vu de la Philosophie".[20] De son côté, dans une lettre adressée à l'érudit calviniste

---

[16] Victor de Swarte, *Descartes directeur spirituel: Correspondance avec la princesse palatine et la reine Christine de Suède* (F. Alcan: Paris 1904), 177-186.

[17] Cette relation est décrite par Jean-François de Raymond, *La reine et le philosophe: Descartes et Christine de Suède* (Lettres Modernes: Paris 1993).

[18] Jacques Chevalier (éd.), *René Descartes. Lettres sur la morale: Correspondance avec la princesse Elisabeth, Chanut et la reine Christine* (Boivin: Paris 1935), 281-285.

[19] Chevalier, *René Descartes*, 296-298.

[20] Chevalier, *René Descartes*, 221-222.

Women's traditions in Europe
Frauentraditionen in Europa
Traditions des femmes en Europe

Claude Saumaise (datée du 9 mars 1650) et récemment se retrouvée, Christine est mordante:

> il est certain qu'il (Descartes) avait de très bonnes parties mais il est vrai qu'il en jugeait lui-même trop à son avantage, et la bonne opinion qu'il avait de soi le fit mépriser tout le monde, il se vanta une fois en ma présence que lui seul connaissait la vérité, et qu'elle était inconnue au reste des mortels ...[21]

Lorsque Christine souligna l'influence de Descartes en termes édifiants dans une lettre à Antoine de Courtin, résident de France à Copenhague (datée du 30 août 1667), elle voulut obtenir une réinhumation du philosophe en terre bénite à Paris:

> et nous certifions mesme par les présentes, qu'il a beaucoup contribué à nostre glorieuse conversion, et que la Providence de Dieu s'est servie de luy, et de son illustre amy, ledit Sieur de Chanut, pour nous en donner les premières lumières que sa grâce et miséricorde achevèrent après à nous faire embrasser la religion catholique, apostolique romaine, que ledit sieur de Cartes a tousjiours constamment professé, et dans laquelle il est mort avec toutes les marques de la vraye piété, que nostre religion exige de touts ceux qui la professent.[22]

Il ne faut donc pas surestimer la responsabilité de Descartes pour la conversion de Christine, tandis que l'influence du catholicisme érudit de Chanut est indubitable.

Mission jésuite

Le 2 août 1651, Christine confia au jésuite Antonio Macedo, en guise de négociant du roi de Portugal, une lettre au Père Général de la Société, demandant de recevoir à sa cour deux savants de l'ordre, déguisés en gentilhommes touristes.[23] Cette stratégie de Christine fut extrêmement audacieuse, parce qu'une reine catholique résidant en Suède aurait risqué sa tête.

La Réforme luthérienne étant confirmée en 1593, il était depuis 1617 defendu pour tous les citoyens suédois, y compris le monarque, d'être catholiques. Il est donc important de noter que Christine annonca devant le Conseil

---

[21] Maryvonne Perrot, "Descartes, Saumaise et Christine de Suède. Une lettre inédite de Christine à Saumaise du 9 mars 1650", in: *Les études philosophiques* (janvier-mars 1984), 1-9, cit. 4.

[22] de Swarte, *Descartes directeur spirituel*, 196-198.

[23] Lettre citée par Garstein, *Rome and the Counter-Reformation in Scandinavia IV*, 635.

Royal son intention d'abdiquer le 7 août, cinq jours après l'envoi de cette lettre à Rome. Le genre apologétique du dossier jésuite officiel ne clarifie pas suffisamment les motifs de sa conversion, toute information essentielle fut sans doute communiquée oralement. Néanmoins, les rapports connus des Pères Paolo Casati et Francesco Malines, qui arrivèrent à Stockholm le 6 mars 1652, offrent quelques renseignements.[24] Casati quitta la Suède déjà en mai, Malines resta encore une année.

Dans une lettre à Alexandre VII (datée du 5 décembre 1655), Casati précise l'évolution intellectuelle de la reine en matière de religion: pendant cinq ans, elle avait exploré les variantes du christianisme, le judaïsme et même l'islam. Néanmoins, sa compréhension perspicace du pluralisme religieux comme phénomène socio-culturel n'avait pas éliminé sa croyance en l'existence de Dieu, c'est pourquoi Christine poursuivit sa recherche d'une foi acceptable pour sa raison. Il est à noter que Malines dans une lettre (en novembre 1655, probablement au Père Général Goswin Nickel) mentionne encore l'influence sur Christine des savants catholiques visitant sa cour. Il est important d'observer que selon le biographe contemporain de Christine, le cardinal jésuite Sforza Pallavicino, la reine proposa d'obtenir la dispense papale d'embrasser la foi catholique secrètement, afin de garder son royaume en communiant une fois par an selon le rite luthérien. Cette possibilité fut exclue *a priori* par Casati et Malines; ainsi, Christine se résigna à abdiquer pour se convertir.[25]

Amazone et fille de l'Eglise

Le 6 juin 1654, la grandiose cérémonie d'abdication en faveur de l'ex-fiancé Charles X Gustave, bientôt transformé en roi très martial, eut lieu devant le *Riksdag* assemblé au château d'Uppsala. Il faut souligner que tout en abdiquant son Règne, sauf quelques territoires pour assurer ses revenus futurs, Christine gardait son autonomie juridique de reine régnante. Quittant aussitôt la Suède en passant par Bruxelles, où elle fut reçue dans l'Eglise romaine *in forma privata* la veille de Noël 1654, Christine entra en triomphe à Rome le 20 décembre 1655. Avant de franchir le territoire pontifical, sa profession officielle de foi catholique eut lieu à Innsbruck le 3 novembre devant l'ex-luthérien Lucas Holstenius, légat du pape et préfet de la Bibliothèque Vaticane.

---

[24] Garstein, *Rome and the Counter-Reformation in Scandinavia IV*, 594-598.

[25] Sforza Pallavicino, *Vita di Alessandro VII*, III, 11 (Prato 1839), 348: "Ed udito di no, perché la simulazione di falso culto è atto intrinseco iniurioso a Dio, soggiunse: adunque bisogna deporre il regno."

Women's traditions in Europe
Frauentraditionen in Europa
Traditions des femmes en Europe

Christine eut l'honneur d'être logée au Vatican jusqu'au 26 décembre, dans la *Torre dei Venti*. Par délicatesse envers cette reine venue du Nord, la citation de Jér 1,14: "Ab Aquilone pandetur omne malum" (tout mal vient du Nord) sur la fresque décrivant le vent septentrional dans la *Sala della Meridiana*, fut couverte. Il est à remarquer que ce même verset fut neutralisé lors de la canonisation de Brigitte en 1391. Dans sa bulle, le pape romain Boniface IX loue cette sainte veuve comme une femme forte venue du Nord pour le renouveau de l'Eglise: "ut etiam ab Aquilone aliquid boni esset".

La reine du Nord fut confirmée par le pape dans la basilique de *San Pietro* le jour de Noël, comme Christina Alexandra Maria. Il est significatif que dans son discours, assise à la droite d'Alexandre VII, Christine se présenta comme amazone nordique et fille du grand Alexandre.[26] En effet, selon une lettre adressée par Holstenius au Secrétaire d'Etat, le cardinal Giulio Rospigliosi (datée du 23 novembre 1655), la reine refusa de rester muette sur la scène, en baisant seulement les pieds et la main du pape. Holstenius suggéra donc de lui accorder la parole pour expliquer sa venue, si possible en respectant l'interdiction apostolique selon I Cor 14,34.[27]

Dans une autre lettre à Rospigliosi (datée du 8 décembre 1655), Holstenius se défend des objections provoquées par la cérémonie de réconciliation de la reine ex-hérétique, qu'il a officiée à Innsbruck. Holstenius explique pourquoi il a permis à la reine d'entrer dans l'église par la porte principale en la faisant baiser un crucifix, conformément au cérémonial utilisé pour les Royaux catholiques d'Espagne et les Princes d'Autriche. Il souligne que Christine était déjà catholique du fait de sa profession secrète à Bruxelles, reconnue par le pape. En perspective oecuménique de notre temps, où le protestantisme n'est plus défini comme hérésie, c'est-à-dire aberration doctrinale, mais plutôt dans le sens de rupture institutionnelle, ce reproche apparaît décidément suranné. La seconde contestation reste pertinente, étant donné que l'incapacité cultuelle du sexe féminin, *impedimentum sexus*, persiste dans la majorité non protestante du christianisme. Par conséquent, les femmes sont encore exclues du sacerdoce et de l'épiscopat dans l'Eglise catholique,

---

[26] *Relazione del Viaggio*: "e recevimento fatto da N.S. Papa Alessandro VII nello Stato Eccl:co, e in Roma alla Maestà di Cristina Alessandra Regina di Suetia." Archivio Segreto Vaticano, Armadio XV, 89, fol. 1-143, ref. 106 r-v.

[27] Archivio Segreto Vaticano, Lettere di Cardinali 99, fol. 134r-135r.

cf. canon 1024 du *Codex Iuris Canonici* (1983), comme dans les Eglises orthodoxes. Il est donc reproché à Holstenius d'utiliser le mot *suspensio*, selon la *Forma absolutionis*: "absolvo te ab omni vinculo excommunicationis, suspensionis et interdicti", parce qu'il s'agit de suspension des fonctions ecclésiastiques, inapplicable à Christine en tant que femme. C'est pourquoi Holstenius souligne que, comme reine régnante, Christine exerçait une juridiction archiépiscopale en tant que chef de l'Eglise luthérienne en Suède: "non sola da regina, ma anche da vescova et arcivescova."[28] C'est-à-dire que par son abdication, Christine s'est déposée elle-même comme archevêque!

En effet, la carrière romaine de la reine reste fortement marquée de cette collision entre l'amazone scandinave et l'ideal méditerranéen de fille bien rangée de l'Eglise. Tout comme la nouvelle convertie n'etait pas conforme à la subordination féminine, elle se montrait aussi étrangère au rôle normatif de femme pieuse, sans doute prévu par Alexandre VII. La réalité vécue à Rome correspondait peu à l'exposé apologétique présenté par les Pères jésuites à Stockholm. Comme Brigitte trois siècles auparavant, Christine montrait une capacité admirable à survivre en exil. Son tempérament autonome et sa largesse tolérante la rendaient peu compatible aux exigences papales, surtout celles du zélé Innocent XI. Néanmoins, en tant que reine défendant la monarchie absolue, Christine endossait le pontificat monarchique en distinguant entre vicaire du Christ et personne du pape: "Les faiblesses, les crimes et les fautes des papes n'effacent pas leur sacré caractère, ni ne peuvent détruire leur autorité, qui mérite nos respects, quoique souvent leurs personnes ne les méritent pas" (L'Ouvrage de Loisir 984, 281). Christine cherchait donc l'unité ecclésiale en faisant front à la fois au séparatisme gallican et au papalisme romain: "Dieu a donné son infaillibilité au pape et non pas aux conciles. Il n'a pas établi une république, mais une monarchie, à laquelle il s'est engagé de tout soumettre un jour" (L'Ouvrage de Loisir 989, 281-282).

Le 19 avril 1689, jour de la mort de Christine, le cardinal Azzolino écrit au cardinal Alderano Cibo, Secrétaire d'Etat, pour obtenir des funerailles solennelles à la basilique de *San Pietro*, où la reine sera enterrée dans la crypte papale. Contre l'instruction testamentaire des cérémonies privées et sans pompe, Azzolino jugea un tel honneur proportionné à la grandeur de la reine

---

[28] Archivio Segreto Vaticano, Lettere di Cardinali 99, fol. 148r-150r.

Women's traditions in Europe
Frauentraditionen in Europa
Traditions des femmes en Europe

Christine morte comme fille fidèle à l'Eglise.[29] Cette formule fait écho aux derniers mots de Thérèse d'Avila, morte en 1582, canonisée en 1622 comme réformatrice anti-protestante et nommée *doctor ecclesiae* en 1970: "Je meurs en tant que fille de l'Eglise." Le placement de l'épitaphe de Christine, insérée sur la colonne de sainte Thérèse dans la basilique de *San Pietro*, est ainsi bien approprié.

Conclusion

L'abdication du royaume en 1654, fut-elle causée par la conversion de Christine, devenue officielle en 1655?

Analysant sa carrière en perspective de *gender*, je trouve cette question souvent mal posée, parce que les deux événements sont chronologiquement disparates, mais existentiellement inséparables. Déjà en 1649, Christine déclara qu'elle ne voulait pas se marier. Lorsqu'elle réussit à imposer son ex-fiancé comme héritier du royaume en 1650, elle assura ainsi son autonomie personnelle et la possibilité d'abdication. Lorsqu'elle déclara vouloir abdiquer en 1651, sa conversion était déjà en cours. Ainsi, Christine a finalement réussi à éviter la subordination du mariage et à se libérer du luthéranisme imposé au monarque. D'autre part, l'abdication a empêché sa sécurité économique en tant que reine exilée, ce qui explique ses efforts sans succès pour régner à Naples, reprendre le trône en Suède ou gagner celui de Pologne. Néanmoins, en insistant sur la suprématie du catholicisme, Christine n'a jamais pu reconnaître qu'elle se soit trompée en abdiquant, un acte indispensable pour sa conversion. Paradoxalement, afin d'obtenir sa liberté corporelle et intellectuelle, Christine s'est placée dans une voie sans issue, bloquée par les axiomes tant androcentriques que confessionnels.

Il est donc important de considérer le destin ambivalent de Christine dans le contexte européen du pouvoir politique des femmes.[30] Régnantes "contra naturam per legem", ces femmes extraordinaires n'invoquaient pas, comme les Mères de l'Eglise médiévale, une autorité charismatique donnée par Dieu.

---

[29] Marie-Louise Rodén, "The Burial of Queen Christina of Sweden in St. Peter's Church", in: *Scandinavian Journal of History* 12 (1987), 63-70, cit. 69: "E morta la Regina, et è morta con dispositione e sentimenti da santa, e da vera e fedelissima figlia di Dio e della Chiesa Cattolica".

[30] Voir l'étude bien documentée sur les femmes régnantes en Europe aux XVe et XVIe siècles, Sharon L. Jansen *The Monstrous Regiment of Women: Female Rulers in Early Modern Europe* (Palgrave Macmillan: New York 2002).

En effet, Christine montrait peu d'intérêt pour *sancta Birgitta*. Selon une anecdote rapportée de Flandre lors de son voyage vers Rome, un bon jésuite à Louvain a flatté la reine en la comparant à la sainte suédoise. Avec ironie, Christine riposta: "J'aime plutôt qu'on me mette entre les Sages."[31] Ainsi, la stratégie rationelle des grandes femmes dans l'histoire de l'Europe peut inspirer la théologie féministe du XXIe siècle à poursuivre la Réforme matristique du christianisme.

In this article the writings – more than 1600 Maxims, an Autobiography, historical essays – by Queen Christina of Sweden (1626-1689) are analysed from a gender perspective. Christina, daughter of the Protestant warlord Gustav II Adolph, inherited her father's kingdom in 1632. Installed as reigning queen in 1644, Christina was crowned as a king in 1650. In 1654, she abdicated in favour of her cousin Charles Gustav, whom she had appointed as her heir before the coronation. After abdication she left Sweden and was officially received into the Catholic Church before entering Rome in 1655. Insisting on her royal autonomy, Christina became patroness of Arts and Letters and influenced curial politics through her intimate friend, cardinal Decio Azzolino. Educated as a prince in order to function as a king, Christina had internalised the Ancient Christian ideal of becoming male, with consequent conflict between her female "body natural" and her male "body politic". Christina's life and writings illustrate her quest for existential and intellectual autonomy. She refused to marry, i.e. to accept wifely submission, pregnancy and childbirth. Her very solid formation in 17th-century philosophy, theology and science made her seek to reconcile faith and reason. Unsatisfied with Lutheranism (compulsory in Sweden since 1617) the queen was impressed by the erudite Catholicism of French *savants* visiting her court. Exiled in Rome until her death in 1689, Christina soon discovered that the ideal *Mater Ecclesia* presented to her in Stockholm did not correspond to ecclesiastical reality.

In diesem Artikel werden die Schriften der Königin Christina von Schweden (1626-1689) – über 1600 Sentenzen, eine Autobiographie und historische Essays – aus einer *gender*-Perspektive analysiert. Christina, Tochter des protestantischen Kriegsherrn Gustav II Adolph, erbte das Königreich ihres Vaters im Jahr 1632. Nachdem sie 1644 als regierende Königin eingesetzt worden war, wurde sie 1650 zum König gekrönt. Im Jahr 1654 dankte sie zu Gunsten ihres Cousins Karl Gustav ab, den sie vor ihrer Krönung zu ihrem Erben bestimmt hatte. Nach ihrer Abdankung verließ sie Schweden und wurde offiziell in die katholische Kirche aufgenommen, bevor

---

[31] Citée dans Curt Weibull, "Om drottning Kristinas tronskifte och tronavsägelse", in: *Scandia* 28 (1962), 197-326, ici 305.

Women's traditions in Europe
Frauentraditionen in Europa
Traditions des femmes en Europe

sie 1655 nach Rom kam. Christina bestand auf ihrer königlichen Autonomie, förderte die schönen Künste und Wissenschaften und beeinflusste die Politik der Kurie über ihren engen Freund Kardinal Decio Azzolino. Da sie als ein Prinz erzogen wurde, der König werden sollte, hatte sie das frühchristliche Ideal des Männlichwerdens internalisiert – mit entsprechenden daraus resultierenden Konflikten zwischen ihrem "natürlichen Körper" und ihrem "politischen Körper". Christinas Leben und ihre Schriften zeigen ihr Streben nach existenzieller und intellektueller Autonomie. Sie weigerte sich zu heiraten, das heißt die Unterwerfung als Ehefrau, Schwangerschaft und Geburten zu akzeptieren. Ihre profunde Bildung in der Philosophie, Theologie und Naturwissenschaft des 17. Jahrhunderts ließen sie nach einer Versöhnung zwischen Glaube und Vernunft suchen. Unbefriedigt von der lutherischen Konfession, die in Schweden seit 1617 obligatorisch war, war die Königin stattdessen beeindruckt vom gelehrten Katholizismus der französischen *Savants*, die ihren Hof besuchten. Allerdings musste sie in ihrem römischen Exil, das bis zu ihrem Tod 1689 währte, schon bald entdecken, dass die ideale *Mater Ecclesia*, die ihr in Stockholm präsentiert worden war, nicht der kirchlichen Realität entsprach.

Kari Elisabeth Børresen (*1932), Senior Professor at the Department of Church History, Oslo University 2003-. Dr. Phil. at Oslo University 1968 with *Subordination et Equivalence. Nature et rôle de la femme d'après Augustin et Thomas d'Aquin*. 1982-2000: Research Professor, Royal Norwegian Ministry of Culture, 2000-2002: Professor of Historical Theology/Gender Studies, Oslo University. She is Theol Dr *honoris causa* at Uppsala University, member of the Norwegian Academy of Science and Letters, and has been visiting professor at a number of European and US universities. She has coordinated several projects and networks in Gender Studies in Religion. Current research interest: Religion, Gender and Human Rights, as is shown in Kari Elisabeth Børresen / Sara Cabibbo (éds.), *Gender, Religion, Human Rights in Europe* (Herder Editrice: Roma 2006).

Journal of the European Society of Women in Theological Research 15 (2007) 177-187.
doi: 10.2143/ESWTR.15.0.2022777

Else-Britt Nilsen

Religious Identity and National Loyalty: Sisters in War

2001 is forever marked by the 11 September attack on the Twin Towers. A few days after the event, a young woman stopped another woman in central Oslo, asking for the nearest bus stop. The young woman had a foreign accent and wore the *hijab*. The second woman was helpful and walked her to the stop. Then her helper received the shock of her life. An older woman stepped out in front of them, looked hatefully at the Muslim girl and spat at her – "every Muslim is a terrorist!"

This was not the first time veiled women have met with scepticism or open hostility in Norway. The Reformation came to Norway mainly as a result of the conversion of King Christian III of Denmark-Norway, who in 1537 by force established the Evangelical-Lutheran faith as the official and only religion of the country.[1] All the monasteries had to be suppressed. By the mid-19th century however things had changed. The first women religious wearing their habits and veils were seen on the streets of the capital in 1868. They had a different outlook on Christian life from what was considered normal at the time, and they were not only Catholics; they belonged to obscure religious orders.

The "foreignness" of the sisters, their Catholic background, language, religious habit and unmarried state, all went against the Norwegian, Protestant sense of national identity. They represented a counter-culture that at best was exotic and charming, but quite often just meaningless or downright unattractive: "An unsettled and foreign population whose way of life was antithetical to that of the 'Norwegian mainstream'."[2]

The young Muslim woman mentioned in the introduction was humiliated by being associated with atrocities committed on a different continent. What

---

[1] Oskar Garstein, *Rome and the Counter-Reformation in Scandinavia* I-II, Studies in the history of Christian thought vol. 46-47 (Leiden: Brill 1992). Overview, see: http://www.kirken.no/english/engelsk.cfm?artid=5730

[2] Here I am paraphrasing an observation on Arabs in Britain today. See Caroline Nagel, "Constructing difference and sameness: the politics of assimilation in London's Arab communities", in: *Ethnic and Racial Studies* 25 (March/2002), 258-287, here 268.

Women's traditions in Europe
Frauentraditionen in Europa
Traditions des femmes en Europe

happens when the atrocities occur in the same country and are directed against the people with and for whom you are working? What happens when this continues for a long period, and when the declared enemy is your compatriot, maybe your own brother?

This study is focused on a group of Catholic sisters who found themselves in such an extreme situation, i.e. during the occupation of Norway during World War II. Sources for this enquiry include material collected by the author: interviews, correspondence, questionnaires, archival material.

When we choose to present individual experiences in a specific situation, this indicates a micro-historical approach,[3] but the macro-historical perspective should not be forgotten.[4] For obvious reasons macro-history is close to events of political or ecclesiastical relevance, events that are central to our context. Nevertheless, macro-history tends to be both centralist and linear. However, micro-history has its obvious limitations as well. To what extent may one generalise from just one or a few cases? Micro-history is narrative by nature, and may – at worst – degenerate into romantic and fictitious stories.[5] Nor can we avoid failures of individual memory.

In this article, we alternate between an individual micro-historical and a general macro-historical level. Thus, we hope to shed light on a hitherto unknown fragment of the history of religious sisters in Norway during the Second World War. Our limited material will not allow us to draw firm conclusions; several themes are only touched upon in passing or not at all.

Thunderclouds over Europe

After the German attack on Poland on 1 September 1939, France and Great Britain declared war on Germany. Two days later, the Catholic Bishop of Oslo, Jacob Mangers, wrote a letter addressed to the Catholics of his Vicariate asking the faithful to give and to do more in order to allow the work of the Church

---

[3]   The expression "micro-history" is borrowed from the social sciences, especially social anthropology. The Norwegian anthropologist, Fredrik Barth, has often used the expression "microlevel" for an individually related scale and "macro-level" for society's aggregate scale. Fredrik Barth (ed.), *Scale and social organization* (Universitetsforlaget: Oslo 1978).

[4]   On the relation between the two approaches, see Birgitta Odén, *Leda vid livet. Fyra mikrohistriska essäer om självmordets historia* (Historiska media: Lund 1998), 9-15. For a more detailed study of the emergence of micro-history in post-modern opposition to the earlier very popular sociohistorical macro-history, see Georg Iggers, *Historiography in the twentieth century: From Scientific Objectivity to the Postmodern Challenge* (Hanover, NH: University Press of New England 1997).

[5]   Odén, *Leda vid livet*, 13.

to continue. Until then, foreign financial aid had supported this work; now that this was no longer possible, the sisters and other Catholics were expected to do their best in order to let the Church continue its work in the various cities and towns of the country.

The spiritual welfare of the people was Mangers' primary concern. From now on, prayers for peace were to be included in all masses. The faithful were asked to practice charity when they were among others, friends and enemies. The Bishop, a native of Luxembourg, warned the clergy not to take sides for or against either of the warring parties in their public statements; Norway was still a neutral country.

The growth of Catholicism had been very slow but continual, from about one hundred Catholics in 1850, to about 3.000 in 1940, i.e. one tenth of one percent of the total population (2.9 million).[6] The Catholic infrastructure, however, had expanded much faster than one might expect, given the relatively small number of Catholic faithful. For a long period, there were more Catholic health and educational institutions than there were parishes. This was partly due to the active involvement of various foreign congregations of women religious in the country.

After difficult years during and after the First World War, the sisters modernised and developed their various institutions. Nevertheless, just when the building efforts had reached their peak, war broke out.[7] At the beginning of 1940, there were 560 women religious in Norway.[8] They worked all over the country, from the extreme north to the south. In every city or town where there were sisters, there was a Catholic hospital and often a Catholic school as well. The sisters played a considerable part in the medical system of the country. They also looked after the priests, worked as sacristans, assured the maintenance of the parish churches, and contributed financially to their upkeep. In short, at the beginning of 1940, the sisters were invaluable members of the

---

[6] In 2005 there were 42.500 registered Catholics out of a total population of 4.6 million. (The number of women religious was 180). http://www.katolsk.no/norge/#Statistikk

[7] Else-Britt Nilsen, "Med Vår Herre selv og Norges legestand i ryggen: De katolske hospitaler", in: *Kirke og Kultur* 98 (1993), 101-121, here 117.

[8] About a half belonged to the Congregation of Saint Joseph of Chambéry, a quarter to the Norwegian Congregation of Francis Xavier, the rest to different congregations from Germany, Netherlands and France. See Susanne Malchau and Else-Britt Nilsen, "Tables and Figures," in: Yvonne Maria Werner (ed.), *Nuns and Sisters in the Nordic Countries after the Reformation: A Female Counter-Culture in Modern Society* (Studia Missionalia Svecana XC; The Swedish Institute of Mission Research [SIM]: Uppsala 2004), 419-436, here 424-425.

Women's traditions in Europe
Frauentraditionen in Europa
Traditions des femmes en Europe

Church under *ordinary* conditions, but even more so when an aggressive war machine like the German *Wehrmacht* invaded the country.

Only a few of the sisters were Norwegian by birth – twenty seven! The others came mainly from France, the Netherlands and Poland. But the majority of the foreign sisters came from Germany, the country that was to occupy Norway for five years. German sisters made up approximately sixty per cent of all women religious in the country at the time.[9] This was particularly so for the Sisters of Saint Joseph. They belonged to a French congregation, but at the beginning of 1940, nearly ninety percent of the Sisters of Saint Joseph in Norway were German. Only five per cent of them were French.

It is reasonable to assume that the large number of Germans among the Sisters of Saint Joseph presented a challenge to the local environment. The German soldiers spoke their mother tongue, and since many of them were Catholics, they visited both the Catholic churches and the sisters' oratories.[10] It is easy to imagine the tensions, uncertainty and conflicting loyalties both within the multinational communities and in relation to society around them. The universality of the Catholic Church did not imply that Catholics did not love their own country. Conflicting loyalties are always possible when the country of one's birth and the country where one is currently living are not only different, but especially so when they are at war with each other.

After its return to Norway following the Reformation, the Catholic Church was regarded as a foreign element for a long time. Would society regard the Church and its adherents as allies in a crisis, as being as "Norwegian" as everybody else? Or, were they still seen as foreigners and strangers, whose loyalty was an unknown quantity?

The invasion of Norway – Material damage and confiscations
On 8 April 1940, a Polish submarine off the Norwegian south coast torpedoed a German troop transport ship, the "Rio de Janeiro". During the afternoon and evening, the Norwegian navy and fishing boats brought living and

---

9   319 were actually born in Germany. Usually the sisters became Norwegian citizens when they had been in the country for the required number of years. The exceptions were the Dominican sisters and the sisters of Saint Anthony. See Else-Britt Nilsen, "Religious Identity and National Loyality: Women Religious in Norway during the Second World War", in: Werner (ed.), *Nuns and Sisters*, 213-253, here 218.
10 Johs. J. Duin, *Elisabethsøstrenes historie i Norge 1880-1980* (Elisabethsøstrene: Oslo 1980), 21.

dead soldiers to the nearby towns and villages. In Kristiansand the town's Catholic hospital got involved: "What were these foreign ships doing in Norwegian waters? What was the 'Rio de Janeiro' doing just off the Norwegian coast? [...] The white nurses went quickly along the corridors, they reacted humanely to human beings, they did not know of any enemy – yet."[11]

The following day, war broke out. The public and their political leaders had believed that Norway would be able to stay out of the war. They thought that the country was strategically situated on the periphery, protected by British naval power, and that keeping Norway neutral would be in the interest of the warring nations on both sides. It was not immediately clear who was the aggressor.

Catholic and non-Catholic properties were damaged indiscriminately during the fighting. Immediately after the occupation of Kristiansand, the Sisters of Saint Joseph received a call from an officer belonging to the German army medical corps, who wanted the hospital cleared of Norwegian patients. Shortly afterwards, the *Wehrmacht* confiscated the whole building, and gave it a new name: *Ortslazarett*. German doctors and medical staff took charge of treatment and care. The sisters who were nurses had to work under German military command. But when the new "hospital administration" took it upon themselves to remove the crucifixes from the wards, the prioress ordered that they were to be put back in place. This was done immediately.[12]

Saint Elisabeth's Hospital in Tromsø in the far North was also taken over by German forces early on. Their doctors and patients respected the sisters, although the sisters (most of them German) did nothing to hide their attitude.[13] In addition to hospitals, other Catholic properties were taken over by the Germans, such as schools, parish halls, and vicarages.

Life must go on

The shock of being occupied faded and everyday life continued. Work was resumed at the hospitals that had been closed temporarily. Those sisters who

---

[11] Gottlieb Rieber-Mohn, "Vi var med. Glimt av den katolske kirke i Norge under okkupasjonen", in: *St. Olav* 57 (1945), 83-86, 93-95, here 83-84.

[12] Informant Marie-Kristin Riosianu (1935-), Norwegian Joseph Sister.

[13] Duin, *Elisabethsøstrenes*, 23. Johannes Mertens, *Geschichte der Kongregation der Schwestern von der Heiligen Elisabeth 1842-1992* II (Kongregation der Schwestern von der Heiligen Elisabeth: Reinbek 1998), 770.

Women's traditions in Europe
Frauentraditionen in Europa
Traditions des femmes en Europe

had to work under German command must have felt alienated at their own hospitals, but by continuing their work they were able to help some civilian patients as well. Daily life was burdensome: the number of patients needing treatment and care was at a record high, and the sisters were overworked.

But what about the unavoidable tensions caused by the occupation? The sisters were human beings, living at close quarters in small, enclosed communities. When the war broke out, the general prioress of the Sisters of Saint Francis Xavier, Beata Höfling, said: "We are sisters from different nations; the war is not to be discussed among ourselves." Aase adds: "The German sisters knew what was going on in Germany, but did not agree with it. And Mother Beata, who was German herself, was a good example to everybody."[14]

Others realised however that the combination of German and Dutch sisters in the same community was not always easy.[15] The Saint Elisabeth Sisters' superiors had to take into account the occasional tensions between the Polish and the German sisters when setting up communities. For them and for others, it was difficult having relatives fighting on opposite sides during the war. When the Sisters of Saint Joseph look back on the war years, it is always with reference to their provincial prioress, Marie Zoé Ducruet. She was French by birth, but her sisters regarded her as being neutral. One of their older sisters said afterwards: "She set a good example. We had to help wherever we could. She never spoke disparagingly of the Germans and tried to help whenever it was needed, regardless of nationality [...]. Marie Zoé tackled this situation, although many people outside the community regarded her as pro-German. If she gave this impression, it was only for the sake of peace and Christian charity."[16]

When one realises how strong her own national feelings were, and how much her own country meant to her, her difficult balancing act during the war was thoroughly heroic. The Sisters of Saint Joseph were nevertheless asked by their superiors not to speak German, even among themselves. If someone from outside addressed them in German, they were to answer in Norwegian. That was a great help vis-à-vis the occupation forces; it kept them at a distance.[17]

---

[14] Informant Aase Raff (1908-1996), Norwegian Francis Xavier Sister.
[15] Informant Valfrida Riemersma (1907-2001), Dutch Francis Xavier Sister.
[16] Informant Magdalene Sophie Niehoff (1900-1994), German-Polish Joseph Sister.
[17] Informant Irene Kleff (1900-1999), German Joseph Sister.

Illegal work

When the arrest of Norwegian Jews for deportation to German concentration camps started in the autumn of 1942,[18] the Churches faced a serious dilemma. Through the Ministry of the Interior, Bishop Mangers sent an appeal for the release, at least of Jews who had been baptised, and who belonged to Catholic parishes.[19] The Bishop received a call from a prominent Lutheran theologian, the same day. He asked Mangers to sign a petition to Quisling, the infamous Norwegian Nazi leader, along with the Protestant bishops, in order to obtain the release of the Jews.[20] Mangers told him that he himself had already sent an application, and was waiting for a reply before he would sign any further petitions.[21] He never received a reply from the authorities to this or later requests.

The illegal work of the Sisters specifically concerned the Jews. During the war a German Sister of Saint Joseph, Irene Kleff, worked in the office of Our Lady's Hospital in Oslo. She showed great care for patients who were in trouble. A number of Jews were admitted as patients under false names and were kept hidden or were helped to escape. When it became known that the Jews were about to be deported, Irene warned the Jewish patients and left the doors of the hospital unlocked during the night in order to give them a chance to escape. "We were given orders from the Nazis all the time, and we were obliged to inform the police when one of the Jews was about to be discharged," she said later.[22]

---

[18] There were about 2,000 Jews in Norway at the time of the invasion in 1940. Approximately 1300 of them managed to flee to Sweden, while 767 were deported to Germany. 26 persons survived the deportation. See Oskar Mendelsohn, *Jødenes historie i Norge gjennom 300 år* II (Universitetsforlaget: Oslo 1987). Arne Hassing, "The Churches of Norway and the Jews, 1933-1943", in: *Journal of Ecumenical Studies* 26 (1989), 496-522.

[19] Bernt I. Eidsvig, "Den katolske kirke vender tilbake", in: John W. Gran (ed.), *Den katolske kirke i Norge: Fra kristningen til idag* (Aschehoug: Oslo 1993), 143-426, here 350. – As far as we know, there were no religious of Jewish descent.

[20] In a letter dated 14 February of that year, the bishops of the Church of Norway protested to the Ministers of Education, and of Work and Sports, respectively, about the National Youth Service. The parents, not the State, had the right to guide their children. Mangers supported his Lutheran colleagues in this matter when he signed the document.

[21] Probably Mangers was aware of the horrible effects of the official protest in August 1942 of the Dutch Bishops against the persecution of the Jews: The immediate arrest and deportation of 40,000 Jews, the majority finishing their lives in the gas chambers. Rieber-Mohn, "Vi var med," 94.

[22] Informant Irene Kleff.

Women's traditions in Europe
Frauentraditionen in Europa
Traditions des femmes en Europe

For obvious reasons, the illegal activities of the sisters were not written down in the chronicles of the different congregations. Their work was done in secret, above and beyond the call of duty. This poses another question: Would illegal activities conflict with the sisters' vow of obedience? In Bergen, there was no conflict, since their superior was fully aware that some of her sisters co-operated with the underground in helping Jewish children escape. However, within the community, this was a well-guarded secret – some of the Sisters only heard of it forty years later![23] The sisters in Kristiansund read illegal papers and listened avidly to the news from the BBC, even though they were afraid of being discovered by the Nazi police.[24]

At Saint Catherine's in Oslo,[25] some of the sisters and several young girls who lived there worked to help Jews reach the Swedish border, so that they might escape to a neutral country. One episode during the mass arrests of the Jews was particularly scary. When a group of Jewish refugees had safely crossed the border to Sweden, one of the sisters who had been engaged in the operation thought she was being shadowed by an unknown man, and thought it best to inform her superior. Their French prioress had been severely traumatised at the news that the German forces had captured Paris in June 1940. She was now terrified and contacted Bishop Mangers, who came straight to St Catherine's and ordered the sisters to keep away from all kinds of illegal work immediately.[26]

In critical situations, however, when they had to choose religious obedience or helping a person in need, the latter was seen as the more important. The sisters followed their conscience. The sisters knew for example that the lives of Jews were in danger, and were not willing to abandon them. But their work with the resistance also included other fields. During a conversation with one of the French sisters at Saint Catherine's several years later,[27] this issue was brought up in a straightforward manner. "We were all engaged in illegal activities, with something the others did not know about", she said. "We never talked about it, so that nobody would be tempted to reveal it if they were brought in for questioning. One of the priests asked me to hide some documents." When asked whether she told her prioress, she answered: "No, I did

---

[23] Informant Maria Merethe Jeuken (1917-2003), Dutch Francis Xavier Sister.
[24] Informant Gudulina Fokker (1911-2002), Dutch Charles Borromeo Sister.
[25] Saint Catherine's was a home for young girls as well as the convent of the Dominican Sisters.
[26] In a confidential letter to the priests on September 1942 Mangers underlined that they did not have an opportunity to work politically. Eidsvig, "Den katolske kirke", 349.
[27] Informant Marie du Christ Soulier (1899-2000), French Dominican Sister.

not speak about it to anybody. We realised only much later that everybody had been doing something ..."[28]

When liberation finally came, on 8 May 1945, the sisters in Stavanger were the first to fly the Norwegian flag from the roof of their hospital. It had been banned during the war years. In Saint Hallvard Church in Oslo, the sisters let the church bells chime for a full hour, until one of their neighbours called to say: "Enough is enough!"[29] Allied troops, who arrived in the country shortly after the German surrender agreement had been signed, were to make new demands on Catholic hospitals and properties; also, there was rehabilitation to be taken care of. The sisters' solidarity with the Norwegian people was never in doubt during the war.

Then and now

At the beginning of this article, we met three women, two young ones and an older one. One of the young women wore her *hijab*, an unmistakable sign of her religious affiliations. The incidents on September 11, 2001 made her a terrorist in the eyes of the older woman.

The story of another group of veiled women, the Catholic women religious of Norway during the Second World War, may serve to show how quickly "we" may draw the wrong conclusions about "them", in critical situations as well as in daily life. The way "the others" were different, in this case the nuns, and the fact that they might even have the same nationality as the enemy, proved to be an asset, not a threat, to the society in which they lived and worked. They were neither traitors nor passive observers, but loyal co-workers who had never before shared a common fate with other Norwegians in the way that they did during wartime, and who had never had an opportunity to express their loyalty in this way before.

"Diaspora" is a useful concept in contemporary social sciences frequently used in the current Norwegian debate about immigrants.[30] It is used independently of national borders and expands one's field of vision towards new

---

[28] The sisters' work of resistance in Norway, was similar to what sisters from religious orders carried out in e.g. Denmark, France and Italy; see Anders Bjørnvad, *På vej mod hjemstavnsret: Den Katolske Kirke i Danmark under den tyske besættelse 1940-45* (Odense Universitetsforlag: Odense 1993), 112-132; Charles Molette, *Prêtres, religieux et religieuses dans la résistance au nazisme 1940-1945* (Fayard: Paris 1995); Francesco Santucci, *The strategy that saved Assisi* (Editrice Minerva: Assisi 2000).

[29] Johs. Bruce, *Fra Urtegaten til Enerhaugen: St. Hallvard menighet 100 år* (St. Hallvard Menighet: Oslo 1990), 59.

[30] Marianne Gullestad, *Det norske sett med nye øyne* (Universitetsforlaget: Oslo 2002), 310.

Women's traditions in Europe
Frauentraditionen in Europa
Traditions des femmes en Europe

processes and contexts. The concept of diaspora is a theoretical construct formerly associated with the historical experiences of the Jews. The Jews are often citizens of the country in which they live while they participate in their own institutions and networks across nation states, and they have a special relationship to Israel as their mythical homeland.[31] By stretching the term a little, this may also apply to women religious, citizens of the country in which they live, participants in their own institutions and international networks, and with a special relationship to the Kingdom of Heaven, their real goal. Thus they are to be found in an interesting position of tension between integration and difference.

From a majority perspective, such minority experiences are often seen as negative aberrations. But, as a Norwegian social anthropologist Marianne Gullestad points out, they may just as well be regarded as exemplars of new tendencies, especially in contemporary societies, rife with tensions between the "natives" and new immigrants and refugees.[32]

In 2002 there was an ongoing debate in two national newspapers between Gullestad and Shabana Rehman, a Pakistani-born writer and stand-up artist, concerning the role of the latter in the current multicultural debate. This discussion illustrates clearly the need for the voices and experiences of immigrant women to be heard. Against this backdrop, it would be neglectful to overlook the experiences and the knowledge of our women religious of yesteryear, in meeting some of the greatest challenges of today's society.

Après la Réforme en Europe au seizième siècle, les prêtres catholiques romains et les religieux n'eurent plus le droit de se rendre en Norvège jusque dans les années 1840. La suspicion concernant les papistes était intense. Pendant les sept ou huit décennies suivantes, différentes communautés religieuses féminines établirent des hôpitaux à travers le pays. La plupart des religieuses et des prêtres étaient étrangers. Lors de la seconde guerre mondiale, la Norvège fut occupée par l'armée allemande pendant cinq ans. Presque 60 % des sœurs étaient d'origine allemande. Les relations devinrent tendues au sein de l'Église catholique. Dans plusieurs communautés religieuses, certaines des sœurs étaient issues des pays en guerre les uns contre les autres. Cet article tente d'analyser la façon dont elles ont fait face à cette situation exceptionnelle. Outre le fait qu'il dépeint une période intéressante dans la vie des congrégations religieuses, cet épisode a une certaine valeur paradigmatique au regard

---

[31] According to Gullestad, *Det norske sett med nye øyne*, 309-310
[32] This coincides with my own conclusion in Else-Britt Nilsen, *Nonner i storm og stille: Katolske ordenssøstre i Norge i det 19. og 20. århundre* (Solum Forlag: Oslo 2001).

des différents conflits se produisant actuellement dans une société de plus en plus multiculturelle, et du besoin de mécanismes adéquats pour y remédier.

Nach der Reformation im Europa des sechzehnten Jahrhunderts waren römisch-katholische Priester und Ordensleute in Norwegen bis in die 1840er-Jahre nicht zugelassen. Misstrauen gegenüber den Papisten war weit verbreitet. Während der folgenden sieben oder acht Jahrzehnte errichteten mehrere Frauenorden eine Reihe von Hospitälern in verschiedenen Teilen des Landes. Die Mehrheit der Schwestern wie auch der Priester stammte aus dem Ausland. Während des Zweiten Weltkriegs war Norwegen während fünf Jahren von deutschen Truppen besetzt. Fast 60% der Schwestern waren deutscher Abstammung. Diese Situation führte in der katholischen Kirche zu ernsten Spannungen. In mehreren religiösen Gemeinschaften gab es Schwestern, die zu den unterschiedlichen Kriegsparteien gehörten. Dieser Artikel will verdeutlichen, wie die verschiedenen Ordensfrauen diese außergewöhnliche Situation bewältigten. Neben der Beleuchtung eines interessanten Abschnitts im Leben der Kongregationen haben die beschriebenen Phänomene einen gewissen Übertragungswert hinsichtlich verschiedener aktueller Konfliktsituationen in einer immer stärker multikulturellen Gesellschaft sowie hinsichtlich der Notwendigkeit angemessener Bewältigungsstrategien.

Else-Britt Nilsen (*1946) has been a member of the Congregation of the Dominican Sisters of Notre Dame de Grâce (Chatillon, France) since 1971, and Prioress of the Congregation since 2003. She has studied sociology and theology in Norway and France. Dr. Theol., University of Oslo, 1990 with a thesis on marriage and divorce praxis among Lutheran ministers in the Church of Norway. Nilsen has a Norwegian State Scholarship and lectures in Catholic Social Teaching at the University of Oslo and the Norwegian Lutheran School of Theology. She has been active in ecumenical work for a long time, and was Vice-president of the Christian Council of Norway until 2006. Recent publications include "Rites for Perpetual Commitment to Monastic and Religious Life in the Nordic Countries", in: Hans Raun Iversen (ed.), *Rites of Ordination and Commitment in the Churches of the Nordic Countries: Theology and Terminology* (Museum Tusculanum Press: Copenhagen 2006), 327-352 and "Religious Identity and National Loyality: Women Religious in Norway during the Second World War", in: Yvonne Maria Werner (ed.), *Nuns and Sisters in the Nordic Countries after the Reformation: A Female Counter-Culture in Modern Society* (Studia Missionalia Svecana XC; The Swedish Institute of Mission Research [SIM]: Uppsala 2004), 213-253.

Journal of the European Society of Women in Theological Research 15 (2007) 189-197.
doi: 10.2143/ESWTR.15.0.2022778

Elina Vuola

Study of Religion and Feminist Theory: Dialogue or Silence?[1]

I belong to the generation of feminist scholars in Finland which saw the outburst of feminist research in Finnish universities, became acquainted with feminist research while still students and started to both demand courses and do research. Unlike in many other European and Nordic countries, feminist research in theology or feminist theology in Finland never really took off and has not created a critical mass, even if small, of scholars who later would be able to teach and supervise and get their doctoral degrees in this area. It is unnecessary to go through the reasons why this is so. I am more interested in looking at the consequences of the situation, which may have relevance also in other European countries, in which there are great differences in the situation of feminist theological research.

I will reflect on the situation in Finland from a quite personal perspective. That includes having also lived and worked in Central America (mostly Nicaragua and Costa Rica) and the United States, which is why I will look at the Finnish context also from the perspectives of those two regions which form a natural long-term part of my overall "context". In this sense, my perspective is multicultural and multicontextual, which I am sure is the case with many other feminist theologians in Europe, even if the "multis" are different from mine. I also want to stress that "European" or "Latin American" or "North American" feminist theologies are always *de facto* practised in a global context, consciously or not, which is why the context should also always be considered in a more global perspective. Feminist theological work done in other cultural and geographical settings should always be of relevance for feminist

---

[1] This is a revised version of my keynote lecture delivered at the II Christina Conference on Gender, Religion and Theory at the University of Helsinki, Finland, 3 March 2005. My purpose was to give a broad overview of the situation of feminist research on religion in Finland for the international participants of the conference.

theologians in other contexts, even with a critical eye. No feminist theology is more (or less) universal than any other.

In Finland, I have worked as a researcher for ten years at the Institute of Development Studies, which is part of the Faculty of Social Sciences, as well as in close contact with the departments of women's studies and Latin American studies. For a theologian, not to work primarily in a faculty of theology, is certainly not without importance. It can be both a strength and a weakness.[2] In relation to what I say above, doing feminist theology is almost by definition a multidisciplinary effort, in some cases more than in others. Here again, I assume that other European feminist theologians can relate what I am saying to their own specific experiences of working in multidisciplinary contexts.

Issues of religion were present already in the first years of feminist scholarship in Finland. This is important to remember when we write the historiography of feminist research in our country. However, issues of religion and gender were present mainly as part of folkloristics and, to some extent, comparative religion, but less so in theology. In the former case when re-reading and re-interpreting the vast sources of collected oral poetry, laments and folklore, the feminist perspective has meant a new, positive valuation of our history and cultural identity, reflected also in its simultaneous artistic, especially musical, revival mostly or often by female musicians. For me, an outsider in the field, it seems that in folkloristics the critical feminist eye has produced a paradigm shift, even if not always recognized as such. It is about re-reading the founding national myths from a gender perspective. An interest in religion was always part of that research. One reason for that may be that Finland became independent as late as 1917, having been part of Russia for over a hundred years. Part of the late 19th century and early 20th century nationalism and nation building was the revival of folklore.

At the same time, the lack or weakness of feminist research in theology – especially systematic theology – has meant that in Finland the development of new theoretical insights, stemming also from our own cultural heritage and context and not imported from outside, in the area of gender and religion has taken place mainly in contexts and disciplines other than theology. Unlike in

---

[2] Since this is not a scientific article *per se* but rather a reflection and commentary based on my own professional experiences, I will not include bibliographical references. I understand that in some cases this may look like making unsubstantiated claims. However, the reader can consult my previously published works some of which are included in the selected bibliography of Scandinavian feminist theology in the end of this journal.

many other countries, a living relationship between feminist theological research and the principal church (Lutheran) has been practically non-existent, meaning that few new insights and changes have been introduced into the texts, liturgy, rituals and other practices of the church. As far as I know, when this is so in the case of the majority church, it is even more so in the Orthodox and other minority churches.

Possibly related to that, the fact that, in Finland, academic theology is prac tised only in the context of the secular state university, and not in church-run seminaries, seems to be a double-edged sword in the case of feminist scholarship. On the one hand, the secular context gives theology an academic freedom and scholarly respectability, which frees theology from the role of a mere servant of a specific religious community. On the other hand, this same reason can easily result in a detachment from both secular and religious realities and issues, often important and even burning to people, especially in the area of ethics. In the specific case of feminist research, this has by and large not so much meant a religiously-based negative attitude to feminist theology (as being somehow godless or heretical) but rather a theoretical rejection: feminist research is seen as something biased, non-scholarly, and not philosophically or theoretically interesting. Often this is something quite implicit, since the whole construction of what counts as science and what does not and on what grounds is seldom explicated.

Thus, the lack or meagerness of feminist research in theology in Finland – together with the overall distance of academic theology from the church and society – has also meant that there is practically no positive correlation between the existence of women pastors in the church and reinterpretations of liturgy, texts, prayers, sacraments etc. from a gender perspective. To put it rather bluntly, women do it just as it was always done by men, or even better. Pastors, both men and women, are not trained in feminist theology, which they then could choose to either use or not use in their practice as pastors. They would also get an idea of what feminist critique of religion could mean in different theological disciplines.

The situation has at least four inter-related consequences. Firstly, there is a considerable lacuna of feminist research in theology – especially in systematic theology, while the situation is less so in Biblical studies and church history – and it seems not to be changing radically. Secondly, feminist theological research, when it exists, does not easily translate into practical changes and innovations either in the church or ethical issues. Thirdly, for those of us who do work in feminist theology and feminist research in religion, the most immediate intellectual community has been with feminist scholars from other fields.

And, fourthly, feminist research in religion in Finland has been mainly realized in the context of other disciplines than that of theology, such as comparative religion and folkloristics.

I do not see this situation only or mainly as a problem. It has happened for certain reasons. It also means that there has been more positive synergy between feminist scholars of religion and feminist scholars from other fields than in many other countries and contexts.[3] Thus, those of us who work with issues of gender and religion from a feminist perspective in Finland have become truly interdisciplinary because of the circumstances. Our identity as theologians is possibly weakened because of this, but the other side of the coin is a self-understanding of our scholarship as being part of the core of feminist interdisciplinary theorizing. This reality may in fact be quite exceptional as well as very different from, for example, the situation in the United States, where it is only very recently that (Christian) feminist theologians have started to dialogue more with feminist theory. However, this group of scholars is still surprisingly small considering the size of the United States.

Interestingly, even when that is the situation, U.S. feminist theology is (too) often taken as something normative and universal. We "import" feminist scholarship in theology, just as we do in other fields, into our own cultural contexts, not always paying enough critical attention to the context in which it was originally born and created – to the extent that concepts such as "gender" are practically impossible to translate into Finnish, or the Finnish equivalent has a quite different connotation from the English one. In Scandinavian languages (even though Finnish is not an Indo-European language unlike Swedish, Icelandic, Danish and Norwegian) the word "gender" does not make the conceptual differentiation between the biological and the social. There is only one word (*sukupuoli* in Finnish, *kön* in Swedish, *køn* in Danish, *kjønn* in Norwegian) which includes both[4], which is why feminist scholars here sometimes add "biological" and "social" in front of the indigenous word.

---

3   The conference in which this paper was first delivered is an example of that dynamic. The first scientific conference in Finland on gender and religion was organized by the interdisciplinary community of feminist researchers under the auspices of the Christina Institute for Women's Studies of the University of Helsinki.

4   Icelandic differs somewhat: feminist researchers in Iceland (with a few execeptions) use different words for sex and gender: *kynferði* for sex and *kyngervi* for gender. *Kyn* is linguistically the same as *kön/køn/kjønn*. In Sweden today, "genus " is the word most commonly used in the academic world at large for "gender" in an inclusive sense (although the precise definitions

All this does not mean that there are no problems or possibilities for more cooperation between feminist scholars of different disciplines. There is an obvious lack, especially internationally and between different religious traditions as well, of a more substantial, more critical and more theoretical dialogue between feminist scholars of religion and feminist scholars from other fields.

However, a situation in which feminist scholars of religion, including feminist theologians, work as part of the larger academic community of feminist scholars is a fruitful situation. This is how feminist theology becomes respected for what it is, namely a critical feminist reinterpretation of different religious traditions, and not for trying to be some sort of general feminist theorizing. The latter often ends in an arbitrary and superficial borrowing from other fields, reinterpreting feminist theology through the theories and concepts of other fields, but not necessarily the other way round.

In my other professional geographical context, Latin America – largely Roman Catholic – the situation is different from both the United States and the Scandinavian countries. Feminist theologians can make a truly revolutionary input in societies where arguments against women's autonomy, reproductive and sexual freedom and education are largely religious. There is a positive correlation between women's access to theological education and the critique and reinterpretation of sacred texts and religious and ethical beliefs from women's perspective. To be able to do this is especially important in societies where religious elites control or strongly influence national legislation and politics as is the case with many Latin American countries.

There are four important issues related to this. Firstly, a feminist critique of religion – of any religion, in any culture or society – stresses the dismantling of religious legitimization for certain political and cultural practices and beliefs. Secondly, it critically analyzes the power structures of religious communities, such as theological education, access to positions of power, right to interpretation, and so on. And thirdly, it reminds us that there is not *one* Christianity, Islam or Hinduism, but different forms and interpretations of them, and that religious communities are often internally divided; and, fourthly, that the determinant role of religion in society should be questioned in general. Thus, a critical analysis of religion is important, but women's struggle is not only with religion. Feminist reinterpretation and critique of different religious traditions has

---

of "genus" differ). It may deserve to be noticed that many Swedish theologians still stick to the terminology "feminist research", some of them even to "kön".

to a large extent included these elements in very different cultural, religious and political contexts.

In my ongoing research, which concentrates on contemporary feminist scholarship from and on Latin America, I have been claiming that much of contemporary social scientific research on religion and women is often guided by two opposite stereotypes. On the one hand, there is a kind of feminist "blindness" of, or resistance to, the importance of religion for women, especially in its possible positive or liberatory aspects, even when women from different religious traditions claim this to be true for them. On the other hand, there is something that could be called a "religious paradigm" type of feminist studies in which women are seen mainly or only through the lense of religion. Religion – Islam, Catholicism, etc. – is not ignored or bypassed as in the first case but, instead, seen as the sole or main signifier of women's lives. Women in a certain country or region are *defined* through their religion, for examples as Muslim women. Curiously, this happens most often in reference to a culture which is not one's own: European feminist scholars, even scholars of religion, very seldom label European women as *Christian*. This is of course based on our internalization of our own region as heterogeneous and diverse. The problem is that we do not always apply the same logic to other cultural and geographical contexts.

The above-mentioned polarity of stereotypes has some interesting and important consequences for women, feminism, and feminist studies. I only will mention three. All of these have relevance also in the Latin American context. Firstly, the historical, social, political and ethical importance of a given religious tradition is negated, because secularization is considered to have won the battle with religion in modern societies, when in fact the kind of secularization that social scientists have predicted has in fact happened only in Western Europe, and not even in the United States or other parts of Europe. The situation may be changing rapidly even in Western European countries.

Secondly, many people in different cultures are deprived of their agency if their religious traditions are considered immutable and unchangeable. If contemporary forms of, for example, Islam or Catholicism are seen as powerful, immutable power systems dominating people's decision making and possibilities to change them, both the dialogue and critique *inside* these religious traditions are ignored, as well as their historical changes over the centuries.

Thirdly, we are witnessing a rise of fundamentalism in all major religious traditions. This "social fundamentalism" (the term used by John Stratton Hawley) is creating new political alliances between, for example, the Vatican and some Muslim governments, especially over issues that have to do with women's rights. If at the same time there is a feminist inability to analyze this phenomenon adequately, which includes taking seriously women's own positive identities as Muslim or Catholic, and if we only see secularisation as the inevitable path, we are not able to understand the complex and often contradictory relationship between women and their religious traditions, identities and beliefs.

Thus, I am arguing for a nuanced, critical, comprehensive understanding of the interplay of women's lives and religious traditions. A feminist perspective should not only include feminist (re)interpretations of those religious traditions, using adequate tools of analysis. There is a substantial group of feminist scholars from different religious backgrounds and traditions realizing that task, even if their work is not always well-known beyond their field. A feminist perspective should also be careful not to judge religion as *per se* oppressive for women, without listening to the different voices of women all over the world who are balancing between their identities as women and their places in religious communities.

The multidisciplinarity of feminist studies seems often to somebody from religious studies or theology to be more wishful thinking than real dialogue between disciplines. Even if what I said above is true about the positive synergy between feminist studies of religion and feminist theory, it is also true that feminist studies in religion are often neglected by (feminist) theorists in other fields, and again I now speak internationally and not just from the specific Finnish context.

I only want to point out two general problems with this neglect of feminist studies in religion. They are related to the stereotypical way many feminists see religion, as mentioned earlier.

Firstly, not only is an important, well scrutinized and critical body of research on religion (not just in and on Christianity) excluded from much of social sciences, although it may be one of the most important parts of religious studies for today if we want to understand the dynamic between religion and society. As was said earlier, the whole controversy about religious fundamentalism and religiously motivated political conflicts often has at its center different understandings of human rights, especially the rights of women. Secondly, if feminist studies in religion are not included in the larger body of feminist theory, the latter runs the risk of excluding important voices of women who are not willing to give up their religious traditions but who are also at the forefront of changing and challenging them, often in extremely difficult circumstances.

Even if I have taken my own research in Latin America as an example here, I believe similar issues are relevant in our Scandinavian contexts. Indeed, because our societies are so secularized, we might in fact be even blinder to the multifaceted roles religion plays in them than in countries where this is more obvious and direct. If feminist study of religion, including feminist theology, is not in substantial dialogue with both theology and feminist theory, both will suffer from a blind spot to an important area of culture which has relevance for women's lives.

J'examine la situation des études féministes sur la religion en Finlande, à partir d'une perspective personnelle, ayant aussi vécu et travaillé en Amérique Centrale et aux États-Unis. En Finlande, la recherche théologique féministe est pauvre, surtout dans le domaine de la théologie systématique. Les questions de genre et de religion ont surtout été traitées par des disciplines autres que la théologie. Les chercheuses féministes en religion et les théoriciennes féministes dans d'autres spécialités ont cependant eu des contacts étroits. Je pose aussi la question de savoir pourquoi un dialogue plus substantiel et critique entre les spécialistes féministes en religion et les spécialistes féministes dans d'autres spécialités est nécessaire. Il semble qu'il y ait une image quelque peu stéréotypée de la religion et des femmes croyantes dans les théories féministes. Il nous faut adopter une compréhension plus globale des connexions entre le vécu des femmes et leurs traditions religieuses.

Ich betrachte die Situation feministischer Forschung auf dem Gebiet der Religionswissenschaften und der Theologie in Finnland aus einer persönlichen Perspektive, zu der es gehört, dass ich auch in Zentralamerika und in den Vereinigten Staaten gelebt und gearbeitet habe. In Finnland gibt es einen Mangel an feministisch-theologischer Forschung, speziell in systematischer Theologie. Themen von *gender* und Religion wurden hauptsächlich außerhalb der theologischen Disziplinen untersucht. Es gab einen recht engen Kontakt zwischen feministischen Religionswissenschaftlerinnen und feministischen Theoretikerinnen aus anderen Gebieten. Ich denke auch über die generelle Notwendigkeit eines substanzielleren und kritischeren Dialogs zwischen feministischen Religionswissenschaftlerinnen und feministischen Wissenschaftlerinnen aus anderen Disziplinen nach. Feministische Theorie tendiert häufig zu etwas stereotypen Bildern über Religion und religiöse Frauen. Wir brauchen ein umfassenderes Verständnis des Wechselspiels zwischen dem Leben von Frauen und ihren religiösen Traditionen.

Elina Vuola (*1960) is Research fellow of the Academy of Finland at the Institute of Development Studies, University of Helsinki. 2002-2003 she was a visiting scholar at the Women's Studies in Religion Program at the Harvard Divinity School, Cambridge, USA. Among her publications can be mentioned *Limits of Liberation*.

Feminist Theology and the Ethics of Poverty and Reproduction (Sheffield Academic Press / Continuum: Sheffield, U.K. / New York 2002; Spanish edition: *Teología feminista, teología de la liberación. Los límites de la praxis*. IEPALA Editorial: Madrid 2000) and "Seriously Harmful for Your Health? Religion, Feminism and Sexuality in Latin America", in: Marcella Althaus-Reid (ed.), *Liberation Theology and Sexuality: New Radicalism from Latin America* (Ashgate: London 2006).

Journal of the European Society of Women in Theological Research 15 (2007) 199-207.
doi: 10.2143/ESWTR.15.0.2022779

Hanna Stenström

Feministische Theologie in Schweden

Im Laufe meiner Arbeit an diesem Band ist mir schmerzlich bewusst geworden, wie unterschiedlich die Bedingungen für eine feministische Theologie selbst in den Nordischen Ländern sind. In diesem kurzen Artikel möchte ich eine Geschichte erzählen, die sich von der finnischen unterscheidet, und einige Probleme und Möglichkeiten in meinem Land, Schweden, aufzeigen.[1]

Aus Platzgründen werde ich mich vornehmlich auf die akademische feministische Theologie konzentrieren. Doch einiges muss auch über die feministische Theologie in der Kirche von Schweden (lutherisch) gesagt werden.[2] Aufgrund des nicht-konfessionellen Charakters der theologischen Fakultäten in Schweden gibt es keine natürliche Verbindung zwischen der akademischen feministischen Theologie und der feministischen Theologie in den Kirchen.[3]

Ebenso wie in Finnland war auch die Ordination von Frauen in der Kirche von Schweden nicht das Ergebnis eines ausdrücklichen feministischen Kampfes, wenngleich es gewiss einen Kampf gegeben hat, an dem einige Frauen der Ersten Frauenbewegung beteiligt waren, und zwar unter anderem mit theologischen Argumenten des liberalen Protestantismus. Selbst in Schweden

---

[1] Ich stütze mich wesentlich auf Anne-Louise Eriksson, „Från mäns dominans till kvinnors dans", in: Håkan Eilert u. a., *Modern svensk teologi: strömningar och perspektivskiften under 1900-talet* (Verbum: Stockholm 1999), 325-348, Anne-Louise Eriksson, *Genusperspektiv på teologi* (Högskoleverket / National Agency of Higher Education: Stockholm 2004).

[2] Zur Kirche von Schweden heute vgl. Anders Bäckström u. a., *Religious Change in Northern Europe: the Case of Sweden. From state church to free church. Final report* (Verbum: Stockholm 2004), mit einem Kapitel über die Situation von Frauen (141-167). Ich konzentriere mich auf die Kirche von Schweden, da das die Kirche ist, die ich am besten kenne, und sie die dominierende Kirche in Schweden ist. Man darf jedoch nicht vergessen, dass ein Großteil der feministischen Arbeit ökumenisch war, und dass es auch Beispiele dafür gibt, dass die feministische Theologie andere protestantische Kirchen beeinflusst hat, z.B. im Bereich der liturgischen Erneuerung.

[3] Eriksson, „Från mäns dominans till kvinnors dans", 345-346.

war es für die ersten Pastorinnen nicht möglich, kritische Fragen an die christliche Theologie zu stellen.[4] Die feministische Theologie kam in den späten 1970er Jahren nach Schweden und gehört seitdem zur kirchlichen Landschaft.[5] Den sichtbarsten und vielleicht auch einflussreichsten feministischen Beitrag stellen die vielen Formen feministischer Liturgien und liturgischer Tänze dar.[6]

Heute ist man sich im Allgemeinen der Probleme bewusst, auf die die feministischen Theologinnen in der Kirche von Schweden und auch in einigen anderen protestantischen Kirchen aufmerksam gemacht haben. Fragen der inklusiven Sprache sind Bestandteil der Diskussionen über neue Liturgien und Gebetbücher, wenn auch die Ergebnisse eher bescheiden sind und keinen radikalen Wandel darstellen. Ich möchte die Situation in meinem Land nicht idealisieren: Es gibt immer noch einen lautstarken Widerstand gegen die Ordination von Frauen, gegen die Anerkennung gleichgeschlechtlicher Beziehungen, inklusive liturgische Sprache und alles andere, was nach Feminismus aussieht. Schweden hat sicher seinen Anteil am wachsenden Fundamentalismus, überlebenden Konservatismus, christlicher Homophobie und männlichem Chauvinismus – neben all denen, die sich einfach nicht für feministische Probleme interessieren. Doch feministische Fragen stehen auf der offiziellen Tagesordnung in der Kirche von Schweden und in einigen anderen protestantischen Kirchen. Feministische Theologinnen, einschließlich einer zunehmenden Anzahl von promovierten Frauen, beteiligen sich an Diskussionen und

---

[4]   Die erste Ordination von Frauen in der Kirche von Schweden wurde 1960 vollzogen. Zur Ordination von Frauen in der Kirche von Schweden vgl. Brita Stendahl, *The Force of Tradition. A Case Study of Women Priests in Sweden,* mit einem Anhang von Constance F. Parvey (Fortress Press: Philadelphia 1985). Vgl. auch Eriksson, „Från mäns dominans till kvinnors dans", 324-330.

[5]   Eriksson, „Från mäns dominans till kvinnors dans", 326; 341-345, wo auch Beispiele aus römisch-katholischem und ökumenischem Kontext aufgenommen sind.

[6]   Zur feministischen liturgischen Bewegung in der Kirche von Schweden vgl. Anders Bäckström u. a., *Religious Change in Northern Europe,* 154-158, Ninna Edgardh Beckman, „Lady Wisdom as Hostess for the Lord's Supper", in: Teresa Berger (Hg.), *Dissident Daughters: Feminist Liturgies in Global Context* (Westminster John Knox Press: Louisville Kentucky 2001), 159-174. Ninna Edgardh Beckman, „Mrs Murphy's Arising from the Pew: Ecclesiological Implications", in: *Ecumenical Review* 53/1 (Januar 2001), 5-13.
     Zur Arbeit in der Kirche von Schweden im Rahmen der vom Ökumenischen Rat der Kirchen ausgerufenen Dekade *Kirchen in Solidarität mit den Frauen 1988-1998* vgl. Ninna Edgardh Beckman, *Folkkyrka – i solidaritet med kvinnor?* (Tro&Tanke 1998:2; Svenska Kyrkans Forskninsgråd: Uppsala 1998), besonders die englische Zusammenfassung 126-131.

Entscheidungsprozessen in der Kirche von Schweden. Das ist ein entscheidender Wandel.[7]

In der akademischen Theologie begann die Geschichte der feministischen Theologie im modernen Sinne in den späten 1970er Jahren. Zu der Zeit waren die theologischen Fakultäten so stark von Männern beherrscht, dass die ersten Initiativen für die Aufnahme feministischer Theologie und theologischer Frauenforschung in das Theologiestudium von Männern ergriffen wurden. Ragnar Holte beispielsweise[8], Professor für Ethik in Uppsala, nahm in den späten 1970er Jahren ein Forschungsprojekt in Angriff, an dem auch weibliche Wissenschaftler[9] auf dem Gebiet der Bibelexegese, der Religionsgeschichte und der frühchristlichen Geschichte[10] beteiligt waren. Er arbeitete auch mit der norwegischen Theologin Kari Elisabeth Børresen zusammen. Die Tatsache, dass

---

[7] Eine wichtige Diskussion muss hier beiseite gelassen werden; sie sei nur kurz erwähnt. Es ist die Frage, ob ein Großteil der neuen Liturgien, genannt „Frauengottesdienste", nicht Gefahr laufen, die Klischees über Frauen zu verstärken, wenn sie die Erfahrungen der Frauen sichtbar machen und das bekräftigen, was aufgrund seiner Verbindung mit Frauen traditionell unterdrückt wird – nämlich den Körper. Man ist sich heute dieses Risikos auch in der feministischen liturgischen Bewegung bewusst. Doch es gibt heute in Schweden eine Spannung zwischen der Arbeit in den Kirchen einerseits, die die Frauen bestätigen und die Erfahrung von Frauen sichtbar machen will, und der akademischen feministischen Theologie andererseits, bei der die traditionellen Vorstellungen von *Gender* und der mögliche essentialistische Bezug auf den Begriff „Frauenerfahrung" auf Kritik stößt. Zu einer solchen Spannung siehe: Eriksson, „Från mäns dominans till kvinnors dans", 345-346.

[8] Zu weiteren Beispielen siehe: Eriksson, „Från mäns dominans till kvinnors dans", 330-334.

[9] Die Wahl des Begriffes „weiblich" statt „feministisch" ist hier bewusst. Ich möchte nicht sagen, dass das biologische Geschlecht – weiblich – die Wissenschaftlerin notwendigerweise zur Feministin macht. Was ich vielmehr sagen möchte, ist dies: Die an dem Projekt beteiligten Wissenschaftlerinnen – Inger Ljung, Kerstin Aspegren, Lilian Portefaix – waren *weibliche* Fachleute, die – nach ihren Veröffentlichungen zu urteilen – mit Forschungsarbeiten begannen, in denen es vornehmlich darum ging, Frauen in der Geschichte sichtbar zu machen, und die dann nach und nach ein mehr oder weniger feministisches Programm entwickelten. Ihre Arbeiten gehören in den feministischen Bereich, wenn man ihn weit definiert, das heißt Frauenstudien mit einbezieht, die darauf hinzielen, Frauen und ihre Lebensumstände in der Geschichte sichtbar zu machen.

[10] Kerstin Aspegren (Hg. René Kieffer), *The Male Woman. A feminine ideal in the Early Church* (AUU Uppsala Women's Studies A: Women in Religion 4; Universität Uppsala 1990, Nachdruck 1995); Inger Ljung, *Silence or Suppression. Attitudes Towards Women in the Old Testament* (AUU Uppsala Women's Studies A: Women in Religion 2; Almqvist&Wiksell International: Stockholm 1989); Lilian Portefaix, *Sisters Rejoice! Paul's Letters to the Philippians and Luke-Acts as Seen by First-Century Philippian Women* (CB NT 20; Almqvist&Wiksell International: Stockholm 1988).

das Projekt den Schwerpunkt auf historische, deskriptive Arbeit legte, ist zweifellos auf das damalige Verständnis von „Theologie" an der theologischen Fakultät in Uppsala zurückzuführen: nichtkonfessionelle, objektive, beschreibende Religionswissenschaft.[11] Doch die Dinge änderten sich, als 1990 eine andere norwegische Akademikerin, Eva Lundgren – Soziologin und Theologin – eine Forschungsstelle in Uppsala erhielt, die sie sechs Jahre lang innehatte.

Eva Lundgren und ihre Doktorandinnen nahmen das Recht für sich in Anspruch, ihre Forschungen als feministisch zu bezeichnen; sie nahmen die Fragen von *Gender* und Macht in ihr Forschungsprogramm auf und entwickelten ihre eigenen theoretischen Instrumente im Dialog mit der allgemeinen feministischen Theorie. Einige der ersten Arbeiten, die man als „skandinavische Kritik an der anglo-amerikanischen feminstischen Theologie" bezeichnen kann, wurden durchgeführt. Der Schwerpunkt verlagerte sich von historischen Fragen auf Fragen feministischer Theorie und auf Fragen, die von der allgemeinen feministischen Agenda her bekannt sind – beispielsweise Göttin-Spiritualität, Schwangerschaftsabbruch und sexuelle Gewalt –, und vom Sichtbarmachen der Frauen auf Analyse und Kritik von *Gender*-Theorien.[12] Wenn auch diese Gruppe feministischer Theologinnen etwas Neues darstellte, so trug sie doch die Merkmale der schwedischen akademischen Theologie: ihr nichtkonfessioneller Charakter, ihre starke Betonung der intellektuellen Stringenz; und sie zeigte zugleich, dass intellektuelle Stringenz nicht verloren geht, wenn das Ideal einer deskriptiven, rein objektiven Forschung aufgegeben wird.

Was kann über die akademische feministische Theologie in Schweden heute gesagt werden?

An der theologischen Fakultät der Universität Uppsala, wo ich lehre, benutzen wir für die Studierenden beim Einführungskurs in die Religionswissenschaften (*religious studies*) ein chronologisches Diagramm. Auf diesem Diagramm wird die Entwicklung des Judentums, des Christentums und des Islam in parallelen Linien dargestellt, auf denen die wichtigsten Ereignisse wie die Reformation, die Vollendung des Talmud und das Osmanische Reich verzeichnet sind. Die Linie, die das Christentum darstellt, beginnt mit Jesus und führt als letztes Ereignis die „feministische Theologie" auf, mit einem Pfeil, der nach vorne oder nach oben zeigt.

---

[11] Vgl. Eriksson, „Från mäns dominans till kvinnors dans", 332.
[12] Eriksson, „Från mäns dominans till kvinnors dans", 332-333.

Ich glaube, dass diese chronologische Darstellung ein eindrucksvolles Beispiel dafür ist, dass in der akademischen Theologie ein allgemeines Bewusstsein von der Bedeutung der feministischen Theologie und der von ihr aufgezeigten Probleme vorhanden ist. Es ist kein Zufall, auch kein völlig isoliertes Phänomen, dass die „feministische Theologie" bei einer chronologischen Darstellung für den Einführungskurs in die Religionswissenschaft einen solchen Platz in der Geschichte des Christentums, neben Konstantin dem Großen und der Reformation, erhalten hat.

An der theologischen Fakultät in Uppsala – um nur ein Beispiel zu nennen – gilt der Grundsatz, dass alle Kurse in einem bestimmten Umfang auch Literatur aus einer „*Gender*-Perspektive" mit einbeziehen sollen. Wenn auch die Richtlinien vielleicht nicht an allen Universitäten und Universitäts-Colleges, an denen man eine theologische Grundausbildung erhalten kann, genau die gleichen sind, so weiß ich doch, dass „feministische Theologie" und „*Gender*-Perspektive" in allen Lehrplänen ihren Platz haben, wenn auch an manchen Orten mehr als an anderen. Gewiss, es besteht immer eine Spannung zwischen Theorie und Praxis. Selbst in Uppsala gibt es Kurse, in denen man nur einen kleinen Artikel auf der Literaturliste findet, über den der Professor nie ein Wort verliert, ebenso wie Kurse, in denen eine *Gender*-Perspektive unübersehbar ist, und Kurse, in denen die „feministische Theologie" das Thema des gesamten Kurses ist. Trotz all der Unterschiede zwischen den verschiedenen Universitäten und Universitäts-Colleges kann man sagen, dass die absolute Mehrheit der Theologiestudierenden in Schweden heute zumindest eine gewisse Basisinformation über feministische Theologie und die Forschungsergebnisse im Bereich Feminismus und *Gender* erhalten. Und viele Studierende erhalten mehr als das.

Zugleich ist es heute sehr schwierig, etwas über schwedische feministisch-theologische Forschung im Allgemeinen zu sagen.

Schon die richtige Bezeichnung zu wählen, ist nicht ganz einfach, da die allgemein akzeptierte offizielle Bezeichnung an der Universität (in ganz Schweden) „*gender studies*", „*gender research*" lautet. Einige gebrauchen diese Bezeichnung ohne Zögern, andere (darunter auch ich) würden sich lieber „feministische Theologinnen" nennen. Es ist schwer zu sagen, ob dieser Unterschied nur ein sprachlicher ist. Ich glaube, dass Anne-Louise Eriksson eine zutreffende Beobachtung macht, wenn sie sagt, dass eine gewisse Tendenz unter Theologinnen, an der (deutlicher politischen) Bezeichnung „feministisch" festzuhalten, darauf zurückzuführen ist, dass man sich unter feministischen Lehrkräften in den theologischen Disziplinen der engen Beziehung zwischen *Gender* und Macht bewusst geworden ist, ebenso wie der Rolle, die die

Religionen für die Legitimierung der patriarchalen Ordnung gespielt haben und immer noch spielen.[13]

Außerdem sind wir viele – und bestimmt keine homogene Menge. Als wir im September 2006 versucht haben, alle schwedischen WissenschaftlerInnen auf dem Gebiet *Gender* und Theologie zusammen zu bringen, sind von über 50 Eingeladenen schließlich nur 25 gekommen; und mindestens fünf bis sieben weitere hatten ihr Interesse bekundet. Unter den 25 Teilnehmenden waren zwei Männer. Wir vertraten verschiedene akademische Disziplinen und verschiedene akademische Einrichtungen. Wir bedienen uns im Blick auf Theorie und Methode vieler unterschiedlicher Instrumente. Einige von uns – wie diejenigen aus der Universität Karlstad – gehören zu einer Gruppe von WissenschaftlerInnen, die in ihrem alltäglichen Beruf zusammenarbeiten. Die meisten von uns arbeiten alleine, selbst wenn es andere an unserer Universität gibt, die feministisch-theologische Forschung treiben.

In ihrem Referat über „*Gender*-Perspektiven auf die Theologie",[14] einer kurzen Arbeit in einer Serie über den Beitrag der *Gender*-Perspektiven in verschiedenen akademischen Disziplinen, die von der Schwedischen Nationalen Organisation für Höhere Bildung veröffentlicht wurde, macht Anne-Louise Eriksson eine wichtige Beobachtung zur heutigen Situation: „Es ist uns zweifellos gelungen, ein allgemeines Bewusstsein der „*Gender*-Probleme" zu erreichen. Doch das darf nie eine Entschuldigung dafür sein, nicht die Grundlagenforschung zu unterstützen, die die theoretische Reflexion vorantreibt und in Neuland vorstößt.[15] Ich meine, dieses Risiko sollte von den akademischen feministischen Theologinnen in Schweden heute ernsthaft ins Auge gefasst werden.

Diese Diskussion kann man zumindest in Schweden in Zusammenhang mit einer Diskussion über allgemeine Studien im Bereich feministische/*Gender* Fragen, nicht nur in der Theologie, sehen. Dabei geht es um folgende Fragen:

Sollten feministische/*Gender* Studien als eine eigene Disziplin aufgebaut werden, mit einem eigenen Forschungszentrum, eigenen Professoren und Professorinnen, Kursen für nichtgraduierte Studenten usw.? Oder wäre es besser, bei den traditionellen Disziplinen zu bleiben und unsere Perspektiven, Theorien und Erkenntnisse zum Bestandteil des theoretischen Repertoires und des Allgemeinwissens der Disziplin zu machen?

---

[13] Eriksson, *Genusperspektiv på teologi,* 47.
[14] Eriksson, *Genusperspektiv på teologi.*
[15] Eriksson, *Genusperspektiv på teologi,* 47.

Die am meisten verbreitete Antwort in Schweden lautet: Es ist keine Frage von entweder – oder, sondern von sowohl – als auch. Die erste Variante – die getrennten Forschungszentren usw. – bietet die Möglichkeit, bei der Entwicklung neuer feministischer theoretischer Instrumente zusammen zu arbeiten, sich zu spezialisieren und damit in der feministischen Forschung in Neuland vorzustoßen. Die zweite Variante ermöglicht es, die Arbeit in den traditionellen Disziplinen zu verändern und den Wissensbestand, der an die Studierenden weitergegeben wird, zu erweitern. Ohne die erste Variante gibt es keine neuen Erkenntnisse und kein neues Fachwissen. Ohne die zweite Variante läuft die feministische Forschung Gefahr, in der Welt allgemein nichts zu bewirken. Wir brauchen beide und einen ständigen Austausch zwischen ihnen.

Das spiegelt sich auch in der Organisation von Forschung und Lehre an den schwedischen Universitäten wider. Alle haben ihre Zentren für feministische/*Gender* Forschung (wenn auch die Namen variieren mögen) mit Forschungsstellen, Kursen, Bibliotheken usw. Zugleich gibt es eine Reihe von WissenschaftlerInnen im Bereich feministische/*Gender* Studien, die in Forschung und Lehre in den traditionellen Disziplinen arbeiten; und es wird viel getan, um ihre Erkenntnisse in den allgemeinen Wissensbestand der Disziplinen, der an die Studierenden weitergegeben wird, zu integrieren. Einzelne Fachleute beteiligen sich sowohl an der Arbeit der gesonderten Zentren für feministische/*Gender* Studien, als auch an der Arbeit ihrer eigenen Disziplin – ein Beispiel für „sowohl – als auch".

Doch, um auf Anne-Louise Eriksson zurückzukommen, können wir die Situation der akademischen feministischen Theologie in Schweden heute so beschreiben, dass es uns gelungen ist, in vielen theologischen Disziplinen das allgemeine Bewusstsein für *Gender*-Fragen zu wecken. So sind neue Erkenntnisse Teil des allgemeinen Wissensbestandes geworden; und die feministische Perspektive wird in vielen theologischen Disziplinen als eine der vielen möglichen Perspektiven akzeptiert. Das ist wirklich gut.

Was uns jedoch noch fehlt, ist der andere Teil des „sowohl – als auch". Es genügt nicht, dass es Zentren für feministische/*Gender* Studien im Allgemeinen gibt, wir brauchen auch Stellen für WissenschaftlerInnen mit Kompetenz sowohl im Bereich feministische/*Gender* Theorie als auch in den theologischen Disziplinen an unseren theologischen Fakultäten.[16] Es gibt auf unserem

---

[16] Wie an anderer Stelle in diesem Band gezeigt wird, bildet die Karlstad Universität eine Ausnahme mit ihrer engen Zusammenarbeit zwischen den religionswissenschaftlichen Studien (*religious studies*) und dem Zentrum für *Gender*-Studien unter der Leitung der systematischen Theologin Cristina Grenholm. Es gibt an manchen Orten – so zum Beispiel in Uppsala –

Fachgebiet in Schweden bislang noch keinen hauptamtlichen ordentlichen Professor oder keine hauptamtliche ordentliche Professorin und auch keine offizielle nationale Infrastruktur, die alle diese verstreuten WissenschaftlerInnen zusammen bringen könnte. Da feministische/*Gender* Perspektiven offiziell akzeptiert sind, könnte man meinen, alles sei in Ordnung. Doch ein allgemeines Bewusstsein, das es uns ermöglicht, unseren Studierenden beizubringen, dass das Kommen der feministischen Theologie ein Meilenstein in der Geschichte des Christentums ist, kann nicht eine Forschung ersetzen, die ständig in Neuland vorstößt. Das ist keine Kritik an der Arbeit meiner KollegInnen. Wir leisten viel interessante Arbeit, selbst unter den gegenwärtigen Umständen. Doch um noch weiter zu kommen, brauchen wir mehr Mittel.

Es ist offensichtlich, dass die feministische theologische Forschung, auch wenn sich schon viel verändert hat, immer noch vom guten Willen derer abhängt, die die Macht haben. Zu wenige von uns haben Anteil an dieser Macht. Die Geschichte der feministischen Theologie in Schweden zeigt, dass Veränderung möglich ist, dass aber selbst in einem so wohlwollenden Milieu noch ein langer Weg vor der feministischen Theologie liegt, um von der Annahme zu wirklicher und dauerhafter Veränderung und zu einer wirklichen Teilhabe an der Macht zu kommen.

The article presents the development of feminist theological research in Sweden, from the 1970s to the present. It shows, on the one hand, that feminist research is today a visible presence in the theological academic landscape and that feminist/gender perspectives have been integrated into the curricula of theological studies. On the other hand, there is still no full time, permanent position in feminist theology at any Swedish university. Thus, although the situation of feminist theological research in Sweden is relatively good, we still lack resources for long-term work to establish feminist research as a permanent and fully recognized member of the theological community.

L'article suivant présente l'évolution de la recherche théologique féministe en Suède, à partir des années 1970 jusqu'à aujourd'hui. Il montre, d'une part, que la recherche féministe jouit d'une certaine visibilité dans le paysage théologique académique, et que les perspectives féministes/de genre ont été intégrées dans le curriculum des études théologiques. D'autre part, il n'existe toujours aucune chaire de

ForscherInnen, die ein Forschungsseminar für *Gender*-Studien als Teil ihrer Arbeit anbieten. Doch es gibt niemanden, der als hauptamtlicher Professor oder hauptamtliche Professorin für feministische Theologie oder *Gender* und Religion arbeitet.

théologie féministe permanente et à plein temps, dans les universités suédoises. Aussi, bien que la situation de la recherche théologique féministe en Suède soit relativement satisfaisante, nous manquons de ressources pour qu'un travail à long terme soit accompli afin de permettre à la recherche féministe d'être reconnue à part entière dans la communauté universitaire.

Hanna Stenström (*1963) promovierte 1999 an der Theologischen Fakultät der Universität Uppsala in Neutestamentlicher Exegese mit der Arbeit *The Book of Revelation. A Vision of the Ultimate Liberation or the Ultimate Backlash? A study in 20th Century interpretation of Rev. 14,1-4, with special emphasis on feminist exegesis.* Sie lehrt Neues Testament an der Universität Uppsala und arbeitet als wissenschaftliche Mitarbeiterin an der Forschungsstelle der Kirche von Schweden. Unter den von ihr veröffentlichten Artikeln sei folgender erwähnt: „Historical-Critical Approaches and the Emancipation of Women – Unfullfilled Promises and Remaining Possibilities", in: Caroline Vander Stichele / Todd Penner (Hg.), *Her Master's Tools? Feminist and Postcolonial Engagements of Historical-Critical Discourse* (Global Perspectives on Biblical Scholarship 9; Society for Biblical Literature: Atlanta 2005), 31-45.

Journal of the European Society of Women in Theological Research 15 (2007) 209-230.
doi: 10.2143/ESWTR.15.0.2022780

I. SELECTED BIBLIOGRAPHY: FEMINIST RESEARCH IN THEOLOGY IN THE NORDIC COUNTRIES

Hanna Stenström

Research on gender and religion is done in the context of a variety of disciplines. However, this bibliography covers only theology, since we did not want it to grow too big, and since the whole Journal is concerned with theology.

We want to mention that Temenos – Nordic Journal of Comparative Religion 1/2006 is a special issue of feminist research of religion, containing the four keynote papers delivered at the conference Gender, Religion and Theory in Dialogue, held at the University of Helsinki, Finland, in March 2005 (Morny Joy, Saba Mahmood, Grace M. Jantzen and Melissa Raphael). It also includes an overview of recent feminist research in comparative religion in Finland.

We have used a wide and inclusive definition of feminist research, i. e. including both works with a developed feminist theoretical framework, and works mainly aiming at making women visible.

Some of the works listed below are interdisciplinary collections of articles. We have chosen to include them to give our readers a glimpse of work made beyond the borders of theological research.

One aim of the bibliography is to show which themes have been dealt with in the five Nordic countries. Therefore, articles or books in our native languages have been included, with an English translation in brackets. Finally, a number of unpublished academic theses have been included. They are available at the respective university library.

Abbreviations:
AUU   Acta Universitatis Upsaliensis
CBNT   Coniectanea Biblica New Testament Series
WUNT Wissenschaftliche Untersuchungen zum Neuen Testament

I.1 General

Kari Elisabeth Børresen (ed.), **Image of God and Gender Models in Judaeo-Christian Tradition**, Oslo: Solum Forlag 1991
A collection of articles by an interdisciplinary international group of scholars, including Scandinavian theologians (also published as: **The image of God: Gender models in Judaeo-Christian tradition**, Fortress Press: Minneapolis 1995).

Eriksson, Anne-Louise, "Från mäns dominans till kvinnors dans", in: Håkan Eilert etal, **Modern svensk teologi – strömningar och perspektivskiften under 1900-talet**, Stockholm: Verbum 1999, 325-348
About the history of feminist theology in Sweden. In Swedish.

Eriksson, Anne-Louise, **Genusperspektiv på teologi**, Stockholm: Högskoleverket 2004
A short introduction in Swedish to "gender perspective in theology". Published by the Swedish National Agency for Higher Education, as part of a series on gender studies in different academic fields.

Eriksson, Anne-Louise (ed.), **Var kan vi finna en nådig Gud?** Om könsmaktsordning i kyrka och teologi, Working papers in theology 2, Uppsala: Uppsala Universitet 2002
Six articles in Swedish by Swedish scholars, in feminist theology as well as the Lutheran tradition of the Church of Sweden, the Church of Sweden in the 20th Century and 20th Century New Testament Exegesis in Sweden. The theme of the work is the subordination of women in church and theology.

Feministisk teologi Kvinnovetenskaplig tidskrift 2, 1989
An issue on feminist theology of a Swedish interdisciplinary magazine for gender studies. Articles by Scandinavian scholars as Lone Fatum and Dagny Kaul and a translated text by Rosemary Radford Ruether. In Swedish with short summaries in English.

Feministteologi idag. Sju föreläsningar till Kerstin Aspegrens minne, Religio 30,
Teologiska Institutionen: Lund 1989
The published versions of seven lectures delivered 1988 in memory of Kerstin Aspegren, the first contact woman for ESWTR in Sweden. One of them, by Kari Elisabeth Børresen, is in English, the rest are in Norwegian – by Astri Hauge, Dagny Kaul, Eva Lundgren – in Danish – by Lone Fatum – and in Swedish – by Ylva Wramming and Ulla Carin Holm. Together, the articles form an introduction to the state of feminist theology in the late 1980s.

Gud och Genus, Kvinnovetenskaplig tidskrift 3-4, 2003
An issue on "God and Gender" – studies of different kinds of religious material with gender perspectives – of a Swedish interdisciplinary magazine for gender

studies. Articles by scholars from different disciplines, including some theologians (Mikael Sjöberg in Old Testament Exegesis, Erica Appelros in Philosophy of Religion, Anne-Louise Eriksson in Studies in Faith and Ideologies, an article on feminist theology and theory). In Swedish with short summaries in English.

Jarl, Ann-Cathrin, "Feminist Liberation Theology from a Swedish Perspective", Journal of Feminist Studies in Religion 18,1 (2002) 93-98

Kainulainen, Pauliina / Aulikki Mäkinen (eds), **Näen Jumalan toisin. Kristinuskon feministisiä tulkintoja**, Helsinki: Kirjapaja 2006
A collection of feminist theological articles in Finnish.

Kaul, Dagny / Anne Hilde Laland / Solveig Østrem (eds), **Feministteologi på norsk**, Oslo Cappelen Akademisk Forlag 1999
An introduction to feminist theology and to Norwegian feminist research in theology by 18 authors. All articles in Norwegian, although two written by non-Norwegian authors, Anne-Louise Eriksson and Ursula King, who have been important for the development of feminist theology in Norway. The work covers a wide range of authors, from the first generation – as Kari Elisabeth Børresen via Dagny Kaul and Astri Hauge – to young scholars – as Åse Røthing. It also covers a wide range of themes, including for example feminist theory, feminist critique of Christian theologies, ethics, biblical studies, inclusive language and women in the history of the Church. The preface is written by bishop Rosemarie Köhn, the first female bishop in Norway.

Lundgren, Eva (ed.), **Kvinnor, vi måste vara med och skapa kunskap! Sex föreläsningar till Gunnel Larssons minne** [Women, Let's Compose Knowledge! Six lectures in memory of Gunnel Larsson], AUU Uppsala Women's Studies A: Women in Religion 5, Stockholm: Gotab 1994
In Swedish. Gunnel Larsson was at the time of her death a doctoral student in ethics at the Faculty of Theology, Uppsala, and contact person for ESWTR.

Raudvere, Catharina (ed.), **Stigma, status, strategier, Genusperspektiv i religionsvetenskap**, Lund: Studentlitteratur 2002
A collection of nine articles by scholars in religious studies and theology from the University of Lund. The aim is to give an introduction to gender studies in religion, with examples from different disciplines. In Swedish.

Stenström, Hanna (ed.), **Kan vi tro på Gud Fader?**, Tro&Tanke 8, Uppsala: Svenska Kyrkans forskningsråd 1992
A collection of influential feminist theological texts in English, and some newly written articles in Swedish, with introductions in Swedish. An introduction to feminist theology.

I.2 Feminist theory and feminist theology

Erica Appelros, "Religion och intersektionalitet" [Religion and intersectionality], Kvinnovetenskaplig tidskrift 2-3 (2005) 69-80
In Swedish.

Anne-Louise Eriksson, "Who and what are 'Women' in Theology? Some reflections on gender theory and its implications for feminist politics", in: Charlotte Metheun / Angela Berlis (eds), **The End of Liberation? Liberation in the End! Feminist Theory, Feminist Theology and their political implications**, ESWTR Yearbook 10/2002, 11-22

Sari Lehti, **"The Otherworld journey". Mary Daly's radikalfeministiska verklighetsuppfattning** [Mary Daly's Radical Feminist Understanding of Reality], Unpublished, Åbo Akademi Library
In Swedish.

Eva Lundgren, **Det får da være grenser for kjønn**. Voldelig empiri og feministisk teori, Oslo: Universitetsforlaget 1993
In Norwegian.
A revised version is published in English: **Feminist Theory and Violent Empiricism**, Avebury: Aldershot & Brookfield 1995
Develops Lundgren's feminist theory, which was influential especially in Swedish feminist theological research in the 1990s, when Lundgren was leader of the Seminar for feminist research at the Faculty of Theology, University of Uppsala.

Jorunn Økland, "Sex, gender and ancient Greek: A case-study in theoretical misfit", Studia Theologica 57 (2003) 124-142
The article takes feminist theory as its point of departure, and relates especially to works by Scandinavian scholars, especially in feminist theology and exegesis.

Elina Vuola, "Remaking Universals? Transnational Feminism(s) Challenging Fundamentalist Ecumenism", Theory, Culture and Society 19/1-2 (2002) 175-195

I.3 The Bible, including theological reflection on biblical authority

Marianne Bjelland Kartzow, "Female Gossipers and their reputation in the Pastoral Epistles", Neotestamentica 39/2 (2005) 255-272

Annika Borg, **Kön och bibeltolkning. En undersökning av hur Nya testamentets brevtexter om kvinnors underordning tolkats i bibelvetenskapliga kommentarer** [Sex/gender issues and biblical interpretation. A study of the interpretations of women's subordination in exegetical work during the twentieth century], Unpublished dissertation, University of Uppsala, 2004. In Swedish with 3,5 pp summary in Swedish.

Anne-Louise Eriksson, "Bibelns auktoritet och kvinnors erfarenhet" [The Authority of the Bible and Women's Experience], in: Per Block (ed.), **Om tolkning V. Bibeln som auktoitet**, Tro&Tanke 1, Uppsala: Svenska Kyrkans forskningsråd 1998, 134-146 In Swedish.

Anne-Louise Eriksson, "Radical Hermeneutics and Scriptural Authority", in: Charlotte Metheun etal (eds), **Holy Texts: Authority and Language**, ESWTR Yearbook 12/2004, 47-52

Lone Fatum, "Image of God and Glory of Man: Women in the Pauline Congregations", in: Kari Elisabeth Børresen (ed.), **Image of God and Gender Models in Judaeo-Christian Tradition**, Oslo: Solum Forlag 1991, 56-137

Lone Fatum, **Kvindeteologi og arven fra Eva**, Gyldendal Intro, Copenhagen: Gyldendal 1992
An introduction to feminist theology for the general public, mainly consisting of analyses of biblical texts where Fatum's critique of Fiorenza's form of feminist biblical scholarship is visible and her programme for "gender hermeneutics" is carried out in practice. In Danish.

Lone Fatum, "1 Thessalonians", in: Elisabeth Schüssler Fiorenza (ed.), **Searching the Scriptures. Volume Two: A Feminist Commentary**, New York: Crossroad 1994 / London: SCM Press 1995, 250-262

Lone Fatum, "Christ Domesticated: The Household Theology of the Pastorals as Political Strategy", in: Jostein Ådna (ed.), **The Formation of the Early Church**, WUNT 183 Tübingen: Mohr Siebeck 2005, 175-207

Mette Marie Ladekær Gräs, **Kønshermeneutik. Metodediskussion og eksegese af Joh 3,1-21; 4,4-42** [Gender Hermeneutics. Discussion of method and an exegesis of Joh 3:1-21; 4:4-42], Tekst &Tolkning 11, Copenhagen: Akademisk Forlag 1994. In Danish.

Cristina Grenholm / Daniel Patte (eds), **Gender, Tradition and Romans. Shared Grounds, Uncertain Borders**, Romans Through History and Culture Series, London: T&T Clark 2005

Hans Jacob Hansen / Jakob Schow Madsen (eds), **"Thi Gud er jeg, ikke mand". Studier over kvindebilleder i Det gamle Testamente**, Aarhus: FK-tryk 1982
A collection of articles on the images of women in the Old Testament. In Danish.

Birgitte Graakjær Hjort, "Gender hierarchy or religious androgyny? Male-Female interaction in the Corinthian community – a reading of 1 Cor 11,2-16", Studia Theologica 55 (2001) 58-80

Inger Ljung, **Silence or Suppression. Attitudes Towards Women in the Old Testament**, AUU Uppsala Women's Studies A: Women in Religion 2, Stockholm: Almqvist & Wiksell International 1989

Inger Ljung "'Vad händer då om det är en kvinna som läser?' – några tankar runt auktoritet, tolkning och ansvar", in: Per Block (ed.), **Om tolkning V. Bibeln som auktoritet**, Tro&Tanke 1, Uppsala: Svenska Kyrkans forskningsråd 1998, 122-133 In Swedish. The article takes reader-oriented biblical exegesis as its point of departure, and moves on to introducing the international exegetical discussions of ethics of biblical interpretation – where Elisabeth Schüssler Fiorenza and Daniel Patte are important – for the Swedish public, and to formulating the author's own model for responsible biblical scholarship.

Talvikki Mattila, **Citizens of the Kingdom. Followers in Matthew from a Feminist Perspective**, Helsinki: The Finnish Exegetical Society / Göttingen: Vandenhoeck & Ruprecht 2002

Cecilia Nahnfeldt, **Kallelse och kön. Schabloner i läsning av Matteusevangeliets berättelser**, Karlstad University Studies 25, Karlstad: Karlstad University 2006. In Swedish with 8 pp summary in English: "Vocation and Gender Reinterpreted: Patterns in the Narrative of the Gospel of Matthew"

Kirsten Nielsen, „Kvindens stilling i det gamle testamente. I Jura og teologi II: Teologi og gyldighed", in: Hans Jacob Hansen / Jakob Schow-Madsen J. (eds), **Thi Gud er jeg, ikke mand**, Aarhus: FKTryk 1982, 69-90 On women in the Old Testament, in Danish.

Jorunn Økland, **Women in Their Place. Paul and the Corinthian Discourse of Gender and Sanctuary Space**, London: T&T Clark International: 2004 The published version of Økland's dissertation with the same name at the University of Oslo in 2000.

Karin Friis Plum, **Kvindehistorie og kvindehistorier – i det gamle testamente**, Copenhagen: Hans Reitzels Forlag 1984 On women stories and women's history in the Hebrew Bible. For the general public. In Danish.

Karin Friis Plum, **Den tilslørede frihed.** Kvindehistorie og kvindehistorier i det nye testamente, Copenhagen: Hans Reitzels Forlag 1984
On women stories and women's history in the New Testament. For the general public. In Danish.

Lilian Portefaix, **Sisters Rejoice! Paul's Letters to the Philippians and Luke-Acts as Seen by First-Century Philippian Women,** CBNT 20, Stockholm: Almqvist & Wiksell International, 1988

Turid Karlsen Seim, "Ascetic Autonomy? New Perspectives on Single Women in the Early Church", Studia Theologica 43 (1989) 125-140

Turid Karlsen Seim, **The Double Message. Patterns of Gender in Luke-Acts,** Studies of the New Testament and its World, London: T&T Clark 1994
A new edition was published in 2004. The published version of Seim's dissertation – written in Norwegian – from the Faculty of Theology, University of Oslo, 1989.

Turid Karlsen Seim, "The Gospel of Luke", in: Elisabeth Schüssler Fiorenza (ed.), **Searching the Scriptures. Volume Two: A Feminist Commentary,** New York: Crossroad 1994 / London: SCM Press, 1995, 728-762

Mikael Sjöberg, **Wrestling with Textual Violence. The Jephtah Narrative in Antiquity and Modernity,** The Bible in the Modern World 4, Sheffield: Sheffield Phoenix Press 2006

Hanna Stenström, **The Book of Revelation: A Vision of the Ultimate Liberation or the Ultimate Backlash? A study in 20th Century interpretations of Rev 14:1-5, with special emphasis on feminist exegesis,** Unpublished dissertation, University of Uppsala, 1999

Hanna Stenström, "Grandma, Räisänen and the Global Village: A Feminist Approach to Ethical Criticism", in: Ismo Dunderberg etal, **Fair Play: Diversity and Conflicts in Early Christianity. Essays in Honour of Heikki Räisänen,** Supplements to Novum Testamentum vol CIII, Leiden: Brill 2002, 521-540

Hanna Stenström, "Is A Feminist Liberating Exegesis Possible Without Liberation Theology?" lectio difficilior 1 (2002), n.p. online: http://www.lectio.unibe.ch

Hanna Stenström, "Historical-Critical Approaches and the Emancipation of Women – Unfullfilled Promises and Remaining Possibilities", in: Caroline Vander Stichele / Todd Penner (eds), **Her Master's Tools? Feminist and Postcolonial Engagements of Historical-Critical Discourse,** Global Perspectives on Biblical Scholarship 9, Atlanta: Society for Biblical Literature 2005, 31-45

215

Studia Theologica. Scandinavian Journal of Theology, 43/1 (1989)
An issue on the theme "Feminist Reconstruction of Early Christian History", with its origins in a Nordic conference on the methodological and hermeneutical issues connected with feminist reconstruction of Early Christian history. The collection of essays, as well as the conference, is cross-disciplinary, involving biblical scholars as well as social anthropologists and scholars in philosophy and classical studies. Two essays are written by Elisabeth Schüssler Fiorenza and the others by Nordic scholars.

Rut Törnkvist, **The Use and Abuse of Female Sexual Imagery in the Book of Hosea. A Feminist Critical Approach to Hos 1-3**, AUU Uppsala Women's Studies A. Women in Religion 7, Uppsala: Uppsala University 1998

Anni Tsokkinnen, "Elisabeth Schüssler Fiorenza on the Authority of the Bible", in: Charlotte Methuen etal (eds), **Holy Texts. Authority and Language**, ESWTR Yearbook 12/2004, 133-142

I.4 Christian theology, including feminist theology

Kari Elisabeth Børresen, **Subordination et équivalence: Nature et rôle de la femme d'apres Augustin et Thomas d'Aquin**, Oslo: Universitetsforlaget / Paris: Maison Mame 1968
Published in English as **Subordination and Equivalence. The Nature and Role of Woman in Augustine and Thomas Aquinas**, Washington: Edition University Press of America 1981, reprinted as **Subordination and Equivalence. The Nature and Role of Woman in Augustine and Thomas Aquinas: A Reprint of a Pioneering Classic**, Kampen: Kok Pharos / Mainz: Grünewald 1995 with a new foreword, some additional bibliographical information about the author's later publications and an interview with the author.
There is also a revised Italian version of the book, published by Citadella Editrice, Assisi 1979.

Kari Elisabeth Børresen, **From Patristics to Matristics. Selected Articles on Christian Gender Models. Published on Occasion of her 70th Anniversary 16 October 2002**, edited by Øyvind Norderval / Katrine Lund Ore, Rome: Herder 2002

Anne-Louise Eriksson, **The Meaning of Gender in Theology. Problems and possibilities**, AUU Uppsala Women's Studies A: Women in Religion 6, Uppsala: University of Uppsala 1995

Anne-Louise Eriksson, **Kvinnor talar om Jesus. En feministisk kristologisk praxis**, Nora: Nya Doxa 1999
On feminist christology. In Swedish.

Cristina Grenholm, **Barmhärtig och sårbar. En bok om kristen tro på Jesus**, Stockholm: Verbum 1999
On christology, in Swedish.

Cristina Grenholm, **Moderskap och kärlek. Schabloner och tankeutrymme i feministteologisk livsåskådningsreflektion** [Motherhood and Love: Stereotypes and Space of Thought in Feminist Theological Reflections on Life], Nora: Nya Doxa 2005
In Swedish with a short abstract in English.

Arnfríður Guðmundsdóttir, **Meeting God on the Cross. An Evaluation of Feminist Contributions to Christology in Light of a Theology of the Cross**, Unpublished dissertation, The Lutheran School of Theology at Chicago 1995
Will be published by Oxford University Press, most probably in 2008.

Astri Hauge, "Har lutherdommen rom for feministisk nytenkning?", in: Dagny Kaul / Anne Hilde Laland / Solveig Østrem (eds), **Feministteologi på norsk**, Oslo: Cappelen Akademisk Forlag 1999, 17-37
On the possibility of making room for feminist renewal in the Lutheran tradition.
In Norwegian.

Tuija Numminen, **God, Power and Justice in Texts of Simone Weil and Dorothee Sölle**, Unpublished, Åbo Akademi Library

Else Marie Wiberg Pedersen, "'The Holy Spirit shall come upon you' Mary – the Human 'Locus' for the Holy Spirit", in: Else Marie Wiberg Pedersen / Johannes Nissen (eds), **Cracks in the Walls. Essays on Spirituality, Ecumenicity and Ethics. Festschrift for Anna Marie Aagard on the Occasion of her 70th Birthday**, Frankfurt: Peter Lang 2005, 23-41

Pamela Slotte, **"Att förmedla liv". Dorothee Sölles syn på teologins språk och det hermeneutiska uppdraget** [Dorothee Sölles Understanding of Theological Language and the Hermeneutical Task], Unpublished, Åbo Akademi Library.
In Swedish.

Elina Vuola, **Limits of Liberation. Feminist Theology and the Ethics of Poverty and Reproduction**, Sheffield: Sheffield Academic Press / New York: Continuum 2002
The published version of the dissertation: **Limits of Liberation. Praxis as Method in Latin American Liberation Theology and Feminist Theology**, The Finnish Academy of Science and Letters No. 289, Helsinki 1997
Also published as: **Teología feminista, teología de la liberación. Los límites de la praxis**, Madrid: IEPALA Editorial 2000 and **La ética sexual y los límites de**

la praxis. **Conversaciones críticas entre la teología feminista y la teología de la liberación**, Quito: Editorial Abya-Yala 2001

Elina Vuola, "El derecho a la vida y el sujeto femenino" [The Right to Life and the Female Subject], Pasos 88 (2000) 1-12

Elina Vuola, "Option for the Poor and the Exclusion of Women – The Challenges of Postmodernism and Feminism to Liberation Theology", in: Joerg Rieger (ed.), **Opting for the Margins. Postmodernity and Liberation in Christian Theology**, Oxford: Oxford University Press 2003, 105-126

Elina Vuola, "Thinking *Other*wise: Dussel, Liberation Theology, and Feminism", in: Linda Martín Alcoff / Eduardo Mendieta (eds), **Thinking from the Underside of History. Enrique Dussel's Philosophy of Liberation**, New York: Rowman and Littlefield Publishers 2000, 149-180

Elina Vuola, "Jungfru Maria och alla övriga kvinnor. Om möjligheterna av en feministisk befrielsemariologi" [Virgin Mary and the Rest of Women. On the Possibilities of a Feminist Liberation Mariology], in: Sigurd Bergmann / Carl Reinhold Bråkenhielm (eds), **Vardagskulturens teologi i nordisk tolkning**, Falun: Bokförlaget Nya Doxa 1998, 45-81
In Swedish.

I.5 Ecofeminism, theology and/or ethics

Maria Jansdotter, **Ekofeminism i teologin: Genusuppfattning, natursyn och gudsuppfattning hos Anne Primavesi, Catherine Keller och Carol Christ** [Ecofeminism in Theology: Views of Gender, Nature and God in Anne Primavesi, Catherine Keller and Carol Christ], Karlstad University Studies 14, Karlstad: Karlstad University 2003
In Swedish with 6 pp summary in English.

Pauliina Kainulainen, **Maan viisaus. Ivone Gebaran ekofeministinen käsitys tietämisestä ja teologiasta** [The Wisdom of the Earth. Ivone Gebarás Ecofeminist Concept of Knowing and Theology], University of Joensuu Publications in Theology 13, Joensuu: University of Joensuu 2005
In Finnish.

Dagny Kaul, "Ecofeminism in the Nordic Countries", in: Mary Grey / Eliszabeth Green (eds), **Ecofeminism and Theology**, ESWTR Yearbook 2/1994, 102-109

David Kronlid, **Ecofeminism and Environmental Ethics: An Analysis of Ecofeminist Ethical Theory**, AUU, Uppsala Studies in Social Ethics 28, Stockholm: Elander Gotab 2003

I.6 Ethics

Malena Björkgren, **I nöd och lust. Feministiska perspektiv på mäns våld mot kvinnor inom kristen tradition**, Unpublished, Åbo Akademi Library, Finland
About feminist perspectives on men's violence towards women in the Christian Tradition. In Swedish.

Sólveig Anna Bóasdóttir, **Violence, Power and Justice. A Feminist Contribution to Sexual Ethics**, AUU, Uppsala Studies in Social Ethics 20, Uppsala: Uppsala University 1998

Sólveig Anna Bóasdóttir, "Cultural Violence. Interpretation of men's violence in feminist theological ethics", in: **Kön och våld i Norden. Gender and Violence in the Nordic Countries. Rapport från en konferens i Köge, Danmark, 23-24 november 2001**, TemaNor 545, Nordiska Ministerrådet: Köbenhavn 2002, 441-450

Sólveig Anna Bóasdóttir, "Feminist sexual ethics", in: Carl-Henric Grenholm / Normunds Kamergrauzis (eds), **Feminist Ethics. Perspectives, Problems and Possibilities**, AUU Uppsala Studies in Social Ethics 29, Uppsala: Uppsala University 2003, 101-118

Sólveig Anna Bóasdóttir, "Auktoritet – sociala visioner – feministisk samlevnadsetik" [Authority – social visions – feminist sexual ethics], Tidskrift for Teologi og Kirke 75/2-3 (2004) 183-192
In Swedish.

Sólveig Anna Bóasdóttir, "Samkynhneigð og kristin siðfræði" [Homosexuality and Christian Ethics], in: Ólafur Páll Jónsson / Albert Steinn Guðjónsson (eds), **Andspænis sjálfum sér. Samkynhneigð ungmenni, ábyrgð og innsæi fagstétta** [Against Yourself. Homosexual adolescents, responsibility and the intuition of professionals], Reykjavík: Háskólaútgáfan 2005, 65-96
In Icelandic.

Sólveig Anna Bóasdóttir, "Sexuality and Social Justice. Feminist Theological Discourse of Sexual Pleasure", Sexologi. Et magasin for det sexologiska fagmiljöet 1 (2006) 18-21

Sólveig Anna Bóasdóttir, "Hvað er guðfræðileg siðfræði? Samspil kynjafræði og guðfræði" [What is theological ethics? A Conversation between Gender Studies and Theology], Glíman. Óháð tímarit um guðfræði og samfélag 1 (2006) 35-55
In Icelandic.

Elisabeth Gerle, **In search of a global ethics: theological, political and feminist perspectives based on a critical analysis of JPIC and WOMP**, Lund Studies in Ethics and Theology 2, Lund: Lund University Press 1995

Carl-Henric Grenholm / Normunds Kamergrauzis (eds), **Feminist Ethics: Perspectives, Problems and Possibilities**, AUU Uppsala Studies in Social Ethics 29, Uppsala: Uppsala University 2003
Papers from a Nordic Conference on the theme given in the title of the book, with contributions by international feminist ethicists and one nordic, Sólveig Anna Bóasdóttir, as well as by Nordic ethicists who are not specialised in feminist ethics but still want to enter into dialogue with feminist ethics.

Johanna Gustafsson, **Kyrka och kön. Om könskonstruktioner i Svenska Kyrkan 1945-1985**, Stockholm / Stehag: B. Östlings bokförlag Symposion 2001
On the discussions of gender, sexuality and marriage in the Church of Sweden 1945-1985. In Swedish with a 13 pp summary in English.

Ann Heberlein, **Den sexuella människan. Etiska perspektiv**, Lund: Studentlitteratur 2004
A popular work on sexual ethics, in Swedish.

Anna Höglund, **Krig och kön. Feministisk etik och den moraliska bedömningen av militärt våld** [War and Gender. Feminist Ethics and the Moral Judgement of Military Violence], AUU Uppsala Studies in Social Ethics 26, Uppsala: Uppsala University 2001
In Swedish, with about 10 pp summary in English.

Ann-Cathrin Jarl, **In Justice. Women and Global Economics**, Minneapolis: Fortress Press 2003
A published version of: **Women and Economic Justice. Ethics in Feminist Liberation Theology and Feminist Economics**, AUU, Uppsala Studies in Social Ethics 25, Uppsala: University of Uppsala 2000

Suvielise Nurmi, "Who We Are? The Question of a Moral Agent in Environmental Ethics", Sustaining Humanity Beyond Humanism, Societas Ethica Annual 39 (2002) 113-126

Karin Sporre, **Först när vi får ansikten – ett flerkulturellt samtal om feminism, etik och teologi** [First when we have faces. A cross-cultural conversation on feminism, ethics and theology], Lund Studies in Ethics and Theology 9, Stockholm: Atlas 1999
The partners in the conversation are Katie G. Cannon, Chung Hyun Kyung and Mary Grey. In Swedish with a 26 pp summary in English.

Karin Sporre, "Women's Human Rights in Sweden: A Feminist Ethical Perspective", in: Karin Sporre / H. Russel Botman (eds), **Building a Human Rights Culture. South African and Swedish Perspectives, Report from Arts and Education,** Falun: Högskolan Dalarna 2003, 288-310

Marja Suhonen, **Mary Dalyn sukupuolen ja seksuaalisuuden etiikka Simone de Beauvoirin ajattelun valossa** [Mary Daly's Ethics of Gender and Sexuality in the Light of Simone de Beauvoir's Thinking], Unpublished, University of Helsinki Library. In Finnish.

Elina Vuola, "Beyond Machos and Madonnas? Issues of Sexual Ethics in Latin American Liberation Theology", in: Red. Sigurd Bergmann (ed.), **Man får inte tvinga någon. Autonomi och relationalitet i nordisk tolkning,** Nora: Bokförlaget Nya Doxa, 2001, 235-246

Elina Vuola, "Seriously Harmful for Your Health? Religion, Feminism and Sexuality in Latin America", in: Marcella Althaus-Reid (ed.), **Liberation Theology and Sexuality. New Radicalism from Latin America,** London: Ashgate 2006, 137-162

I.7 Philosophy of Religion

Erica Appelros, "Finns Gud? Feministiska förhållningssätt till en omdebatterad fråga", Genus och Gud Kvinnovetenskaplig tidskrift 3-4 (2003) 71-75
A discussion of religious realism and anti-realism from a feminist perspective. In Swedish with a short summary in English.

Kirsten Grønlien Zetterqvist, **Att vara kroppssubjekt. Ett fenomenologiskt bidrag till feministisk teori och religionsfilosofi** [Being a Body Subject. A phenomenological contribution to feminist theory and philosophy of religion], Studia Philosophiae Religionis 23, Uppsala: University of Uppsala 2002
In Swedish with 2,5 pp summary in English.

Annukka Kalske, "Katsaus feministisen uskonnonfilosofian lähtökohtiin", Teologinen Aikakauskirja 1 (2006) 5-12
An outline of Feminist Philosophy of Religion, in Finnish.

I.8 Women in the churches in past and present

Kerstin Aspegren, **The male woman. A feminine ideal in the Early Church,** AUU Uppsala Women's Studies A: Women in Religion 4, Uppsala: University of Uppsala 1990 (reprinted in 1995, edited by René Kieffer)

Ninna Edgardh Beckman, **Folkkyrka – i solidaritet med kvinnor?**, Tro&Tanke 2, Uppsala: Svenska kyrkans Forskningsråd 1998
About the work during The Ecumenical Decade Churches in Solidarity with Women 1988-1998 in the Church of Sweden. In Swedish with 5,5 pp summary in English.

Kari Elisabeth Børresen / Kari Vogt, **Women's Studies of the Christian and Islamic Traditions: ancient, medieval and Renaissance foremothers**, Dordrecht: Kluwer Academic Publishers 2003

Kari Elisabeth Børresen (ed.), **Christian and Islamic Gender Models in Formative Traditions**, Rome: Herder 2004
By an international group of scholars, including four Norwegians.

Ruth Franzén, "Kvinnoperspektiv på kyrkohistorisk forskning", in: **Kirkko ja politiikka. Festschrift für Eino Murtorinne**, Veröffentlichungen der Finnischen Gesellschaft für Kirchengeschichte 153, Helsinki Suomen Kirkkohistoriallinen Seura/Finnische Gesellschaft für Kirchengeschichte: 1990, 113-129.
In Swedish with short summary in German "Kirchengeschichtliche Forschung aus der Sicht von Frauen".

Arnfríður Guðmundsdóttir, "Kristnisaga með eða án kvenna" [A Church History with or without Women], in: **Kristni á Íslandi. Útgáfumálþing á Akureyri og í Reykjavík** [Christianity in Iceland. Papers and procedures from a Conference concerning the publication of a new Icelandic Church History, held in Akureyri and Reykjavik], 2001, 93-100.
In Icelandic.

Arnfríður Guðmundsdóttir, "'Kristur var minn eini vinur.' Þjáning og trú í lífi Guðríðar Símonardóttur" ['Christ was my only Friend.' Suffering and Faith in the life of Guðríður Símonardóttir], Studia Theologica Islandica 15 (2001) 11-24
In Icelandic.

Gunilla Gunner, **Nelly Hall: uppburen och ifrågasatt. Predikant och missionär i Europa och USA 1882-1901** [Nelly Hall: Esteemed and questioned as Preacher and a Missionary in Europe and United States 1882-1901], Studia Missionalia Svecana XCII, Uppsala University of Uppsala 2003
In Swedish with 6,5 pp summary in English.

Dagny Kaul, "Femmes-pasteurs et theólogie féministe au sein de 'l'association norvégienne des théologiennes'", in: Angela Berlis et al (eds), **Women Churches: Networking and Reflection in the European Context**, ESWTR Yearbook 3/1995, 142-155

Tulikki Koivunen Bylund, **Frukta icke, allenast tro. Ebba Boström och Samariter-hemmet 1882-1902** ["Fear not, believe only". Ebba Boström and the Samaritan Home 1882-1902], Bibliotheca Theologiae Practicae 52, Stockholm: Almqvist & Wiksell International 1994
In Swedish with about 11 pp summary in English.

Gunvor Lande, **Visjonen om likeverdet. Det økumeniske tiåret 1988-1998. Kyrkjer i solidaritet med kvinner i El Salvador, Noreg, Kenya og Japan** [The Vision of Like-Worthiness. The Ecumenical Decade 1988-1998 – Churches in Solidarity with Women in El Salvador, and Norway, Kenya and Japan], Bibliotheca Theologiae Practicae 67, Lund: Lund University 2002
In Norwegian with 4,5 pp summary in English.

Pirjo Markkola (ed.), **Gender and Vocation. Women, Religion and Social Change in the Nordic Countries 1830-1940**, Studia Historica 64, Helsinki: SKS-FLS 2000
A collection of articles by historians and church historians.

Else-Britt Nilsen, "Religious Identity and National Loyality: Women Religious in Norway during the Second World War", in: Yvonne Maria Werner (ed.), **Nuns and Sisters in the Nordic Countries after the Reformation: A Female Counter-Culture in Modern Society**, Studia Missionalia Svecana XC, The Swedish Institute of Mission Research Uppsala [SIM] 2004, 213-253

Ellen Nielsen, **Kvinden i mandens kirke**, København: Samleren 1978
On women in church history, from the beginning to the present. For the general public. In Danish.

Inger Marie Okkenhaug (ed.), **Gender, Race and Religion. Nordic Missions 1860-1940**, Studia Missionalia Svecana XCI, Uppsala: University of Uppsala 2003
An interdisciplinary collection of articles.

Else Marie Wiberg Pedersen, **Gudsbillede – Mariabillede – Kvindebillede: Om teologi og spiritualitet hos Beatrice of Nazareth (1200-1268)** [Image of God – Image of Mary – Image of Woman: On the Theology and Spirituality of Beatrice of Nazareth (1200-1268)], Unpublished dissertation, University of Aarhus, 1991
In Danish.

Else Marie Wiberg Pedersen, "Image of God – Image of Mary – Image of Woman: On the Theology and Spirituality of Beatrice of Nazareth", Cistercian Studies Quarterly 29/2 (1994) 209-221

Else Marie Wiberg Pedersen, "Gottesbild – Frauenbild – Selbstbild. Die Theologie Mechthilds von Hackeborn und Gertruds von Helfta", in: M. Bangert / Hildegund

Keul (eds), **Vor dir steht die leere Schale meiner Sehnsucht**, Leipzig: Benno Verlag 1999, 46-68

Else Marie Wiberg Pedersen, "The In-Carnation of Beatrice of Nazareth's Theology", in: J. Dor etal (eds), **New Trends in Feminine Spirituality: The Holy Women of Liège and Their Impact**, Turnhout: Brepols Publishers 1999, 61-81

Else Marie Wiberg Pedersen (ed.), **Se min kjole. De første kvindelige præsters historie** [See my Gown. The History of the First Women Pastors in Denmark], Copenhagen: Samleren 1998
In Danish.

Eeva Raunistola-Juutinen, **Äiti ja nunna. Kirkkojen Maailmanneuvoston naisten ekumeenisen vuosikymmenen pan-ortodoksisten dokumenttien naiskuva** [The Image of Women in the Pan-Orthodox Documents of the Ecumenical Decade of Women of the World Council of Churches], Unpublished, University of Joensuu Library.
In Finnish.

Päivi Salmesvuori, "Kirkko ja yhteiskunta: Uskonnon vaikutus naiskuvaan Suomessa" [The Church and Society. How Religion affects Images of Women and Humanity], in: Anna Moring (ed.), **Sukupuolen politiikka – Naisten äänioikeuden 100 vuotta Suomessa** [Politics of Gender. A Century of Women's Suffrage in Finland], Helsinki: Otava 2006, 117-126
In Finnish. The book is also published in Swedish as **Kön och politik. 100 år av kvinnlig rösträtt i Finland**

Päivi Salmesvuori, "Birgitta – aatelisneidosta kosmopoliitiksi" [Birgitta of Sweden – from a Noble Maiden to a Cosmopolitan], in: Päivi Setälä / Eva Ahl (eds), **Pyhä Birgitta – Euroopan suojeluspyhimys** [Saint Birgitta – the Patroness Saint of Europe], Helsinki: Otava 2003, 9–54
In Finnish.

Päivi Salmesvuori, "Birgitta, Hemming ja Naantalin luostari" [Birgitta, Hemming, and the Cloister of Naantali], in: Tuomas M. S. Lehtonen / Timo Joutsivuo (eds), **Suomen kulttuurihistoria I, Taivas ja maa** [Finland's Cultural History], Helsinki: Tammi 2003, 177–182; 185–189.
In Finnish.

Päivi Salmesvuori, "Hildegard Bingeniläinen miesten maailmassa" [Hildegard of Bingen in Men's World], in: Meri Heinonen (ed.), **Ikuisuuden odotus. Uskonto**

keskiajan kulttuurissa [Waiting for Eternity. Religion in the Medieval Culture], Helsinki: Gaudeamus 2000, 59–87
In Finnish.

Karin Sarja; **"Ännu en syster till Afrika". Trettiosex kvinnliga missionärer i Natal och Zululand 1876-1902** ["Yet another Sister for Africa". Thirty-six female missionaries in Natal and Zululand 1876-1902], Studia Missionalia Svecana LXXXVIII, Uppsala: Uppsala university 2002
In Swedish with 14 pp summary in English.

Nina Sjöberg, **Hustru och man i Birgittas uppenbarelser** [Wife and husband in the Revelations of St. Birgitta], AUU Studia Historico-Ecclesiastica Upsaliensa 41, Uppsala: University of Uppsala 2003
In Swedish with 8,5 pp summary in English.

Synnøve Hinnaland Stendal, **"...under forvandlingens lov". En analyse av stortingsdebatten om kvinnelige prester i 1930-åren**, Bibliotheca Theologica Practicae 70, Lund: Arcus 2003
In Norwegian with 10pp summary in English: "Undergoing a Metamorphosis: An Analysis of the Debate in the Storting in the 1930s on Women Ministers". *Stortinget* is the Parlament in Norway.

Elina Vuola, "Sor Juana Inés de la Cruz. Rationality, Gender, and Power", Journal of Hispanic/Latino Theology August (2001) 77-97
Swedish translation "Sor Juana Inés de la Cruz. Rationalitet, genus och makt", in: Sigurd Bergmann / Cristina Grenholm (eds), **Makt i nordisk teologisk tolkning**, Trondheim: Tapir akademisk forlag & NTNU 2004, 77-97

Cecilia Wejryd, **Svenska Kyrkans syföreningar 1844-2003** [Sewing Circles in the Church of Sweden from 1844 until 2003], Forskning för kyrkan 1, Stockholm: Verbum 2005
In Swedish.

I.9 Liturgies, preaching, christian feminist spirituality, ecclesiology

Ninna Edgardh Beckman, "Sophia – a possible Christian and Feminist Wisdom", Feminist Theology 16 (1997) 32-54

Ninna Edgardh Beckman, **Feminism och liturgi. En ecklesiologisk studie**, Stockholm: Verbum 2001

A study of feminist liturgies celebrated in Sweden during The Ecumenical Decade Churches in Solidarity with Women 1988-1998. In Swedish with 10,5 pp summary in English "Feminism and Liturgy – an Ecclesiological Study".

Ninna Edgardh Beckman, "Lady Wisdom as Hostess for the Lord's Supper", in: Teresa Berger (ed.), **Dissident Daughters. Feminist Liturgies in Global Context**, Louisville Kentucky: Westminster John Knox Press 2001, 159-174

Ninna Edgardh Beckman, "Mrs Murphy's Arising from the Pew: Ecclesiological Implications", Ecumenical Review 53/1 (2001) 5-13

Ninna Edgardh Beckman, "The Theology of Gathering and Sending; a Challenge from Feminist Liturgy", International Journal for the Study of the Christian Church 6/2 (2006) 144-165

Ninna Edgardh Beckman, "The Relevance of Gender in Rites of Ordination", in: Hans Raun Iversen (ed.), **Rites of Ordination and Commitment in the Churches of the Nordic Countries. Terminology and Theology of Ordination in Churches in the Nordic Countries**, Copenhagen: Museum Tusculanum Press 2006, 539-549

Arnfríður Guðmundsdóttir, "Auður Eid Vilhjálmsdóttir og feministisk teologi", in: Sven-Åke Selander / Christer Palmblad (eds), **Luthersk påskpredikan i Norden II**, Copenhagen: Nordisk Ministerråd 2002, 543-555
An article on Auður Eid Vilhjálmsdóttir – pastor in the Women's Church, a group in the Lutheran Church of Iceland – and feminist theology, in a work on Lutheran Easter Sermons in the Nordic Countries. In Danish.

Else Marie Wiberg Pedersen, "Lutheran Ecclesiologies Today – Custodians of the Past or Guides to the Future?", in: Else Marie Wiberg Pedersen etal (eds), **For All People. Global Theologies in Contexts. Essays in Honor of Viggo Mortensen**, Grand Rapids Michigan: Eerdmans 2002,128-148
The article takes ordination of women as its point of departure.

Lise Tostrup Setek, "When Good Friday Seems No Good, Still Rays of the Easter Sun Break the Fog of Suffering", in: Annette Esser etal (eds), **Revisioning Our Sources. Women's Spirituality in European Perspectives**, Kampen: Kok Pharos 1997, 193-206

I.10 Inclusive language in worship and Bible translations

Arnfríður Guðmundsdóttir, **"Hvenær eru konur menn?"**. **Um kynjað tungutak og þörfina á endurskoðun málfars í boðun og starfi kirkjunnar** ["When are women men?" About Gendered Language and the Need for a Re-evaluation of the

Language used by the Church], Orðið. Rit félags guðfræðinema [The Word. The Journal of the Theological Students's Association] 36/1 (2001)

Fredrik Ivarsson, **Evangelium enligt Markus och Maria: Förslag till revidering av NT 81:s översättning av Markusevangeliet utifrån en diskussion om inklusivt språk**, Tro & Tanke 4, Uppsala: Svenska Kyrkans Forskningsråd 1999
An introduction to the discussion of inclusive language, especially inclusive language in translations of the Bible, and a revised version of the latest Swedish translation of the Gospel of Mark using inclusive language. In Swedish.

Marit Rong, "'Like sant som Gud er vår far, er han vår mor' Inkluderande språk i kirken", in: Kaul, Dagny / Anne Hilde Laland / Solveig Østrem (eds), **Feministteologi på norsk**, Oslo: Cappelen Akademisk Forlag 1999, 195-211
On inclusive language in Christian services, with special focus on the Lutheran Church in Norway. The subject of the article is also the focus of the author's doctoral project. In Norwegian.

I.11 Interfaith dialogue and theology of religions

Helene Egnell, **Other Voices. A Study of Christian Feminist Approaches to Religious Plurality East and West**, Studia Missionalia Svecana C, Uppsala: Uppsala University 2006

Anne Hege Grung, "Kvindeperspektiv på kristen-muslimsk dialog" [Women's perspectives on Christian-Muslim Dialogue], in: Lissi Rasmussen / Lena Larsen (eds), **Islam, Kristendom og det Moderne** [Islam, Christianity and Modernity], Copenhagen: Tiderne skifter 2004, 164-179
In Norwegian.

Anne Hege Grung, "Religionsdialog og kjønn: Kan interreligiøse dialoger føre til større kjønnsrettferdighet?" [Interfaith Dialogue and Gender: Will interfaith dialogue promote gender justice?], Norsk Tidsskrift for Misjon 3/4 (2006) (*Festschrift* for professor Notto Thelle), 269-282
In Norwegian.

Anne Hege Grung / Lena Larsen, **Dialog med og uten slør**, Oslo: Pax Forlag 2000
On interfaith dialogue between Muslim and Christian women in Norway. In Norwegian.

I.12 Postchristian feminist spirituality

Jone Salomonsen, **Når gud bli kvinne. Blant hekser, villmenn og sjamaner i USA**, Oslo: Pax Forlag 1991

A presentation for the general public of the author's research on post-christian religious movements in the US, including feminist witches. In Norwegian.

Jone Salomonsen, **Enchanted Feminism. Ritual, Gender and Divinity among the Reclaiming Witches of San Francisco**, Religion and Gender, London: Routledge 2002

I.13 Women's Religious Experiences and Psychology of Religions

Valerie M. DeMarinis, "Psychology of religion and the impact of feminism", Svensk religionshistorisk årsskrift 9 (2000) 174-191

Valerie M. DeMarinis, **Critical Caring. A Feminist Model for Pastoral Psychology**, Louisville Kentucky: Westminster John Knox Press 1993

Ulla Carin Holm, **"Hennes verk skall prisa henne." Studier av personlighet och attityder hos kvinnliga präster i Svenska Kyrkan** ["Let her own works praise her." Studies in Personality and Attitudes of Women Ministers in the Church of Sweden], Studies in Religious Experience and Behavior 3, Vänersborg: Plus Ultra 1982
In Swedish with 6 pp summary in English.

Petra Junus, **Den Levande Gudinnan. Kvinnoidentitet och religiositet som förändringsprocess** [The Living Goddess. Women's identity and religiosity as a process of change], Nora: Nya Doxa 1995
In Swedish with 7 pp summary in English.

Lene Sjørup, **Du er gudinden**, Copenhagen: Hekla 1983
In Danish.

Lene Sjørup, "Response to Elisabetta Donini", in: Elizabeth Green / Mary Grey (eds), **Ecofeminism and Theology**, ESWTR Yearbook 2/1994, 80-83

Lene Sjørup, "Mysticism and Gender", Journal of Feminist Studies in Religion 13/2 (1997) 45-68

Lene Sjørup, **Oneness. A Theology of Women's Religious Experiences**, Leuven: Peeters 1998

I.14 Religion in contemporary societies and culture

Ninna Edgardh Beckman (ed.), **Welfare, Church and Gender in Eight European Countries. Working Paper 1 from the project Welfare and Religion in a**

European Perspective, Diakonivetenskapliga institutets skriftserie 9, Uppsala: DVI 2004

Ninna Edgardh Beckman / Thomas Ekstrand / Per Pettersson, "Welfare, Church and Gender in Sweden", in: Ninna Edgardh Beckman (ed.), **Welfare, Church and Gender in Eight European Countries. Working Paper 1 from the project Welfare and Religion in a European Perspective**, Diakonivetenskapliga institutets skriftserie 9. Uppsala: DVI 2004, 26-62

Kari Elisabeth Børresen et al (eds), **Religion, Gender, Human Rights in Europe**, Rome: Herder Editrice 2006

Arnfríður Guðmundsdóttir, "Female Christ-figures in Films: A Feminist Critical Analysis of Breaking the Waves and Dead Man Walking", Studia Theologica 56 (2002), 27-43

Eva Lundgren, **Gud og Hver mann. Seksualisert vold som kulturell arena for å skape kjønn**, Oslo: Cappelen 1990
An empirical study of wife battering in Christian communities in Norway, and a contribution to the development of feminist theory. In Norwegian. Published in Swedish as Gud och alla andra karlar: en bok om kvinnomisshandlare, Natur och Kultur: Stockholm 1992

Åse Røthing, **Sex, kjønn og kristentro** [Sexuality, gender and Christian faith], Oslo: Verbum 1998
A study based on interviews with 22 Christian female teenagers on sexuality, gender roles and relations with men. In Norwegian.

Madeleine Sultán Sjöqvist, **"Vi blev muslimer" Svenska kvinnor berättar. En religionssociologisk studie av konversionsberättelser**, Acta Universitatis Upsaliensis Psychologia et Sociologia Religionum 19, Uppsala: University of Uppsala 2006
A sociological study of Swedish women's stories about their conversion to Islam. In Swedish with 18 pp summary in English.

I.15 Theological education

Arnfríður Guðmundsdóttir, "Theological Education from a feminist perspective", in: **Teologisk utdannelse på kanten af det gamle Europa**, Nordiska Ekumeniska Rådet 2001, 33-42

Arnfríður Guðmundsdóttir, "Feminist Perspectives in Theology Transforming Curriculum: A Regional Update – The European Situation", in: **Lutheran World**

Federation Global Consultation on Engendering Theological Education for Transformation. Report from a meeting in Montreux, Switzerland, 5-8 November 2001, LWF Publication 2002, 57-59

Journal of the European Society of Women in Theological Research 15 (2007) 231-239.
doi: 10.2143/ESWTR.15.0.2022781

II. BIBLIOGRAPHIE – BIBLIOGRAPHY – BIBLIOGRAPHIE[1]

Ursula Rapp

II.1 Exegese (Erstes Testament, Neues Testament, Jüdische und frühchristliche Schriften) und Hermeneutik / Biblical Studies (Old Testament, New Testament, Literature of early Judaism and early Christianity) and hermeneutics / Etudes bibliques (Ancien Testament, Nouveau Testament, littératures juives et chrétiennes) et hermeneutique

Gerlinde Baumann, **Gottesbilder der Gewalt im Alten Testament verstehen**, Darmstadt: Verlag Wissenschaftliche Buchgesellschaft 2006, 240 p., ISBN: 3-534-17933-1, € 49,90

Andrea Bieler / Luise Schottroff, **Das Abendmahl. Essen zum Leben**, Gütersloh: Gütersloher Verlagshaus 2007, ca. 240 p., ISBN: 978-3-579-08017-8, € 24,95 D / 25,70 A / CHF 44,60

Linda Day / Caroline Pressler (eds), **Engaging the Bible in a Gendered World. An Introduction to Feminist Biblical Interpretation in Honor of Katherine Doob Sakenfeld**, Louisville: Westminster John Knox Press 2006, 288p. ISBN-10: 0-664-22910-7, $ 29,95

*Detlef Dieckmann / Erbele-Küster, Dorothea (Hgg.), „**Du hast mich aus meiner Mutter Leib gezogen". Beiträge zur Geburt im Alten Testament**, Biblisch-Theologische Studien 75, Neukirchen-Vluyn: Neukirchener 2006, 196 p., ISBN: 3-7887-2140-5, € 24,90 D / 25,60 A / CHF 44,50

Ute E. Eisen, **Die Poetik der Apostelgeschichte. Eine narratologische Studie**, NTOA/StUNT 58, Fribourg: Academic Press 2006, 294 p., ISBN: 3-525-53961-4, € 50,30

Elaine Fantham, **Julia Augusti**, Women in the Ancient World, London: Routledge 2006, 176 p., ISBN: 9780415331463, £ 18,99

---

[1] Zu Büchern mit * siehe unter "Rezensionen" – Books marked * are reviewed below – Pour les livres avec * voire sous "Critique des livres".

*Irmtraud Fischer, **Gotteslehrerinnen. Weise Frauen und Frau Weisheit im Alten Testament**, Kohlhammer: Stuttgart 2006, 210 p., ISBN: 3-17-018939-5, € 19,00

*Tikva Frymer-Kensky, **Studies in Bible and Feminist Criticism**, JPS Scholar of Distinction Series, Jewish Publication Society: Philadelphia 2006, 350 p., ISBN: 0827607989, US$ 39,95

Robert Goss / Deryn Guest / Mona West, **The Queer Bible Commentary**, London: SCM Press 2006, ISBN: 978-033-4-040-217, £ 64,99

Anni Hentschel, **Diakonia im Neuen Testament. Studien zur Semantik mit besonderer Berücksichtigung der Rolle von Frauen**, Wissenschaftliche Untersuchungen zum Neuen Testament 2. Reihe; 226, Tübingen: Mohr 2006, 500 p., ISBN: 3-16-149086-X, € 75,00

*Claudia Janssen, **Anders ist die Schönheit der Körper. Paulus und die Auferstehung in 1 Kor 15**, Gütersloh: Gütersloher Verlagshaus 2005, 358p., ISBN: 978-3-579-05210-6, € 34,95 D / 36,00 A / CHF 61,00

*Renate Jost, **Gender, Sexualität und Macht in der Anthropologie des Richterbuches**, BWANT 164, Stuttgart: Kohlhammer 2006, 390 p., ISBN: 3-17-018556-X, € 40,00

*Renate Jost, **Frauenmacht und Männerliebe. Egalitäre Utopien aus der Frühzeit Israels**, Kohlhammer: Stuttgart 2006, 180 p., ISBN: 3-17-019511-5, € 19,00 / CHF ca. 33,60

J. Ellsworth Kalas, **Strong was Her Faith. Women of the New Testament**, Nashville: Abingdon Press 2007, ISBN: 0687641217, $ 13,00

*Tarja S. Philip, **Menstruation and Childbirth in the Bible. Fertility and Impurity**, Studies in Biblical Literature 88, New York: Peter Lang, 2005, 153p., ISBN: 978-0-8204-7908-8, € 52,10 D / 53,60 A / CHF 76,00

Dagmar Pruin, **Geschichten und Geschichte. Isebel als literarische und historische Gestalt**, OBO 222, XII, Fribourg: academic Press 2006, 498 p., ISBN: 3-525-53022-6, € 89,90

*Adele Reinhartz, **Freundschaft mit dem Geliebten Jünger. Eine jüdische Lektüre des Johannesevangeliums**, Zürich: Theologischer Verlag 2005, 245 p., ISBN: 3-290-17358-5, € 22,50 D / 23,20 A / CHF 36,00 (aus dem Englischen übers. von Esther Kobel)

Eleonore Reuter (Hg.), **Frauen-Körper**, FrauenBibelArbeit 18, Stuttgart: Verlag Katholisches Bibelwerk 2007, 88 p., ISBN: 978-3-460-25298-1, € 9,50 D / € 9,80 A / CHF 17,50

*Ilona Riedel-Spangenberger / Erich Zenger (Hgg.), **"Gott bin ich, kein Mann". Beiträge zur Hermeneutik der biblischen Gottesrede**. Fs. für Helen Schüngel-Straumann zum 65. Geburtstag, Paderborn: Schöningh 2006, 454 p., ISBN: 3-506-71385-X, € 58,00 / CHF 98,00

Jane Shaberg, **Mary Magdalene Understood**, Edinburgh: T&T Clark 2006, 176 p., ISBN: 0826418996, £ 12,95

Vander Stichele / Todd Penner (eds), **Her Master's Tools? Feminist and Postcolonial Engagements of Historical Citical Discourse**, Global Pespectives on Biblical Scholarship 9, Society of Biblical Literature: Atlanta 2005, 390 p., ISBN: 1 58983 119 5

Elsa Tamez, **Struggles for Power in Early Christianity. A Study of the First Letter to Timothy**, Maryknoll / New York: Orbis 2007, 192 p., 978-1-57075-708-2, $ 20,00

II.2 Kirchen- und Religionsgeschichte / Church history and history of religions / Histoire de l'église et des religions

Mieke Bal (ed.), **The Artemisia Files. Artemisia Gentileschi for Feminists and Other Thinking People**, Chicago: University of Chicago Press 2006, 245 p., ISBN: 978-0-226-03582-6, $ 18,00

*Gisa Bauer, **Kulturprotestantismus und frühe bürgerliche Frauenbewegung in Deutschland. Agnes von Zahn-Harnack (1884-1950)**, Leipzig: Evangelische Verlagsanstalt 2006, 420 p., ISBN: 3374023851, € 58,00

Lydia Bendel-Maidl (Hg.), **Katholikinnen im 20. Jahrhundert. Bilder, Rollen, Aufgaben**, Beiträge zu Theologie, Kirche und Gesellschaft im 20. Jahrhundert 2, Münster: LIT 2007, 320 p., ISBN: 978-3-8258-5540-6, € 24,90 D

Katja Boehme, **Madeleine Delbrêl. Die andere Heilige**, Freiburg u.a.: Herder 2005, 125p., € 14,90

*Doris Brodbeck (Hg.), **Dem Schweigen entronnen – Religiöse Zeugnisse von Frauen des 16. bis 19. Jahrhunderts**, Würzburg / Markt Zell: Religion & Kultur Verlag 2005, 339 p., ISBN: 3-933891-17-5, € 19,90 / CHF 34,90

Sonja A. Buholzer, **Solange du liebst**. **Botschaften einer Rebellin** (Mechthild von Magdeburg), Zürich: efeF 2007, CHF 36.00 / € 24.00

Sarah Coakley, **Macht und Unterwerfung**. **Spiritualität zwischen Hingabe und Unterdrückung**, Gütersloh: Gütersloher Verlagshaus 2007, 240 p., ISBN: 978-3-579-05235-9, € 24,95 D / 25,70 A / CHF 44,60

Irene Fleiss, **Als alle Menschen Schwestern waren**. **Leben in matriarchalen Gesellschaften**, Rüsselsheim: Christel Göttert 2006, 405 p., ISBN: 3-922499-84-8, € 19,80 / CHF 36,00

Ute Gause / Cordula Lissner (Hgg.), **Kosmos Diakonissenmutterhaus**. **Geschichte und Gedächtnis einer protestantischen Frauengemeinschaft**, Leipzig: Evangelische Verlagsanstalt ²2005, 293 p., ISBN: 978-3-374-02267-0, € 22,00

Margaret L. King / Albert Rabil Jr. (eds), **Teaching Other Voices**. **Women and Religion in Early Modern Europe**, Chicago: University of Chicago Press 2007, 208 p., ISBN: 978-0-226-43632-6, $ 21,00

*Marion Kobelt-Groch, **Judith macht Geschichte**. **Zur Rezeption einer mythischen Gestalt vom 16. bis 19. Jahrhundert**, Wilhelm Fink Verlag: München 2005, 310 p., ISBN: 3-7705-3959-1, € 34,90

Heike Köhler, **Deutsch – Evangelisch – Frau**. **Meta Eyl – eine Theologin im Spannungsfeld zwischen nationalsozialistischer Reichskirche und evangelischer Frauenbewegung**, Neukirchen-Vluyn: Neukirchener ²2007, 357 p., ISBN: 978-3-7887-1923-4, € 39,90 D / 41,10 A / CHF 69,00

*Julie Kirchberg / Judith Könemann (Hgg.), **Frauentraditionen**. **Mit Elisabeth Gössmann im Gespräch**, Ostfildern: Schwabenverlag 2006, 144 p., ISBN: 3-7966-1258-X, € 16,90 D

*Marion Kobelt-Groch, **Judith macht Geschichte**. **Zur Rezeption einer mythischen Gestalt vom 16. bis 19. Jahrhundert**, München: Wilhem Fink Verlag 2005, 310 p., ISBN: 3-7705-3959-1, € 34,90

*Adelheid M. von Hauff (Hg.), **Frauen gestalten Diakonie 2. Vom 18. bis zum 20. Jahrhundert**, Stuttgart: Kohlhammer 2006, 560 p., ISBN: 3-17-019324-4, € 29,00 D / CHF 50,70

Rajah Scheepers, **Regentin per Staatsstreich? Landgräfin Anna von Hessen (1485–1525)**, Königstein: Ulrike Helmer Verlag 2007, 360 p., ISBN: 978-3-89741-227-9, € 39,90 / CHF 63,00

Verena Scholl, **Rembrandts biblische Frauenporträts. Eine Begegnung von Theologie und Malerei**, Zürich: Theologischer Verlag Zürich 2006, 192 p., ISBN-10: 3-290-17384-4, ISBN-13: 978-3-290-17384-5, € 20,80 D / 21,40 A / CHF 32,80

II.3 Systematische Theologie, Ökumene und Interreligiöser Dialog / Systematic Theology and Interreligious Dialogue / Etudes œcuméniques

Marcella Althaus Reid (ed.), **Liberation Theology and Sexuality**, Aldershot: Ashgate 2006, 192 p., ISBN: 0754650804, $ 99,95

Marcella Althaus Reid / Lisa Isherwood, **Controversies in Feminist Theology**, SCM Press 2007, 188 p., ISBN: 978 0334 040507, £16,99

Bieberstein, Sabine / Buday, Kornélia / Rapp, Ursula (eds), **Building Bridges in a Multifaceted Europe. Religious Origins, Traditions, Contexts, and Identities - Brücken bauen in einem vielgestaltigen Europa. Religiöse Ursprünge, Traditionen, Kontexte und Identitäten – Construire des ponts dans une Europe multiforme. Origines, traditions, contexts et identités religieux**, Jahrbuch der europäischen Gesellschaft für theologische Forschung von Frauen 14/2006, Leuven: Peeters 2007, € 23,00

Kari Børresen / Sara Cabibbo (eds), **Gender, Religion, and Human Rights in Europe. The Impact of Cultural and Religious Gender Models in the European Formation of Socio-Political Human Rights. Exploratory Workshop – Roma, 11-13 November 2004**, Roma: Herder 2006, 307p., ISBN: 88-89670-15-X, € 38,00

*Margit Eckholt / Sabine Pemsel-Maier, **Räume der Gnade. Perspektiven auf die christliche Erlösungsbotschaft**, Ostfildern: Schwabenverlag 2006, 192 p., ISBN-10: 3-7966-1299-7 / ISBN-13: 978-3-7966-1299-2 € 18,90

Monika Egger / Livia Meier / Katja Wißmüller (Hgg.), **WoMan in Church. Kirche und Amt im Kontext der Geschlechterfrage**, Theologische Frauenforschung in Europa 20, LIT: Münster 2006, 152 p., ISBN: 3-8258-9220-4, € 19,90

*Helene Egnell, **Other Voices. A Study of Christian Feminist Approaches to Religious Plurality East and West**, Studia Missiolina Svecana C, Uppsala 2006, 369 p., ISBN: 91-85424-92-7, SEK 265 / € 29,25

Magdalene L. Frettlöh, **Gott Gewicht geben. Bausteine einer geschlechtergerechten Gotteslehre**, Neukirchen-Vluyn: Neukirchener 2006, 378 p., ISBN: 978-3-7887-2072-8, € 34,90 D / 35,90 A / CHF 61,00

Ute Gahlings, **Phänomenologie der weiblichen Leiberfahrungen,** Freiburg: Verlag Karl Alber 2006, 720 p., ISBN-13: 978-3-495-48173-8, € 56,60 A / CHF 94

Michelle A. Gonzalez, **Created in God's Image. An Introduction to Feminist Theological Anthropology,** Maryknoll / New York: Orbis 2007, 176 p., 978-1-57075-697-9, $ 20,00

Elisabeth Hartlieb, **Geschlechterdifferenz im Denken Friedrich Schleiermachers,** Theologische Bibliothek Töpelmann 136, Berlin: de Gruyter 2006, 390 p., ISBN: 3-11-018891-0, € 98 / CHF 157,00

Ursula Hepperle, **Die Stellung der Frau im islamisch-sunnitischen und römisch-katholischen Eherecht. Ein Rechtsvergleich,** Tübinger Kirchenrechtliche Studien. Kleine Wissenschaftliche Reihe 1, Münster: LIT 2006, 168 p., ISBN: 3-8258-9834-2, € 17,90

Anne Joh Wonhee, **Heart of the Cross. A Postcolonial Christology,** Louisville: Westminster John Knox Press 2006, 184 p., ISBN-10: 0-664-23063-6, $ 24,95

Mirja Kutzer, **In Wahrheit erfunden. Dichtung als Ort theologischer Erkenntnis,** Regensburg: Pustet 2006, 368 p., ISBN: 987-3-7917-2010-4, € 39,90 D / 41,10 A / CHF 69,40

Monica Migliorino, Miller, **Sexuality and Authority in the Catholic Church,** Chicago: University of Chicago Press / University of Scranton Press 2006, 320 p., ISBN: 978-1-58966-128-8, $ 28,00

*Elisabeth Moltmann-Wendel / Renate Kirchhoff (Hgg.), **Christologie im Lebensbezug,** Göttingen: Vandenhoeck & Ruprecht 2005, 240 p., ISBN: 3-525-56958-0, € 29,90

Muriel Orevillo-Montenegro, **The Jesus of Asian Women,** Women from the Margins, Maryknoll / New York: Orbis 2007, 192 p., ISBN: 978-1-57075-533-0, $ 18,00

Kathleen McPhillips / Lisa Isherwood (eds), **Post-Christian Feminisms. A Critical Approach,** Aldershot: Ashgate 2007, c. 256 p., ISBN: 978-0-7546-5380-6, $ 99,95

Ida Raming, **Gleichrangig in Christus anstatt: Ausschluss von Frauen „im Namen Gottes". Zur Rezeption und Interpretation von Gal 3,27f in vatikanischen Dokumenten,** Theologische Plädoyers 1, Münster: LIT 2006, 80 p., ISBN: 3-8258-9706-0, € 10.00

Laurel Schneider, **Beyond Monotheism. Divine Multiplicity in a World of Difference**, London: Routledge 2007, 224 p., ISBN: 9780415941914, £ 19,99

*Hanna Strack, **Die Frau ist Mit-Schöpferin. Eine Theologie der Geburt**, Rüsselsheim: Christel Göttert Verlag 2006, 357 p., ISBN: 3-922499-85-6, € 19,80 / CHF 36,00

*Doris Strahm / Manuela Kalsky (Hgg.), **Damit es anders wird zwischen uns. Interreligiöser Dialog aus der Sicht von Frauen**, Mainz: Grünewald 2006, 160 p., ISBN: 3-7867-2604-3, € 16,80 D / € 17,30 A / CHF 29,90

II.4 Praktische Theologie, Spiritualität, Liturgiewissenschaft, Religionspädagogik, Homiletik, Ethik / Pastoral theology, teaching, homiletics, spirituality, liturgy, ethics / Théologie pastorale, Scienes liturgiques, Pédagogie religieuse, Théologie morale et d'Ethique

Kirsten Armbruster, **Starke Mütter verändern die Welt. Was schiefläuft und wie wir Gutes Leben für alle erreichen**, Rüsselsheim: Christel Göttert Verlag 2007, 230 p., ISBN: 978-3-922499-97-8, ca. € 19,80 / CHF 36,00

Regina Ammicht-Quinn, **Glück der Ernst des Lebens?** Herder: Freiburg u.a. 2006, 144p., ISBN: 3-451-05652-6, € 8,90 / CHF 16,50

Claudia Bandixen / Silvia Pfeiffer / Frank Worbs (Hgg.), **Wenn Frauen Kirchen leiten. Neuer Trend in den reformierten Kirchen der Schweiz**, Beiträge zu Theologie, Ethik und Kirche 2, Zürich: Theologischer Verlag Zürich 2006, 172 p., ISBN: 978-3-290-17418-7, € 12,80 D / 13,20 A / CHF 20,00

*Sybille Becker, **Leib – Bildung – Geschlecht. Perspektiven für die Religionspädagogik**, Theologische Frauenforschung in Europa 13, Münster: LIT 2005, 360 p., ISBN: 3-8258-6628-9, € 19,90

Lena Behmenburg / Mareike Berweger / Jessica Gevers / Karen Nolte / Anna Schnädelbach / Eva Sänger (Hgg.), **Wissenschaf(f)t Geschlecht. Machtverhältnisse und feministische Wissensproduktion**, Frankfurter Feministische Texte – Sozialwissenschaften 9, Königstein: Ulrike Helmer 2007, 300 p., ISBN: 978-3-89741-225-5, € 30,00

Anke Edelbrock, **Mädchenbildung und Religion in Kaiserreich und Weimarer Republik. Eine Untersuchung zum evangelischen Religionsunterricht und zur**

Vereinsarbeit der Religionslehrerinnen, Neukirchen-Vluyn: Neukirchener Verlag 2006, 490 p., ISBN: 3-7887-2152-9, € 39,90 D / 41,10 A / CHF 69,00

Regine Froese, **Zwei Religionen eine Familie. Religionspädagogik in pluraler Gesellschaft**, Religionspädagogik in pluraler Gesellschaft 7, Gütersloh: Gütersloher Verlagshaus 2005, 336 p., ISBN: 3-579-05297-7, € 39,95 D / € 41,10 A / CHF 69,00

*Andrea Günter (Hg.), **Frauen – Autorität – Pädagogik. Theorie und reflektierte Praxis**, Königstein/Taunus: Ulrike Helmer Verlag 2006, 241 p., ISBN: 978-3-89741-217-0, € 22,00

Hanna Habermann / Ute Wannig / Barbara Heun / Iren Steiner / Andrea Günter, **selbstbestimmt und solidarisch. Frauen und das Alter**, Rüsselsheim: Christel Göttert Verlag 2005, 80p., ISBN: 3-922499-81-3, € 5,00 / CHF 9,80

Sandra Lassak / Katja Strobel (Hgg.), **Von Priesterinnen, riot girls und Dienstmädchen. Stimmen für eine feministische Globalisierung von unten**, Münster: Institut für Theologie und Politik 2005, 190 p., € 13,00 D

*Silke Leonhard, **Leiblich lernen und lehren. Ein religionsdidaktischer Diskurs**, Praktische Theologie heute 79, Stuttgart: Kohlhammer 2006, 530 p., ISBN: 3-17-019321-X, € 39,00 / CHF 67,50

*Heike Knops (Hg.), **Kunst und Theologie im Dialog. MenschSein im Zeitalter der Gentechnik**, Interdisziplinäres Forum Wissenschaft, Sprockhövel: Verlag Dr. Eike Pies 2006, 88 p. (mit DVD), ISBN: 3-928441-60-4, € 19,80

Maria Katharina Moser, **Opfer zwischen Affirmation und Ablehnung. Feministisch-ethische Analysen zu einer politischen und theologischen Kategorie**, Studien der Moraltheologie 34, Münster: LIT 2006, 544 p., ISBN: 3-8258-9417-7, € 44,90

Maria Katharina Moser, **Von Opfern reden. Ein feministisch-ethischer Zugang**, Königstein: Ulrike Helmer 2007, 160 p., ISBN: 978-3-89741-224-8, € 14,90

Carola Möller / Ulla Peters / Stiftung Fraueninitiative (Hgg.), **Dissidente Praktiken. Erfahrungen mit herrschafts- und warenkritischer Selbstorganisation**, Konzepte / Materialien 4, Königstein: Ulrike Helmer Verlag, 240 p., ISBN: 3-89741-214-4, € 19,90

Isabel Mukonyora, **Wandering a Gendered Wilderness. Suffering and Healing in an African Initiated Church**, New York u.a.: Peter Lang 2007, 154 p., ISBN: 978-0-8204-8883-7, € 56,20 D / 57,80 A / CHF 82,00

Mary Nyangweso Wangila, **Female Circumcision. The Interplay of Religion, Culture and Gender in Kenya**, Maryknoll / New York: Orbis 2007, 192 p., ISBN: 978-1-57075-710-5, $ 25,00

Elisabeth Naurath, **Mit Gefühl gegen Gewalt. Mitgefühl als Schlüssel ethischer Bildung in der Religionspädagogik**, Neukirchen-Vluyn: Neukirchener 2007, 330 p., ISBN: 978-3-78872218-0, € 29,90 D / 30,80 A / CHF 52,90

*Ina Praetorius (Hg.), **Sich in Beziehung setzen. Zur Weltsicht der Freiheit in Bezogenheit**, Königstein: Ulrike Helmer Verlag 2006, 124 p., ISBN: 3-89741-182-2, € 24,90

Justyna Sempruch / Laura Shook / Katharina Willems (Hgg.), **Multiple Marginalities. An Intercultural Dialogue on Gender in Education Across Europe and Africa**, Königstein: Ulrike Helmer Verlag 2007, 498 p., ISBN: 3-89741-208-X, € 49,90

Marie-Theres Wacker / Stefanie Rieger-Goertz (Hgg.), **Mannsbilder. Kritische Männerforschung und theologische Frauenforschung im Gespräch**, Theologische Frauenforschung in Europa 21, Münster: LIT 2006, 392 p., ISBN: 3-8258-9267-0, € 19,90 D

Sylvia Grevel / Mieke Korenhof / Barbara Leijnse (Hgg.), **Theologische Ikonographien. Kunst und Religion im Dialog**, Theologische Frauenforschung in Europa 22, Münster: LIT 2007, 136 p., ISBN: 3-8258-9407-X, € 16,90

Susanne Opfermann (Hg.), **Unrechtserfahrungen. Geschlechtergerechtigkeit in Gesellschaft**, Recht und Literatur – Frankfurter Feministische Texte – Sozialwissenschaften 8, Königstein: Ulrike Helmer 2007, 180 p., ISBN: 978-3-89741-226-2, € 17,90

Sabine Plonz, **Arbeit, soziale Marktwirtschaft und Geschlecht – Studienbuch Feministische Sozialethik**, Neukirchen-Vluyn: Neukirchener 2006, 153p., ISBN: 978-3-7887-2154-1, € 22,90 D / 23,60 A / CHF 41,10

*Annegret Reese, **"Ich weiß nicht, wo da Religion anfängt und aufhört". Eine empirische Studie zum Zusammenhang von Lebenswelt und Religiosität bei Singlefrauen**, Religionspädagogik in pluraler Gesellschaft 8, Gütersloh: Gütersloher Verlagshaus / Freiburg: Herder 2006, 581 p., ISBN: 3-451-28951-2, EUR 49,95 D / EUR 51,40 A / CHF 84,00

Christa Spilling-Nöker, **Wir lassen Dich nicht, Du segnest uns denn. Zur Diskussion um Segnung und Zusammenleben gleichgeschlechtlicher Paare im Pfarrhaus**, Geschlecht – Gewalt – Gesellschaft 6, Münster: LIT 2007, 408 p., ISBN: 3-8258-9610-2, € 29,90

Journal of the European Society of Women in Theological Research 15 (2007) 241-292.
doi: 10.2143/ESWTR.15.0.2022782

III. Rezensionen – Book Reviews – Critique des Livres

III.1 Exegese (Erstes Testament, Neues Testament, Jüdische und früh-christliche Schriften) und Hermeneutik / Biblical Studies (Old Testament, New Testament, Literature of early Judaism and early Christianity) and hermeneutics / Etudes bibliques (Ancien Testament, Nouveau Testament, littératures juives et chrétiennes) et hermeneutique

Detlef Dieckmann / Erbele-Küster, Dorothea (Hg.), *„Du hast mich aus meiner Mutter Leib gezogen".* *Beiträge zur Geburt im Alten Testament,* Biblisch-Theologische Studien 75, Neukirchen-Vluyn: Neukirchener 2006, 196 p., ISBN 3-7887-2140-5, € 24,90 D / 25,60 A / CHF 44,50

Der Band ist die zweite Publikation des „Arbeitskreises Rezeption des Alten Testaments" (AKRAT) und versammelt exegetisch-bibeltheologische Studien sowie eine mit philosophisch-ethischem Schwerpunkt zum Thema Geburt.

Die Einführung (1-9) betont, dass das Thema Geburt zwar in biblischen Anthropologien vernachlässigt wird, trotzdem aber als Grundfaktum menschlichen Daseins und menschlicher Erfahrung – auch von göttlichem Wirken – in den biblischen Texten zum Ausdruck kommt. Mit unterschiedlichen Fragestellungen und Zugängen wird dies in den einzelnen Beiträgen beeindruckend dargestellt.

Im ersten Beitrag, der sich Gen 3,16 und damit dem Thema Geburt aus der Sicht der Mutter zuwendet, hebt Detlev Dieckmann zunächst die verschiedenen Übersetzungsmöglichkeiten des Verses mit ihren theologischen Implikationen und schließlich die ambivalente Verheißung von Nachkommen und Schmerz, die sich im Gebären zeigen, hervor. Diese Spannung von Nachkommensfreude und Mühsal wird dem menschlichen Elternsein also nicht abgesprochen, aber die göttliche Zusage des Überlebens und der Fortpflanzung gegeben.

Dorothea Erbele-Küster wendet sich dem *gender trouble* im Alten Testament zu. Sie untersucht drei sehr unterschiedliche Texte daraufhin, wie soziales und biologisches Geschlecht durch die Begriffe „männlich" und „weiblich" ausgedrückt werden. Während die beiden Sichtweisen von Geschlechtlichkeit nach Gen 1,27 in der Schöpfung vorgegeben sind, werden sie in Lev 12 normiert und im Ritual aktualisiert (52). Jeremia dagegen bricht diese Festlegungen auf: in Jer 30,6 liegt Unheil darin, dass Männer eine weibliche Geschlechterrolle übernehmen. Das biologische Geschlecht wird so stark mit kulturspezifischen Rollen verbunden, dass die Vorstellung von Männern, die sich wie Frauen benehmen, ein Ausdruck der Unordnung der bestehenden Machtverhältnisse darstellt. Nach Jer 31,22, aber entstehen Rettung und Neuschöpfung gerade dadurch, dass Frauen ihre biologistisch zugeteilten Muster aufbrechen.

Stefan Fischer zeigt in seinem Beitrag über das Hohelied, wie soziale und persönliche Identität der Liebenden im Text auseinanderklaffen und dadurch die Beziehung zu einer illegitimen machen. Durch die Initiative der Frau, die den Mann an den Ort ihrer Zeugung und Geburt bringt, dorthin, wo Identität beginnt, können neue Identitäten geschaffen werden, die die Beziehung legitimieren.

Marianne Grohmann beschreibt Ps 22,10f als biblische Annäherung an das altorientalische Bild von Gott als Hebamme und stellt eindrücklich heraus, dass, wenn man den Psalm vom Thema der Geburt her liest, in V. 30-32 nicht von einer „Auferweckung der Toten", sondern vielmehr davon die Rede ist, dass Gott manche sterben lässt, noch bevor sie leben. Dann spricht der Vers aber von Fehlgeburten und zieht eine Verbindung zum Thema Geburt in V. 10f.

Alexandra Grund betont die rettungsgeschichtliche und identitätsstiftende Bedeutung von Geburt für das Volk Israel. Sie stellt dar, dass die Schöpfung selbst durch Geburt geschieht, und dass die Israelitinnen und Israeliten Kinder Gottes sind, weil sie aus Gott geboren sind (Dtn 32,18). Wenn Krisenzeiten im AT mit Geburtswehen verglichen werden, dann u.a. deshalb, weil in ihnen die Geburt eines rettenden Herrschers angesagt wird (z.B: Jes 7,14; 9,5). Ps 2,7; 110,3 werden dann aufgrund ägyptischer Parallelen konsequent so verstanden, dass Gott den König gebiert.

Raik Heckl lässt sich vom Aufruf, „wie die Kinder zu werden" zum versprochenen Himmelreich und von dort zum verheißenen Land führen, das ja die Kinder erben werden (Num 14,30; Dtn 1,39), die nicht Gut und Böse unterscheiden und deshalb schuldunfähig sind. Kindsein hat deshalb etwas zu tun mit Sündenvergebung und Neubeginn.

Stefan Heuser liefert als einziger Autor, der nicht am AT forscht, den am meisten systematischen Beitrag, indem er Vorstellungen von Geburt als Erwählung und damit Machtlegitimation von Herrschergestalten (Jes 9,6) sowie als Aufgabe zur Kooperation mit Gott versteht. Diese verbindet er mit der Kategorie des Geborenwerdens in der politischen Ethik. Seine anschließende Kritik an Hanna Arendt bezieht sich darauf, dass sie nicht angeben kann, woher Handeln in Freiheit und Vergebung ermöglicht sind. Diese Frage beantwortet Heuser wieder vom AT her.

Der Beitrag von Benjamin Ziemer stellt anhand von Vorkommen und Verwendung des Verbs *jalad* (gebären, zeugen) fest, dass das Buch Genesis seine Zeitrechung entlang von Schwangerschaftsperioden strukturiert. Darüber hinaus stellt er den inhaltlich ambivalenten Vers Gen 3,16 nachvollziehbar als Segen zur Fortpflanzung der Menschen dar, von der die Genesis in ihrem weiteren Verlauf ständig erzählt.

Der Band stellt eine sehr gelungene exegetische und bibeltheologische Sammlung zu einem zentralen Thema der Anthropologie dar und ist aufgrund seiner zugespitzten Fragen und klaren Abhandlungen daran auch Nicht-BiblikerInnen zu empfehlen.

Ursula Rapp (Linz/Feldkirch – Austria)

Irmtraud Fischer, *Gotteslehrerinnen. Weise Frauen und Frau Weisheit im Alten Testament*, Stuttgart: Kohlhammer 2006, 221 Seiten, ISBN: 3-17-018939-5, € 19,00

Gotteslehrerinnen ist ein faszinierend leichtfüßig geschriebenes Buch. Ob biblische Geschichte, ob Einblicke in die neuere Forschungslage oder sozialgeschichtliche Details – die Texte sind einfach und gut zu lesen. Die Leserin wird mitgenommen und verführt, sich auf die Vielzahl biblischer Texte einzulassen, die in diesem Buch besprochen werden. Irmtraud Fischer stellt eine Fülle biblischer Frauenfiguren vor: In der ersten Hälfte des Buches ist Abigajil, der weisen Frau aus Tekoa, der weisen Frau aus Abel-Bet-Maacha und der Königin von Saba je ein Kapitel gewidmet. Ester, Judit und Debora kommen vor, die Frau Hiobs, Königsmütter, die als Ratgeberinnen tätig sind, aber auch schlechte Ratgeberinnen, wie Seresch, die Frau Hamans aus dem Esterbuch. Der zweite Teil widmet sich der Auslegung des Sprüchebuches. Hier vermittelt Fischer Einblicke in die Lehrtätigkeit von Müttern, und geht der „Frau Weisheit" nach, einer Figur, „die aus der alltäglichen Lebenswirklichkeit von

Frauen der gehobenen Bevölkerungsschicht in persischer Zeit entwickelt wurde" (201), und einen wichtigen „Hinweis auf die weibliche Herkunft der Weisheitsliteratur" (203) gibt.

Nicht immer bin ich mit Irmtraud Fischers Auslegung der biblischen Texte einverstanden – im Hiobbuch wird m.E. nicht gewettet, auch will Batseba nach meinem Verständnis der Geschichte nicht Adonija oder Abischag loswerden. Doch auch bei inhaltlichen Differenzen nimmt Irmtraud Fischer mich mit in die Spannung der biblischen Erzählung, die nachzuzeichnen ihr immer wieder gelingt. Bei der Darstellung der biblischen Texte setzt sie sich mit deren Auslegungsgeschichte auseinander, weist frauenfeindliche Stereotypen zurück, wie z.b. die Trivialisierung der Geschichte Abigails als „Familiengeschichte", und stellt die neuere Forschung, insbesondere die feministische, vor. Außerdem vermittelt sie eine Fülle sozialgeschichtlicher Informationen über das Leben von Frauen in biblischer Zeit. Z.B. stellt Fischer die Frau, über die in Sprüche 31 gesprochen wird, als eine Geschäftsfrau im persischen Großreich vor, die nicht mit Kleinkrämerei, sondern mit Welthandel beschäftigt ist, und sie verweist auf Dokumente aus persischer Zeit, die beweisen, dass Frauen im internationalen Handel tätig waren.

Diese Geschäftsfrau ist ein typisches Beispiel der in dem Buch präsentierten weisen Frauen, insofern „das soziale Milieu, aus dem die weisheitlichen Texte überwiegend stammen, nicht die verarmte Unterschicht, sondern vielmehr die wohlhabende Mittel- und Oberschicht ist", die zu gesellschaftlicher Verantwortung auffordert (218). Als ein weiteres Charakteristikum der weisheitlichen Texte und ihrer Protagonistinnen arbeitet Fischer ihren kreativen Umgang mit der als heilsrelevant erachteten Schrift heraus. „Stellt die Prophetie eine Aktualisierung der Tora dar, so die Weisheit die lebenspraktische Verwirklichung der Weisung Israels. Während Prophetie die zeitgemäße Gotteswahrheit präsent hält, sorgt sich die Weisheit um die Lebbarkeit der göttlichen Weisung" (215f).

Besonders bemerkenswert an diesem Buch über weise Frauen und ihre Weisheit finde ich, dass Irmtraud Fischer sich nicht zurückhält, ihrerseits Rat zu erteilen und z.B. in der Auseinandersetzung mit der Geschäftsfrau aus Sprüche 31 zu dem Ergebnis kommt: „Ohne Arbeit geht das nicht. Nur die eigenständige, kontinuierliche, aber auch lustvoll getane Arbeit schafft die Unabhängigkeit. Wer von den Frauen sich zurücklehnt und versorgen lässt, der muss als Preis dafür die eigene Selbständigkeit zahlen." (171f)

Klara Butting (Uelzen – Germany)

Tikva Frymer-Kensky, *Studies in Bible and Feminist Criticism*, JPS Scholar of Distinction Series, Philadelphia: Jewish Publication Society, 2006, 350 p., ISBN: 0827607989, US$ 39,95

This book gathers thirty articles that Tikva Frymer-Kensky, professor at the University of Chicago Divinity School, published from 1972 to 2006, the year in which she passed away after four years of fighting breast cancer. The volume begins with an introductory essay, "A Retrospective", in which the author describes and reflects on her life and career as a Jewish feminist Bible scholar. This is my favorite piece of the book and I wish I had known about her story earlier. The chapter weaves biographical information together with descriptions about her career and scholarship, which creates a charming, impressive, lively, and thoroughly engaging narrative. For instance, we learn that Frymer-Kensky had been a "whiz kid" who was ridiculed and attacked by her classmates in public schools in Queens, New York. Her educational "oasis" (p. xi) was Hebrew school where she "first began to associate religious studies with intellectual challenge and stimulation" (p. xii). Eventually she learned, "much to my surprise" (p. xiii), that she did not want to study nuclear engineering, and realized: "I had my priorities backward: I should read science for fun and study Bible as a profession. And so I began to prepare for a career in biblical studies" (xiii). Yet soon she understood that "[t]he field of biblical studies was no more open to women than high school physics had been, and I had no female role models" (p. xiii). Yet she persevered, and the present volume demonstrates that it was worthwhile indeed – for all of us who benefit from her work now.

Six sections organize the volume, reflecting Frymer-Kensky's wide-ranging research interests and impressive scholarly accomplishments in Assyriology, Sumerology, Hebrew Bible, Jewish and women's studies. The first section, "Comparative Culture I: Ancient Near Eastern Religions", investigates ancient Near Eastern and biblical creation, flood, and goddess myths. The second section, "Comparative Culture II: Judaism and Christianity", showcases the author's interests in Jewish-Christian dialog and biblical studies, such as "Biblical Voices on Chosenness" and "Jesus and the Law". The third section, "Feminist Perspectives I: Gender and the Bible", includes an evaluative discussion on the relationship between biblical and women's studies, illuminating Frymer-Kensky's controversial conviction that "preexilic Israel had no ideology of gender differences" (p. 167). The fourth section, "Feminist Perspectives II: Gender and the Law", addresses patriarchal family relationships and ancient Near Eastern legislation, sex in the Bible, and Halakhah and feminism. The fifth section, "Theologies I: Biblical Theology", investigates connections between the Hebrew Bible and revelation, Moses, justice, ecology, and Levitical laws. The sixth section, "Theologies II: Constructive Theology", covers Jewish biblical theologies, healing, "feminine God-talk", Jewish women, and giving birth, a somewhat unusual topic for a Bible scholar but one that the author also tackled elsewhere. This volume is a treasure and required reading for anybody interested in Bible, Judaism, feminism, and this scholar's life-time work.

Susanne Scholz (North Andover, MA – U.S.A.)

Claudia Janssen, *Anders ist die Schönheit der Körper. Paulus und die Auferstehung in 1 Kor 15*, Gütersloh: Gütersloher Verlagshaus 2005, 358p., ISBN: 978-3-579-05210-6, € 34,95 D / 36,00 A / CHF 61,00

Claudia Janssens Arbeit zu Paulus leistet einen wichtigen Beitrag, damit wir Paulus neu denken, neu entwerfen und hören können. Sie gehört mit zu den ForscherInnen, die am Konzept des „Paulus" arbeiten, die ihn aus seiner besserwisserischen hohen Warte befreien und ihn in das lebendige und konfliktreiche Leben der ersten christlichen Gemeinden stellen. So wurde das Konzept „Paulus und seine Brüder" in feministischer Bibelwissenschaft nicht einfach zu „Paulus und seine Brüder und Schwestern", sondern vielmehr zu „Paulus' Stimme im Chor der Gemeinde", denn seine Stimme ist nie allein zu hören, sondern immer nur gebrochen und unterstützt von Stimmen aus den Gemeinden.

Diese Veränderung macht Paulus als Glied in einer Kette derer fassbar, die ihn die Hoffnung lehrten, und derer, die mit ihm und in Auseinandersetzung mit ihm das neue Leben zu gestalten suchten. Damit liegt das Augenmerk nicht mehr darauf, was der große Denker und Theologe Paulus zu diesem oder jenem Thema zu sagen hatte – sondern es wird versucht, den Diskurs in der Gemeinde zu verstehen, worüber nachgedacht und gekämpft wurde, und wie miteinander gestritten, gekämpft, nachgedacht wurde – wobei deutlich wird, dass sich auch Frauen stark an diesem Diskurs beteiligten – gerade die paulinischen Briefe bringen diese Frauenstimmen zum Vorschein.

Brigitte Kahl machte in ihrem Kommentar zum Galaterbrief darauf aufmerksam, dass der Gal wie kein anderer Brief von männlicher Körpersprache bestimmt ist: 22mal begegnen Worte wie Vorhaut, Beschneidung, beschneiden, sperma, Kastration. Paulus spricht sogar vom *Evangelium der Vorhaut* und *Evangelium der Beschneidung.* Spätere Übersetzer haben diese nackte Männlichkeit versucht zu kaschieren durch Übersetzungen wie „Evangelium für die Heiden/die Juden", oder „Evangelium für die Unbeschnittenen/ Beschnittenen". Solche Kaschierungen trugen dazu bei, den männlichen Körper als zentralen Ort des theologischen Ringens im Gal unsichtbar zu machen.

Wie Brigitte Kahl verblindet auch Claudia Janssen mit der genauen Lektüre paulinischer Schriften gegenwärtige Diskussionen um Körper und Körperlichkeit. Paulus lässt sich nicht nur aus der Antike lesen, sozusagen unter Ausblendung gegenwärtiger Probleme. Die Lektüre wird spannender, wenn das Körperbild der Antike, genauer: des Paulus, mit demjenigen der Gegenwart konfrontiert wird. Das bedingt natürlich ein Aufarbeiten des höchst ambivalenten, gerade für Frauen problematischen Körperbildes des Christentums. Die neuplatonische Scham, im Leibe zu sein, prägte die christliche Theologie stärker als die alttestamentliche Lebenszugewandtheit. Mit der Abwertung des Körpers wurde meist auch die Frau abgewertet, denn in ihren Körper projizierte man Sünde, Anfälligkeit, Schwäche, Sexualität.

Seit den achtziger Jahren setzte unter feministischen Denkerinnen eine Körperdebatte ein. Was heißt das, einen weiblichen Körper zu haben? In einen weiblichen Körper geboren worden zu sein? Welchen Stellenwert hat der Körper, wie kommt er in verschiedenen kulturellen Entwürfen zur Sprache? Welche Politik wird ihm auf den Leib geschrieben?

Die Autorin konfrontiert diese Fragestellungen aus der Gegenwart mit dem Körperbild des Paulus. Sie zeigt, dass Paulus die erniedrigten und geschundenen Körper der Menschen in den Mittelpunkt seiner Überlegungen stellt. Er spricht nicht einfach von der Schwäche des Fleisches, sondern von den Menschen, die als schwach, als Abschaum gelten.

Damit kommt ein neuer Paulus zum Vorschein. Einer, der wahrnimmt, was um ihn herum geschieht, der die hungrigen Menschen sieht und sich selbst zu ihnen zählt. Er stellt auch seinen Körper als verletzt, als erniedrigt und schwach daneben. Er schreibt nicht unter Ausblendung der eigenen Erfahrungen, sondern bezieht diese ganz wesentlich mit ein. Und von diesem Ausgangspunkt beginnt er, Gott zur Sprache zu bringen. Sie zeigt, wie seine Rede von Gott dieser Realität der hungrigen, angstbeladenen Körper stand zu halten versucht.

Wenn Paulus so sehr das Leiden um ihn herum wahrgenommen hat, wie kommt er dann dazu, vom Körper als Tempel Gottes zu sprechen? Oder umgekehrt gefragt: haben diejenigen Paulusinterpreten nicht recht, die seine Rede von der Auferstehung für futurisch halten? Hier das Leiden und die Vergänglichkeit – dort, im Jenseits die Herrlichkeit und Unvergänglichkeit?

Ich habe meine helle Freude daran gehabt, zu lesen, wie CJ sich gegen eine solche dualistische Auferstehungsvorstellung wendet, wie sie ihr zu Leibe rückt und Auferstehung ins Leben holt. Denn bei Paulus sind die Körper nicht nur Schauplatz von Gewalt und Krankheit, sie sind auch Ort der Offenbarung Gottes. Die Körper sind durchlässig, offen für die Verwandlungskraft Gottes. Denn sie sind aus Gottes Händen, das haftet ihnen gleichsam an, sie bleiben immer Gottes schöne Geschöpfe und ihr Glanz geht nicht verloren.

Janssen zeigt, dass sich Paulus in 1Kor 15 stark auf den Schöpfungsbericht aus Gen 1 bezieht, wie auch auf Schöpfungspsalmen. Er zählt die Fülle der Geschöpfe auf, um die Zusage Gottes zum Leben, zu den Kreaturen aller Art, in Erinnerung zu rufen: Und siehe es war sehr gut! Diese Freude Gottes wird zum Garant der Auferstehung allen Lebens: denn die Todesstrukturen, die ihr Unwesen auf den Körpern austoben, die sie hungern und leiden lassen, stehen gegenüber Gott auf schwachen Füssen.

Sie übersetzt 1Kor 15,39-41 so:

Nicht jedes Geschöpf ist dem anderen gleich,
denn eines sind die Menschen,
ein anderes Geschöpf sind die Haustiere,
ein anderes Geschöpf die Gefiederten,
ein anderes die Fische.
Und es gibt Körper am Himmel und Körper auf der Erde.
Aber unterschieden ist die Schönheit derer am Himmel,
unterschieden die derer auf der Erde.
Eine andere ist die Schönheit der Sonne
Und eine andere die Schönheit des Mondes
Und eine andere die Schönheit der Sterne;
Ein Gestirn unterscheidet sich nämlich von einem anderen in seiner Schönheit.

So klingt Paulus als Poet, als Sänger und Dichter in der Neuübersetzung von Claudia Janssen. Damit übersetzt sie nicht nur neu, sie transformiert nicht nur das Bild des hochintellektuellen und wetternden, schwer verständlichen Theologen, sie arbeitet gleichzeitig an einer Transformation der Theologie überhaupt.

Luzia Sutter Rehmann (Basel – Switzerland)

Jost, Renate, *Gender, Sexualität und Macht in der Anthropologie des Richterbuches*, Beiträge zur Wissenschaft vom Alten und Neuen Testament 164,

Stuttgart: Kohlhammer 2006, 390 p., ISBN: 978-3-17-018556-2, € 40,00
(Habilitationsschrift)

Jost, Renate, *Frauenmacht und Männerliebe. Egalitäre Utopien aus der Frühzeit Israels*, Stuttgart: Kohlhammer 2006, 191 p., ISBN: 978-3-17-019511-0,
€19,80

Renate Jost, Professorin für Theologische Frauenforschung/Feministische Theologie an der Augustana-Hochschule in Neuendettelsau, legt im Jahr 2006 zwei Bücher zum Geschlechterverhältnis im alttestamentlichen Buch der Richter vor. Während das erste ihre Habilitationsschrift repräsentiert, ist das zweite lediglich die stark gekürzte Fassung derselben, allerdings mit einem anderen, etwas plakativeren Titel: ‚Frauenmacht und Männerliebe', entspricht dabei weitgehend der Vorlage der Habilitation. Auch der wissenschaftliche Stil wird beibehalten; die hebräischen Buchstaben werden allerdings ausgetauscht und in Umschrift wiedergegeben. Leider wird im Vorwort auf die enge Verwandtschaft der beiden Bücher nicht hingewiesen.

Renate Jost geht von der Beobachtung aus, dass im Richterbuch Frauen eine auffallende Rolle spielen: sowohl von mächtigen Frauen (zum Beispiel Debora) als auch von Situationen größter Frauenohnmacht (Ri 19) wird erzählt. Die sich daraus ergebenden Fragen nach Sexualität und Gender verbindet Jost mit den Diskussionen um Macht und Herrschaft, und bringt damit zwei in der Forschung häufig getrennte Fragestellungen zusammen. Jost verwendet den Begriff der ‚Wildnis' als heuristische Kategorie, indem sie gleichermaßen an die positiven Konzepte der biblischen Traditionen, die Konzepte innerhalb der europäischen Geistesgeschichte, sowie der womanistischen und der feministischen Befreiungsgeschichte anknüpft. Diese Kategorie hat zwar eine gewisse Unschärfe, birgt aber gerade darin ein großes Potential. In ihrer Habilitationsschrift definiert sie 'Wildnis' ausführlich und weist mithilfe ethnologischer Modelle einen Zusammenhang von Wildnis und egalitären Gesellschaften nach, die sie für die Exegese des Richterbuches fruchtbar macht. Der Interpretation der biblischen Texte gehen recht lange Begriffsklärungen voraus, die aber nötig scheinen, um die verschiedener Diskurse, methodischen Zugänge und hermeneutischen Modelle zu erläutern. So werden z.B. auch die Begriffe Macht, Herrschaft, Gewalt, Sexualität und Gender ausführlich erörtert. Die Verfasserin nennt ihre Auslegung eine ‚integrative Exegese', die offen ist für die Vielfalt der kulturell bedingten Deutungsmöglichkeiten, die die Fremdheit der Texte akzeptiert und gleichzeitig gegenwärtige Fragestellungen mit den biblischen Texten ins Gespräch zu bringen versucht. Leider gibt die Kurzfassung diesen für das Verständnis des ganzen Ansatzes wesentlichen methodischen Überlegungen nur wenig Raum, obgleich sie (im Unterschied zur Habilitationsschrift) eine Graphik zu integrativen Exegesen montiert (30). Am Ende eines jeden Kapitels gibt es kurze, spannende Abschnitte, die die Relevanz der jeweiligen biblischen Texte für die Gegenwart problemorientiert bedenken.

Nach einer Analyse der Texte Ri 4-5; 11-12,7; 13; 16; 19 und ausführlichen Darstellungen von und Diskussion mit anderen Auslegungen kommt die Verfasserin zu dem Ergebnis, dass die staatenlose Zeit der Richterinnen und Richter als egalitäre, geschlechtssymmetrische Zeit verstanden werden kann, gleichermaßen als Erinnerung und als Utopie einer ‚Wildnis', die sich als kritisches Potential gegen Hierarchien erweisen kann. Dieses kritische Potential gilt auch jenen Texten des Richterbuches, die vehement für das Königtum plädieren und das Geschlechterverhältnis extrem asymmetrisch zeichnen. Die Utopie einer Gesellschaft ohne Staat mit Geschlechtersymmetrie, bzw. sogar Geschlechterasymmetrie zugunsten von Frauen hinterfragt die herrschende Vorstellung, der zufolge das biblische Israel eine patriarchalische Gesellschaft par exellence sei.

Die Ausführungen Josts eröffnen neue Blicke auf die Texte des Richterbuches, die in ihrer Spannung von Macht und Ohmacht, Gewalt und Schwäche, sex and crime oft so schwierig zu lesen sind. Wer an einer Auseinandersetzung mit der Vielzahl möglicher (auch kulturell bedingter) Deutungen der Figuren und Erzählungen im Richterbuch interessiert ist, der/dem sei diese/s Buch/ Bücher empfohlen.

Ulrike Bail (Bochum – Germany)

Ilse Müllner, *Das hörende Herz. Weisheit in der hebräischen Bibel*, Stuttgart: Kohlhammer 2006, 159 p., ISBN: 3-17-018287-0, € 16,80

Der in Kassel lehrenden Alttestamentlerin ist ein gut lesbares und verständliches Werk gelungen. Das Buch will ausdrücklich nicht als Beitrag zur wissenschaftlichen Fachdiskussion verstanden sein (5) und auch nicht die vorhandene ausführlichere Überblicksliteratur ersetzen, sondern möchte eine knappe Einführung in die Weisheitsliteratur und die Forschungspositionen auch für Menschen außerhalb der bibelwissenschaftlichen Fachwelt geben. Eigene Akzente setzt die Autorin dabei, wenn sie beispielsweise bei der Auslegung biblischer Textpassagen die historische Perspektive mit literaturwissenschaftlichen Einsichten verknüpft, wenn spätere rabbinische Aufnahmen der biblischen Weisheitstexte zur Sprache kommen, oder wenn den Frauen und weiblichen Figuren in den Texten besondere Aufmerksamkeit zuteil wird. Die neueste und wichtigste Sekundärliteratur wird jeweils diskutiert.

Im ersten Kapitel umreißt die Autorin den besonderen Charakter weiser Menschen, um einen Zugang zu den Subjekten der weisheitlichen Texte auch für heutige bibelferne Menschen zu ermöglichen. Kapitel 2 führt in wichtige Einzelaspekte der Weisheit in der hebräischen Bibel ein. So werden etwa weisheitliche Kompetenzen geschildert, das Herz als Ort der Weisheit benannt, oder Salomo als beispielhaft Weiser in den Blick genommen. In den drei folgenden Kapiteln konzentriert sich die Autorin auf jeweils eines der drei Weisheitsbücher der hebräischen Bibel: das Sprüchebuch, das Buch Ijob [Hiob] und das Buch Kohelet. Das sechste Kapitel ist der personifizierten Weisheit des Sprüchebuchs gewidmet. Das abschließende Kapitel 7 hebt die didaktischen Aspekte der Weisheitsliteratur hervor und schlägt Brücken zum heutigen Lehren und Lernen.

Trotz des knappen Zuschnitts des Buches enthält es auch für die Fachfrau interessante Anregungen, so etwa aus dem Bereich der Neurolinguistik zur Verarbeitung der Sprichwörter oder aus der Kognitionspsychologie zur besseren Einordnung der sprachlich knappen weisheitlichen Weltdeutung (35f). Bei Ijob hebt die Autorin hervor, dass sich gerade in der Vielzahl von Umgangsweisen mit dem Schicksal Ijobs im Buch die Erkenntnis spiegelt, dass tiefes Leid nicht auf einfache Weise beantwortet werden kann (68f). Das Buch Kohelet ist als Auseinandersetzung mit griechisch-philosophischen Fragestellungen wie der nach dem menschlichen Glück anerkannt. Neu ist, dass die Betonung der Unverfügbarkeit Gottes bei Kohelet sich nur als Weiterentwicklung älterer alttestamentlicher Traditionen angemessen würdigen lässt. Im Kapitel über die personifizierte Weisheit in Spr 1-9 wird auch ihre Gegenspielerin, die „fremde Frau", sowie als eine Art Synthese von beiden die „Frau der Stärke" in Spr 31,10-31 betrachtet. Die Autorin unterstreicht dabei zweierlei (121): Die Weisheitsgestalt lebt auch von patriarchalen Klischees und ist deshalb nicht uneingeschränkt positiv zu bewerten. Die Männlichkeit des israelitischen Gottesbildes wird durch die Weisheitsgestalt allerdings aufgebrochen. Das abschließende Kapitel über die Weisheitsliteratur als didaktische Literatur hebt unter anderem hervor, dass es sich bei der Rede von den „Unbelehrbaren" nicht um eine Wesenszuschreibung handelt, sondern um eine situative Einordnung.

Durchgängig knüpft die Autorin an die Lebenswirklichkeit heutiger Menschen an und setzt sich mit ihr auseinander. Dabei erhält die alttestamentliche Weisheit gelegentlich die Rolle einer kulturkritischen Stimme. So wird sie von einem alten, fremden Text zu einem Instrument der Reflexion für heutige

Lesende auf ihre eigene Kultur. Solch ein Einsatz ihrer Erkenntnisse wäre vermutlich ganz im Sinne der alttestamentlichen Weisen.
Gerlinde Baumann (Marburg/Langenselbold – Germany)

Tarja S. Philip, *Menstruation and Childbirth in the Bible. Fertility and Impurity*, Studies in Biblical Literature 88, New York: Peter Lang, 2005, 153 p.,
ISBN: 978-0-8204-7908-8, € 52,10 D / 53,60 A / CHF 76,00

Das Buch widmet sich einem Thema, dem erst in jüngster Zeit mehr Beach-
tung geschenkt wird: dem Körperzyklus der Frau und der Geburt in biblischen
Texten. Zuerst wird die Menstruation behandelt, in Kapitel vier und fünf der
Geburtsvorgang und die Geburtsmetaphorik in der Hebräischen Bibel. Die
Autorin will die Texte einer genauen Re-Lektüre, einem close reading unter-
ziehen (19). Sie unterscheidet zwischen priesterlichen und nichtpriesterlichen
Texten, wobei sie mit letzteren einsetzt. Das Skopus der erzählenden Texte, die
vom Körperzyklus der Frau handeln, sei Fruchtbarkeit. Rahel etwa will, indem
sie auf den Hausgöttern sitzt, ihre Unfruchtbarkeit überwinden (Gen 35). Wenn
der Weg der Frauen aufgehört hat, ist Sara unfruchtbar (Gen 18). Die Schlussfolgerung der Autorin ist, dass der Sprachgebrauch der Reinheitstorot in Lev 15
sich in diesen Texten jedoch nicht findet.

Der kurze Forschungsüberblick zu Beginn des Buches und die Kritik altorientalischer und kulturanthropologischer Vergleiche, da letztere vielfach nur
auf Textfragmenten beruhen (5-8), führt die Notwendigkeit der Re-Lektüre der
Texte vor Augen. In den Fragen von Tarja Philip liegt Potential für eine Re-
evaluierung des Paradigmas „Unreinheit" mit Blick auf die Menstruation bzw.
der Rede von einem universalen Menstruationstaboo. Desto mehr verwundert
daher der Untertitel „Fertility and Impurity" (Fruchtbarkeit und Unreinheit).
Erfassen diese Begriffe die Spannbreite der Texte der Hebräischen Bibel zum
Thema? Geben sie kulturübergreifende Erfahrungen von Frauen bzw. Kate-
gorisierungen von Geburt und Menstruation wieder, wie in den ersten Zeilen
der Einleitung evoziert wird (1)?

Im Folgenden beschränke ich mich auf einige Beobachtungen zum Thema
Menstruation und "Unreinheit" ausgehend von Tarja Philips Ausführungen:

Angesichts des Textbefundes stellt sich generell die Frage nach der Praxis
der Reinheitsvorschriften in vorexilischer Zeit. Im Unterschied zu anderen
Auslegungen innerhalb der jüdischen Exegese fällt die scharfe Trennungslinie
auf, die Tarja Philip zwischen dem biblischen Text und der nachbiblischen

Literatur im Blick auf die Reinigungsvorschriften für eine Frau nach der Menstruation zieht. Ein Bad nach der Menstruation werde in Lev 15 gerade im Unterschied zu dem Mann mit Ausfluss nicht gefordert und der Gang zur Miqveh ist erst in rabbinischer Zeit belegt bzw. gefordert. Die Autorin untersucht u.a. die Verwendung des hebräischen Begriffs *niddah*, der wörtlich Menstruation und in metaphorischer Hinsicht Unreinheit bedeute. Bedingt durch die Aufteilung des Buches werden zuerst Stellen analysiert, wo *niddah* in übertragener Weise verwendet wird. Ausgangspunkt einer grundlegenden Untersuchung des Begriffs müssten allerdings Lev 15 und 12 bilden, denn diese Kapitel prägen *niddah* zum kultischen Fachbegriff für den Zustand der Frau während der Menstruation. In dieser Hinsicht ist *niddah* in Beziehung zu kultischer Unreinheit, d.h. Kultunfähigkeit zu setzen, ohne allerdings synonym mit diesem zu werden.

In der Analyse von Tarja Philip verschmelzen die beiden Begriffe Unreinheit und Menstruation (*niddah*). Der metaphorische Gebrauch von *niddah* in Ez 7:19-20; 36:17; Esra 9:11 und an anderen Stellen führe dazu, dass *niddah* synonym zu Unreinheit gebraucht werde (35.37.64). Doch ist Unreinheit/impurity die treffende Wiedergabe? Lässt sich *niddah* nicht eher als kultische Grenzziehung und Absonderung in wörtlichem Sinne und dann auch im übertragenen verstehen? Entsprechend hätte das von der Autorin mit Blick auf die Menstruation beäugte Thema Unreinheit einer Explizierung und Problematisierung bedurft.

Ihre Schlussfolgerung für die Bewertung des Menstruationsbluts in den „priesterlichen" Texten, dass diesem Unreinheit aufgrund seiner Natur inhärent sei (73), bleibt damit leider trotz einzelner wertvoller Einsichten ihrer Textanalysen hinter den Fragestellungen und Erkenntnissen, wie sie sich programmatisch im Titel der Monographie von Charlotte Fonrobert „Menstrual Purity" bzw. in dem des Sammelbandes „Wholly Women, Holy Blood" spiegeln, zurück.

Dorothea Erbele-Küster (Kampen – The Netherlands)

Adele Reinhartz, *Freundschaft mit dem Geliebten Jünger. Eine jüdische Lektüre des Johannesevangeliums*, Zürich: Theologischer Verlag 2005, 245 p., ISBN: 3-290-17358-5, € 22,50 D / 23,20 A / CHF 36,00 (aus dem Englischen übersetzt von Esther Kobel)

Der Jünger, den Jesus liebte (Joh 13,23), kenne ich von Abendmahlsdarstellungen her: ein besonders junger, zarter Mann liegt irgendwie über Jesus. Manchmal schmiegt er sich an ihn an, manchmal sitzt er auf seinem Schoss.

Was soll frau davon halten? Schön, dass Männer auch zarte Seiten haben...
Und sonst?

Man sagt auch, dass der Lieblingsjünger derjenige gewesen sei, der mit
Petrus einen Wettlauf unternommen und gewonnen hatte (Joh 20,4). Kein
Wunder, wenn er so jung und leicht war, während Petrus doch eher älter und
derber und schwerer war. Jedenfalls versteht er als Erster, was das leere Grab
bedeutet, Petrus braucht da noch einen Moment.

Und langsam dämmert es der Leserin, dem Leser: dieser geliebte Jünger
hat das Evangelium des Johannes geschrieben (Joh 21,20-24). Er ist die Linse,
durch den wir von der johanneischen Gemeinde erfahren, von ihren Konflikten und ihrem Glauben. Oder: er ist das Nadelöhr, durch den alles, was in der
johanneischen Gemeinde erinnert und weitererzählt wurde, passieren musste.
Ich weiß einfach nicht, ob ich ihn mag, diesen Jüngling. Bin ich etwa eifer-
süchtig? Wohl kaum, es ist eher meine Erfahrung von aufstrebenden Schüler-
typen, die sich dem Meister hingebungsvoll an die Brust werfen, und dabei mit
ihrer Karriere so wunderbar vorankommen. Aber das hat ja nichts mit dem
Johannesevangelium zu tun. Oder doch?

Adele Reinhartz geht der rätselhaften Gestalt dieses Jüngers nach, indem sie
sorgfältig literaturwissenschaftlich analysiert, wie unsere Haltung als LeserIn
die Wahrnehmung dieser Gestalt beeinflusst. Sie typisiert vier Lektüren (die
„zustimmende", die „widerständige", die „wohlwollende" und die „betei-
ligte"). Geschärft wird diese Typisierung durch die Fokussierung auf den
Antijudaismus des vierten Evangeliums, auf die Darstellung der „Juden" als
die Anderen, die Gegner, die Ungläubigen. Adele Reinhartz ist jüdische Neu-
testamentlerin. Sie ist am Johannesevangelium interessiert und bereit, mit dem
Geliebten Jünger ins Gespräch zu kommen – was sie immer wieder mit der
Metapher eines gemeinsamen Abendessens durchblicken lässt. Doch wer sitzt
ihr da gegenüber? Ein Mentor, ein Kollege, ein Gegner oder ein Anderer?

Das Gespräch, das sie entwickelt, ist durch den grundsätzlichen Widerspruch
der johanneischen Christologie erschwert: Der Geliebte Jünger behauptet, dass
Jesus der Sohn Gottes, der Christus, sei und sie ist nicht willens, diesen
Anspruch anzuerkennen. Dazu kommt die Exklusivität dieser Christologie:
alle, die diesen Anspruch nicht anerkennen, werden in der binären Rhetorik des
Geliebten Jüngers als Lügner abqualifiziert.

„So verlangt meine Bemühung, wirklich Raum für den Geliebten Jünger zu
schaffen, einen weniger direkten, weniger konfrontativen Weg... Es bleibt
dabei, dass der Geliebte Jünger und ich bezüglich Wahrheit und des Wertes seines Geschenkes, das er mir auf dem Weg seines Evangeliums anbietet, nicht

einer Meinung sind. Es bleibt auch dabei, dass ich die Makrometapher, innerhalb derer er sich bewegt, mit Sorge betrachte..." (207)

Doch wie steht es jetzt mit mir und dem besagten Jünger? Mir ist er nicht
näher gekommen, im Gegenteil. Ich mag ihn nicht. Er ist so stur und über-
zeugt, stellt sich selbst nur ins beste Licht und Maria Magdalena lässt er
schließlich in ein Schweigen gehüllt, das ihrer Autorität großen Abbruch tut
(160). Eigentlich wusste ich das schon zu Beginn von Reinhartz Untersuchung.
Die Historikerin in mir hat nicht wirklich neue Erkenntnisse gewonnen, weder
ist mein Verständnis für die johanneische Gemeinde verändert worden, noch
sind irgendwelche externe Bezüge geschaffen worden zu Gemeinschaften in
vergleichbaren Situationen. Die Konzentration auf das fiktive Nachtessen mit
dem Geliebten Jünger hat seinen Preis: um viele sorgfältige Überlegungen
reicher, aber mit einem Gefühl der Leere verlasse auch ich die Szene.

Doch woher kommt diese Leere? Was habe ich denn erwartet? Erzeugt
nicht der Geliebte Jünger selbst dieses Unbehagen, wenn er so schwarz-weiß
argumentiert, wenn er sich selbst als „geliebt" darstellt, wenn er etwas anbietet, was auch ich als nicht-jüdische Leserin so nicht annehmen kann? Gehört
diese Leere zum Johannesevangelium und seiner Makroebene, zu mir, weil
ich Nahrung möchte, zu Adele Reinhartz, die nur analysiert, spiegelt, nach-
denkt und keine Brötchen backen will?

Dennoch beeindruckt das Ringen der Autorin um eine Freundschaft mit
dem „impliziten Autor" des vierten Evangeliums, weil es die eigenen Vorga-
ben und Einstellungen offenlegt, die aus ihnen resultierenden Konsequenzen
und schließlich zeigt, was eine *ethische Lektüre* eigentlich auszeichnet, resp.
was ein einander anerkennendes Verhältnis grundsätzlich belastet oder unmöglich macht. Für alle, die eine respektvolle Lektüre suchen und weder der Meinung sind, dass die Juden vom Teufel abstammen (Joh 8,44), noch diese Aussage (u.v.a.) als nicht so schlimm abtun wollen – ist dieses Buch ein Muss.

Luzia Sutter Rehmann (Basel – Switzerland)

Ilona Riedel-Spangenberger / Erich Zenger (Hg.), *"Gott bin ich, kein Mann"*.
Beiträge zur Hermeneutik der biblischen Gottesrede. FS für Helen Schüngel-
Straumann zum 65. Geburtstag, Paderborn: Schöningh 2006, 454 p., ISBN: 3-
506-71385-X, € 58,00

"Gott bin ich und kein Mann". Hier wird eine Programmatik formuliert, mit der
Helen Schüngel-Straumanns Lebenswerk gewürdigt wird. Eine nachträgliche

Genugtuung der von Ilona Riedel-Spangenberger und Erich Zenger herausgegebenen Festschrift wird für die Jubilarin sein, dass dieses Buch dank der Druckkostenfinanzierung verschiedener Diözesen (Freiburg, Basel, Fulda, Mainz, Rottenburg-Stuttgart) und der Katholischen Frauengemeinschaft zustande kam. Im Reigen der gratulierenden AutorInnen finden sich nicht nur Kollegen der Bibelwissenschaften (E. Zenger, O. Keel, S. Schroer, J. Marböck, I. Müllner, M. Häusl, F.-L. Hossfeld, M.-Th. Wacker, E. S. Gerstenberger usw.), Mitstreiterinnen der Europäischen Gesellschaft für Frauen in der Theologie (V. Ferrari Schiefer, R. Ammicht-Quinn, A. Günter, A. Jensen, E. Moltmann-Wendel, I. Praetorius, A. Valerio, C. Vander Stichele), Schwestern auf dem gemeinsamen Weg (T. Berger, W. Herbstrith, E. Gössmann, Ch. M. Maier, A. Ohler), sondern auch Stimmen aus Praxisfeldern (J. J. Meier, A. Loretan, M. Bogner, W. Bühlmann, M. Raske, H. Kohler-Spiegel, U. King, I. Löffler, M. Heimbach-Steins, U. Gerhard). Im ersten Teil des Buches (17-173) gruppieren sich Artikel, die die Gottesrede in Beziehung zur Anthropologie der Geschlechter setzen, im zweiten Teil (177-334) finden wir spannende Exegesen, im dritten Teil (337-454) werden die Praxisfelder und unterschiedlichen theologischen Perspektiven (Ethik, Religionspädagogik, Liturgie) im Hinblick auf biblische Texte entfaltet.

Die Festschrift beginnt mit einem Beitrag von A. Franz, der Antonio Da Corregios Bild 'Die Heilige Nacht' (17-26) dazu benutzt, die metaphorische Rede von Gott als Licht und Vater als Botschaft des göttlich Unsichtbaren im Menschen zu entschlüsseln. Allerdings meint er damit auch die Frage des Geschlechtes Gottes erledigt zu haben. Er zitiert den Roman von Dan Brown 'Das Sakrileg' als einzige Gewährsquelle feministisch-theologischer Diskussion (17) sowie eine Publikation der Jubilarin im Schlepptau, um seine Polemik zu untermauern. Kein Wunder, dass hier Selbstverständliches wiederholt wird. Da trifft der sehr kurze Beitrag von Anne Jensen 'Hat Gott einen Enkelsohn?' (82-85) schon eher den Kern der feministisch-theologischen Debatte. Die Autorin stellt die letzte der fünf theologischen Reden (von 380) des Gregor von Nazianz, die die Beziehung zwischen Vater und Geist zu verstehen sucht, heraus. "Wenn der Heilige Geist dagegen vom Sohn gezeugt ist, dann haben wir es mit einem Enkelgott zu tun" (84). Gregor geht es um die Unmöglichkeit, Gott auf der Bildebene zu treffen. Sonne, Strahl und Licht konjugiert er durch und kommt zu dem Schluss, dass alle Bilder trügerisch sind. Hier vertritt Jensen mit Hilfe von Gregor die entgegen gesetzte Position zu Franz im ersten Beitrag. Es folgt ein sehr sympathischer Beitrag von Elisabeth Moltmann-Wendel 'Gott, eine alte Frau' (86-95), die unter Bezugnahme auf vier sehr unterschiedliche Textverweise diesen Gott kreativ und lebendig porträtiert. Die ihrem Beitrag vorangestellte These, dass die in der feministischen Forschung tätigen Frauen – "meist jung an Jahren" – den Aspekt der 'alten, weisen Frau' nicht sehen wollten, teile ich nicht. All die über fünfzig-jährigen Forscherinnen, die ich im deutschsprachigen Raum kenne, sind ja über die Matriarchatsforschung, die den Zyklus von jungem Mädchen, reifer Frau, weise Alte hervorhebt, stimuliert worden, um in der christlichen Tradition nach weiblichen Bildern Gottes zu suchen. Zu den profiliertesten gehört wohl hier Marie-Theres Wacker, die auch in der Festschrift mit einer mutigen Exegese zu 2 Makk 7 (259-270) vertreten ist. Wissend um die historische Schwierigkeit der männlichen Präferenz christlicher Gottesbilder hat Valeria Ferrari Schiefer eine wunderbare Analyse einer Vision der Predigerin Domenica Narducci da Paradiso (1473-1553) vorgelegt (156-161), in der sie die Inklusivität des Sprechens über Gott dieser Italienerin nachzeichnet. Auch der italienischsprachige Beitrag von Adriana Valerio geht in diese Richtung (156-161). Mit detektivischem Scharfsinn machen die Beiträge von Othmar Keel (105-123) sowie von Silvia Schroer und Thomas Staubli (124-155) auf die Bedeutung altorientalischer (Miniatur-)Kunst für die Benennung weiblicher Gottheiten aufmerksam. Forschungsmäßig für mich als systematischer Theologin zwei 'Sahnehäubchen'! Ina Praetorius steuert wie immer inspirierend einen Beitrag über 'Gott, die Welthausfrau' bei (96-104), Waltraud Herbstrith eine Rekonstruktion des Gottesgedankens bei Edith Stein (162-173). Im Buch finden sich einander widersprechende Beiträge, so wenn man Caroline Vander Stichele 'Der Herr? Das geht nicht mehr!' (318-327) und Theodor Schneider (40-54) vergleicht, der dem Titel 'Herr' einen zärtlichen Klang verleihen möchte. Gerne liest man die bibelwissenschaftlichen Beiträge, die allesamt zeigen, dass die theologischen Frauenforschung Eingang in den allgemeinen Fachdiskurs gefunden hat. Ob E. Zenger, F.-L.Hossfeld, E. Gerstenberger oder I. Müllner und alle Nichterwähnten, sie alle bezeugen diesen Standard im wissenschaftlichen Diskurs, den andere theologische Disziplinen noch längst nicht erreicht haben. Im letzten Teil der Festschrift kommen Stimmen zu Wort, die den Ertrag der Forschungen der Jubilarin in verschiedenen Praxisfeldern bezeugen, wie z.B. der Beitrag von I. Löffler (411-419). Ursula King macht in ihrem Artikel 'Geist und Geschlecht' auf die Früchte des Religionsvergleiches in der internationalen Frauenforschung aufmerksam, eine Wohltat in diesem doch sehr 'deutschsprachig' orientierten Buch. Insgesamt ist diese Festschrift ein exegetisches Juwel! Den HerausgeberInnen ist es zu danken, dass sich die Lehr- und Lebensspuren von Helen Schüngel-Straumann auch als eine Art

Zwischenbilanz feministischer Theologie im deutschsprachigen Raum lesen lassen.

Hedwig Meyer-Wilmes (Nijmegen – The Netherlands)

III.2 Kirchen- und Religionsgeschichte / Church history and history of religions / Histoire de l'Eglise et des religions

Gisa Bauer, *Kulturprotestantismus und frühe bürgerliche Frauenbewegung. Agnes von Zahn-Harnack (1884-1950)*, Arbeiten zur Kirchen- und Theologiegeschichte 17, Leipzig: Evangelische Verlagsanstalt 2006, 417 p., ISBN-10: 3374023851, € 48,50

Die Frauenrechtlerin, Lehrerin und Publizistin Agnes von Zahn-Harnack, so wird man wohl urteilen dürfen, war eine der bemerkenswertesten Frauen der ersten Hälfte des 20. Jahrhunderts. Während viele Theologiestudierende ihren Vater, Adolf von Harnack, kennen, wissen heute wohl die wenigsten, dass seine Tochter die erste immatrikulierte Studentin an der Friedrich-Wilhelms-Universität (heute Humboldt-Universität) zu Berlin war.

Gisa Bauer hat mit ihrer 2005 in Leipzig eingereichten Dissertation eine wichtige Forschungslücke geschlossen. Die Arbeit wurde von dem inzwischen verstorbenen Kirchenhistoriker Prof. Dr. Dr. Kurt Nowak angeregt und von dessen Nachfolger Prof. Dr. Klaus Fitschen betreut. Ausgehend von der Biographie Agnes von Zahn-Harnacks stellt sie eine wichtige Epoche deutscher Geistes- und Frauengeschichte dar. Dabei geht es der Vf. darum, der „Korrelation von Kulturprotestantismus und früher bürgerlicher Frauenbewegung" (9) nachzugehen, und diese in der „biographischen Erörterung von Leben und Werk Agnes von Zahn-Harnacks" (ebd.) zuzuspitzen.

In der Einleitung (Kapitel I) legt die Vf. das Schwergewicht auf die Bedeutung der Verknüpfung von Kulturprotestantismus und Frauenbewegung: Durch die bisherige gegenseitige „Ignoranz" von Theologie- und Kulturgeschichte (14) sei Agnes von Zahn-Harnack bislang nur einseitig gewürdigt worden, nämlich entweder als Protagonistin der Frauenbewegung oder als Biographin ihres Vaters. Gisa Bauer möchte nun durch eine fächerübergreifende Synopse aller Publikationen von Zahn-Harnack „sowohl das frauenemanzipatorische Wirken Zahn-Harnacks für die Theologiegeschichtsschreibung aufbereiten, als auch das liberal-protestantische Movens der Protagonistin der frühen Frauenbewegung für die Frauengeschichtsschreibung verdeutlichen" (15).

Das zweite Kapitel widmet sich der soziologischen und strukturellen Vernetzung von liberalem Protestantismus und bürgerlicher Frauenbewegung. Hier zeigt die Vf. die personellen, strukturellen und institutionellen Wechselwirkungen auf, die sich z.b. in der Anzahl von Vertreterinnen der Frauenbewegung verfassten Artikel in den ersten beiden Auflagen des Handwörterbuchs für Theologie und Religionswissenschaft „Religion in Geschichte und Gegenwart" niederschlugen (u.a. Gertrud Bäumer, Paula Mueller-Otfried, Else Zurhellen-Pfleiderer). Auch in den liberalprotestantischen Medien wurden Frauenfrage und Aspekte der Frauenbewegung diskutiert (etwa in Martin Rades „Die christliche Welt", den Mitteilungen des Evangelisch-Sozialen Kongresses oder Friedrich Naumanns „Die Hilfe").

Der Vater der Porträtierten, der berühmte Theologe und Kirchenhistoriker Adolf (von) Harnack (1851-1930), sowie sein Verhältnis zur Frauenemanzipationsbewegung sind Gegenstand des dritten Kapitels. Harnacks Bedeutung für die Frauenbewegung schlug sich z.B. in einem Telegramm Getrud Bäumers, Vorsitzende des Bundes Deutscher Frauen (BDF), zu seinem 60. Geburtstag nieder, in dem sie ihn als den vielleicht größten Helfer, „den die preußische Frauenwelt je gehabt hat, ihre Rechte zu verteidigen" apostrophierte (71). Harnack setzte sich zeitlebens für verbesserte Bildungschancen für Mädchen und Frauen ein – was unmittelbar auch seinen Töchtern zugute kam (s.o.).

Das Hauptkapitel der Studie widmet sich unter der Überschrift „Frauenemanzipation aus protestantischem Geist" Agnes von Zahn-Harnack (Kapitel IV). Dargestellt werden ihr Leben und ihr Werk als Publizistin und Leiterin von Frauenorganisationen. Agnes von Harnack kam 1884 in Gießen als älteste Tochter Adolf Harnacks und seiner Frau Amalie, geb. Thiersch, zur Welt. Nach einem kurzen Aufenthalt in Marburg zog die Familie im Jahr 1888 nach Berlin. Agnes wuchs in Berlin in einem intellektuellen Milieu auf, das reich an Kontakten zu den Geistesgrößen dieser Zeit war. Sie besuchte die Höhere Mädchenschule, absolvierte die Ausbildung zur Lehrerin für diese Schulform und begann schließlich 1908 das Studium der deutschen und englischen Philologie sowie Philosophie (und nicht der Theologie, wie oft fälschlicherweise zu lesen ist). 1912 beendete sie ihr Studium mit der Promotion und wurde Lehrerin. Während des Ersten Weltkrieges engagierte sie sich in der Berliner Kommission des Nationalen Frauendienstes und stand damit an der Spitze der weiblichen Kriegshilfe, worüber ihr Vater folgendermaßen urteilte: „ein Witz der Preuß[ischen] Geschichte: die erste Frau in einem Ministerium findet sich im

Kriegsministerium!" (126). 1919 schloss sie sich der liberalen Deutschen Demokratischen Partei (DDP) an. Im selben Jahr heiratete sie den promovierten Juristen Karl von Zahn (1877-1944), Ministerialrat beim Reichsarchiv in Potsdam. Aus der Ehe gingen drei Kinder hervor. Die Heirat beendete von Zahn-Harnacks gerade erst wieder aufgenommene Tätigkeit im Schuldienst. So wirkte sie fortan freischaffend publizistisch. Im Jahr 1926 engagierte sie sich führend für die Gründung des Deutschen Akademikerinnenbundes (DAB) und wurde dessen erste Vorsitzende. Das Ziel des DAB war es, die universitäre Frauenbildung weiter zu fördern. Der DAB war eine der einflussreichsten Frauenorganisationen der Weimarer Republik. In den Jahren 1931-33, als Vorsitzende des BDF, wurde sie so zur öffentlichen Stimme von rund zwei Millionen Frauen. In der NS-Zeit zog sich Agnes von Zahn-Harnack weitestgehend aus der Öffentlichkeit zurück. Nach Kriegsende wirkte sie an der Gründung des Berliner Frauenbundes mit. 1949 erhielt sie in Marburg den Ehrendoktor für die Biographie ihres Vaters. Ihr zweites wichtiges Werk war eine Darstellung der Frauenbewegung: „Die Frauenbewegung. Geschichte, Probleme, Ziele" (1928). In dieser Studie untersuchte sie die Geschichte der Frauenbildung, das Mädchenschulwesen, Frauenwahlrecht und die internationale Einbindung der deutschen Frauenorganisationen. Ergänzt wurde das Werk durch eine umfangreiche Bibliographie, die eines der zentralen Hilfs- und Arbeitsmittel für die Frauenforschung im 20. Jahrhundert darstellen sollte.

Rajah Scheepers (Hannover/Berlin – Germany)

Doris Brodbeck (Hg.), *Dem Schweigen entronnen. Religiöse Zeugnisse von Frauen des 16. bis 19. Jahrhunderts*, Würzburg/Markt Zell: Religion Kultur Verlag 2006, 328 p., ISBN: 3-933891-17-5, € 19,90 / CHF 34,90

Frauen haben sich immer zum eigenen Glauben geäußert, ihr religiöses Leben reflektiert und sich aktiv daran beteiligt, eine am Evangelium orientierte Praxis zu gestalten. Der von Doris Brodbeck herausgegebene Sammelband bietet dafür neunzehn anregende, zum Teil bislang weniger bekannte Zeugnisse von Frauen des 16. bis 19. Jahrhunderts, Frauen aus verschiedenen christlichen Konfessionen, die in der Schweiz mit viel Engagement und zum Teil gegen den Widerstand ihrer Umwelt wirkten. So hat beispielsweise Catherine Both-Clibborn (1858-1955) das Werk der Heilsarmee 1882 in Genf und Sophie von Wurstemberger (1809-1878) das Diakonissenhaus in Bern gegründet. Die russische Baronin Juliane von Krüdener (1764-1824) und die radikalpietistische

Prophetin Ursula Meyer (1682-1743) gingen einer Predigtätigkeit nach, die öffentliches Aufsehen erregte. Unter den vorgestellten Frauen finden sich auch die durch ihr Buch *Heidi* bekannt gewordene Johanna Spyri-Heußer (1827-1901) und die Menzinger Oberin Bernarda Heimgartner (1822-1863) sowie die redegewandte und gebildete Marie Dentière, die vor ihrem Übertritt zum protestantischen Glauben als Priorin einer Augustinerinnengemeinschaft vorstand und sich dann in Genf mit allen Kräften für die Reformation einsetzte. Aber auch Zeugnisse von mehr im Hintergrund wirkenden Frauen werden vorgestellt, wie Elise von Liebenau und Josephine Schwytzer, die die Tagebücher des Marienvereins von Luzern führten und somit einen Einblick in die Religiosität junger Frauen des schweizerischen katholisch-konservativen Milieus des 19. Jahrhunderts erlauben (84).

Vier Überschriften gliedern das Buch und ordnen somit diese breite Vielfalt unterschiedlicher Textzeugnisse und deren Autorinnen für die Leserinnen und Leser thematisch. Im ersten Teil *Zwischen Auflehnung und Anpassung* finden sich Frauen, die für die religiöse Emanzipation der Frau eintreten, etwa die Bernerin Helene von Mülinen (1850-1924), die in ihrem Briefwechsel mit ihrem Lehrer Adolf Schlatter in theologischer Auseinandersetzung einen Weg sucht, sich aus den engen Gesellschaftsrollen zu befreien. Angeregt von ihrer Freundin Josephine Butler, die in Norden Englands seit 1870 gegen die Prostitution kämpfte, prangerte auch Emilie de Morsier (1843-1896) die soziale Ungerechtigkeit und die Doppelmoral an. Sie verfolgte das Ziel der Befreiung von Frauen, die Hebung menschlicher Moral und den Schutz der Familie und wollte damit eine umfassende Sozialreform erreichen (34).

Im zweiten Teil *Religiöse Hingabe und Armut* werden unter anderem ausgewählte Texte der Schwester Trinette Binschedler (1825-1879), die erste Oberin des Diakonissenhauses in Riehen, und der Schwester Maria Wiborada Treichlinger (1736-1765), die erste Chronistin des Klosters Libingen-Glattburg im Kanton St. Gallen, vorgestellt.

Im dritten Teil *Glaubensentwürfe zwischen Pietismus und Rationalismus* kommen die Dichterinnen Meta Heußer-Schweizer (1797-1876), Pfarrerstochter und Arztfrau, und die aus St. Gallen stammende Anna Schlatter-Bernet (1773-1826) zu Wort, die Ursulinin Katharina Schmid (1759-1831), die bereits benannte Radikalpietistin Ursula Meyer, Marie Huber (1695-1753), die in ihren Schriften die Züge einer natürlichen Religion zeichnete, und die hochadelige Hortensia von Salis (1659-1692). Die Verschiedenheit dieser Frauen zeigt das breite Spektrum auf, das im Spannungsfeld zwischen Pietismus und Rationalismus besteht (14).

Im letzten Teil *im Schatten der Reformation* ist von zwei sehr unterschiedlichen Zeugnissen die Rede, (und zwar) zum einen von der bereits oben genannten ehemaligen Klosterfrau Marie Dentière, die dem Christentum kritisch gegenüber stand, heiratete und während der Reformation öffentlich auftrat, und (sich) zum anderen von der Chronistin und späteren Äbtissin Jeanne Jussie (1503-1561), die Marie Dentière stark kritisierte, sich mit ihren Mitschwestern den Forderungen der Reformation, aus dem Kloster auszutreten und zu heiraten, widersetzte und im Exil in Frankreich ihr Ordensleben fortführte.

Mit ihrer kleinen Chronik des Konvents St. Klara in Genf verfasste Jeanne Jussie einen der interessantesten Berichte über den Widerstand eines Frauenklosters und über die Gräuel der Gewalt in den Umwälzungen der Reformationszeit. Mit ihren Schilderungen leistete sie Widerstand gegen das Vergessen der Opfer (14).

In die Textzeugnisse der vorgestellten Frauen aus vier Jahrhunderten führen hochqualifizierte Fachfrauen, vor allem Theologinnen und Historikerinnen, aber auch Philosophinnen und Sprachwissenschaftlerinnen, sehr sorgfältig ein, bieten weiterführende Literatur und wecken somit Interesse, noch mehr über die Protagonistinnen und ihre Zeit zu erfahren. Indem neben den emanzipatorischen auch den weniger beachteten und den von heute aus vielleicht eher angepasst und konservativ erscheinenden Stimmen Platz gegeben wird, indem Glaubenskonflikte von Frauen, Überzeugungen und Widersprüche zu Tage kommen können, wird ein einzigartiger Einblick in die Kirchengeschichte der Schweiz geboten, der der Vielfalt und Verschiedenheit religiösen Lebens von Frauen Rechnung trägt.

Valeria Ferrari Schiefer (Ludiano-Sion – Switzerland / Bobingen – Germany)

Julie Kirchberg / Judith Könemann (Hg.), *Frauentraditionen. Mit Elisabeth Gössmann im Gespräch*, Ostfildern: Schwabenverlag 2006, ISBN: 3-7966-1258-X, 142 S., € 16,90

Die Beiträge des vorliegenden Sammelbandes gehen auf ein Symposium zu Ehren Elisabeth Gössmanns im November 2004 zurück. Dessen Anliegen war es, Früchte sowie Neuansätze und Herausforderungen der theologischen Arbeit von Frauen sichtbar zu machen und dabei nicht nur universitäre und pastorale Arbeitsfelder sondern auch verschiedene Frauengenerationen ins Gespräch miteinander zu bringen.

Der Band enthält außer dem Vorwort der Herausgeberinnen und einem Grußwort der Leiterin des Seelsorgeamts im Bistum Osnabrück, Dr. Daniela

Engelhard, zwei Teile mit drei bzw. sieben Beiträgen. Im ersten Teil „Elisabeth Gössmann – Pionierin theologischer Frauenforschung" würdigt zunächst eine Pionierin der feministischen Theologie, Elisabeth Moltmann-Wendel, Gössmanns Arbeit auf dem Gebiet der theologischen Frauenforschung. Anschließend kommt Gössmann selbst in zwei Beiträgen zu Wort: eine Frau, die ihre Lebenserfahrung in zwei Kontinenten gewonnen hat und diese fruchtbar auch für ihr theologisches Arbeiten macht. Dies tritt etwa dort zutage, wo sie sich kritisch mit der Entwicklung der (römisch-katholischen) Mariendogmen von 1854 und 1950 auseinandersetzt und ihren Leserinnen und Lesern die japanische Rezeption Marias in der Figur der *Kannon-sama* vorstellt. Der zweite Teil „Früchte, Neuansätze und Herausforderungen theologischer Arbeit von Frauen – Gespräch zwischen den Generationen" beginnt ebenfalls mit einem Beitrag Gössmanns. Sie behandelt anhand der Auslegung von Gen 1-3 von ihr wiederentdeckte „Frauentraditionen im Christentum" und verschafft so Einblick in ihre kritisch-theologiegeschichtliche, quellenorientierte Arbeitsweise, die ihren Niederschlag in dem seit 1984 von ihr herausgegebenen „Archiv für philosophie- und theologiegeschichtliche Frauenforschung" gefunden hat. Im Anschluss daran folgen Reaktionen jüngerer Frauen; der Beitrag von Stefanie Rieger-Goertz und das Interview Julie Kirchbergs mit Irene Porsch zeigen, dass „Mechanismen der Ungerechtigkeit" (98) heute viel subtiler als früher geworden sind und diese von jungen Frauen oft erst im Übergang zum Berufsleben erfahren werden. Ingeborg Tiemann verbindet das zurückgehende Interesse an Feminismus und feministischer Theologie nicht nur mit dem bereits angedeuteten Brisanzverlust aufgrund verminderten Leidensdrucks, sondern auch mit einem wachsenden Desinteresse an der Auseinandersetzung mit kirchlichen Strukturen und einer veränderten Männerrolle. Ihrem bündigen Schluss, die „soziale Lage veränderte die Interessenlagen und damit auch die Prioritätensetzungen von Frauen" (111) ist zuzustimmen. Die Einschätzung Tiemanns, dass der Ruf nach mehr Frauen in Führungspositionen in der römisch-katholischen Kirche derzeit nicht chancenlos sei, wird von Heinrich Jacob, dem ehemaligen Leiter des Seelsorgeamtes der Osnabrücker Diözese, geteilt. Martina Blasberg-Kuhnke, Professorin an der Universität Osnabrück, zieht Bilanz hinsichtlich feministischer Ansätze in der Praktischen Theologie/Pastoraltheologie und Religionspädagogik und nennt Desiderate und Zukunftsaufgaben feministischer Praktischer Theologie. Feministische Theologie und Theologie sowie die Frauenbewegung sind „Bezugsgrößen praktisch-theologischen Denkens", denn: „Kirchliche Praxis ist als eine Praxis von Frauen zu reflektieren" (126). Die Praxis von Frauen hat ihre konkreten Orte.

Mit der Metapher des Ortes – als Ausgangspunkt oder Ankerplatz, als verlassener Ort, oder als Stelle, zu der frau aufbricht – schließt die in Bamberg lehrende Professorin für Christliche Soziallehre und Allgemeine Religionssoziologie, Marianne Heimbach-Steins, den Band mit einer Ortsbestimmung heutiger feministischer Theologie ab. Wer aufbreche, brauche Geschichtsbewusstsein und die Rückbindung an Quellen, müsse Grenzen überschreiten und ziehen und sich der Begegnung mit dem Fremden stellen, „bewohnbare Orte" (136) – Zelte, Wohnhäuser, Brutstätten, Marktplätze – finden und dabei das Paradox einer zugleich nomadischen und sesshaften, etablierten und prekären, randständigen und mittigen Existenzweise leben.

Die Beiträge des Bandes sind gut lesbar und für einen breiten Leser/innenkreis geeignet; die Verbindung von Geschichte und Praktischer Theologie hätte – was mich angeht – vertieft und weiter konkretisiert werden können, ebenso das Gespräch zwischen den Frauengenerationen.
Angela Berlis (Utrecht – The Netherlands)

Adelheid M. von Hauff (Hg.), *Frauen gestalten Diakonie. Band 2: Vom 18. bis zum 20. Jahrhundert*, Stuttgart: Kohlhammer 2006, 567 p., ISBN: 3-17-019324-4, € 29,80 / CHF 50,70

Während es den Theologinnen in den verfassten Kirchen erst mit der Zulassung der Frauen zum Amt der Vikarin möglich wurde, hauptberuflich in der Kirche tätig zu werden, stellte die Diakonie den Frauen schon früher einen Wirkungsraum zur Verfügung. Wobei, auch dies sei vorweg bemerkt, der eigenständige Gestaltungsraum der Frauen in den meisten Fällen stark eingeschränkt war, lag doch die Leitungsmacht in der Diakonie meist beim Vorsteher bzw. hauptamtlichen Geistlichen.

Den Frauen in der Diakonie ist der von Adelheid von Hauff, Lehrbeauftragte am Diakoniewissenschaftlichen Institut der Universität Heidelberg und an der dortigen Pädagogischen Hochschule, herausgegebene Band gewidmet. Dieser zweite Band behandelt die drei letzten Jahrhunderte, während Band 1 sich den Frauen in der Diakonie zu Zeiten des Alten Testaments bis zum Pietismus widmet. Über die Problematik eines derart weiten Begriffs von „Diakonie" wird noch etwas zu sagen sein.

Beide Bände sind für den Gebrauch in der Praxis, insbesondere der schulischen Arbeit, gedacht. Begleitet werden sie von zwei Bänden mit

Unterrichtsmaterialien, die den Stoff für das 1. bis 6. Schuljahr bzw. die Sekundarstufe 1 erschließen sollen.

Eröffnet wird der vorliegende Band mit einem Geleitwort der Herausgeberin, in dem sie das Verhältnis von Männern und Frauen in der weiblichen Diakonie reflektiert. Der Hg.' geht es darum, jene Frauen zu porträtieren, die „eigenständig initiativ wurden und damit als Frauen diakonische Zeitgeschichte schrieben" (10). Auf Grund dieses Kriteriums werden die beiden Ehefrauen Theodor Fliedners bewusst nicht dargestellt, wohl aber andere Frauen, bei denen Männer eine „Vorreiterrolle spielten" (11). Dadurch wird Vf.' Friederike und Karolines Lebenswerk nicht gerecht, – auch bleibt die auf die Fliedners zurückgehende weibliche Diakonie Kaiserswerther Prägung unbeachtet.

In der Einleitung fokussiert eine der bekannten älteren Vertreterinnen der feministischen Theologie, Elisabeth Moltmann-Wendel, unter der Überschrift „Frömmigkeit und autonomes Handeln" die Zusammenhänge von Frauengeschichte und Diakoniegeschichte. In ihrem aufschlussreichen Überblick beleuchtet sie u.a. „Die Ordnung der Mütter": Die meisten der dargestellten Frauen erhielten im Laufe ihres Lebens den Titel „Mutter" zuerkannt – unabhängig davon, ob sie im biologischen Sinn Mutter, Jungfrau, Witwe oder allein lebende Frau waren. „Mütterlichkeit" war ein wichtiges Kennzeichen der Krankenpflege und der Sozialarbeit. Auch die erste deutsche Frauenbewegung hob die „Mütterlichkeit" auf ihr Schild. Dies ist insbesondere deswegen von Interesse, da es um die Jahrhundertwende vom 19. zum 20. Jahrhundert zu einer heftigen Auseinandersetzung um das „richtige Verständnis" von Mütterlichkeit zwischen Frauenbewegung und weiblicher Diakonie kommen sollte.

Die 35 Porträts sind chronologisch angeordnet, sie reichen von Louise Scheppler (geboren 1763 wirkte sie an der Seite Friedrich Oberlins im Bereich der Kleinkinderpädagogik) bis zu Brigitte Schröder (gestorben 2000, Gründerin des Krankenhausbesuchsdienstes der „Grünen Damen") und umfassen damit fast 250 Jahre Frauengeschichte. Die Autoren und Autorinnen decken viele Bereiche des Spektrums von Kirche und Diakonie ab, darunter landeskirchliche Archive, Universitäten, Kirchengemeinden, Fachhochschulen, Diakonissenmutterhäuser, Kirchenmusik und Journalismus. Die Aufsätze sind von unterschiedlicher Qualität und Tiefenschärfe. Während manche Biogramme aus den Quellen gearbeitet sind und damit neue Erkenntnisse bringen, beschränken andere Beiträge sich lediglich darauf, Bekanntes zu wiederholen. Eine historische Kontextualisierung des Dargestellten erfolgt nicht in jedem Fall, wäre aber hilfreich gewesen.

Erfreulich ist der Umstand, dass die Herausgeberin sich nicht auf Deutschland beschränkt, sondern auch einige Biographien aus dem Ausland berücksichtigt: so z.B. die Engländerin Elizabeth Fry, die als Expertin für Gefängnisreformen schon Theodor Fliedner inspirierte, und ihre Landsmännin Josephine Butler (Kampf für Frauenbildung und gegen eine staatliche Reglementierung der Prostitution), der bereits Anna Paulsen 1964 ein eigenes Kapitel in ihrer Untersuchung zum Verhältnis von Frauendiakonie und Frauenbewegung gewidmet hatte. Aber auch in Deutschland weniger bekannte Frauen aus dem osteuropäischen Raum wie Wilhelmina Clasina Blazejewski, die innerhalb der Gemeinschaftsbewegung wirkte, oder Kristina Royová, religiöse Schriftstellerin und eine der bedeutendsten Frauen der slowakischen Diakonie, werden in dem Band gewürdigt.

Für die weitere Forschungsarbeit wären Literaturangaben am Ende der Artikel sowie ein Register hilfreich gewesen, auch um die zahlreichen Verflechtungen zwischen den Protagonistinnen der weiblichen Diakonie aufzuzeigen.

Als Resümee bleibt zu ziehen, dass es sich hierbei um ein überwiegend gut geschriebenes Buch mit vielfältigen Porträts handelt, das – obschon primär an Lehrkräfte adressiert – allen an Frauen– oder Diakoniegeschichte Interessierten empfohlen werden kann. Die Herausgeberin schließt eine Lücke in unseren diakoniegeschichtlichen Kenntnissen, indem sie einen sehr weiten Begriff von Diakonie anlegt, um auch Frauen außerhalb der Diakonie Kaiserswerther Prägung in den Blick nehmen zu können. Diese Vielfalt ist die Stärke des Buches, gleichzeitig aber auch seine Schwäche. Wenn die Hg.' Diakonie „als Dienst der praktischen Nächstenliebe wie auch als Dienst am Wort" (Klappentext) versteht, wird eine Zuordnung schwierig. So war Bertha von Suttner als erste Trägerin des Friedensnobelpreises (1905) ohne Zweifel eine wichtige Frauengestalt, aber ob ihre Arbeit die Etikettierung „diakonisch" zu Recht trägt, scheint fraglich.

Rajah Scheepers (Hannover/Berlin – Germany)

Marion Kobelt-Groch, *Judith macht Geschichte. Zur Rezeption einer mythischen Gestalt vom 16. bis 19. Jahrhundert*, München: Wilhelm Fink Verlag 2005, 310 p., ISBN: 3-7705-3959-1, € 34,90

Der Titel „Judith macht Geschichte" bezieht sich eigentlich nur auf die ersten beiden Kapitel des Buches, in denen zunächst der Mythos Judith allgemein und dann fokussiert auf das Werk Sacher-Masochs thematisiert wird. Im dritten Teil beschäftigt sich Marion Kobelt-Groch nämlich mit der bisher in der Forschung vernachlässigten Nebenfigur der Magd Judiths.

Nicht die theologische Wirkungsgeschichte der biblischen Judith und ihrer Befreiungstat – die Enthauptung des Holofernes – ist Thema der Untersuchung, sondern die interdisziplinäre Rezeption der mythischen Gestalt Judith in künstlerischen, literarischen und musikalischen Bearbeitungen vom 16. bis 19. Jahrhundert. Dabei arbeitet Kobelt-Groch Judith als eine Gestalt heraus, die für alle sozialen Schichten und für beiderlei Geschlechter relevant ist, weil sie bereit war, für alles und jeden zu kämpfen (26). Judith kann demnach allumfassend eingesetzt werden, sie kann konservieren und revolutionieren. Die Autorin entwickelt überzeugend, dass in der Betrachtung Judiths nicht ein Dualismus der Geschlechter vorherrscht, sondern dass sie aus individuellen Motiven im jeweiligen Lebenskontext begriffen wird. So wird Judith etwa in einem Drama des 16. Jahrhunderts einfach zum Mann erklärt, ein Lied besingt sie als großmütiges Werkzeug Gottes, sie ist barocke Heldin und in Gustav Klimts Gemälde Femme fatale. Bedeutende Frauen wie Elisabeth I. werden mit ihr verglichen und andere, etwa Angela Merici, solidarisieren sich mit ihr, eine dritte Gruppe wird nach Meinung der Autorin durch denselben Vornamen in eine Allianz mit Judith gezwungen (70). Nach den unterhaltsamen Erläuterungen über die Verwendungsmöglichkeiten der biblischen Gestalt Judith werden erstmals auch Leichenpredigten über getaufte „Judiths" auf ihren Identifikationscharakter hin befragt. Die Ergebnisse der Untersuchung fallen nach Aussage der Autorin eher hypothetisch aus und weisen oft nur oberflächliche Parallelen, aber auch biographische Übereinstimmungen auf (114).

Nach Beispielen für die Sehnsucht nach der grausamen Powerfrau richtet Kobelt-Groch ihre Aufmerksamkeit auf die sexuellen Phantasien von Leopold von Sacher-Masoch. Der galizische Schriftsteller stilisiert Judith in seinem fast vergessenen literarischen Werk in zeitlos anmutenden Frauengestalten zum „masochistischen" Ideal, zur kaltblütigen Mörderin, die ihrem Opfer höchsten Genuss schenkt (146). Interessant zu lesen sind seine progressiven Aussagen zur weiblichen Emanzipation und zum Verhältnis von Mann und Frau sowie die dekadenten Gedanken des Fin de siècles, wenn Männer sich danach sehnen, von erfahrenen Frauen im Bordell getötet zu werden (195). Kobelt-Grochs gründliche Recherche der bildnerischen und historischen Judith im Schaffen Sacher-Masochs beeindruckt, auf der anderen Seite macht sie deutlich, dass sich dessen Judithbild ständig wiederholt.

Die Rezeptionsgeschichte der Magd wird interessant und kurzweilig erläutert. Weil die namenlose Magd in der fiktiven biblischen Erzählung nur im Hintergrund agiert, lässt sie Raum für kreative Spekulationen und künstlerische Schöpfungen in Literatur und Kunst. So ist sie bei Lucas Cranach

vornehm gekleidet und Vertraute ihrer Herrin, bei Veronese eine dunkel-
häutige Afrikanerin und bei Cariani gar Inkarnation des Todes. Sie ist mit
allen Negativklischees einer Magd belastet, erscheint aber auch als ideali-
sierte Dienerin; als Hexe, Kupplerin, alte Vettel dient sie als Kontrast zur
schönen Judith oder beide werden allegorisch als Glaube und Vernunft pola-
risiert; die Magd ist Zeugin, Helferin oder sie greift selbst zum Schwert.
Instrumentalisiert und didaktisch gestaltet erhält die Magd ein multiples Profil und eignet sich für moralische Botschaften aller Art (232). Theologisch
betrachtet repräsentiert sie unter der Führergestalt Judith das jüdische Volk
bei der befreienden Heilstat Jahwes. Während Judith rezeptionsgeschicht-
lich festgelegt ist auf ihre Schönheit und die befreiende Bluttat, erscheint
ihre Magd facettenreich und beleuchtet auch neue Dimensionen Judiths.

Der Mord Judiths am Feldhauptmann Nebukadnezars entfacht heute keine
aufgebrachten Auseinandersetzungen mehr, Kinder leiden aus Unkenntnis
des Bibeltextes nicht mehr unter ihrem Namen und einen wirklich aktuellen
Sitz im Leben – ein Kupferstich von 1495 verlegt die assyrische Belagerung
nach Neuss – gibt es kaum noch. Dennoch taucht das Judithmotiv auch heute
noch auf, etwa bei der Wahl des Künstlernamens „Judith Holofernes" einer
Popsängerin.

Kobelt-Groch gelingt es in ihrer akribischen Bestandsaufnahme (mit über
800 Anmerkungen) des Judith-Motivs nachzuweisen, wie der Mythos Judith
gelebt hat, sie kann mit ihrem Buch dazu beitragen, dass er ein lebendiger
Mythos bleibt.

Helene Neis (Saarbrücken – Germany)

III.3 Systematische Theologie, Ökumene und Interreligiöser Dialog /Syste-matic Theology and Interreligious Dialogue / Etudes ecuméniques

Margit Eckholt / Sabine Pemsel-Maier (Hg.), *Räume der Gnade. Interkulturelle
Perspektiven auf die christliche Erlösungsbotschaft*, Ostfildern: Schwabenverlag 2006, 188 Seiten, ISBN-10: 3-7966-1299-7 ISBN-13. 978-3-7966-1299-2

"Gnade", dieses Grundwort christlicher Theologie, aus der Sicht von Theologinnen aus verschiedenen Kulturen zu reflektieren, leitet die Aufsatzsammlung,
die Margit Eckholt, Professorin für Dogmatik an der Hochschule der Salesia-
ner in Benediktbeuren und Sabine Pemsel-Maier, Professorin für Katholische

Theologie und Religionspädagogik an der Pädagogischen Hochschule Karlsruhe vorlegen. Drei Texte deutscher Theologinnen, die die Überwindung der Lehrverurteilungen der Reformationszeit durch die 1999 verabschiedete "Gemeinsame Erklärung zur Rechtfertigungslehre" umkreisen, bilden den von klassischer europäischer Theologie geprägten Ausgangspunkt. Davon gehen Wege aus nach Argentinien, Bolivien, Kamerun und wieder zurück nach Europa. Gemeinsam ist ihnen die lebensgeschichtliche Entfaltung dessen, was Gnade im Leben von Frauen (und auch Männern) bedeutet, wo und wie im Leben der Einzelnen, der Kirche und der Gesellschaft "Räume der Gnade" aufbrechen.

Die drei ersten Beiträge ergänzen sich, indem Friederike Nüssel die Etappen der Entstehung und die kontroverse Debatte um die "Gemeinsame Erklärung" darstellt, Sabine Pemsel-Maier darauf reflektiert, wie die Rechtfertigungsbotschaft angesichts veränderter Gottesvorstellungen und eines gewandelten Sündenbewusstseins für die Gegenwart verständlich übersetzt werden muss und Dorothea Sattler den Gedanken der Wandlung des Menschseins durch Gottes Annahme weiblich-erfahrungsbezogen akzentuiert.

Die argentinische feministische Befreiungstheologin Virginia Raquel Azcuy stellt ihre von globalen Spannungen und "Vermengungen verschiedener Realitätsbereiche" (61) gezeichnete Biographie und die Alltagswelt als theologische Orte vor – ein Konzept, das mit den Beiträgen von María José Caram und Ursula Silber über das Leben der peruanischen Andenbäuerin Isabel Choque konkret entfaltet wird. Silber fordert die Wertschätzung der alltäglichen Menschen gerade auch für die deutsche Pastoral ein. In Carams Text wird sichtbar, wie durch die Inkulturation in die kleinbäuerliche Kultur der indianischen Andenbevölkerung "Gnade" eine neue befreiende Gestalt annimmt, die nicht einfach in die Begrifflichkeit einer Rechtfertigungstheologie gefasst werden kann, deren prägender Kontext die frühneuzeitlich mitteleuropäische Ständegesellschaft war. Der Aufsatz von Eugénie Tchéugoué bringt die biblische Botschaft der Rechtfertigung mit dem gesellschaftlichen Problem der Hexer und Hexerinnen in Afrika zusammen und entwickelt daraus die Forderung nach Bildung und kirchlichem Engagement für die als Hexen angeklagten Frauen.

Die protestantische Argentinierin Nancy Elizabeth Bedford zeigt Kirche und Arbeitsleben als Räume der Gnade auf, die sie als spirituelle und politische Räume, nicht als Privatsache versteht. Ihre feministisch-befreiungstheologische Wahrnehmung und Analyse findet zwischen den Strukturen der Sünde die verwandelnden Zwischenräume der Gnade unter dem Leitgedanken des "Vergnügens/enjoyment" (79). Die deutsche Ethikerin Regina Ammicht-Quinn lässt sich von Bedfords Text anregen, der Fremdheit des Wortes Gnade außerhalb der Theologie- und Kirchensprache nachzugehen. Das Verschwinden des Wortes Gnade aus der Alltagswelt und -sprache lässt sich, – so Ammicht-Quinn – teilweise einholen durch die Besinnung auf das Wort Glück, das – von der theologischen und philosophischen Hochkultur lange vernachlässigt – alltagssprachlich und in der Populärkultur seinen festen Platz hat. Als "geerdetes Glück", bezogen auf menschliches Gedeihen und transzendenzoffen sei Glück "ein legitimer und häufig notwendiger Schritt hinein in das Abenteuer der Gnade" (95). Bernadette Carmen Caero Bustillos entdeckt in ihrer Auslegung von Hosea 2,16–25 "Räume der Gnade", die auf JHWHs leidenschaftlicher Liebe ruhen und die mit Schalom ausgefüllt sind.

Mirjam Schambeck skizziert knapp und zugleich eindrucksvoll Erfahrungen, mit der Brüchigkeit des Lebens umzugehen und stellt sie in eine theologische Deutung der menschlichen Existenz, die auch als brüchige und fragmenthafte schon von den Spuren der Gnade Gottes durchdrungen und "zugunsten der Gnadenbestimmtheit des Menschen entschieden" sei (156). Religiöse Bildung habe diese "Identität im Fragment" (H. Luther) anzuerkennen und ein Reservoir von Deutungen zu eröffnen, die Wahrnehmungen des eigenen Lebens als "Ermutigungen zu einem Leben 'trotzdem'" (160) ermöglichen. Annegret Langenhorst stellt vor, wie in John von Düffels Roman "Houweland" Gnade zum Leitmotiv einer Familiengeschichte wird, wenn man mit Ammicht-Quinns Arbeitsdefinition Gnade anthropologisch zurückgenommen als Chiffre für das Verlorene versteht, als Bewusstsein dessen, dass etwas gut sein könnte. Margit Eckholt beschließt die Aufsatzsammlung, indem sie die Aufmerksamkeit auf die neu aufgebrochenen, nicht nur auf die Kirche begrenzten Gnadenräume mit der klassisch-theologischen Tradition verbindet und einen neuen systematisch-theologischen Blick einfordert, der die Gnadentheologie aus spannungsvollen Lebensgeschichten heraus formuliert. Wer dafür Anstöße sucht, kann in diesem Band fündig werden.

Elisabeth Hartlieb (Berlin – Germany)

Helene Egnell, *Other Voices. A Study of Christian Feminist Approaches to Religious Plurality East and West,* Studia Missionalis Svecana C, Uppsala (Sweden) 2006, 369 p., ISBN: 91-85424-92-7, SEK 265 / € 29,25

In this dissertation, Helene Egnell explores the contribution of feminist theology in interfaith dialogue. The field of this study is Intercultural Theology within Mission Studies, with special attention to Asian feminist theology. The dissertation is primarily intended as a contribution to the intra-Christian discussion on religious plurality. The objectives are to summarise experiences of women in interfaith dialogue and to investigate whether Christian feminist theologians use specific approaches, themes and methodologies that could be useful for the development of theologies of religions and interfaith dialogue praxis.

The Introduction gives detailed information on the material and method used, limitations, terminology, and theoretical considerations. Egnell explains having chosen for the term "interfaith" dialogue, because in interfaith dialogue persons exchange "personal beliefs", and her/his version of their religious tradition. She describes "interreligious" dialogue as having a more institutional connotation. Here participants are seen as representatives of a religious tradition. Egnell indicates that Carol Gilligan's publication *In a Different Voice* and her theory about women's moral development have strongly influenced feminist theology and theory, and the women's movement. She uses Gilligan's publications as a theory upon which women in this dissertation build their praxis and explains: "They are then part of a cycle, where their praxis affirms Gilligan's theories and contributes to new theories around women and relationality" (37).

Part I *Possibilities of Praxis* starts with the Case Study: *The Women's Interfaith Journey*. This study is based on interviews with the project co-ordinator and participants, and written material of three Women's Interfaith Journeys, organised by the international research centre *Henry Martin Institute* in Hyderabad (India). The aim of this project: to include women in interfaith dialogue and to explore women's way of participating in interfaith dialogue. During three weeks, women from different religions and two different countries travelled together in the countries of the participants, where they also met women's organisations. From 1993 – 2003 the Journeys took place in India, Canada, Kenya, Sri Lanka and South Africa.

Two of the five key insights from this Case Study are "The Messiness of Actual Life" and "Emphasis on Relationships". Egnell explains that these two themes are connected and writes that "Messy" is a recurring term in her material and a central theme in feminist theologies of religion. It is the realisation that religious realities cannot be contained in neat categories or in boxes. "Messiness" is also described as the awareness that things do not fit, like the term "interfaith/interreligious dialogue". Participants in the Journey expressed they had a different way of doing interfaith dialogue, than ever tried before.

They perceived interfaith dialogue as practised by men as very formal and talking on a theoretical level, while women live it.

In the second section: *Feminist Approaches to Interfaith Dialogue*, Egnell studied nine different international conferences: two organised by the World Council of Churches; two by Harvard University and Berkely University on *Women Religion and Social Change* (WRSC), and five Asian conferences. This study is based on publications, videotapes, archive material and interviews with participants of these conferences. Egnell concludes from the conference material "Feminist approaches to interfaith dialogue call the whole concept of interfaith dialogue into question" (167). Participants of the WRSC conferences rejected the label of "interfaith dialogue" for their conferences. Many participants also distanced from malestream dialogue, which they considered as very cerebral and verbal, and too abstract and divorced from reality. They expressed that interfaith dialogue needs to be based on care, justice and personal relations, and to lead to transformation of individuals, society and religious traditions. Egnell indicates that this is the kind of dialogue that has taken place in the conferences of her material. She remarks that most of the participants did not have much experience in malestream dialogue, and were speaking from a general impression of malestream conferences. Egnell notices that these women are not only excluded from interfaith dialogue, they have rejected it and created their own field. She express not having participated in any of the conferences and projects of her dissertation. However having taken part in other women's conferences, she recognises much of what is described. Her own experiences affirm what she found in the material of the women's interfaith conferences.

In her reflection on these conferences, Egnell describes "marginality" and "otherness" as important themes, because women share the experience of being "the other" in their religious traditions. It creates a bond when women meet in this shared experience, but it may also reify women's marginality and prevent women from influencing the centre and the larger interfaith field, and from including feminist analysis in interfaith dialogue.

Part II *Theoretical Challenges* starts with describing the challenges Christian feminist theology has been facing from its beginning. The assumptions of early pioneers, white middle-class women, were challenged by women of colour, who challenged their assumptions about women's experiences for not taking issues of race and class seriously. Themes in the discussion on difference and diversity include the acknowledgement of differences while not reifying the differences and turning the dialogue partner into an "other". It also includes the acknowledgement of power relations between feminists from different ethnic communities.

This section is followed by the sections: The Challenge of Jewish-Christian Dialogue, The Asian Challenge, Western Feminist Challenges to Malestream Theologies of Religions, and Malestream Responses to the Feminist Challenge. Each section ends with conclusions.

Part III *Synthesis* is divided in two sections. The first section reflects on whether the Margins is a good place for dialogue. In the second section, Egnell proposes "hermeneutics of difference" as the best strategy for the way forward. She concludes that "An intercultural feminist theology of difference" is needed to create theology in today's world.

This dissertation is based on an impressive amount of conference material and published and unpublished literature on the voices of women in interfaith dialogue. Though the women interviewed for this study express not having participated in interfaith/interreligious conferences with male participants, they express a negative view on male colleagues in the dialogue and on the term "dialogue". This negative attitude makes it difficult to integrate feminist theology in the interreligious dialogue. Having participated since more then ten years in the interreligious dialogue with male colleagues and in the founding of a new interreligious organisation, I experience the interreligious dialogue with male colleagues as necessary and as inspiring. It is the right place to raise awareness about the worldwide religiously motivated violations of the human rights of women and children and to inspire us to develop ways to stop it.

Annie Imbens-Fransen (Eindhoven – The Netherlands)

Elisabeth Moltmann-Wendel / Renate Kirchhoff (Hg.), *Christologie im Lebensbezug*, Göttingen: Vandenhoeck & Ruprecht 2005, 240 p., ISBN: 3-525-56958-0, € 29,90

Die Christologie ist für feministisch-theologische Forschung ein problematisches Feld. Die Anfang der 80er Jahre von Rosemary Radford Ruether formulierte Frage „Kann ein männlicher Erlöser Frauen erlösen?" verweist auf Machtstrukturen, die einen Verbund mit der traditionellen Christologie eingegangen sind: auf eine gleichsam göttliche Vorrangstellung des Mannes aufgrund des männlichen Geschlechts des Gottessohnes, auf die Verklärung des Leidens von Frauen unter Bezugnahme auf das Kreuzesleiden Jesu. Feministische Forschung hat von der im Glaubensbekenntnis formulierten Christologie wie jeglicher Kreuzestheologie denn auch weitgehend Abstand genommen. Ins Zentrum des Interesses rückte der irdische Jesus und damit vor allem sein ethisches Handeln, während die Spekulationen um Inkarnation und Tod weitgehend außen vor blieben. Aber, und diese Frage stellt das Buch: Ist die Christologie tatsächlich etwas, das feministische Theologie ausblenden muss, um nicht in patriarchale Strukturen zu verfallen und damit auch die Botschaft Jesu von Gerechtigkeit und Heilung zu verstellen? Mit Monika Fander gesprochen: „Wollen wir als feministische Theologinnen sie [die Christologie] wirklich aufgeben oder uns nicht trotz aller berechtigter Kritik mit ihr neu auseinandersetzen?" (156)

Acht Autorinnen verschiedener Konfessionen formulieren aus der Perspektive unterschiedlicher theologischer Disziplinen ihr Nein, indem sie eines der zentralen Anliegen feministischer Theologie an die Christologie herantragen, das gleichzeitig eine methodische Vorgehensweise markiert: Sie setzen die Symbolisierungen des Glaubens zu konkreten Lebenssituationen in Beziehung und dadurch die gewohnte Wahrnehmung sowohl der traditionellen Texte wie der eigenen Erfahrungen aufs Spiel. Dies geschieht zunächst auf einem für feministische Theologie klassisch gewordenen Weg: Erinnert werden die Lebensgeschichten von Frauen und ihre weitgehend vergessenen theologischen Zugänge zu Jesus Christus. Elisabeth Moltmann-Wendel widmet ihren Beitrag der Sozialpädagogin Henriette Schrader-Breymann (1827-1898), der Historikerin Ricarda Huch (1864-1947) sowie der jüdischen Philosophin und Politologin Hannah Arendt (1906-1947). Elisabeth Gössmann erzählt die Geschichte der Malwilda von Meysenburg (1816-1903), die in einem regen Austausch mit Friedrich Nietzsche über Frauenbild und Christusbild stand. Wie sehr dabei oft gegenwärtige Problemstellungen und Lösungsversuche vorweggenommen werden, wird beeindruckend deutlich an der Lebensgeschichte und den theologischen Reflexionen der Béatrice Kimpa Vita (1864-1706), die Valeria Ferrari Schiefer beleuchtet. Die Kongolesin war für ein befreiendes Christentum eingetreten, das in Zeiten von Kolonialismus und Sklavenhandel auf der Seite der Entrechteten steht. Aktiv und kreativ bezog sie dabei die Kultur der Kongolesen in die Verkündigung mit ein, denn ein Christentum ohne Inkulturation leistete dem Rassismus der Eroberer Vorschub.

Um konkrete Erfahrung von Leid und Gewalt geht es auch Monika Fander. Angestoßen von Begegnungen mit Menschen, die durch Kriege, sexuellen Missbrauch oder Prügeldelikte traumatisiert sind, liest sie das Markusevangelium als Zeugnis der Auseinandersetzung mit dem Jüdischen Krieg und der

Tempelzerstörung 70 n. Chr. Damals wie heute scheint angesichts schier grenzenloser Kriegsgräuel jede Hoffnung an eine Ordnung der Schöpfung obsolet, ist der Glaube an die Auferstehung als Zeichen der Gerechtigkeit schaffenden Macht Gottes gefährdet. Für Fander ist es gerade eine Kreuzestheologie, die nicht nur zum Engagement für Gerechtigkeit und gegen Gewalt aufruft, sondern die auch mit dem Unvermeidbaren und Unbegreiflichen umzugehen lehrt.

Einen in der Christologie unterbelichteten Gedanken greift Elisabeth Naurath auf. Gott kam als Kind zur Welt. Ist aber, wenn Jesus Christus wie alle anderen Menschen eine Kindheit hatte, nicht auch Entwicklung ein notwendiges Moment von Christologie? Und verändert dies nicht den Blick auf die Entwicklung von Kindern und auf ihre in ihrer Unmittelbarkeit oft erstaunlich innovative Theologie?

Den möglichen Anstößen der Christologie für die kirchliche Praxis widmen sich die Beiträge von Renate Kirchhoff, Brigitte Enzner-Probst und Ute Grümbel. Renate Kirchhoff liest Mk 10,35-45 als einen Text, in dem Machtkonstellationen und Konfliktbewältigungsstrategien der markinischen Gemeinden diskutiert werden, und untersucht seine Relevanz für feministisch-theologische Gruppen. Brigitte Enzner-Probst lässt sich von Frauenliturgien dazu inspirieren, einen Blick auf die Verbindungen von Schöpfungstheologie und Christologie zu werfen und verweist auf die biblische Rede von Schöpfung und Neuschöpfung in den Bildern der Geburt. Um die gottesdienstliche Praxis geht es auch Ute Grümbel. Sie bemüht mit Gal 3,26-28 einen Schlüsseltext feministischer Theologie und nimmt gerade dessen oft ausgeblendeten christologischen Bezug zum Anstoß dafür, „geschlechtsspezifische Festlegungen, traditionelle Klischees und deren Begründung zu hinterfragen" (209).

Das Buch setzt einen neuen Anfang, die Christologie für die feministische Theologie zurückzugewinnen, und bietet dabei eine Reihe von Perspektiven, die sich weiterzudenken lohnen. Gleichzeitig zeigt es eine nach wie vor bestehende Differenz zwischen feministischem Zugang zu Jesus Christus und der „klassischen" Christologie an. Viele Themen sind noch kaum berührt – die Präexistenz, die Zwei-Naturen-Lehre, der Kenosis-Gedanke. Der in den Beiträgen weitgehend gelungen hergestellte Lebensbezug gibt das Programm für die Zukunft vor: Will Theologie dem Christus-Ereignis gerecht werden, kann sie es nicht in überzeitliche Wahrheiten hinein auflösen, sondern muss sich auf konkretes Leben einlassen.

Mirja Kutzer (Wien – Austria)

Hanna Strack, *Die Frau ist Mit-Schöpferin. Eine Theologie der Geburt*, Rüsselsheim: Christel Göttert Verlag 2006, 357 p., ISBN: 3-922499-85-6, € 19,80 / CHF 36,00

Die existentielle Bedeutung der Geburt, die spirituellen Erfahrungen, die mit Gebären verbunden sind und die Entwicklung einer beziehungsfördernden Geburtskultur – daraus entwickelt Hanna Strack einen neuen theologischen Ansatz.

Ein dreifacher Perspektivenwechsel steht zu Beginn: – von der Konzentration auf die Sterblichkeit zum Geborensein als existentielle Grundkategorie (Hannah Arendt); – vom disziplinierenden Eva-Mythos zur biblischen Eva als Mutter alles Lebendigen und zu Frauen als Mitwirkenden an der Schöpfung; – vom auf medizinische Aspekte eingeschränkten Blick hin zur Geburt als kulturell-gesellschaftlich und religiös eingebettete Erfahrung. Ziel der Autorin ist eine phänomenologisch begründete Theologie der Geburt. Grundlage dafür bilden Interviews mit Hebammen, die als Expertinnen eine Vielzahl von Geburten begleitet haben.

Die Autorin gibt einen Überblick über die Geschichte des Hebammenberufs und befasst sich unter anderem mit der Beziehung von Kirche und Hebamme. Ein besonderes Augenmerk gilt dem Wandel der theologischen Bedeutung des Hebammenberufs und der frühneuzeitlichen protestantischen Gebets- und Liedliteratur rund um die Geburt. Androzentrische Theologie – so die Konklusion von Hanna Strack – hat zur Konstruktion der Gebärenden als schwacher Patientin in der heutigen Geburtsmedizin beigetragen und den Körper der Frau als Ort der Kraft und der Schöpfung vergessen lassen. Die Analyse von Geburtserfahrungen zeigt, dass die Beteiligten in Kategorien des Heiligen – Ergriffenheit, Seligkeit, Grenze, Schweigen, Schmerz, … – von ihren Erfahrungen berichten. Dies ermöglicht es Hanna Strack, das Gebären in den sakralen Bereich zurückzuholen und eine Theologie der Geburt zu entwerfen, die Frauen als Mitwirkerinnen Gottes würdigt.

Dem Hauptteil der Publikation folgen die Endnoten zu den jeweiligen Kapiteln, ein ausführliches Literaturverzeichnis sowie der zweiteilige Anhang. In diesem befinden sich Segensliturgien für Hebammen und für Schwangere, meditative Texte und Gebete (Schwangerschaft, Fehl- oder Todgeburt, Schwangerschaftsunterbrechung, Kinderlosigkeit, Begrüßung des Kindes, Taufe). Beispielhaft zeigen sie einen frauenfreundlichen Umgang mit Geburt, der die Dimension des Religiösen thematisiert. Die Niederschrift der Interviews mit den Hebammen, zwei Geburtsberichte sowie ein historischer Text bilden den zweiten Teil des Anhangs.

Hanna Strack bietet eine ermutigende neue theologische Perspektive. Die Publikation zeugt von einer Theologie mit Erfahrung, Herz und Engagement. Das anregende Werk thematisiert ein breites Spektrum an Aspekten rund um Geburt und Hebammentätigkeit. Es verbindet die historische Aufarbeitung mit der zeitkritischen Analyse und weist Wege in eine theologische und pastorale Zukunft, die noch zu gehen sind. Es ist zu hoffen, dass es nicht nur Hebammen und Gebärende anspricht, sondern für TheologInnen und die Theologie als Ganzes fruchtbar wird.

Anmerkungen und Kritik können bei dem hier begangenen Neuland nicht ausbleiben: Manchmal speisen sich die provokanten Thesen aus einer zu idealisierten beziehungsweise zu polarisierten Sicht von Vergangenheit und Gegenwart zugunsten der positiven Zielformulierung; die Ambivalenz von Geburtserfahrungen und von historischen Entwicklungen kommt zu kurz. Nach wie vor scheint es schwierig zu sein, die Erfahrungen des Gebärens aus der Sicht der Mütter zu thematisieren und zu theologisieren: Hier wird der objektivierende Zugang über die Erfahrungen von Hebammen gewählt. Das Werk hat einen klaren protestantisch-theologischen Fokus. Eine katholische Aufarbeitung des Themas ist ausständig und müsste auch die Mariologie bearbeiten. Eine editorische Kritik zum Schluss: Es ist mühsam, im Literaturverzeichnis nach dem Erscheinungsjahr von ansonsten vollständig in den Endnoten angeführten Publikationen suchen zu müssen.

Ich wünsche der „Theologie der Geburt" weitere vertiefende theologische und historische Arbeiten.

Gertraud Ladner (Innsbruck – Austria)

Doris Strahm/ Manuela Kalsky (Hg.), *Damit es anders wird zwischen uns. Interreligiöser Dialog aus der Sicht von Frauen*, Ostfildern: Matthias-Grünewald-Verlag bei Schwabenverlag 2006, 159 p., ISBN: 3-7867-2604-3, € 16,80

Als Horizont der versammelten Beiträge identifizieren die Herausgeberinnen eine "Wiederkehr des Religiösen als gesellschaftlicher Kraft" (7), sei es zur Legitimierung von Gewalt oder der Durchsetzung von Machtinteressen, oder zur Identitätsmarkierung und Abgrenzung gegenüber 'anderen'. Angesichts dessen stelle sich die Frage, wie "ein friedvolles und gerechtes Zusammenleben in unseren multikulturellen und multireligiösen Gesellschaften" (7) möglich sein und welchen Beitrag dazu der interreligiöse Dialog leisten könne. Hierbei, so die das Buch initiierende These, seien die "Grundfragen", die

"Erfahrungen und Sichtweisen von Frauen" (7) bislang zu wenig beachtet worden. Das entstandene Buch will diesem Defizit begegnen.

Beweggrund und Ziel des interreligiösen Dialogs werden hier also konkret anwendungsbezogen, 'lebenspraktisch', bestimmt. Dem entspricht die Definition seines Inhalts und seiner Aufgabe, nämlich als Abbau von Vorurteilen und Beförderung wechselseitigen Verstehens (7), als die "Suche nach einem 'dialogischen Verstehen'" (8). Dabei stellen sich den Herausgeberinnen Multikulturalität und Multireligiosität, die Frage interreligiösen und interkulturellen Verstehens, als ebenso verbunden dar, wie Wert auf eine Verbindung zwischen jeweiligen persönlichen und fachlichen Hinsichten gelegt wird.

Entsprechend der traditionsbildenden Religionen im europäischen Kontext beschränken sich die Beiträge auf Dialoge zwischen den drei großen monotheistischen Religionen – das 'Multi' des -religiösen Ansatzes entpuppt sich bei näherem Hinsehen also als ein 'Tri' –. Dem Umfeld dieser Religionen, indes aus ganz unterschiedlichen fachlichen Hintergründen – Religions- und Islamwissenschaft, jüdischer Religions- und Geistesgeschichte, christlicher Theologie, Soziologie, Interkulturalität und Geschlechterstudien –, entstammen denn auch die 13 Autorinnen der insgesamt neun Beiträge:

Diese sind in vier Sektionen unterteilt. Der *erste Teil* ist der Erörterung der Voraussetzungen und Rahmenbedingungen für Dialog, Begegnung und interreligiöse Kommunikation (8 und 16) gewidmet. Als erfolgreich ausgewiesen wird der Orientierungsrahmen "Mehr-von-einander-wissen-und-verstehen-wollen" (20), der respektvollen, gleichberechtigten Umgang (29, 37) und "den Willen zum Perspektivenwechsel" (25) beinhalte, ohne dabei Verschiedenheiten zu nivellieren. Der Erfolg dieser Herangehensweise wird anhand zweier erfolgreicher Dialogprojekte, eines christlich-islamischen und eines auf jüdische und nicht-religiöse Frauen erweiterten, dargestellt.

Der *zweite Teil* konzentriert sich auf die "Herausforderungen einer pluralistischen, multikulturellen und multireligiösen Gesellschaft für die religiöse Identitätsfindung" (9). Es geht hier um die Frage der eigenen religiösen Identität in einer religiös und kulturell nichthomogenen Gesellschaft und um die Wechselbeziehungen zwischen säkularen Überzeugungen und den i.d.R. eher patriarchal geprägten religiösen Traditionen. Beteiligen sich Frauen an der Gestaltung und Modifikation der Traditionen der eigenen Religionsgemeinschaft, so eine These, können sie auf ein friedliches Zusammenleben religiös und kulturell verschiedener Menschen hinwirken.

Im *dritten Teil* werden spezifisch aus der Gender-Perspektive Zusammenhänge zwischen Migration, Integration, Identität, Religion und (moderner, säkularer) Gesellschaft thematisiert. Hier geht es darum, wie sich der Faktor Religion, konkret, der Faktor Islam, auf die Integration junger Migrantinnen und ihre Identifikation mit oder ihre Ablehnung von traditionellen Geschlechterrollen auswirkt. Die wechselseitige Beeinflussung zwischen Identitätsausbildung, Hinwendung zum Islam, Verhüllung (mit Hidjab, dem Tschador) und dem Gewinn an Status, Autorität, Emanzipation und Freiheit wird für letzt genannte insgesamt als positiv markiert.

Der einzige Beitrag des *vierten Teils* ("Nachdenken über Religion und Ethik") schließt explizit an die Intention und das Grundanliegen des Buches an und führt gleichzeitig praktisch aus, worüber bislang berichtet und reflektiert wurde: Eine Muslima, eine Jüdin und eine Christin beginnen einen Dialog mit der Frage, ob geteilte Glaubensüberzeugungen für eine gemeinsame Handlungsfähigkeit notwenig vorausgesetzt werden müssten, und kommen von dort aus zu einer Fülle von Fragen u.a. politischer, kultureller, philosophischer (gerechtigkeitstheoretischer) Natur. Der Band schließt so mit einem interreligiösen Gespräch *in actu*, deren Wortmeldungen sich anders als die in vielen anderen solcher Gespräche deutlicher als Such- und Denkprozess präsentieren. Es passt zu einem Buch, dessen AutorInnen ein Bewusstsein für die Grenzen menschlicher Denkversuche erkennen lassen und die Leserin nicht mit ihrer Sicht der Dinge erschlagen, sondern zu eigenem Weiterdenken einladen wollen.

Das oben erwähnte Grundanliegen der Anwendungsbezogenheit, sprich, "Theorie und Praxis des interreligiösen Dialogs sowie gelebte Religion und deren theoretische Reflexion miteinander zu verbinden" (8), schlägt sich in den Beiträgen so nieder, dass jeweils konkrete Projekte gelebten interreligiösen und interkulturellen Dialogs und/oder spezifische lebensweltliche Erfahrungen den Bezugspunkt darstellen. Das Buch enthält Texte von und über Frauen und Projekte, die nicht unbedingt als erste gefragt respektive ausgewertet werden, wenn es gilt, etwas zur Verständigung zwischen den Religionen und zum Aufbau einer möglichst konfliktarmen Zivilgesellschaft beizutragen. Darin, sodann in den verschiedenen Herangehensweisen und den verschiedenen fachliche Kompetenzen, die in ihm versammelt sind, und in der erwähnten besonderen Dialogbereitschaft, liegt zweifelsohne die große Stärke dieses Buches.

Indes: Leider ist "'die' Sicht von Frauen" trotz der eben beschriebenen religiösen und fachlichen Weite des Buches in einer entscheidenden Hinsicht wieder einmal relativ monoform: Referenzpunkt ist eine (sic!) letztlich doch eher 'klassische' weibliche Identität in 'klassischen' Beziehungskonstellationen. Das in allen drei Religionen prävalente Genderkonzept

einer an Varianten des Differenzmodells orientierten Anthropologie wird
m.E. insgesamt zu wenig hinterfragt, und an keiner Stelle (*apologies* falls
ich eine Seitenbemerkung übersehen haben sollte) wird die in allen drei
Religionen extrem problematische Position von Menschen mit transgender
Identitäten und/oder anderen Beziehungskonstellationen in die Überlegungen mit einbezogen.

Und leider präsentiert sich "'die' Sicht von Frauen" wieder einmal als pra-
xisorientierte Erfahrungs- und Projektberichte samt sehr durchdachten, manchmal aber auch etwas vagen Interpretationen und Argumentationen (die 'Rück-
seite' der Offenheit und Dialogbereitschaft, vielleicht?). Zu kurz kommt mir
jedenfalls die Metareflexion; ich wünsche mir ferner stärker Anschluß an, heißt:
Auseinandersetzung mit sonstigen theologischen Diskursen zu Fragen der Viel-
heit der Religionen (z.B. die 'Theologie der Religionen', die es in der einen oder
anderen Form in allen der drei Religionen gibt), und manchmal vermisse ich
auch einfach wesentliche theologische Informiertheit. – Wie *z.B.* kann man das
"verbalinspirierte Schriftverständnis des Koran" (22) schlicht als "einen jener
kulturellen Bestandteile, in denen sich die muslimischen Frauen einmal mehr
nicht akzeptiert und verstanden fühlen" (23) betrachten, ohne bzw. anstatt
(zumal im Rahmen des Themas "Jesus im Koran") den entscheidenden *theo-*
logischen Unterschied zwischen dem Verständnis einer Schrift als Offenbarung
und dem einer Schrift als Offenbarungszeugnis zu benennen, und diesen in der
weiteren Erörterung zu berücksichtigen?

Was den Anschluß betrifft: Nicht, dass frau sich Topoi und Ebenen des Dis-
kurses vorgeben lassen sollte, gerade wenn sie dessen Beschränkungen erkannt
hat. Doch wenn frau deutlich sieht, dass die "zweitrangige Stellung der Frau (...)
im Widerspruch zu unseren ethischen Vorstellungen von Gerechtigkeit und Recht
[steht], *welche sich vom biblischen Konzept her entwickelt hat*" und wenn sie sich
so – *mutatis mutandis* – im Falle aller drei Religionen "mit einer patriarchalen
Religion konfrontiert [sieht], die ihre eigenen Ansprüche nicht verwirklichen
kann" (146, Hervorhebungen dh), so reicht es m.E. nicht, dieses festzustellen.
Den selbsternannten Verfechtern von guter und stringenter Argumentation die *de*
facto bestehenden internen Inkohärenzen ihrer Argumente ausführlicher und
expliziter *vorzuführen* wäre m.E. ein noch durchschlagenderes Remedium gegen
Gewalt und Unterdrückung im Namen der Religion, das nicht leichten Herzens
verschenkt werden sollte. Zumal solche (Ein-)Sichten in interne Inkohärenzen
meist nur denjenigen zukommen, die unter ihnen zu leiden haben.

Kurzum: Ein nötiges, ein sehr lesenswertes, erhellendes und sehr empfeh-
lenswertes, aber ein unbedingt – mit den Einsichten und Ergebnissen dieser

Projekte – auch auf anderen Terrains und auf anderer Diskursebene fortsetzungsnotwendiges Buch!
Diana Heß (Heidelberg – Germany / Basel – Switzerland)

III.4 Praktische Theologie, Spiritualität, Liturgiewissenschaft, Religionspädagogik, Homiletik, Ethik / Pastoral theology, teaching, homiletics, spirituality, liturgy, ethics / Théologie pastorale, Scienes liturgiques, Pédagogie religieuse, Théologie morale et d'Ethique

Sybille Becker, *Leib – Bildung – Geschlecht. Perspektiven für die Religionspädagogik,* Theologische Frauenforschung in Europa 13, Münster: LIT Verlag 2001, 359 p., ISBN: 3-8258-6628-9, € 19,90

Leiblichkeit ist in den letzten Jahren zu einem inhaltlichen Schnittpunkt im interdisziplinären feministischen und Gender-Diskurs geworden. Becker macht ihn zum Fokus ihrer Arbeit, indem sie die philosophischen, soziologischen, pädagogischen und theologischen Fachdiskurse unter einer religionspädagogischen Perspektive evaluiert. Die Dimensionen der Leiblichkeit bilden auch das strukturelle Grundgerüst der Argumentation: von der subjektiven Leibwahrnehmung über die Sozialität des Leibes bis hin zur geschlechtlichen Dimension, werden jeweils aus dem Blickwinkel der verschiedenen Disziplinen beleuchtet. Den Abschluss der Arbeit bilden bildungstheoretische und religionspädagogische Überlegungen.

Die (religions)pädagogische Fragestellung ergibt sich durch die Tradition einer immer noch wirksamen leibfeindlichen Theologie, sowie durch die traditionelle Leibvergessenheit oder sogar –feindlichkeit schulischer Lernformen. In den letzten Jahren gibt es im methodisch-didaktischen Bereich vermehrt Konzepte mit ganzheitlichem Anspruch, die wenigstens die sinnliche Komponente in den Lernprozess mit einbeziehen (E. Buck/E.M. Bauer). Allerdings sind diese weitgehend genderunsensibel.

Das Buch behandelt alle einschlägigen Namen und Theorien zum Thema Leiblichkeit. Der Versuch, aus den Anregungen der unterschiedlichen Disziplinen ein religionspädagogisches Ganzes zu weben, erweist sich als schwierig, ein Problem, das in der inhaltlichen Disparität der Referenzliteratur begründet ist und die sich zudem nicht ohne weiteres religionspädagogisch verwerten lässt. Die religionspädagogischen Ansätze im Themenfeld hingegen sind eher dem methodischen verhaftet oder denken Leiblichkeit nicht konsequent zu

Ende (wie Biehl). Hier stellt sich die Frage, inwieweit „Sinnliches", „Gestische Symbolisierung" (127) und coenästhetische Lernwege (Rumpf) schon den Weg hin zur Leiblichkeit in der Religionspädagogik aufzeigen können. Mit J. Moltmann und S. Heine werden zwei hochinteressante theologische neue Zugänge zur Leiblichkeit in der Theologie aufgezeigt, die aber nicht religionspädagogisch gedacht sind. In pädagogischer Sicht wiederum ist K. Meyer-Drawes Ansatz bemerkenswert, vermag sie doch die – phänomenologisch begründete – Ambiguität des Leibes zum Ausgangspunkt einer Bildungstheorie zu machen.

Der Schlüssel zur gesamten Arbeit findet sich erst spät (Kap. 5) im Zusammenhang mit der Thematik der Geschlechtlichkeit des Leibkörpers. Hier wird deutlich, dass Merleau-Pontys Unterscheidung von Körper und Leib, die Kategorien der Ambiguität und Opazität des Leibes und das Verständnis des Leibes als Leib als „Sein zur Welt" die gesamte Argumentation prägen. Bis dahin behilft Becker sich mit dem Wortungetüm „Leib-bzw. Körperlichkeit". Es ist zu empfehlen, das fünfte Kapitel zuerst zu lesen.

Am Schluss werden eine Reihe von religionspädagogischen Anknüpfungspunkten vorgeschlagen: Die „leibkörperliche Wahrnehmung als besonderer Zugang zu religiösem Erleben", die Einbettung des Leibkörpers in der Gemeinschaft, sowie religiöse leibhaftige Praxis als „Eindruck wie Ausdruck" von Glauben. Als eine echte Entdeckung erweist sich die amerikanische Theologin Paula Cooey (311ff.), die Aussen- vs. Selbstwahrnehmung des Körpers einerseits sowie Materialität vs. leibliche Gestaltungsfreiheit auf den Begriff „sign and site" bringt. Das Feld Leib – (religiöse) Bildung – Geschlecht wird in diesem Buch erstmals umrissen, bedarf aber einer weiteren Klärung und Zuspitzung. Interessant wäre es z.B., das nur am Rande erwähnte Bibliodrama im Hinblick auf das Leibkonzept zu untersuchen. Weitere Fragen drängen sich auf: Wie „existenziell" darf Lernen, gerade auch im Kontext religiöser *Bildung* sein? Darf Religionsunterricht in einer pluralen Gesellschaft auf „religiöses Erleben" (341) zielen? Eine Unterscheidung von Lernkontexten ist hier dringend notwendig. Zeigt leibliches Lernen einen methodischen Paradigmenwechsel, oder führt es zur Ergänzung herkömmlicher Methoden? Wie kann die Überwindung der Trennung zwischen Kognition, Emotion und Körper, wie sie sich im Begriff des „reflexiven Leibes" ausdrückt, religionspädagogisch zum Tragen kommen?

Monika Jakobs (Luzern – Switzerland)

Andrea Günter (Hg.), *Frauen – Autorität – Pädagogik. Theorie und reflektierte Praxis*, Königstein/Taunus: Ulrike Helmer Verlag 2006, 241 p., ISBN: 978-3-89741-217-0, € 22,00

„Heute sollen das betriebswirtschaftliche Modell und der neoliberale Markt, deren kulturelles Paradigma als das siegreiche Modell ausgegeben wird, alle komplexen sozialen Aufgabenfelder organisieren, einschließlich der Schule und der Erziehung. (…) Die Terminologie des Banken- und Kontenverkehrs – Schulden, Kredite, Buchführung der Kompetenzen, Humankapital, Ausgaben, Akkumulation, Zertifizierung – bringt eine Vorstellung von Erziehung zu Tage, die vom ersten Lebensjahr an flexible Arbeiter und Konsumenten funktional heranbilden und selektieren will. Bildungsangebote werden mobilisiert und modularisiert, wie ein Warenangebot im Supermarkt. Weshalb sich die Lehrenden in Verkäufer verwandeln sollen, in ‚intelligente' Produktlieferanten, die zugleich selbst wiederum Kunden von irgendwelchen Produkten anderer sind." Eine eindrückliche Beschreibung einer aktuellen Tendenz in der Pädagogik von Anna Maria Piussi (41).

Nun gibt es aber immer noch (ein bisschen erinnert die Situation an den Beginn jedes Asterix-Comics) Menschen, die in ihrer Erziehungsarbeit keine Ökonomisierung und Rationalisierung wollen oder diese nicht mitmachen können: Menschen, die mit kleinen Kindern leben, ReformpädagogInnen, kritische ErziehungswissenschafterInnen – und nicht zuletzt die feministische Pädagogik plädieren für ein anderes Bildungs- und Erziehungsmodell: tätige Menschen mit der Lust und Fähigkeit, Welt zu gestalten wollen sie hervorbringen – oder besser: im Aufwachsen begleiten. Was bedeutet das aber in Zeiten der Postmoderne, in der sich viele vormalige Sicherheiten und Gegebenheiten verflüssigt haben? „Im Zufälligen und Vergänglichen Notwendigkeiten und Gültigkeiten finden, durch ebenfalls zufällige und vorläufige Interaktionen verbindliche Maßstäbe für das Zusammenleben der Menschen entwickeln und als Orientierung für junge Menschen weitergeben: mit diesen Tätigkeiten lässt sich die Aufgabe von Eltern, Pädagogen und Pädagoginnen insbesondere in sich verändernden, postmodernen Zeiten fassen." (Günter 7) Autorität bedeutet dabei, „Orientierung immer wieder herzustellen und herbeizuführen", bezeichnet „die Wandlungsmacht, aus Zufällen, Unterschieden, Besonderheiten etwas Neues, Orientierendes und wenigstens vorläufig Bestand Habendes zu gewinnen." (Günter 10) Die Gebürtigkeit und die (Generationen)Beziehung sind dabei die Grundlagen der Autorität. Wie sich Autorität in pädagogischen Beziehungen in der Rezeption der „Italienerinnen" in unterschiedlichen Praxisfeldern im deutschen Sprachraum darstellt, darum geht es im dem vorliegenden Band, der Beiträge der Tagung „Frauen – Autorität – Pädagogik. Reflektierte Praxis in Deutschland und in Italien" an der Evangelischen Akademie Arnoldshain im Sommer 2003 dokumentiert. Die Pädagogin Anna Maria Piussi zeichnet in ihrem grundlegenden Beitrag den Weg (auch ihren eigenen) zu einer „Pädagogik der sexuellen Differenz" nach. Ihr Beitrag ist eine prägnante Einführung in das Denken der Philosophinnengruppe DIOTIMA und vor allem die Konsequenzen für die Pädagogik mit vielen kritischen Anmerkungen zu derzeitigen bildungspolitischen Programmen. In einem weiteren grundlegenden Beitrag stellt Andrea Günter die Diskussion über Autorität im letzten Jahrhundert in Pädagogik, politischer und feministischer Theorie dar und stellt das Lehren der „Kunst des Hörens" in die Mitte von Erziehung und Bildung. Das Problem der (ja freiwillig zugesprochenen) Autorität in Blick auf Kinder und Jugendliche, deren pädagogische Kontexte auch von Unfreiwilligkeit geprägt sind, reflektiert Martina Haasis.

Neben diesen grundlegenden Beiträgen berichten Frauen, wie sie in ihrem jeweiligen pädagogischen Feld (kirchliche Pastoral und Frauenseelsorge, Mädchen- und Jungenarbeit, Universität, Mentoring und Entwicklungspolitik) mit Autorität, Beziehung und weiblicher Genealogie umgehen und den Ansatz der Pädagogik der Geschlechterdifferenz rezipieren. Das Begehren der Frauen, Freiheit in Abhängigkeit, weibliche Genealogie und die Verschiedenheit der Frauen sind hier immer wiederkehrende wichtige Stichworte, die so manches „Aha-Erlebnis", neue Blickwinkel und ein neues Denken und Handeln ermöglichen. Dies scheint am erfolgreichsten in Zusammenhängen zu geschehen, in denen (erwachsene) Frauen mit (erwachsenen) Frauen zu tun haben – was wiederum auf die Entstehungsgeschichte des Denkens der Geschlechterdifferenz im Mailänder Frauenbuchladen hinweist.

Welche beim Lesen Lust auf mehr bekommen hat, findet dazu genügend Anregung in einer kleinen, aber feinen Literaturliste zu Autorität und zur Pädagogik der sexuellen Differenz am Ende des Buches.

Silvia Arzt (Salzburg – Austria)

Heike Knops (Hg.), *Kunst und Theologie im Dialog. MenschSein im Zeitalter der Gentechnik,* Interdisziplinäres Forum Wissenschaft, Sprockhövel: Verlag Dr. Eike Pies 2006, 88 p. (mit DVD), ISBN: 3-928441-60-4, € 19,80

Die Herausgeberin hat im Jahr 2005 in Wuppertal eine beeindruckende Ausstellung durchgeführt, die mit diesem Bändchen dokumentiert wird. Das

Außergewöhnliche ihres Projektes liegt darin, dass Kunst und Theologie für ein hoch aktuelles Thema in einen Dialog getreten sind. Dass dies nicht immer und nicht von Anfang an ohne Probleme und Komplikationen funktioniert hat, versteht sich dabei fast von selbst. Insofern ist dieses Resümee am Ende des Projektbandes evident, da es letztlich nur vor Augen führt, wie starr und unbeweglich Theologie dort sein kann, wo die Wissenschaft auf andere Ausdrucksformen als die des Wortes trifft.

Diese Problematik macht sich auch dort bemerkbar, wo die Herausgeberin versucht, so viele Eindrücke wie möglich in dem vorliegenden Band zum Thema „Mensch und Gentechnik" in schriftlicher Form festzuhalten. Ein Kabarett kann aber nicht schriftlich dargestellt werden, um den Leserinnen und Lesern einen Eindruck über diesen Teil des Projektes zu vermitteln; die Vorträge hingegen, die in der vierwöchigen Projektphase gehalten wurden, lassen sich sehr gut nachvollziehen und vermitteln einen guten Überblick über die verhandelten Themen und die aktuellen Anfragen. Vor allem die Bilder, die Heike Knops im Anhang den Betrachterinnen und Betrachtern in diesem Band vorstellt, bieten einen erstaunlich eindrucksvollen Kontrast zu den hochtheoretischen und ausführlichen Vorträgen von Frederik de Lange und Horst Schwebel. Genau in dieser Gegenüberstellung ist der Herausgeberin also das gelungen, was der Titel dieses Projekt-Berichts verspricht: Die Theologie tritt mit der Kunst in einen Dialog; und dort, wo man den Worten von de Lang nicht mehr folgen kann oder will, vermag ein Bild, wie das von Leif Skoglöf mit dem Titel „DNA-Verstrickungen", die interessierten Leserinnen und Leser auf andere Weise anzusprechen. Gentechnik hat viele Facetten. Kunst und Theologie sind mannigfaltig in ihrer Ausgestaltung. Und so, wie das Klonen von Tier und Mensch unterschiedliche Gesichter zeigt, so zeigen auch Theologie und Kunst verschiedene Bilder ein und desselben Themas. Dies hat Xenia Marita Riebe in ihrer Bilderserie beeindruckend ausgearbeitet.

Welche Themen und Beiträge von der Podiumsdiskussion erarbeitet bzw. erörtert wurden, bleibt leider offen, da auch dieser Punkt des Projektes nur schlecht für eine Verschriftlichung zugänglich ist. Hingegen zeigt der Gottesdienst mit der Predigt zum Sabbat sehr eindrücklich und überzeugend, in welcher Form Gentechnik zum Thema in der Kirche gemacht werden kann. Dass dies nicht nur in Form eines Gottesdienstes mit Worten funktioniert, ist von Heike Knops von Beginn an gezeigt worden. Denn die Initiatorin dieses spannenden Projektes hat einen ganz anderen Raum als die Universität gesucht: eine Kirche. Die Bioethik trifft die Theologie also dort, wo Theologie am Sonntag stattfindet – im Andachtsort. Dies scheint den Dialog von Wissenschaft und Kunst am ehesten voranzutreiben. Dass dabei viele andere Faktoren eine Rolle spielen und gerade die neuen Medien ihren Platz in der Vermittlung haben müssen, versteht sich hier von selbst. Insofern wäre es schön gewesen, die Texte und Bilder mehr für sich sprechen zu lassen, als jede Erfahrung und Empfindung deskriptiv nachzuzeichnen. Dies nimmt der überzeugenden Aussage des Projektes ein wenig von ihrer Kraft. Für künftige Bioethik-Debatten ist die Arbeit von Heike Knops allerdings richtungsweisend und kann nicht unbeachtet bleiben.

Meike Rieckmann (Bonn – Germany)

Silke Leonhard, *Leiblich lernen und lehren. Ein religionsdidaktischer Diskurs,* Praktische Theologie heute 79, Stuttgart: Kohlhammer Verlag 2006, 526 p., ISBN: 978-3-17-019321-5, € 39,00 D / 40,10 A / CHF 67,50

Silke Leonhards Dissertation geht von den Prämissen aus, dass die Leiblichkeit menschlichen Lebens unhintergehbar ist, auch wenn sie wissenschaftlich selten reflektiert wird, und dass „körperlich-sinnliche Erscheinungsformen von Religion (zu) wenig ernstgenommen (werden)" (15). Ziel der Arbeit ist „die Entwicklung eines Lehrkonzepts, welches die Leiblichkeit des Menschen im Licht der Leibhaftigkeit Gottes als Basis religionspädagogischer Anthropologie, religiöser Bildung und schulischen Religionsunterrichts würdigt" (93). Leonhard wählt erkenntnistheoretisch zum einen ein phänomenologisches Vorgehen, das sie in ihrer Bedeutung für die Religionspädagogik und Theologie im Anschluss an ausgewählte Vertreter skizziert (94-107), zum anderen qualitativ-empirische, historische und interpretative Erweiterungen. Folgende Untersuchungsperspektiven sind leitend: die „Frage nach der Dimension von Leiblichkeit religiöser Lehr- und Lernprozesse", die „Suche nach dem Verbindungsstück zwischen gelebter und gelehrter Religion" und die „Suche nach Darstellungswegen (...) personbezogene Wissenschaft zu betreiben" (110).

Die Arbeit gliedert sich in vier Teile. Hinführend zur Zielformulierung wird in Teil I eine „Topographie" der „Leiblichkeit in religions-pädagogischer Landschaft" gezeichnet (19-112). Leonhard untersucht, welcher Raum Religion an den Lernorten Gesellschaft, Kirchenraum und Schule zukommt und wie Leiblichkeit in diesen Kontexten berücksichtigt wird. Anschließend skizziert sie Leiblichkeit im Kontext heutiger Kultur und in philosophischen Ansätzen (Edmund Husserl, Gabriel Marcel und Maurice Merleau-Ponty) mit dem Ergebnis, dass sich mit diesen Ansätzen „die Bezogenheit der Existenz, die

Liminalität des Leibes und seine Medialität als Elemente leib-räumlicher Subjektkonstitution herausarbeiten" (54) lassen. Ansatzpunkte für Leiblichkeit werden nicht nur in religionspädagogischer Praxis, sondern auch in der Tradition religionspädagogischer Theorieentwürfe, exemplarisch anhand von drei Ansätzen protestantischer Religionspädagogik des 20. und 21. Jahrhunderts, dargestellt, die sich durch eine Nähe zur Phänomenologie auszeichnen: Martin Rang, ein Vertreter der sog. Evangelischen Unterweisung, dessen unterrichtliche Konzeption auf Anschauung zielt (65); Martin Stallmann dessen Konzeption des Hörens eine leibliche Dimension der angezielten Betroffenheit nur implizit beachtet und Peter Biehl, dessen Symbol(isierungs)didaktik offen für die leibliche Dimension ist, auch wenn sie eher implizit bleibt (vgl. 87).

Teil II „Focusing: ein Gefährt(e) leiblichen Lernens" (112-236) beginnt mit „Streifzüge(n) in die pädagogische Aufmerksamkeit", die für jugendliche Körperinszenierungen, den pädagogischen Umgang mit Körper und die reformpädagogische Achtsamkeit für den Körper sensibilisieren. Es folgt die Aufzeichnung eines Gesprächs zwischen der Autorin und dem Begründer des Focusing, Eugene T. Gendlin, das Grundlage für die Darstellung des Ansatzes ist, der in besonderer Weise für die „Leibräumlichkeit des Lebens" (128) aufmerksam macht. Im Zentrum des Focusings steht laut Deutschem Ausbildungsinstitut für Focusing und Focusing-Therapie „das achtsame Wahrnehmen des körperlichen Erlebens. Aus diesem entfalten sich unter bestimmten Bedingungen lösungsorientierte Schritte – Denkschritte und Heilungsschritte zugleich. Focusing bedeutet, der Stimme des Körpers zu folgen." (www.daffocusing.de, Zugriff am 05.03.07). Es ist „ein anthropologischer Ansatz, der sich erkenntnistheoretisch zwischen Phänomenologie, Ästhetik und Hermeneutik bewegt" (207) und er wird unter Bezugnahme auf hermeneutisch und phänomenologisch orientierte Philosophieansätze von Leonhard als „hermeneutischer Weg zum produktiven Verstehen" (176) als „ästhetisches Handwerkszeug" (199) und als „Instrument zur Gestaltbildung" (207) begründet. Pädagogisch korreliert Focusing mit Konzepten personaler Erziehung und ästhetischer Bildung, religionspädagogisch ermöglicht es eine subjektorientierte Wahrnehmung von Religion (vgl. 236).

Teil III (237-418) titelt mit „Auf dem Weg zu religiöser Bildung: Leibliches Symbolisieren". Da Religionsdidaktik in der Spannung zwischen Theologie und Lebenswelt steht, prüft Leonhard zunächst lebensweltlich orientierte Ansätze der „gelebten Religion" (vgl. Wolf-Eckart Failing, Hans-Georg Heimbrock, Henning Luther, Dietrich Zilleßen), des Zusammenhangs von Religion und Initiation als „erlebter Religion" (Manfred Josuttis) und ästhetische

Zugänge zu christlicher Religion (Albert Grözinger, Hans-Georg Heimbrock und Peter Biehl) jeweils auf ihre Anschlussfähigkeit für eine leib-räumlich orientierte Religionsdidaktik. Nach Überlegungen zu einem leibräumlichen Symbolisieren anhand biographischer Erfahrungen und verschiedener Formen, wie Religion als Gestalt zu Wort kommt (Kirchenbau, Lied, Psalm, Arie, Abendmahl) formuliert Leonhard als „Perspektiven personaler Bildung von Religion" eine religionspädagogische Anthropologie, die Leibsein ernst nimmt und eine prozesshaft zu denkende Bildung, die sich ästhetisch signiert (vgl. Joachim Kunstmann). Dabei kommt dem liturgischen Lernen eine große Bedeutung zu, da Liturgie in besonderem Maß die leib-räumliche Dimension von Religion verkörpert. Weitere Elemente sind Ausführungen zu Kirchenpädagogik, Bibel als Wortraum und kultischen Vollzügen als Verleiblichung von Religion.

Teil IV: „Mit dem Fuß in der Tür: Unterricht zwischen gelebter und gelehrter Religion" (419-492) wendet die theoretischen Überlegungen auf Unterrichtspraxis an. Auf der Basis eigener Lehrerfahrungen formuliert die Verf. Beispiele einer leib-räumlichen Schulkultur, einer Unterrichtsplanung unter Bezugnahme des Focusing und lebendiger Vollzüge im Unterricht. Abschließend zieht Leonhard den Bogen „vom Handwerk zum Kunstwerk" (479) als einem religionspädagogischen Ansatz, der Raum für religiöses Lehren und Lernen gibt, im Unterricht sowohl Freiraum als auch Struktur berücksichtigt und dessen Unterrichtsprinzipien „Erfahrungs-, Bewegungs-, Handlungs- und Wahrnehmungsorientierung" (484) sind und in dem Leiblichkeit Gegenstand des Lernens und Unterrichtsstil ist.

Die Arbeit zeugt von einer äußerst fundierten und breiten Rezeption – sowohl aktueller als auch geschichtlicher – protestantisch-religionspädagogischer, allgemein-pädagogischer und philosophischer Konzepte, die sie in Bezug zur eigenen Theorieentwicklung setzt. Leider machte diese Fülle und der sich eher spiralförmig dem Thema nähernde Zugang es mir als Leserin streckenweise schwer, den roten Faden in der Gedankenentwicklung vor Augen zu haben. Einführende Zielbeschreibungen oder knappe Zusammenfassungen des Ertrags am Ende eines Kapitels hätten geholfen, die Gedankenstruktur der Autorin nachzuvollziehen. Auffällig ist, dass Fragen bezüglich eines Zusammenhangs zwischen Leiblichkeit und Geschlecht nicht zur Sprache kommen, obwohl Unterschiede zu vermuten sind.

„Eine am Lernort Schule ansetzende Religionspädagogik und schulisch ausgerichtete Didaktik hat letztlich auf die Bedingungen, Möglichkeiten und Grenzen schulischen Religionsunterrichts einzugehen" (59) – so der Anspruch der Autorin. Trotz der didaktischen Bezüge, scheinen mir viele der Überlegungen eher in einer gemeindlichen Katechese, im Rahmen von Kirchenraumpädagogik oder eines schulischen Projektes mit einer kleinen Gruppe realisierbar, als im schulischen Alltag einer Klasse von zwanzig oder mehr Schülerinnen und Schülern.

Insgesamt ist es Silke Leonhard überzeugend gelungen, auf eine religionspädagogische Leerstelle zu verweisen, indem sie die Bedeutung der Leibräumlichkeit für religiöse Vermittlungsprozesse heraus arbeitete und die Anschlussfähigkeit der Leibräumlichkeit an philosophische, (praktisch-)theologische und pädgogische Bezugstheorien differenziert darstellt.

Angela Kaupp (Freiburg – Germany)

Ina Praetorius (Hg.), *Sich in Beziehung setzen. Zur Weltsicht der Freiheit in Bezogenheit*, Königsstein: Ulrike Helmer Verlag 2005, ISBN: 3-89741-182-2, € 14,90

Ina Praetorius, die Herausgeberin, sieht „theologisches Denken (…) als gemeinschaftliche Suche nach dem Sinn des Ganzen" (115), diese Schlussworte des Buches bezeichnen gleicherweise das Motto und die Arbeitsweise der Autorinnen. Die Beiträge der einzelnen Autorinnen beziehen sich in einer Weise aufeinander, wie ich es bisher in keiner anderen Veröffentlichung gelesen habe. Die „denkerische Bezogenheit" zeigt sich nicht nur, aber besonders interessant in den Fußnoten, die ich darum zur genauen Lektüre empfehle.

Die Politologin Antje Schrupp untersucht die Rolle feministischer Sozialistinnen wie Victoria Woodhull im 19. Jahrhundert in der Politik. Sie legt dabei ihr Erkenntnisinteresse offen und lädt die Leserin ein, ihren Forschungs- und Gedankenweg mitzuverfolgen. Denn das Ergebnis der Forschung ist anders als erwartet: über den weiblichen Beitrag zur sozialistischen Ideengeschichte lässt sich kaum etwas herausfinden. Der wichtigste Punkt scheint der Beitritt zur Internationalen als solcher zu sein. Schrupp lässt die Leserin an der Weiterentwicklung ihrer Fragestellung teilhaben. Sie erkennt eine „Politik der Frauen" die auf die Vermittlung der politischen Ideen, auf Beziehungen zwischen den politischen AkteurInnen setzt und Politik weder als kompromisshaften Interessensausgleich noch als Kampf zweier Lager versteht.

Michaela Moser plädiert für eine „erneuerte Politik des Sozialen", die die Bedürftigkeit des Menschen nicht als Ausnahme- sondern als Normalzustand sieht. Dies setzt sie – auch angesichts der sog. Arbeitsmarktreformen – gegen die „gesellschaftliche Lebenslüge" von der Autonomie des Menschen und weitere falsche Annahmen. Maren A. Jochimsen bezieht sich darauf als Ökonomin und bezieht die (partielle) Abhängigkeit des Menschen von anderen bei Krankheit, am Lebensanfang und Lebensende in die ökonomische Theorie mit ein. Maria Katharina Moser entwickelt neue Definitionen von „notwendig" und „arm" und greift aktuelle Debatten um die Globalisierung auf, indem sie Geschichten vom Essen erzählt und aufeinander bezieht. Die „Weltmarktstrukturküche" (56) verringert die Entscheidungsfähigkeit über das eigene Essen; Gastfreundschaft und gemeinsame Mahlzeiten sind keineswegs banal. Reinhild Traitler-Espiritu berichtet von den Erfahrungen mit dem zweijährigen „Europäischen Projekt für interreligiöses Lernen", in dem der Dialog als Methode allmählich die traditionelle Wissensvermittlung abgelöst hat.

Der Beitrag der Biologin Florianne Koechlin bringt die Genforschung mit der Weltsicht der Bezogenheit zusammen. Der Mensch hat „nicht viel mehr Gene als eine Stubenfliege" die menschliche Komplexität ist also durch genetischen Determinismus nicht zu erklären. Sie erwartet ein neues Paradigma, das Gene und Zellen als lernende, interaktive, komplexe Systeme sieht. Im Buch sind auch zwei Erklärungen abgedruckt, die die Autorinnen mit anderen erarbeitet haben: zu Fragen der „sogenannten Bioethik" und rund um die Themen „Geld, Arbeit und Sinn".

Übrigens sollten die Aufsätze des Bandes eigentlich in der Fachzeitschrift „Evangelische Theologie" erscheinen, doch – so erläutert Ina Praetorius – konnte sich der Herausgabekreis mit dem interdisziplinären Ansatz nicht anfreunden. So kam es zu dieser Buchveröffentlichung. Ein Glück, denn auf die Literatur dieser Beiträge hätte ich ungern verzichtet.

Antje Röckemann (Oer-Erkenschwick – Deutschland)

Annegret Reese, *„Ich weiß nicht, wo da Religion anfängt und aufhört". Eine empirische Studie zum Zusammenhang von Lebenswelt und Religiosität bei Singlefrauen*, Religionspädagogik in pluraler Gesellschaft 8, Gütersloh: Gütersloher Verlagshaus / Freiburg: Herder 2006, 581 p., ISBN: 3-451-28951-2, € 49,95 D / € 51,40 A / CHF 84,00

Bei dem vorgelegten Band handelt es sich um eine Promotion, die an der Katholisch-theologischen Fakultät der Ruhr-Universität Bochum in Kooperation mit dem Fachbereich Katholische Theologie der Universität Duisburg Essen im Jahr 2005 erstellt worden ist.

Annegret Reese untersucht auf der Basis von qualitativen Interviews, wie kinderlose Singlefrauen um die 40 Jahre ihren Alltag gestalten und bewältigen. Ausgangsbasis für das Design dieser qualitativen Arbeit ist das Faktum, dass die Zahl der alleinlebenden, kinderlosen Frauen seit mehreren Jahren deutlich ansteigt und eine Abnahme dieses Trends vorläufig nicht zu erwarten ist. Immer mehr Frauen leben freiwillig oder unfreiwillig – jenseits traditioneller Muster (Mutter, Ehefrau, Hausfrau). Zugleich blicken Frauen um die 40 bereits auf das eigene Leben zurück und hinterfragen ebenso ihre Erfahrungen und ihr Handeln in Bezug auf die Zukunft, auf ihre Sehnsüchte und Hoffnungen. Vor diesem Hintergrund fragt die Autorin: Wie sehen diese Frauen sich selbst, wie bewältigen sie ihr Leben? In welchem Ausmaß und in welcher Form spielen Religion und Religiosität dabei eine Rolle?

Die Arbeit gliedert sich in vier Hauptteile: der erste Teil bietet eine theoretische Hinführung, in der zu den wesentlichen Aspekten zur Singleforschung, zu den elementaren Kategorien der Arbeit von „Lebensgestaltung" und „Lebensbewältigung" Bezug genommen wird. Im zweiten Teil folgt die methodologische Hinführung, in der das Forschungsdesign beschrieben wird, welches dann konsequenterweise in den dritten Teil, der empirischen Studie einführt. Der abschließende vierte Teil erfolgt unter den Perspektiven von Zusammenfassung, Diskussion der Ergebnisse und Ausblick.

Ein Ergebnis dieser qualitativen Studie ist es, dass Singlefrauen entgegen so mancher Erwartung vielleicht, nicht einsam und isoliert leben. Die in der Studie zu Wort kommenden Frauen berichten alle von einem tragfähigen Netz sozialer Beziehungen und wichtiger Freundinnenschaften. In ihre sozialen Kontakte stecken die Frauen viel Energie und Zeit. Diese Freundschaften sind ihnen wichtige und wesentliche soziale Ressource in ihrem Leben. Soziale Beziehungen sind es auch, die Familienkontakte (auch zur eigenen Herkunftsfamilie) ersetzen. Daneben fällt auf, dass die Frauen außerordentlich reflektiert sind. Dies ist plausibel, wenn bedacht wird, dass sie alltägliche Bestätigung durch Selbstreflexion ersetzen müssen. In ihrer Selbstreflexion tauchen auch religiöse Fragen auf und in diesem Zusammenhang greifen die Frauen auch auf religiöse Praktiken, wie zum Beispiel Meditationen zurück.

Die Frauen, die in der Studie zu Wort kommen, sind durchaus religiös interessiert und ansprechbar, sie wünschen sich sogar gemeinschaftliche Formen. Zugleich fühlen sie sich von Angeboten der institutionalisierten Kirchen nicht wirklich angesprochen. Ihre Religiosität praktizieren sie privat und alleine.

Dies kann als ein Indiz dafür gewertet werden, dass sie in gemeindlichen Angeboten, die noch immer stark auf Familien zugeschnitten sind, vor dem Hintergrund ihrer eigenen lebensweltlichen Erfahrungen keinen Anschluss finden. Es fehlt an Einübungs- und Kommunikationsräumen, die ihnen bei ihrer Verortung in Gemeinden helfen können.

Die Ergebnisse dieser qualitativen Studie überraschen nicht wirklich, vor allem dann nicht, wenn man sie vor dem Hintergrund der Sinus-Milieu-Studie® liest. Aber mit der vorliegenden Arbeit wird die Wahrnehmung auf eine bestimmte Gruppe im Volk Gottes geschärft und dies ist ein Verdienst an sich und zugleich eine Herausforderung für die Pastoral.

Hildegard Wustmanns (Dornburg-Dorndorf – Germany)

Journal of the European Society
of Women in Theological Research

1 **Luise Schottroff, Annette Esser**, *Feministische Theologie im europäischen Kontext – Feminist Theology in a European Context – Théologie féministe dans un contexte européen*, 1993, 255 p., ISBN: 90-390-0047-6
[out of print]

2 **Mary Grey, Elisabeth Green**, *Ecofeminism and Theology – Ökofeminismus und Theologie – Ecoféminisme et Théologie*, 1994, 145 p., ISBN: 90-390-0204-5   23 EURO

3 **Angela Berlis, Julie Hopkins, Hedwig Meyer-Wilmes, Caroline Vander Stichele**, *Women Churches: Networking and Reflection in the European Context – Frauenkirchen: Vernetzung und Reflexion im europäischen Kontext – Eglises de femmes: réseaux et réflections dans le contexte européen*, 1995, 215 p., ISBN: 90-390-0213-4   23 EURO

4 **Ulrike Wagener, Andrea Günter**, *What Does it Mean Today to Be a Feminist Theologian? – Was bedeutet es heute, feministische Theologin zu sein? – Etre théologienne féministe aujourd'hui: Qu'est-ce que cela veut dire?*, 1996, 192 p., ISBN: 90-390-0262-2   23 EURO

5 **Elisabeth Hartlieb, Charlotte Methuen**, *Sources and Resources of Feminist Theologies – Quellen feministischer Theologien – Sources et resources des théologies féministes*, 1997, 286 p., ISBN: 90-390-0215-0   23 EURO

6 **Hedwig Meyer-Wilmes, Lieve Troch, Riet Bons-Storm**, *Feminist Pespectives in Pastoral Theology – Feministische Perspektiven in Pastoraltheologie – Des perspectives féministes en théologie pastorale*, 1998, 161 p., ISBN: 90-429-0675-8   23 EURO

7 **Charlotte Methuen**, *Time – Utopia – Eschatology. Zeit – Utopie – Eschatologie. Temps – Utopie – Eschatologie*, 1999, 177 p., ISBN: 90-429-0775-4   23 EURO

8   Angela Berlis, Charlotte Methuen, *Feminist Perspectives on History and Religion – Feministische Zugänge zu Geschichte und Religion – Approches féministes de l'histoire et de la religion*, 2000, 318 p., ISBN: 90-429-0903-X
[out of print]

9   Susan K. Roll, Annette Esser, Brigitte Enzner-Probst, Charlotte Methuen, Angela Berlis, *Women, Ritual and Liturgy – Ritual und Liturgie von Frauen – Femmes, la liturgie et le rituel*, 2001, 312 p., ISBN: 90-429-1028-9
23 EURO

10 Charlotte Methuen, Angela Berlis, *The End of Liberation? Liberation in the End! – Befreiung am Ende? Am Ende Befreiung! – La libération, est-elle à sa fin? Enfin la libération*, 2002, 304 p., ISBN: 90-429-1028-9
23 EURO

11 Elżbieta Adamiak, Rebeka J. Anić, Kornélia Buday with Charlottte Methuen and Angela Berlis, *Theologische Frauenforschung in Mittel-Ost-Europa – Theological Women's Studies in Central/Eastern Europe – Recherche théologique des femmes en Europe orientale et centrale*, 2003, 270 p., ISBN: 90-429-1378-9
23 EURO

12 Charlotte Methuen, Angela Berlis, Sabine Bieberstein, Anne-Claire Mulder and Magda Misset-van de Weg, *Holy Texts: Authority and Language – Heilige Texte: Autorität und Sprache – Textes Sacrés: Autorité et Langue*, 2004, 313 p., ISBN: 90-429-1528-X
23 EURO

13 Valeria Ferrari Schiefer, Adriana Valerio, Angela Berlis, Sabine Bieberstein, *Theological Women's Studies in Southern Europe – Theologische Frauenforschung in Südeuropa – Recherche théologique des femmes en Europe Méridionale*, 2005, 255 p., ISBN: 90-429-1696-6
23 EURO

14 Sabine Bieberstein, Kornélia Buday, Ursula Rapp, *Building Bridges in a Multifaceted Europe. Religious Origins, Traditions, Contexts, and Identities – Brücken bauen in einem vielgestaltigen Europa. Religiöse Ursprünge, Traditionen, Kontexte und Identitäten – Construire des ponts dans une Europe multiforme. Origines, traditions, contextes et identités religieux*, 2006, 257 p. ISBN 978-90-429-1895-5
23 EURO

All volumes of the Journal of the ESWTR can be ordered from Peeters Publishers, Bondgenotenlaan 153, B-3000 Leuven
Fax: +32 16 22 85 00; e-mail: order@peeters-leuven.be

The volumes of the Journal of the ESWTR are also available online at
http://poj.peeters-leuven.be